The Accidental Slaveowner

The Accidental Slaveowner

Revisiting a Myth of Race and
Finding an American Family

MARK AUSLANDER

THE UNIVERSITY OF GEORGIA PRESS

ATHENS AND LONDON

© 2011 by the University of Georgia Press
Athens, Georgia 30602
www.ugapress.org

Designed by April Leidig-Higgins
Set in New Baskerville by Copperline Book Services, Inc.
Printed digitally in the United States of America

Library of Congress Cataloging-in-Publication Data
Auslander, Mark.
The accidental slaveowner : revisiting a myth of race and
finding an American family / Mark Auslander.
    p. cm.
Includes bibliographical references and index.
ISBN-13: 978-0-8203-4042-5 (hardcover : alk. paper)
ISBN-10: 0-8203-4042-1 (hardcover : alk. paper)
ISBN-13: 978-0-8203-4043-2 (pbk. : alk. paper)
ISBN-10: 0-8203-4043-X (pbk. : alk. paper)
    1. Slavery—Georgia—History—19th century.   2. Women
slaves—Georgia—Social conditions—19th century.   3. Kitty,
1822–1851—Biography.   4. Slaveholders—Georgia—Biography.
5. Andrew, James O. (James Osgood), 1794–1871—Biography.
6. Bishops—Georgia—Biography.   7. Methodist Episcopal Church,
South—History—19th century.   I. Title.
E445.G3A97   2011
975.8'041—dc22   2011012913

British Library Cataloging-in-Publication Data available

Dedicated to

Lee Bradley Caldwell (1925–2010)

Ellen Schattschneider

John Pliny ("J. P.") Godfrey Jr.

and the memory of all enslaved persons
owned by James Osgood Andrew

Contents

Illustrations

Preface and Acknowledgments

THIS BOOK SPANS history and ethnography, moving back and forth between the ethnographic present and multiple points in the past. Drawing on spoken recollections, published and unpublished documents, as well as architectural and landscape forms, I document the history of powerful myths about freedom and unfreedom. I simultaneously attempt to reconstruct historical happenings that these evocative, proliferating narratives may have obscured. As such, this study has been enabled and supported by a great range of communities, institutions, and persons, whom I can only begin to acknowledge or thank adequately.

The Emory University Center for Myth and Ritual in American Life (Alfred E. Sloan Foundation), the Emory Office of University-Community Partnership, and the Norman Fund of Brandeis University funded field and archival research for this project. Parts of chapter 5 were published, in a somewhat different form, as "The Other Side of Paradise: Glimpsing Slavery in the University's Utopian Landscapes," in *Southern Spaces* (May 2010). Parts of chapter 9 were published, in a somewhat different form, as "Saying Something Now: Documentary Work and the Voices of the Dead," in *Michigan Quarterly Review* 44, no. 4 (Fall 2005). Permission to republish is gratefully acknowledged.

I remain deeply grateful to my students at Oxford College of Emory University during 1999–2001, and to our many community partners in Oxford and Covington, Georgia, including Allen Memorial United Methodist Church in Oxford, the historically African American congregations of Rust Chapel United Methodist Church and Mt. Zion Baptist Church in Oxford, and St. Paul's African Methodist Episcopal Church, Bethlehem Baptist Church, and Grace United Methodist Church in Covington. Our shared labor restoring and documenting the historic African American sections of the Oxford City Cemetery has been the enduring inspiration for this study. This work is also anchored in the deep wisdom and historical insights of Newton County's African American community historians, including Mary Gaiter McKlurkin, Mildred Wright Joyner, Sarah Francis Hardeman, Sarah Francis Mitchell Wise, and Emogene Williams. In the local faith community, Rev. Avis Williams, Rev. Hezekiah Benton, Deacon Forrest and Sharon Sawyer, and Deacon Richard and Polly Johnson have been valued sources of support, historical knowledge, and encouragement. State Representative Tyrone Brooks has been a firm supporter of this work and a champion of social justice initiatives in the region. Virgil and Louise Eady shared remarkable family papers that cast the history of slavery in the community in new light. John Pliny "J. P." Godfrey Jr. has been a tireless and intrepid partner in all these inquiries and allied activist adventures; I cannot imagine how this book could have been written without his insight, curiosity, optimism, and friendship.

In Dallas County, Alabama, I am grateful for the support and generosity of the Wayman Chapel AME church membership and to the many other residents of Summerfield, Valley Grande, and Selma who kindly gave of their time, family records, and knowledge. Alston and Ann Fitts, Brenda J. Smothers, and Sister Afriye Wekandodis have been invaluable and generous guides to Selma's storied history. In Augusta, Georgia, I am grateful to Joyce Law, Travis Halloway, and the congregations of Springfield Baptist Church, St. John United Methodist Church, and Trinity Christian Methodist Episcopal Church, all of whom are linked to the story of Miss Kitty in different ways. In Iowa, Doris Secor generously welcomed us to Keosauqua and its Underground Railroad history; Lynn Walker Webster kindly guided me in uncovering Buckner-Boyd family history and the related history of the AME church in the state. In Rockford, Illinois, Rev. Virgil Woods, pastor of Allen Chapel AME Church, kindly guided me to the local descendants of Miss Kitty.

I wish to think the staff at many institutions, including Jane M. Aldrich at the Avery Research Center for African American History and Culture (College of Charleston); Sharon Avery of the Iowa State Archives; the Georgia State Archives; the South Carolina Department of Archives and History; the Alabama Department of Archives of History; the Arkansas History Commission and State Archives; the Manuscripts, Archives, and Rare Book Library (MARBL) of Emory University, especially Ginger Cain and Randall Burkett; Kitty McNeil and her staff at the Oxford College of Emory University library; Debra Madera at the Pitts Theology Library, Emory University; Probate and Superior Court staff in Newberry (South Carolina), Covington, (Georgia), Dallas County (Alabama), Augusta–Richmond County (Georgia), Morgan County (Georgia), and Greene County (Georgia); Nic Butler at the Charleston, South Carolina, public library; the public libraries in Newberry (South Carolina), Pine Bluff–Jefferson County (Alabama), Newton County (Georgia),

Augusta–Richmond County (Georgia), Rockdale County (Georgia), and Greene County (Georgia), as well as the public libraries in Selma and Birmingham (Alabama); the South Carolina Library; the Washingtonia Division, Martin Luther King Jr. Library (Washington, D.C.); Washington Historical Society; Office of Public Archives and D.C. Archives (Washington, D.C.); the Manuscripts division of the Library of Congress; the National Archives and Records Administration, in their Washington, D.C., College Park, Atlanta–Morrow, Georgia, and Waltham, Massachusetts, facilities; the African American Museum of Iowa; and the library of the U.S. Department of State.

Among the many persons and organizations that have kindly assisted me, I should especially acknowledge the Moore's Ford Memorial Committee, especially Rich and Janise Rusk, Waymund Mundy, and Robert Howard; the Newton County African American Historical Association, especially Forrest Sawyer Jr.; the Newton County Historical Society; the Oxford Historical Shrine Society, especially Jim Waterson, Marshall Elizer, Roger Gladden, and Valerie McKibben; Linda Derry of Old Cahawba (Selma, Alabama); and the Augusta Genealogical Society.

At Oxford College and the Druid Hills campus of Emory University, I am grateful to many supportive colleagues, especially Susan Ashmore, Leslie Harris, Francis Smith Foster, Thee Smith, Laurie Patton, Jonathan Prude, Robert Paul, Gary Hauk, and Joe Moon. Bradd Shore's synthetic work on myth and ritual in American society, especially in Georgia's Salem camp meeting, is a vital inspiration for this study. I am also deeply appreciative of the pioneering work on Newton County African American history by emeritus Oxford historian Ted Davis, on whose work I build. Over the years, I have greatly benefited from stimulating conversations about this project with Laurie Kain Hart, Rajeswari Mohan, Jean and John Comaroff, Natasha Barnes, Rick Parmentier, Evelyn Brooks Higgenbotham, Pete Richardson, James T. Campbell, and Alfred Brophy. Scott Schnell, Wyatt MacGaffey, Alan Cattier and Carole Meyers, and Allen and Cynthia Tullos all provided hospitality and intellectual inspiration during our journeys. Lynn Marshall-Linnemeier, Kevin Sipp, and Sister Afriye We-Kandodis have been invaluable interlocutors in reimagining aspects of Miss Kitty's life and the lives of the other enslaved peoples explored in this book. Since 2004 the staff and participants in the Transforming Community Program at Emory University, coordinated by Leslie Harris, Catherine Manegold, Susan Ashmore, and Jody Usher, have been inspiring reminders of the possibilities for reconciliation as institutions grapple with the weight of a common, often painful history. I also wish to express my gratitude to the anonymous reviewers for the University of Georgia Press for their insightful and generous readings, to my editor Derek Krissoff, to the superb copyeditor Bob Land, and to the whole team at the University of Georgia Press.

Since the summer of 2009 it has been a joy and privilege to come to know descendants of Catherine "Miss Kitty" and Nathan Boyd, now in their sixth generation. I have been deeply moved by their generosity and insights as we have together attempted to excavate this complex historical narrative. I am especially grateful to the late Mr. Lee Bradley Caldwell, the great-great-grandson of Miss Kitty, and his daughters Darcell Caldwell and Cynthia Caldwell.

My parents and stepparents, Ruth Auslander, Joe Auslander, Barbara Meeker, and the late Maury Shapiro, as well as my aunt and uncle Judy and Alan Saks, have been unflagging supporters of this project, proving constant encouragement as well as serene places to write. My sister Bonnie Auslander has been a deeply insightful reader and interlocutor, sensitive both to the overall structure of argument and literary inflections.

Above all, I am deeply grateful to my wife and colleague Ellen Schattschneider, who has shared every step of this project. She has driven us thousands of miles across the nation's Southeast and Midwest, helped to scour archives, attended worship services and family reunions, and has critically engaged with every line in the manuscript. She has shared in my intellectual and emotional engagements with the memory of Miss Kitty/Catherine Boyd, the other enslaved persons associated with James Osgood Andrew, and their many descendants, known and unknown. This work is deeply informed by Ellen's brilliance, compassion, curiosity, and humor. It is a privilege to dedicate the book to her, to J. P. Godfrey Jr., to Lee Caldewell, and to the memories of the enslaved people whose story I have attempted to tell.

In this work I try to give voice to a wide range of voices and opinions by persons, past and present, grappling with one of the most vexing conundrums in the American body politic—the enduring legacies of slavery and racial injustice that continue to haunt our private imaginings and our civic life. Recognizing that the contested narratives of Bishop Andrew and the enslaved people he owned are matters of significant concern to multiple religious faiths, I attempt to engage these varied spiritual traditions with care and respect. I have sought to honor diverse perspectives, often passionately held, on the circumstances of slavery in this historical chapter and its long-term implications. In so doing my fervent hope is that I have justly represented both the words and the ethical commitments of each person whom I have cited or quoted. I recognize that not all agree with the interpretations and analyses I advance. Yet my hope is that this study helps to open new areas of dialogue across admittedly difficult terrain of race and difference. Through reflecting upon our most deeply shared capacity, our human ability to generate an endlessly proliferating array of mythic narratives, may we come to celebrate a shared humanity that emerges paradoxically through our unruly, creative impulses toward difference, synthesis, and endless recombination.

A Note on Nomenclature and Terminology

I have generally used the term "slaves" when emphasizing the perspectives or transactions of slaveowners, and "enslaved people" when calling attention to the perspectives or agency of those held in bondage. This is not, to be sure, an entirely satisfactory solution to the challenges of recognizing the objectifying horrors of slavery and the subjectivities of the enslaved. I have used the term "slaveholder" when characterizing a situation in which a person had legal control of another human being, for example as a trustee or administrator, without full legal ownership. I have used the term "slaveowner" in instances when legal possession was unambiguous.

Conscious of the freighted politics of naming in African American historical experience, I continue to grapple with how to refer to the enslaved woman at the heart of this historical drama. For her husband, she appears to have been known as "Catherine Boyd"; as her descendants become acquainted with her story, this is the name by which they have primarily chosen to refer to her. In this book I usually refer to her as "Kitty" when characterizing white representations of her and "Miss Kitty" when foregrounding African American discourses about her in Oxford, where she has long been remembered by that appellation.

Unless they had given explicit permission to be identified by name, living and recently deceased persons mentioned in this text are referred to only through pseudonyms.

Continuing Conversations

This book emerges out of partnership with community members and with the descendants of those whose stories are told here. Readers interested in commentaries by community partners and updates on continuing research, as well as sharing their own reflections on slavery and its legacies, are invited to access the book's website: http://www.theaccidental slaveowner.com.

Prologue

ON A WARM MORNING in July 2009 I found myself nervously mounting the steps of a modest house in Rockford, Illinois, not quite sure what kind of welcome I might receive. I was, in a sense, at the conclusion of a journey I had begun a decade earlier. In September 1999, as I began teaching at Oxford College, the original campus of Emory University in the small town of Oxford, Georgia, I had become fascinated with the often-told story of the enslaved woman known as "Miss Kitty," and her owner, Bishop James Osgood Andrew, first president of Emory's Board of Trustees. "Kitty," I had been half-jokingly told by a number of Oxford residents, "is really the person who caused the Civil War." Bishop Andrew's ownership of slaves, including Miss Kitty, in 1844 had occasioned national controversy, leading to a great schism in the Methodist Episcopal Church that was regarded in local circles as a "dress rehearsal" for the secession of the slaveholding states seventeen years later.

For years I had followed intense debates over the circumstances of Kitty's life and the Bishop's precise connection with slavery. Most white people in Oxford insisted that the Bishop had offered Kitty her freedom in 1841 but that she had refused emancipation out of loyalty to the Bishop and his wife. The Bishop was thus only an "accidental slaveholder," unfairly accused of slaveowning by "hypocritical and fanatical" northern Methodists, who understood nothing of the deep affection and loyalty felt by Kitty and her fellow slaves for their masters and mistresses. To be sure, the town's African American residents had little patience with this version of events. Miss Kitty, they held, was most likely the Bishop's mistress and he the probable father of her children. She had hardly been offered a fair chance at freedom, they insisted. The multiple memorials in town to the story of Kitty and Bishop Andrew, erected by whites over the years, were a constant affront to persons of color. While local whites insisted Kitty had married a free man of color named Nathan Shell, African Americans were skeptical that such a man had ever existed. Yet, across the lines of race and difference, all wondered what had become of Kitty's children and her posterity.

As a social and cultural anthropologist who had primarily done field research in rural southern Africa, it occurred to me that in hearing these contested stories of Bishop Andrew and Miss Kitty I was in the presence of what anthropologists term "the mythic imagination." For anthropologists, myths are not simply falsehoods or misstatements of fact but rather are a culture's continuing, inventive efforts to understand the most fundamental enigmas of the social and natural world around us. Even when they are intensively debated and argued over, mythic forms reveal the underlying aspirations and longings that bind together a human society. To explore a community's deeply cherished or reviled myths is to contemplate its underlying structures of meaning, its hidden networks of power and domination, and its continuing struggles for renewal and transformation.

How, I had long wondered, had these competing versions of the "myth of Kitty" coexisted in this community for over a century and a half? Had the details of the stories altered over time, and had the meanings of the tales themselves shifted? Why had the narrative deeply moved so many whites, and profoundly troubled so many African Americans, across the generations? What in fact was the relationship of James Osgood Andrew to Miss Kitty and to the institution of slavery? How many slaves had Bishop Andrew held or owned during his lifetime, and what had happened to them and their descendants in slavery and freedom?

Seeking answers to these questions had taken me on a long and winding trail. With my students at Oxford College I had worked with community members in documenting and restoring Oxford's historic African American cemetery, where Miss Kitty and others whom Bishop Andrew owned were buried. I had pored through documents in county courthouses, archives, and household attics in Georgia, South Carolina, Alabama, Washington, D.C., and Iowa. Most important, my journey had taken me deep into varying encounters with religious faith in America, which remains, to this day, deeply embedded in the complex tapestry of race and the unresolved legacies of slavery. I had attended scores of worship services, meeting hundreds of people who sensed a profound emotional and spiritual bond to Miss Kitty or Bishop Andrew. A white congregation had hewed to the standard "white" narrative, that Kitty was deeply loyal to James Andrew, and that the Bishop was a martyred victim of northern intolerance. With equal passion, an Afrocentric church had held an ancestral walk to the site of Kitty's renovated slave quarters, pouring out libations to her and giving her a new name in the West African Ewe language, as they heard her spirit declare she was a victim of sexual assault by nineteenth-century white clergymen. In the old Springfield Baptist Church in Augusta, Georgia, within the physical building that Miss Kitty had once worshipped as a child, I was led in a prayer by the elderly pastor that Miss Kitty's "children's children" would someday be found and brought back to Springfield. Such prayers were echoed in churches in Oxford, Georgia; Summerfield, Alabama; and Washington, D.C. Yet in all this work, to my deep disappointment, I had not been able to trace any of Miss Kitty's living descendants, and had become convinced that none existed.

In summer 2009 the trail had suddenly turned hot. A Freedman's Bank record from 1871 had indicated that Kitty really had an African American husband named Nathan who had fathered children with her. The eldest of these children, a man named Alfred (or "Alford") Boyd, had appeared within a year after the Civil War in, of all places, the small Iowa town of Keosauqua. So in July 2009, accompanied by my wife and fellow anthropologist Ellen Schattschneider, I traveled to Iowa and began to trace the career of Kitty's eldest son. Alford had, we soon learned, become a minister in the African Methodist Episcopal (AME) Church and spent his career serving in congregations across the Midwest. With help from church members, archival records, and court documents, I finally located Rev. Alford Boyd's great-grandson, Lee Caldwell, a man in his eighties, who still worshipped at Allen Chapel AME Church, the institution his great-grandfather had pastored a century earlier. The church's current pastor, Rev. Virgil Wood, kindly agreed to accompany me to Mr. Caldwell's home and introduce me.

Standing on the house's threshold, I was enormously excited but also anxious: Would Mr. Caldwell have any interest in his family history, and would his family memories confirm or undercut the histories I had reconstructed? Would he and his family regard my visit as an intrusion? What would it mean to them to learn that their ancestress had for so long been a subject of fascination and debate, a veritable object of myth, in communities so far away from them? What would it mean that the story of Miss Kitty, over which I had so long been obsessed, would now belong, at long last, to her descendants?

Mr. Caldwell opened the door. He was a handsome, smiling man, a little bit unsteady on his cane but with a firm and friendly gaze. He engaged in some raucous repartee with the pastor, whom he had not seen for a while, and invited us into the parlor. As he sat next to me on the sofa, he turned, with a twinkle in his eye and a spirit of fun in his voice, and said, "Now, young man, what can I do for you, and what can you do for me?"

THE BOOK THAT FOLLOWS is my effort to answer Mr. Caldwell's profound and mischievous question. How might a critical excavation of the mythologies that still surround American chattel slavery be mutually enriching and transformative, for the descendants of the enslaved and for the heirs of white privilege? How might revisiting these mythologies help to free all of us from their enduring hold and help us chart a new and more democratic path? Over the course of the book I attempt to revisit this powerful and enduring myth in a number of different ways, drawing on the conceptual toolkits of structuralism, literary studies, history, and anthropology.

Chapter 1 begins with the more or less present moment, with how the stories of Miss Kitty and Bishop Andrew are remembered in Oxford, Georgia, in the early twenty-first century, and then moves on to key interpretive challenges faced in this study, among them the enduring conundrums of race and slavery in the history of American Methodism and the operations of mythology itself in modern society. I propose we may revisit competing versions of the narrative through the lens of the structural study of myth, teasing out transformations of underlying enigmas about kinship, race, sexuality, and gender in the American cultural order. The struggles over this particular myth are illustrative of much broader contests over how slavery is to be represented and remembered in American society, as well as enduring debates over the legacies of slavery and race-based inequality.

Chapter 2 moves back in time, grounding our discussion in terms of the operations of kinship and descent relations in a slavery-based society. Chattel slavery, while predicated on the commoditized buying and selling of human beings, was also embedded in overlapping spheres of white and African American family dynamics that in some respects functioned as an overarching kinship system. I demonstrate these general points through considering slavery and kinship in antebellum Newton County, Georgia, where the key episodes in the Kitty-Andrew story unfolded and where the standard renditions of the narrative were first circulated.

Part 2 traces the mythologization of the historical events involving

Miss Kitty and Bishop Andrew, as they have been circulated and trans-formed across 160 years. Chapters 3 and 4 revisit written and oral texts to tease out their ideological agendas and their enduring force. In chapter 3, I consider how the story of Andrew and Kitty was developed in foundational published texts from the 1840s into the 1880s. Chapter 4 traces how these core texts, in turn, have been selectively drawn upon and modified in successive retellings of the story, through the twentieth century and into the early twenty-first century.

The next two chapters revisit this powerful mythology in a different way, considering how these narratives and counternarratives have been embedded in lived material spaces and landscapes. Chapter 5 explores how these mythic accounts have been embedded and struggled over within and through landscape sites, primarily in the Oxford city cemetery. Chapter 6 concentrates on struggles over the presentation and interpretation of the slave quarters known as "Kitty's Cottage," including a June 2007 ritual held at the site by a visiting Afrocentric congregation from an Atlanta suburb.

Part 3 revisits the myth in a third vein, through what anthropologists term a historical ethnography. I explore the actual social circumstances and historical experiences of the persons and communities subjected to mythologization, including erasure by dominant texts and visible material forms. I thus shift emphasis from mythology, social memory, and ritual practice to the historical circumstances of the slaves whom Bishop Andrew owned and the descendants of these enslaved people. Chapter 7 offers a partial reconstruction of the puzzling life story of Kitty herself and traces the experiences of her children and their descendants, as they traveled to Alabama, Arkansas, Iowa, Washington, D.C., and elsewhere. (Appendices 3 and 4 offer additional historical background on the lives of Kitty, her children, and their descendants.) Chapter 8 attempts to re-construct the lives and trajectories of the other enslaved persons, around forty in number, whom Andrew owned or held, whose histories have been rendered long obscure by the mainstream narrative. (Appendix 5 offers supplementary historical material on the postemancipation experiences of these families.) In the concluding chapter I turn to continuing efforts to develop an inclusive dialogue over this difficult and challenging history, as diverse persons and families ponder the implications of a history of slavery for forging a common future.

Part One

Memory, Myth, and Kinship

Chapter One

The Myth of Kitty

ON A BRIGHT Friday morning in May 2000, a group of about fifty fifth-graders excitedly clambered out of two yellow school buses with their teachers and chaperones and entered into the fabled Old Church in Oxford, Georgia. Giggling and whispering among themselves, they took their seats in old wooden pews, glancing around the beautiful, recently restored structure, which they were told dated back to the 1840s. As they settled down, local historian Martin Porter, a leading member of the town's historical society, began to speak to the group about the story of an enslaved woman named Kitty, who, he told them, had worshipped in this very church and lived next door to it before the Civil War.[1] Porter, an avuncular, vigorous white man in his eighties, was an accomplished raconteur and held most of the children spellbound. Porter recounted the tale he had told hundreds of times over the previous decade:

> Now I wanna tell you a story about a little girl who was just about your age at that time. She was a slave girl, but she was of mixed blood. And the person who owned her was Mrs. Powers in Augusta. And Mrs. Powers thought a great deal of this little girl. Her name was Kitty. And, uh, she wanted to keep Kitty from being used like most slave girls at that time were used. That is, to produce more slaves. So Mrs. Powers had the idea of willing Kitty—that is, putting in her will when she died—that Kitty would belong to a minister's wife. And this minister's wife was Mrs. Amelia Andrew. She's buried up here in the cemetery. And of course Kitty is, too. Now, when Kitty was born in 1822, and when Kitty became the property of Mrs. Andrews in 1834, Kitty was twelve years old. How many of you are twelve years old? The rest of you are what, eleven, thirteen? Well, anyhow, Kitty was about your age, and she became the property of

Mrs. Andrews, but at that time a woman's property was also that of her husband's.

You girls have come a long way . . . you can own property yourself.

Now, there was a law, an ordinance in the Methodist Church that said that a bishop could not own slaves. A lot of people around in this area did not believe in slavery, but at the same time a lot of them did. And the laws of Georgia supported slavery. That is one person owning another. That's a bad idea, isn't it? I'm glad we don't think that way now. But the people back then did, because they could make money that way. You know, however you make money, that's how some people like it.

Well, there came a time when Kitty was nineteen, when the will stipulated that she was to be given the chance to go to Liberia. You know where Liberia is? Anybody know? Tell me where. . . . It's on the west coast of Africa. How would Kitty get there? She'd have to go by boat, and by train before she'd get where she could get on the boat.

Well, Kitty was told what her choices were. She could either go to Liberia and be a free person, make her own living. (She wasn't but nineteen.) I don't know if she could read or write. Or, she could stay with the Bishop's family. Now Kitty loved the Bishop's family. She was treated just like one of the members of that . . . and they loved her.

Kitty said, "I don't know where Liberia is. I might die before I get there. I'd rather stay with the Bishop's family."

Well, the Bishop kinda liked that. He was . . . he said to Kitty, "I'll build you a house and put it right backa my house." And that house is the one on the hill across the creek there. The Bishop's house was . . . and you know where Kitty's house is? It's been moved several times but right . . . the last time it was moved it was moved right backa this church. So you'll see Kitty's Cottage this morning.

Now that building is about 156—7—years old at least, 'cause it was built right after this church was built, the original part of it. And the wings that are suspended from this church were built about forty-five or seven years later. Something like that.

Now, what happened when Kitty wanted to be a member of the Bishop's family? She would have to be his slave, because the laws of Georgia wouldn't permit otherwise. See, if she stayed in Georgia . . . well, it happened in 1844, just two or three years later, this same thing became an issue in the Methodist Church. And the Methodist

Church the next year had such a hassle over this issue, until they split into the Methodist Episcopal Church, South, and the Methodist Episcopal Church, North. That's pretty hard to say, but I say it. And you know how long it remained split? Ninety-five years. Church didn't come back together until 1939. And even then some of the bishops didn't like the idea. And one of them's up at the cemetery. I won't name him, you wouldn't remember him anyhow, I'll betcha.[2]

Any questions, up to this point? Yes?

A white female student asked, "How did she die?" Porter gave her a broad smile and responded,

I'm glad you asked that. I suppose we all got to die, haven't we? Now, Kitty in 1850 was about twenty-eight years old. Now, she had had three children. Incidentally, she had married a free man by the name of Nathan Shell, and she lived, they lived, in that cottage just back of the church. It was on the other side of the hill there. And she had a boy in 1844. A boy in 1846. A little girl in 1848. And, uh, pretty soon after that, Kitty became stricken with disease. Now all kinds of diseases were movin' around here in this part of the country. Yellow fever, diphtheria, malaria, you just name it, and consumption, that sort of thing . . .

And Kitty realized she had a disease that was gonna take her out. So she called to the Bishop and she expressed to the Bishop how much she appreciated what the Bishop's family had done for her. And she commended her little girl who was just a few years old to one of the Bishop's daughters, I'm not sure which one.

But, uh, anyhow, she died we think around 1850-something. She is buried up there in the Bishop's lot. She wanted to be buried next to Miss Amelia, her mistress.

Incidentally, pretty soon after Kitty decided she wanted to stay with the Bishop's family in 1841, uh, Mrs., uh, Andrew, Amelia Andrew, died the next spring. And Kitty waited on her day and night. They could hardly get her to go to bed. And when Miss Andrew realized she was about die, she asked Kitty to come over and kiss her, because she loved her like a daughter. And, uh, Kitty did kiss her.

Any questions? Yes, sir?

A white male student asked, "How old was Kitty when she died?" and Porter responded,

She was in her early thirties, I think. I would give anything if some of you students would find out the year that Kitty did die.[3] I'd give you a . . . I would give anything if I could get a hold of Kitty's descendants. We do know about one of the descendants who went to Washington, D.C., early on to be educated. And, uh, in 1877 a man from Oxford who was writing a book ran across this boy who was carrying messages from one place to another, in Washington between you know the big buildings.[4] Of course [chuckling] I have a pretty good job myself.

The lead white teacher, glancing at her watch, told the students, "OK, one more question," and Porter requested, "And repeat it for me." An African American female student, one of four African American students present, asked, "Did they treat the girl like a slave, or . . . ?" The white teacher repeated the question for Porter, who was cupping his ear, "Did they treat Kitty like a slave. Or was she like one of the family?" Porter responded, "She was like one of the family. They were called 'servants' in the Bishop's house. A lot of families treated people well. Some of them didn't."

The teacher thanked him, and the students shuffled outside as Porter led them around the back of the church. A local white woman dressed in mid-nineteenth-century dress took them through the slave quarters Kitty had resided in, known as "Kitty's Cottage." The children then got back on the buses and returned to school.

Later that afternoon, John Pliny ("J. P.") Godfrey Jr., one of two African Americans on the Oxford City Council, sat in the living room of his cousin Margaret Watkins, as he told her about Martin's Porter presentation, which he had listened to while seated quietly in a rear pew of the church.[5] "Well, Margaret," he sighed, "all I can say is that Martin was in fine form this morning. He had those children eating right out of his hand. Why, did you know, Miss Kitty was just 'one of the family' and they just loved her so much that couldn't get enough of her!"

Margaret laughed ruefully, "I'll say they loved her. Or at least the Bishop did, making her his mistress and all that."

J. P. continued, "And she just wanted to stay in slavery so much, she just pleaded with the Bishop to keep her."

Margaret continued in the same sardonic vein, "That's right, slavery was just a regular social welfare system, just took care of all your needs.

No worries at all." Laughing, she added, "That's why she just needed but a moment to decide, when the chance was offered, that she wanted to be a slave forever!"

J. P. chuckled as he responded, "And I just love the part that Kitty was just too ignorant to know slavery was being argued over all the country, since she was 'just as innocent as could be.' Had no idea about the coming storm clouds. Too busy cooking and cleaning, after all."

Margaret smiled impishly and looked over at me, "It's just like Grandmother used to say: 'What did white people think we were doing all day in the kitchen, just cooking? No, sir, we were. . . .'" She and J. P. then simultaneously delivered the beloved punch line, passed down through the generations of their extended family: "We were *listening*!"

"White people just plumb forgot we were listening to *everything*!" J. P. delightedly repeated, as they both rocked back and forth with laughter.

Then J. P. suddenly stopped smiling as his face took on a look of pain. He leaned forward, his voice now low, "But seriously, Margaret, we have to do something about this. We just can't keep letting these lies get delivered to our children. Somebody has to tell them the truth for a change." Margaret took his hand and held it for a long moment in silence as she looked at him and quietly nodded.

Memory Work in Oxford, Georgia

I take these exchanges as my point of departure for considering the nature of social memory in the small town of Oxford, Georgia, birthplace of Emory University and designated "shrine" of the Methodist Episcopal Church. The modern social geography of this carefully designed community, thirty miles east of Atlanta, foregrounds the story of Miss Kitty, an enslaved mulatto woman who lived in Oxford from 1840 until her death in April 1851. New residents of the town, including students at Oxford College (the initial Emory campus), are frequently taken on tours of the key landscape points associated with "Kitty" (usually termed "Miss Kitty" by African American residents) and her white owner, Methodist Bishop James Osgood Andrew, first president of the board of trustees of Emory College.[6] These sites include the carefully restored house in which Kitty allegedly once lived and the city's long-segregated white cemetery, in which, whites often insist, Kitty is the only person of color buried. In the cemetery stands an elaborate stone tablet, erected in 1939 by a prominent wealthy white segregationist, on which is inscribed the official "white" version of the story of Kitty and Bishop Andrew. Her grave, marked in 2000 with a modest headstone by an all-white private foundation, and her preserved house, renovated by the nearly all-white local historical society, are often spoken of by local whites as the most important historical sites in the county. Over the past century and a half, Kitty's story has been retold in hundreds of local and national publications. Since the 1930s, her "cottage" and grave have come to function as veritable pilgrimage sites for thousands of Georgia's white residents, including weekly busloads of schoolchildren brought in for "educational visits" from throughout the state, of the sort led by Martin Porter in the opening vignette.

I have been struck by how often the Kitty story surfaces in conversations with local whites about the contemporary trials and tribulations of "the family." Many white residents, when bemoaning the current frantic pace of family life and the pervasive air of distrust between neighbors, often bring up the case of Kitty in a nostalgic or elegiac tone, as an illustration of how "things used to be different here." In white versions of the story, Kitty refused manumission when it was offered to her in 1841 and was allowed by her master, Bishop Andrew, to reside in her own small cottage behind his mansion in de facto freedom. There, it is said, Kitty "looked after" local children, white and black, and treated them with warmth and respect. As one white woman noted, "Kitty's story reminds us how families used to be, and how things still should be." Since 1994, many local white families have volunteered time, money, and effort to help restore Kitty's former residence, a process that has not, as of this writing, included any African American residents of the town.

In this book I consider why the Kitty narrative has been so densely embedded in the white-managed local landscape, and explore the long-term consequences of this peculiar mythologized geography for local white and African American families. I also explore why and how the story of Bishop Andrew and his connections with slavery have widely resonated far beyond Oxford and Emory University, finding their way into popular fiction, public commentary, and works of academic scholarship. In so doing, I reflect upon how classical anthropological approaches to myth, ritual, and place—an intellectual tool kit primarily developed for the analysis of small-scale non-Western societies—might be relevant to the analysis of the modern American conundrum of race.

Oxford, Georgia

Oxford, Georgia, is a small town of about twenty-five hundred persons, immediately north of the Newton County seat, Covington. Sixty percent white, 40 percent African American, its citizens dwell in homes ranging from million-dollar restored antebellum mansions to multiple-unit low-income housing. Although many families cherish historical links to agriculture, no working farms remain in the town. Many of those white residents who do not work at Oxford College are employed in the growing financial and biotechnology firms that have relocated to the county, although some commute daily to Atlanta, thirty miles west. About 40 percent of white families consider themselves to be long-term residents of the county. The majority states that they have made a conscious decision to live in Oxford, to get away from the filth, hubbub, and crime of the city.

Until two decades ago, most African Americans residents of Oxford were employed at Emory's Oxford College, the Porterdale Textile mills, or as servants and farm workers; most now work at semiskilled labor in local concrete firms, at factories or in service jobs, or are retired on fixed incomes, although some have managerial positions in local firms. About 80 percent of Oxford's African American citizens consider their families to be long-term residents of the town, and many can trace their ancestry back to persons enslaved by local landowners and Emory College faculty and officials, including Bishop James Osgood Andrew himself.

It will come as no surprise, in this social context, that multiple versions of the Kitty story exist. For the vast majority of Oxford's white residents, the Kitty legend for generations has been understood as a moving tale of loyalty and noble suffering. In the standard white version of the story, Kitty was inherited by an unwilling slaveholder, Methodist Bishop James Osgood Andrew (1794–1871), in the mid-1830s, when she was twelve years old. After she voluntarily refused manumission (conditional on transport to Liberia) at age nineteen in 1841, she was allowed by her benevolent owner to reside in a house that he built for her, adjacent to his own house. There, he allegedly told her, "You may live as free as I am." In time, the story goes, she married a free African American man, Nathan Shell, and bore him three children before her death in the 1850s. Throughout Kitty's short life, it is said, she was intensely loyal to Bishop Andrew and his family. For this reason, she is the only person of color buried in the historically white section of the segregated Oxford City Cemetery. As a further sign of the special bond between Kitty and the Bishop's white family, the story goes, the Bishop's adult daughter Elizabeth took responsibility for caring for Kitty's infant daughter.

Since Andrew's slaveholding was the precipitating cause of the 1844–45 split between the northern and southern Methodist churches (which lasted until the two wings of the church were reunited in 1939), the story of Kitty takes on particular poignancy for many white southerners: Andrew, a reluctant and accidental slaveowner who only sought to preserve Kitty from the sexual depredations of slavery, was unjustly pilloried by his hypocritical northern counterparts. Nearly all long-term white residents of Oxford, as far as I can tell, accept this general version of the story.

As we have seen, African American families in Oxford have a rather different relationship to the Kitty legend. My oldest African American informants recall hearing from the "old people" of the community that Kitty was Bishop Andrew's coerced mistress, and that Andrew was the covert father of her children, whom he never acknowledged. Some profess to be bored by the whole business, which they regard as a puzzling (or, at times, offensive) white obsession. Still others critique local white fascination with Kitty and with the restoration of her small house (referred to as "Kitty's Cottage" by most local whites) as an attempt to paper over the horrors of slavery and to evade full accountability for the city's antebellum slaveowning history. For many local African Americans the persistence of the standard Kitty narrative in the public square is deeply painful and perplexing.

Situating the Research:
Ethnographic Encounters and Partnerships

Although a work of scholarship, this book originates outside of "pure" academic pursuits. In fall 1999 I began teaching at Oxford College of Emory University, a two-year undergraduate institution that functions as a feeder school into the main Atlanta campus of Emory University. I was eager to give my first- and second-year undergraduate students in anthropology and sociology a sense of real-world social problems that might be productively addressed through a combination of practical action and intellectual analysis. I was quickly drawn to the dynamics of race and inequality in the surrounding community. My students and I undertook study projects in Oxford and its environs, documenting how access to material and cultural resources might vary according to race, gender, social class, and ethnicity. We were especially intrigued by the famous dictum of French sociologist Pierre Bourdieu that the most important values and relations of power in society "go without saying, because they come without saying." For Bourdieu and other scholars of practice theory, the most vital organizing features of any particular social community are generally not communicated overtly or verbally, but are rather conveyed silently, through regular actions lodged in the physical, moving human body and its extensions, including adornment and lived space, especially in houses and domestic architecture. Adopting a term coined by the early-twentieth-century anthropologist Marcel Mauss, Bourdieu calls this mass of activities, dispositions, and orientations toward the world the "habitus."[7] For Bourdieu, the habitus is a form of tacit knowledge that may not be explicitly articulated but which structures and is structured by the taken-for-granted practices and environmental spaces of everyday life.

How, we discussed in class, might a habitus be discerned in the community around us, and to what extent might a habitus be amenable to change? Having worked as an anthropologist on the cultural symbolism of landscape in southern Africa, I tried to direct students to pay particular attention to the local organization of social space: how might forms of social inequality be "naturalized" by everyday practices embedded in the layout of land and architecture? As a research fellow attached to Emory's new research center on Myth and Ritual in American Life, an Alfred Sloan Foundation–funded initiative on American working families, I was especially eager to involve students in studying the social and cultural dynamics of the family through attention to the "signifying practices" of everyday life.

We thus began our inquiries in the Oxford City Cemetery, a few blocks north of the campus, an arena in which family memory and the politics of race continuously intersect. As it happened, Martin Porter and J. P. Godfrey Jr. gave us successive tours of the cemetery. Students took careful notes on the implicit social values embedded silently in this complex landscape. They noted the beautiful, elegant lawns and monuments of the white half of the cemetery, in striking contrast to the visibly neglected half of the cemetery where African Americans were buried. This, they were told, "is just the way things are" in southern towns, where race still, as sociologists would put it, "overdetermines" access to resources.

I had thought our trips to the cemetery would simply serve as object lessons in the naturalization of social difference. But rather to my surprise, many of my students—Asian, white, and African American—quickly asked in class, "Why are we just observing? Why can't we do something about this?" Why, I was asked, can't we help restore the historic black cemetery? Why can't we do something to make things right?

We quickly arranged for meetings with J. P. and other leaders of the local African American community, including the two historically black congregations in town. After substantial discussion we were given permission to begin a restoration and documentation project in the "black cemetery." Each Saturday morning, more and more students, faculty, staff members, and community members would gather in the cemetery, trimming back privet, repairing erosion, unearthing stone markers, and recording the locations of gravesites. My wife, Ellen Schattschneider, brought her students out from Emory University's main Atlanta campus and began to plant flower plots. A cedar tree of remembrance was planted in the oldest section of the African American cemetery, and we mounted exhibitions in the college and university libraries on the history of the African American cemetery and the local African American community. The students began to turn their concerted attention to campaigning for the official desegregation of the city cemetery.

Throughout this process, white and black residents repeatedly called our attention to the story of Miss Kitty and Bishop Andrew, commemorated in two memorial markers in the cemetery. That spring, Forrest Sawyer Jr., who had spearheaded the Southern Christian Leadership Conference's struggle in Covington for desegregation in 1970, visited the Oxford campus to talk about race and justice in Newton County. After lecturing on the local civil rights movement, he told my students, "But, if you really want to understand what makes this county tick, you need to go way back in time, before *Plessy*, before Emmett Till, before Little Rock, before Selma and Birmingham. You need to learn the story of a beautiful woman, Miss Kitty, and a white bishop, right here in this town. You learn the *real* story that'll put this whole county in a whole new light. Then you'll understand why some of us feel we've always been on the outside looking in!"

In the weeks that followed, largely in order to answer the students' persistent questions about Miss Kitty, I began to follow Forrest's admonition, trying to tease out both how the mainstream white story of Kitty had developed and what had in fact taken place in Oxford in the 1840s.

A decade later, this book is the result of these inquiries, initially generated by Forrest Sawyer's challenge and by the difficult questions my students posed in 1999–2000 as we began our service learning projects. This study has emerged through extended conversations with African American and white residents of Oxford, as well as what anthropologists term "participant-observation." In addition to the physical labor of helping to restore burial plots, I have attended worship services and family reunions, worked with community members of all ages on genealogy and family history projects, and supervised a community history intern project for low-income minority youth in the region. Although I have remained committed to the values of careful, empirically based research, it has been difficult at times to disentangle my work as a scholar, a teacher, and community advocate.

After my wife and I left Emory University to teach at Brandeis University in Waltham, Massachusetts, my links with the legacies of slavery at Emory unexpectedly deepened. The leaders of a remarkable initiative at Emory, the Transforming Community Project, widely known as TCP, had become interested in the teaching work I had done around race, slavery, and memory on and around campus. For five years they have regularly invited me back to the university to help facilitate seminars for faculty, staff, and students on race and difference.

These regular TCP visits have not only afforded me opportunities for archival and ethnographic research but also encouraged me to explore my own tacit assumptions about race, gender, class, and region. As a white secular Jewish male and the product of an academic family, I had perhaps never given sufficient attention to the operations in white privilege in my own life and scholarship. Through regular presentations and dialogues with TCP participants, I have been asked to reflect critically about my own positionality, about the set of forces that have allowed me over the years to do this kind of research. I have become more and more conscious of the dynamics of power in historical and anthropological research. Whose story is this? What right do I have to presume to tell the story of Miss Kitty, her descendants, and those of other enslaved people, whose life stories have so long been obscured? In turn, as a person whose proximate cultural roots are in the U.S. Northeast, how might I responsibly negotiate the task of critiquing a set of standardized assumptions in the white South? As a largely secular Jew, in turn, how well can I engage imaginatively and respectfully with an overwhelmingly Christian narrative, attempting to understand the motivations and aspirations of white and African American Protestant persons and networks, past and present?

This research has thus in part been a process of critical self-examination and self-discovery that has been, in curious ways, a profound homecoming for me. Although I grew up in Washington, D.C., I primarily knew only the city's white and upper-middle-class neighborhoods. Tracing Miss Kitty's second son, Russell Nathan Boyd, who moved to Washington in the late 1860s, has deepened my appreciation of the city's proud African American heritage and caused me to rediscover anew my hometown. Along the way, I have come to appreciate in many respects how deeply southern the District of Columbia is, long embedded in contradictions of race and class that are often elided or obscured by its cosmopolitan and internationalist aspirations. These emerging insights were intensified during the inauguration of Barack Obama in January 2009, when my mother invited Forrest Sawyer Jr. and his wife Sharon to stay with her to participate in that memorable week. I had the extraordinary opportunity, in effect, to witness the District through Forrest's and Sharon's eyes, as they pondered the mysteries of race and transformation in the nation's capital. Moments after the new president had been sworn in, we met an elderly, wheelchair-bound African American woman from a small southern town. Pinned to her apron were photographs of her four grandparents, all born "in slavery times." She had brought them, in effect, to Washington to see this blessed moment. "I suppose," remarked Forrest with a broad smile, "you could say we're not on the outside looking in anymore. We are here!" The work of witnessing stories of the enslaved, of bringing to light the mythology and the histories of enslavement, had never seemed so urgent.

At the same time, this work has forced me to bridge geographical and historical distances, challenging assumptions about the South I had imbued growing up in the North. The Oxford white community has treated me with extraordinary generosity. Among many others, I remain deeply grateful to Virgil Eady, a direct descendant of one of the leading slaveowners of nineteenth-century Emory College, and to his wife Louise, for generously sharing an extraordinary set of family documents on slavery in Oxford, and for their unflagging support of my research.

Through these partnerships, with J. P. and his wife Mary, with Forrest and Sharon, with Virgil and Louise, with the living descendants of Catherine Boyd/Miss Kitty, and with many others, I have become acutely aware that my work on Oxford, Emory, and the Kitty-Andrew story is part of a long conversation. The interlocutors in this conversation are not only the friends that I have made through this work but many other presences and voices, near and far, some long gone from the scene. A vast range of actors and institutions have overlapped and intersected in the continuing production of the mythic narratives explored in the book, among them the northern and southern Methodist Episcopal churches, the historically black Methodist denominations, abolitionist and pro-slavery advocates, segregationists and civil rights activists, clergy and laity. To be sure, in producing, circulating, and contesting multiple versions of the Kitty-Andrew mise-en-scène, these actors have often talked over one another, or past each other, while operating on distinctly unequal footing. Yet they have, nonetheless, been engaged in a long and winding conversation that spans at least six generations.

Long Conversations: Colonialism, Tacit Knowledge, and Mutual Transformation

My reference to a conversation builds on another study of Methodism, race, and power half a world away from the American South. In their two-volume study, *Of Revelation and Revolution*, Jean and John Comaroff characterize colonialism in southern Africa as a "long conversation" between African and European protagonists.[8] Often operating on profoundly unequal terms, the various parties entered into complex exchanges of practices and significances that were to prove mutually transforming for all concerned. The story of Methodist evangelism and its "civilizing mission" in South Africa cannot be understood simply as the imposition of an alien worldview on local indigenous life worlds but is rather an uneven process of debate, riposte, and continuous reformulation. Building on Bourdieu, the Comaroffs demonstrate that the most dynamic sites of mutual transformation lay in the realm of the habitus, of tacit forms of knowledge that resided in techniques of the body, including adornment and healing, domestic architecture, quotidian practices of agriculture and animal husbandry, and the management of cash and currency. The most potent shifts in political and moral consciousness, among colonizers and colonized alike, came about not solely at the level of explicit discourse but often within and through the realm of that which comes without saying through the silent, meaningful practices lodged in bodily comportment, the fashioning of the self, and the contours of the built en-

vironment. To listen in on these historical conversations requires atten-
tiveness not only to that which is said but also to that which is unsaid, to
the constant play of images, material forms, and bodily action over time.

So too for the evolving, contested narratives of slavery and its legacies
with which this volume is concerned. At first consideration, the circula-
tion and dissemination of stories about Bishop James Osgood Andrew
and slavery may appear more of a monologue than a dialogue, more of
a polemic than a conversation. The dominant narrative has, after all,
shown remarkable staying power over the past century and a half. The
standard white, paternalist version of the tale is the only rendition inscribed in the Oxford built environment, and vastly predominates in the
hundreds of published accounts of the story. Yet if the dominant white
spoken and printed accounts have been manifestly monologic, more nuanced conversations have emerged in the shadows and on the sidelines.
Monuments and restored buildings, while seeming to proclaim a single
version of the story, have unexpectedly opened up fissures in the seemingly taken-for-granted order of things. A long-untended section of the
cemetery may occasion a new, critical insight among persons excluded
for decades from centers of economic and political privilege. Resistance
may not necessarily be lodged in spoken or printed language, but rather
be registered in a nuanced glance, a meaningful gesture. Out of such
signals and reformulations, large and small, are the long conversations
of power and dissent constituted.

Methodism, Slavery, and Race

The Kitty-Andrew story is directly situated in the most difficult set of
conversations in the history of Methodism in North America, those
revolving around slavery and racial justice. Methodism's emergence in
Britain in the context of the early Industrial Revolution was intertwined
with the formation of working-class and petit bourgeois sensibilities that
celebrated free labor and the inviolable sovereign dignity of each human
individual. Methodist founder John Wesley and his brother Charles, who
had resided and preached in coastal Georgia in the 1730s, were passionate opponents of slavery. In Britain, Africa, and the northern United
States during the early and middle nineteenth century, Methodism became increasingly associated with antislavery positions; indeed, many
British Methodists would campaign for British imperial expansion into

Africa precisely to combat the inequities of the slave trade.[9] In the southern United States the picture was more complex, as white slaveowners became more prominent in church leadership and as many whites sought theological legitimation for the peculiar institution.

Throughout the American colonies and in early U.S. history, the Methodist movement was notably egalitarian and multiracial; important African American and woman preachers emerged in congregations that initially were integrated across the spectra of race, ethnicity, and class. Yet contradictions and fractures within these egalitarian impulses quickly came to the fore. As many persons of color sensed themselves marginalized within the faith, separate black churches arose, most notably the African American Episcopal Church, formed in 1816, and the African Methodist Episcopal Zion Church, organized in 1821. Struggles over race, slavery, and inclusiveness within the larger Methodist Episcopal Church continued to rage, leading to the breakaway formation of the abolitionist Wesleyan Methodist Connection in 1843. The next year, in May 1844, matters came to a head at the General Conference of the Methodist Episcopal Church in New York City, when Bishop James Osgood Andrew's status as a slaveowner leaped onto the national stage. After a long series of convoluted parliamentary maneuvers and legalistic debates, the majority of delegates voted to request Bishop Andrew to abstain from exercising his duties as a bishop until he had removed the "impediment" of his slaveholding.

As we shall see, the respectful and moderate language of the resolution was scorned by abolitionist activists, but was nonetheless greeted with outrage by southern delegates, who took rapid steps to dissolve the national church and create the Methodist Episcopal Church, South. Only at the General Conference in Kansas City in 1939 was the Methodist Episcopal Church (MEC) reunited. This reunion was predicated on a racial compromise that many black Methodists viewed as a fundamental betrayal of the faith's egalitarian principles, the creation of a segregated "Central Jurisdiction" to which persons of color were relegated within the national church until the late 1960s.[10]

Conferences within the Methodist Church, it should be noted, are not simply administrative or bureaucratic gatherings for the conduct of church business and assignment of ministers. Since the emergence of the faith, conferences have functioned as complex ritual arenas, through which ordained and lay members reenter a sacred space and time of origins, through which the entire religious movement is resanctified and revitalized.[11] As such they may occasion profound collective experiences of spiritual unity or bitter encounters with division.

It would be hard to overstate the national impact of the New York General Conference of 1844 and the subsequent schism of the MEC. Methodism was at the time the largest religious movement in the United States, deeply interwoven into the nation's political, cultural, and civic life.[12] Morris Davis reports, "Ulysses S. Grant is rumored to have said there were three major political parties in the United States, if you counted the Methodists."[13] Numerous proponents of southern states' rights and nullification would cite the northern censuring of Bishop Andrew as a grave insult against southern honor and an indicator of the ultimate northern intention of eradicating slavery by force.[14] Many white southerners to this day cite the case of Bishop Andrew as a preeminent example of northern intolerance toward their southern brethren.

Having said this, it is important to understand that evangelical outreach to persons of color remained enormously important to white southern Methodists, before and after the 1844–45 schism of the national church, as it was after the Civil War. Like British nonconformist missionaries laboring in Africa during the nineteenth century, white southern Methodists usually viewed conversion of persons of African descent as a profound and sacred duty, even when many powerful whites feared that the Christian message of spiritual liberation might spark insurrection and revolutionary action.[15]

Marriage and the Civilizing Mission

As the Comaroffs demonstrate, a central theme of the long conversation swirling around nonconformist evangelism in early and mid-nineteenth-century southern Africa was the nature of marriage and the domestic sphere. Methodist missionaries hoped to sow the seeds of a virtuous agrarian yeoman peasantry organized through monogamous Christian-sanctioned marriage and bourgeois conceptions of free labor, legitimate commerce, and the loving, well-regulated household.

To be sure, antebellum southern Methodists in the United States differed drastically from their British contemporaries in Africa on the question of chattel slavery. The global struggle against unfree labor was in many respects the defining attribute of British Methodist evangelism during this period, and gradually came to be critical to Methodist self-conceptions in the U.S. free states. In contrast, most southern Methodists by the early nineteenth century had come to embrace the principles and values of the slavery system. Yet for all these differences, which would by 1844 sever American Methodism for nearly a century, the white U.S. southern Methodists shared with their British and northern counterparts a deep belief in the ennobling consequences of sacramental marriage for persons of color. The Methodist mission to plantation slaves continuously emphasized the value of monogamous marriage, within the framework of devotion to the white master.

The standard white rendition of the Kitty story thus encapsulates in mythic form the ideals or fantasies of the "civilizing mission" of antebellum southern Methodism. White evangelical labor among slave populations (which Bishop Andrew termed "the noblest prize of the Gospel") aimed to foster loyalty, humility, and virtue among bondservants, predicated on the sacrament of marriage, even though the bonds of matrimony among the enslaved were not protected by law. Kitty is held up as an exemplary woman who married a proper husband, who had children within the bonds of Christian-sanctioned marriage, and who died a Christian death under the Bishop's benevolent tutelage. Significantly, Kitty's status as a virtual freedwoman in the story is not protected by law, but by the Bishop's own virtue. And this is precisely the point. For white southern Methodists before the Civil War, the rights of slaves, as property, were not to be protected by the instruments and institutions of human law, but rather were safeguarded by the moral virtue of Christian masters exercising their God-given free will. The white story of Kitty and Bishop Andrew thus presents in microcosm the idealized image of the Christian plantation, in which a benevolent white master oversees a community of loyal bondservants bound together in Christian matrimony.

Such spiritual commitments by Christian slaveowners were fraught with contradiction. As Erskine Clarke demonstrates in *Dwelling Place: A Plantation Epic*, many pious slaveholders understood themselves as operating on an imperiled terrain, suspended between neighboring irreligious "infidels" who favored the wholesale expansion of slavery as a "positive good" and northern "radical abolitionism."[16] Christian defenses of matrimony among the enslaved were constantly buffeted by the racialized sexual politics of plantation life, in which even "privileged" married women of color were subjected to rape and sexual exploitation by white men. In this context, religious slaveowners who understood themselves as benevolent masters were especially drawn to stories, such as the narrative of Kitty, of loyal slaves who achieved the holy state of matrimony under the paternalist protection of their white masters.

Slavery and Universities

The Kitty-Andrew story is also caught up in another long-running conversation—that between the institution of slavery and institutions of higher learning. Academic institutions, which largely grew out of monastic and ecclesiastical enterprises, have long been experienced as utopian spaces, prelapsarian gardens enclaved from the cares and travails of the outer world. Yet these earthly paradises rested in most instances upon the systematic and underacknowledged exploitation of bondservants. Scores of antebellum colleges in North America were deeply embedded in the slave trade or in plantation slavery. Many schools profited directly and indirectly from the peculiar institution, directly owning or renting enslaved workers and housing the slaves of students. Many faculty members helped provide legal and theological legitimation for slavery through their teaching and publications, even as others were engaged in abolitionist endeavors.

For more than a century after emancipation, there was little public discussion on most campuses of this hidden history; slavery might be taught as a general topic, but its prior presence on campuses was rarely mentioned. Yet something shifted at dawn of the twenty-first century. At the same time my students and I were researching the history of slavery at Emory College, scholars and students at several other academic institutions, as it happened, were also starting to reflect more publicly upon histories and legacies of enslavement on their home campuses. In 2001 a group of graduate students at Yale University, in the context of organized labor's struggles with the university administration, produced a controversial study on slavery in the institution's history, titled "Yale, Slavery, and Abolition." The report was widely interpreted as a polemic asserting long-term continuities in Yale's exploitation of oppressed workforces. Their report was widely criticized for some inaccuracies, perhaps related to the haste of its production. Lacking administration backing, the report does not seem to have occasioned public soul-searching at an institutional level within Yale. However, the widely publicized report unquestionably encouraged critical reflection at other New England academic institutions, most notably at Brown University, which in 2003 formed a committee on slavery and justice headed by historian James T.

Campbell to examine the intimate links between the early financing of the university and the profits of the Atlantic slave trade. The committee's work, strongly supported by the university president Ruth Simmons, attracted national attention, much of it laudatory and some quite critical. The committee emphasized that from its inception Brown had been a veritable battleground in the global struggle over slavery, with prominent pro-slavery and antislavery voices struggling over the implications of the institution's linkages to the slave trade and plantation slavery.

In subsequent years, faculty at many other colleges and universities, in the North and South, have delved into the intimate linkages between their schools, the slave trade, the everyday conduct of chattel slavery, and antislavery thought. In 2004 the faculty senate of the University of Alabama, inspired by the research and activism of legal historian Alfred Brophy, issued an apology to descendants of slaves who were owned by faculty members or who worked on campus in the years before the Civil War. In 2005 the University of North Carolina–Chapel Hill mounted a major exhibition on slavery in the making of the university; that same year, the UNC graduating class funded an "Unsung Founders" memorial honoring the persons of color who in bondage and freedom built and maintained the university. The College of William and Mary in 2009 initiated "The Lemon Project: A Journey of Reconciliation," named for an enslaved person owned by the college in the early eighteenth century, devoted to researching and publicizing African American labor and contributions at the college.[17] At the University of Maryland, noted historian of slavery Ira Berlin in 2009 taught a course on slavery in the university's forerunner institutions. At Harvard, Sven Beckert and I have each taught classes in which students have researched persons enslaved by Harvard presidents and faculty in the early eighteenth century. The College of Charleston has dedicated a memorial to enslaved persons buried on its campus. Eastern Illinois University is currently engaged in an intense debate over whether or not a residence hall bearing the name of Stephen Douglas should be renamed, in light of Douglas' energetic support of the extension of slavery. In January 2011, Emory University's board of trustees issued a statement of regret in reference to slavery in the school's history. Emerging out of the Transforming Community Project, a group of us organized an international conference on universities and slavery, hosted at Emory University itself in February 2011.

Why, in the early twenty-first century, is serious attention being paid, at long last, to the web of associations between slavery and institutions of higher learning? Several factors seem to have intersected. In the most general sense, late-modern citizenship has increasingly rested on public processes of documented trauma, truth telling, apology, and reconciliation. This tendency to reimagine the nation or community through therapeutic practices of restorative justice, exemplified in South Africa's post-1994 Truth and Reconciliation Commission, has increasingly become a constitutive feature of political life across the global cultural field.[18] Within the United States, a movement of scholarship and activism during the 1990s around the question of reparations brought to larger public awareness the deep linkages between major American corporations, including insurance companies, and the vast profits of the slave trade and slave-based plantation production. (Brophy himself had worked extensively on reparations before turning to the question of academic institutions.) As many universities have become, gradually, more attuned to the larger social and moral imperatives to support community-engaged scholarship and service-learning initiatives, it has become more acceptable for classes to plunge into difficult episodes in proximate history. At the same time, through recent works of literature, art, and cinema—including the films *Amistad*, *Beloved*, and *Glory*—it has become more possible to converse about slavery in public and quasi-public forums. After Brown's initiative in 2004 was covered extensively in the national media, including the *New York Times*, more scholars began to plunge into local histories of slavery on their campuses, at times with the direct support of their administrations, at times in the face of outright condemnation by alumni and senior administrators. In complicated ways, it has become more acceptable, albeit in fits and starts, to reenvision enslaved persons, so long excluded from the academy's self-conception, as members of the university family.

Slavery, Mythology, and Kinship

Nearly a century and a half after slavery's end, painful struggles endure over how the peculiar institution is to be represented and evoked in colleges and other institutions built by the labor of enslaved people, as well as in museums, heritage sites, and monuments. For the purposes of this study, it is important to emphasize that the most fraught debates over representation often revolve around spectacles of kinship and the uncertain contours of domestic space. Reenactments of auctions in which enslaved families are sold apart remain the most fraught of all public performances associated with remembering slavery.[19] Richard Handler reports that a persistent source of friction between historical staff and African American interpreters at Colonial Williamsburg concerns the status of beds in the slave quarters: the staff historians would prefer the beds be unmade, to demonstrate that slaves had to leave for the fields before dawn; in turn, the costumed interpreters who staff the quarters insist on making up the beds, to demonstrate that the enslaved had dignity and self-respect.[20] The well-intentioned 2005 *Unsung Founders* memorial at UNC–Chapel Hill also illustrates how the difficult task of commemorating slavery is intimately bound up with the domestic domain. Depicting scores of small African American male and female figures holding up a large table, in a manner reminiscent of the "Blackamoor" genre of decorative furniture, the work was greeted with scorn by some African American university workers. One food-service worker ruefully remarked, "I know they wanted to do the right thing, but really, just showing us holding up a table? It is like we are still serving those students, after all these years!"

Beyond these forms of public history, I also understand this work as being in dialogue with continuing efforts in literature, the visual arts, and performance to reconstruct the intimate psychic contours of relations between masters and slaves. Suggestively, many of the most important artistic explorations of slavery and its aftershocks have concentrated on the entanglements of kinship relations within scenarios of involuntary servitude. For example, in Winslow Homer's 1875 *Visit from the Old Mistress*, one of the greatest American paintings of the nineteenth century, a single elderly white woman, clearly the former plantation mistress, visits the cabin of five free women of color, each woman representing a different generation of an extended family. Homer signals each generation's different relationship to the white woman and the history she embodies. The central figure is a large black woman whose body bars the door and whose gaze is directly even with that of the white woman on the threshold. A young mother holds an infant girl, unquestionably born in freedom, who eyes the visitor curiously. At the far right, as far as possible from the white woman, sits a very elderly black woman, gazing intently at the white woman. We sense ourselves in the presence of a long-running narrative, reaching deep back into the time of slavery: what precisely do the older women of the family remember as they gaze upon this unwelcome visitor? What memories of sexual assault, children sold off, confidences betrayed, and unspeakable violence hover in the air between these still figures?

If Winslow Homer's painting only whispers these questions, Kara Walker's recent silhouettes shout them out dramatically. In her striking images, some set in complex dialogue with Winslow Homer's works, slavery and the mythic Old South are recast as elaborate, gothic family romances. Her work continuously ruptures the classical opposition outlined by Kirk Savage between canonical white and grotesque black bodies in nineteenth-century public statuary; white and black bodies are unexpectedly conjoined and opened to one another in an exuberant carnival of polymorphous perversity. White and black women give birth to misshapen offspring; sexual couplings are often figured as triangles that cut across the color line, all bound together in enigmatic lines of descent.

Similar categorical ruptures characterize Octavia Butler's novel *Kindred*, as the time-traveling protagonist finds herself oscillating between different positions in a long and complex kinship history spanning the present moment and the antebellum South. She must as a slave save the life of her white owner and rapist in order to ensure her own lineage and eventual existence as a modern-day person.

These literary and artistic meditations, I suggest, point the way forward for scholars seeking to comprehend the enduring mythologies of slavery that haunt contemporary social imaginations. American chattel slavery, although governed by property law and market transactions, was a complex kinship system in which the familial relations of masters and slaves were intricately intertwined and mutually constitutive. To understand and critique persistent habits of judgment about race and difference, it is essential to tease out the hidden assumptions about kinship embedded in popular narratives about slavery, and to reconstruct the long-lost histories of kinship relations that have their origins in the slavery era.

Mythic Transformations

With these thoughts in mind, let us return to the present-day struggles in Oxford, Georgia, and at Emory University over the remembrance of Miss Kitty and Bishop Andrew. For all the manifest contrasts in white and African American renditions of the narrative, and their strikingly different responses to spaces in which the story is memorialized, are these mythic accounts entirely distinct from one another? To consider this question, we should briefly consider these mythic variants as texts through the lens of classic "structural" approaches to myth, divorced from the circumstances of their performance and spatial realization.

In a well-known passage from *The View from Afar*, anthropologist Claude Lévi-Strauss proposes that myths are a culture's "a posteriori (after the fact) attempts to construct a homogeneous system on the basis of disparate rules." Hence, he suggests, "Sooner or later, mythical thinking conceives of these rules as so many possible answers to a question." Lévi-Strauss applies this insight to the diverse cultures of Polynesia, arguing that a vast range of mythic narratives found on diverse Pacific islands can be understood as attempts to answer a basic set of questions throughout the extended Polynesian region about "relations between relations,"[21] about how the relationship between brother and sister is like and unlike that between husband and wife, and so forth.

For all the obvious differences between premodern Polynesia and the contemporary United States, Lévi-Strauss's insight has a good deal of relevance to the case at hand. The various narratives of Kitty, including the manifestly opposed white and African American accounts, can be thought of as varied attempts to answer a common set of questions about the constitution of American society. One aspect of this enduring question is the formulation *E pluribus unum*, the challenge of unity in diversity. While at a manifest level this formulation is formally color-blind, it has long had at its core a set of conundrums about race and personhood. As many scholars have argued, for much of American history, the promise of democratic inclusiveness for an ever-widening group of persons rested upon the systematic exclusion of civil liberties to persons of African descent, whether legally enslaved or free. This core cultural paradox, like so many pivotal paradoxical formulations in the diverse cultures of humanity, is invariably framed in the idiom of kinship. The very system of racial apartheid upon which classic American democratic expansion rested continuously generated a new set of ambiguous kin and quasi-kin relations. Not only were new biogenetically related kin continuously reproduced across putative racial lines, but the emotional configurations of classic family dynamics were continuously recombined and redistributed: as maternal, paternal, and filial roles moved back and forth between formally black and white positions. Paraphrasing Lévi-Strauss, we might argue that the vast range of mythic narratives about American chattel slavery poses a central enigma: how are relations between masters and slaves, or their descendants, like and unlike relations among kin within free families? What forms of love and loyalty, of anger and betrayal, are generated within a national family that is half free, half unfree?

One of the most elegant meditations on these core conundrums is Ralph Ellison's climatic statement in his posthumously published novel *Juneteenth*, a book that Ellison dedicated "To That Vanished Tribe into which I was born: the American Negroes." The black protagonist contemplates his apparently adoptive son, who physically appears white and whom he had raised as "Negro" in the futile hope that the child would become a latter-day Lincoln, a defender of his oppressed brothers and sisters. Instead the boy has grown to be a virulently racist, white supremacist U.S. senator. As the senator lays dying he calls for his lost black "Father," who ponders what Providence has wrought: "There's always the mystery, of the one in the many and many in the one, the you in them and the them in you—ha!"[22]

For Ellison, the core American mystery is one of kinship, in all the rich, mutually entailed biogenetic, poetic, and spiritual dimensions of this complex term. How are we related, yet unrelated? How can we claim that our society rests on universal brotherhood while the very historical process of democratic expansion rested on domination, oppression, and racially based hierarchies? The glory of the American Dream rests in the quest for the transcendent father figure of Abraham Lincoln, yet this very quest seems to simultaneously demand the American tragedy: the repeated death of the father as his sons seek to come into their own and turn against their brothers.

These basic kinship-related cultural paradoxes may be fruitfully considered in light of anthropologist David Schneider's classic study *American Kinship: A Cultural Account*. Schneider argues that American kinship, as an idealized system of shared symbols, is founded upon a fundamental opposition between two structurally opposed cultural categories: Blood and Law. Persons classified as relatives in American culture are either related to one another through "law" or "blood," but never both. Law-based relations, typified by marriage, a human-made construct, demand that the parties not be related by blood. In contrast, blood relations, typified by the parent-child bond, are never simply a matter of law, which is a mere human-made artifice, but are rather "natural," beyond mere human choice or volition. The opposed cultural realms of blood and law are linked (or "mediated") by the core symbol, which Schneider asserts, rather surprisingly, is sexual intercourse. Sexual intercourse,

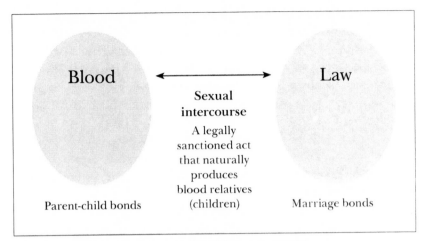

FIGURE 1.1. David Schneider's model of American kinship

which is "natural," can only legitimately occur in the context of the law-sanctioned relationship of marriage, and only sexual intercourse can produce relations founded on blood—that is to say, parent-child relations (see Figure 1.1).[23]

Schneider, concentrating on the "ethnographic present" of mid-twentieth-century North America, never discussed slavery in his model. Yet slavery's historical legacies complicate this cultural model of American kinship, challenging the fundamental structural opposition between categories of blood and law. At one level, the master-slave relationship is legal, founded on the same legal code that legitimates marriage, a formal, contract-based relationship between non-blood-related persons. But slaves also stood in quasi-filial (bloodlike) relationships to their white owners, inasmuch as they were classified as legal minors at best. Not far from Kitty's gravesite, in the otherwise all-white Oxford cemetery, stands a headstone to a white woman:

> In memory of Mary wife of Rev. Osborn Rogers. Embraced Religion August 12, 1812, Died 15 Feb 1856. The morning before her death she called her family, white and black, around her and bade them farewell. From that time as long as she could be understood she continued to praise God.

In many instances, of course, these metaphorical bloodlike relations among white and black members of the same "family" also had biogenetic components. The historical record is replete with cases of slaveowners owning or selling their biological progeny and kin. A famous case in Newton County in the 1820s, often discussed by my African American informants, centered on a young white slaveowner going to court to break his father's will, which had granted freedom and transport to a free state to a young black male slave. As the case proceeded, it became clear that the young white man was suing to retain his half-brother in bondage. This case, of course, was by no means atypical.

The varied versions of the Kitty myth, I suggest, may be understood as a series of attempts to resolve the fundamentally irresolvable paradoxes of blood and law posed by slavery. Take, for example, the common popular assertion in white renditions of the story that Kitty was first inherited by Bishop James Andrew's first wife, Ann Amelia, and that after her death the Bishop therefore was left as her reluctant legal owner. Various historians over the past century and a half have sought to correct this misconception, noting that according to the historical record Andrew directly inherited Kitty from a nonrelative. But for our purposes, the culturally significant fact is that this revised version of the story keeps on reemerging. For anthropologists, this phenomenon can be thought of as the mythic imagination in action.

What is accomplished by this frequent white version of the myth? As illustrated in Figures 1.2 and 1.3, the disturbing violations of the blood/law opposition are resolved, or at least muted, within the comforting framework of the domestic familial unit. This version emphasizes that while all the players remain within the all-embracing penumbra of the Andrew family, under the paterfamilias James Osgood, a strong distinction is preserved between relations by law and relations by blood. In many respects, Kitty and Elizabeth (Andrew's white daughter) are treated as parallel in this myth version. On the left of Figure 1.2, Kitty is inherited by law, as a consequence of the Bishop's marriage, a legal relationship. In contrast, Elizabeth is distinctly a blood relative of the Bishop. Kitty and Elizabeth can thus safely be stated, in the white variant, to have been "like sisters." Indeed, when Martin Porter and the all-white cemetery foundation placed a new headstone for Kitty in 2000 in the Andrew plot, they were careful to locate it near Ann Amelia and Elizabeth's headstones, under the spire of the Bishop Andrew obelisk, ritually reproducing the myth's model of idealized family relations.

The next stage of this myth variant further restores the blood/law distinction: Kitty is married legally to a legally "free" black man (see Figure 1.3), and within the context of this legal relationship, has children by

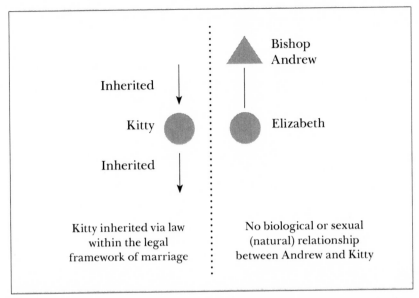

FIGURE 1.2. The white version in terms of Schneider's categorical distinction. Kitty legally inherited by Mrs. Andrew and then by Bishop Andrew. Kitty and Elizabeth said to be "like sisters."

him. As in conventional American kinship, a relationship of law produces legitimate blood relatives in a manner that parallels conventional white bourgeois family relations.

African American Transformations

Conversely, African American versions foreground the violation of the law/blood distinction. Kitty was sexually violated by Andrew and forced to bear his children. These children, in turn, were unacknowledged by their white father, who sought to remove them from the community. In this version of the myth, it becomes impossible to say whether Andrew and Kitty are related through law or blood. (In this light, it may be noteworthy that some African American informants in reconstructing the story emphasize the inevitably violent, bloody nature of master-slave relations that they believe to have characterized these coerced liaisons.) Even less clear is the blood/law distinction in the relations between Kitty, Bishop Andrew, and the products of their union: the children were the legal property of Andrew and his blood progeny; the normally "natural"

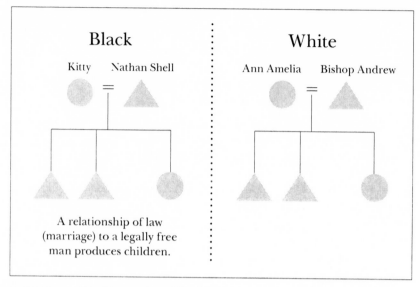

FIGURE 1.3. In white versions, Kitty's marriage to the "legally free" Nathan Shell said to be a relationship of law. Their legal marriage produces their blood or "natural" children.

bonds of blood ties were violated by his refusal to acknowledge "his own flesh and blood."

The white and African American versions of the myth may be regarded, in structuralist terms, as "transformations" of one another, playing with common elements, problems, and questions. One is reminded of the great anthropologist Franz Boas's observation about Northwest Coast Native American mythology, a line quoted by Lévi-Strauss in *The Savage Mind*, "It would seem that mythological worlds have been built up only to be shattered again, and that new worlds were built from the fragments."[21] For all their significant differences, these diverse variants of the myth of Kitty are built up out of the common fragments of American culture. Even when the various parties are not fully listening to one another, they are engaged in a long conversation about many of the fundamental challenges and puzzles in American society.

Unequal Voices?

A formal structuralist reading along the above lines is only the beginning of a full social revisiting of this evocative mythic narrative. In this book I attempt through a range of interpretive lenses to unpack the public and private stories about Bishop Andrew, Miss Kitty, and a related set of enslaved people. We begin with what might be termed the social life of the multiple version of the Andrew-Kitty tale. Why have certain versions of the narrative proliferated in public arenas, while others have been consigned to the background? How did the different variants emerge, and how have they changed over time? What social dynamics are responsible for the differing trajectories of these stories and their meanings? What, as far as can be determined, are the historical facts of the case?

Although, in an abstract sense, these myth variants may be understood as coequivalent transformations of one another, in practice there is a striking disparity in the relative prevalence of the various versions. White renditions of the story, in print or by word of mouth, are commonplace in Oxford, around Emory University, and in the broader white Georgia Methodist community. In contrast, African American renditions of the story are infrequent, often reluctant or halting, and hardly ever delivered in a public or quasi-public context. In practice, not all myth variants are created equal.

Why has the dominant white narrative for so long remained publicly unchallenged? In part, many African Americans are struck by the absence of legitimating texts in support of oral understandings of the story. Other than Bishop Andrew's largely forgotten 1851 obituary of Kitty and a few lines in Rev. George G. Smith's 1882 published hagiography of Andrew, no written accounts of Kitty's own words survive. No recorded words of the at least forty other enslaved people owned by Bishop Andrew have endured. The associated documentary evidence, including census and tax records, is fragmentary and has not been easily accessible or decipherable.

In addition, many African American women and men with whom I have discussed the matter express a desire to see the matter closed, once and for all. Lisa Tompkins, a middle-aged African American woman, sighed, when the Kitty question came up, "Isn't it time we all talked about something else? We have to get beyond all that." An elderly woman, Janet Hastings, told me that she recalls her mother often telling her about Kitty, when she was a girl. "'Miss Kitty this, Miss Kitty that.' I just couldn't take it no more. Well, I was more interested in boys and such. It went in one ear and out the other. But still after all years, I still hear that Kitty story hammering away in my head. I just want that story to stop!"

Similarly, Amos Callahan, an older African American man, grew very quiet when the conversation briefly turned to Kitty. After a long pause, he noted softly, "Sometimes, you know, the dead just need to stay good and buried."

Hearing such comments, one is reminded of the closing refrain of Toni Morrison's novel *Beloved*: "This is not a story to pass on." The narrative of the horrific legacies of slavery and infanticide at one level needs to be told, but retelling ultimately is in the interest of exorcising the spirit and the story, so that they will not be "passed on." Certain tales need to run their course, and then new life needs to take hold.

Even those in the African American community who are intensely interested in researching, uncovering, and broadcasting the facts of the Kitty case find themselves facing fundamental challenges of time, space, and geography. Amos Callahan sighed, "So much time has elapsed, is there any way we could ever really get back there, and determine what really happened to Miss Kitty and all those other people back in slavery times? Is there really any way to get beyond, past the brick wall, between these days and those days?"

MANY OXFORD African Americans, in turn, note that whites have, in effect, colonized the only places where Kitty's story could be retold, especially the cottage and her supposed gravesite. Juliet Haines, a middle-aged African American woman, remarked, "OK, let's say we really could prove everything about Kitty and Bishop Andrew, with DNA or whatever. Where in Oxford would we ever get to tell the truth? Put on a display? Where is there? You tell me."

Margaret Watkins, in a pensive mood after her conversation with her cousin J. P. Godfrey about the Kitty story, posed a related question that went beyond the challenge of recovering the "mere facts" toward the problem of reconstructing the nature of consciousness in the past:

> Sometimes I wonder, how can we ever really know how people thought back then, in slavery times? Did white people here in Oxford really convince themselves of the stories they told about how everyone was so content with their lot? When they put together these tales that have been passed down like gospel truth, all the way down to today, did they really believe all that? Or were they plagued at times by their conscience, by a small, still voice that came to them in the midnight hour? Were all those stories just for show, or did they believe them,

even as they were doing what they were doing? I'd love to know that, but how can we really know what was truly deep in their hearts?

Her cousin J. P., in turn, mulled over a series of related questions:

Each time I hear Martin tell his version of the Andrew and Kitty story, I find myself filled with questions. Not just about Miss Kitty but about everyone else we don't hear about. Was there really a black man in her life, and if they *were* married what did that mean in those days? Could love between men and women of color endure in this town back in those days? What did he think, if he really existed, of the Bishop's nocturnal visits to the "cottage," as they call it, which he would have been powerless to stop? What did her children make of all of this, being torn away, it seems from Oxford, after their mother died? And what went through the minds of the white wives as their husbands pursued their, ah, interests among the women house slaves and the field slaves? Did they rage at home, taking out their anger on the slave-women who looked after them? Did they ever take comfort in the arms of male slaves, as the ultimate form of revenge on their husbands? Each question, you know, just leads to other questions. . . .

In this study, drawing on the intellectual tool kit of anthropology, history, folklore, and literary studies, I attempt to answer the questions posed by Amos, Juliet, Margaret, J. P., and my many other interlocutors in Oxford and beyond. How did the dominant narrative of Bishop Andrew and his slaves come to be so fixed in the local public square, and why has it remained resistant to challenge? To what extent can we reconstruct the actual events of the mid-nineteenth century, and tease out the agendas, aspirations, and private imaginings of the actors, black and white, in this celebrated drama? What other stories, of slavery and the coming of freedom, might be recovered from the shadows cast by the mainstream paternalist story of white beneficence and black loyalty?

Chapter Two

Distant Kin

Slavery and Cultural Intimacy
in a Georgia Community

MYTHOLOGY, as Lévi-Strauss argues, is often generated out of the most enigmatic tensions and contradictions of a social system. For over two centuries, North American chattel slavery, which posed so many fundamental conundrums about personhood, relatedness, and the contours of human freedom and constraint, was highly productive of mythological renderings in white and African American imaginings. Although we might discern "family resemblances" among these many popular narratives, many of their specific details were produced out of local specificities in regimes of coerced labor. The vast plantations of Mississippi helped to generate the mythological renderings of Faulkner's Yoknapatawpha County, just as the hardscrabble small holdings of Kentucky helped inspire the portraits of intimate violence immortalized in Toni Morrison's *Beloved*.

Before exploring in detail how the myth of Kitty developed and transformed over time, it is thus helpful to sketch out the milieu in which this deeply resonant narrative emerged—that is to say, the social matrix of slavery in Oxford and Newton County before the Civil War. This historical case study is not universally applicable to all instances of slavery in the antebellum South, but it does call attention to how intimately intertwined chattel slave ownership was with the overall operations of kinship and descent on both sides of the color line in the wider region. In important respects, slavery functioned as an overarching system organizing social relations within and among white and African American family networks. In order to navigate local social landscapes, free and enslaved actors both needed to be acutely aware of genealogical relations that cut across lines of race, social class, and ownership status. Many enslaved persons tangibly embodied a complex social "map" of white kinship and descent relations, a map that would largely condition their trajectories and life possibilities. Such was dramatically the case with the enslaved persons owned or controlled by James Andrew from the 1830s until emancipation in 1865; each carried, in effect, an intricate microhistory of legal and descent transactions that were often perplexing to external observers, but which were of vital importance to slaveowners and the enslaved alike.

Enslaved people were critical at many levels to the overall project of white social reproduction in the antebellum South. In a material sense, of course, their extracted labor power undergirded the domestic and externally oriented economies of white slaveholding households. At more subtle cultural or ideological levels, slaves functioned as what structural anthropologists have termed "symbolic operators"; they bound together white families, intensifying bonds created through marriage, parenthood, and common descent. To be sure, even when enslaved persons were biogenetic relations of their white masters, they were rarely treated as full kin. Yet they were what might be termed "distant kin," profoundly enmeshed in the intricate social and legal reckonings of antebellum kinship calculus. As dowry gifts, living exchange objects, nurturers, and sentient holders of family memory, enslaved persons actively helped to create white families and white kinship relations. At the same time, the enslaved often bore the brunt of structural tensions and crises in white gender, sexual, and familial relations.

These observations echo in significant respects Lévi-Strauss's discussions of the position of women in his foundational study *The Elementary Structures of Kinship*. In terms of the overall structure of human kinship and descent systems, women may be regarded as foundational exchange objects out of which a social structure is constituted. Through the organized exchange of women between men, male-dominated social units come into being, assume definition in relation to one another, and reproduce themselves over time. In these important respects, women function as "objects" in relation to an overall system of social relations, even though, as Lévi-Strauss freely acknowledges, actual women possess existence in and of themselves as conscious, sentient agents in the world.[1]

A similar doubled existence characterized the existential predicament of enslaved persons within the antebellum family networks explored in this study. As units or tokens of commercial and familial exchange, slaves were clearly rendered objects, manipulated pawns and objects of desire on the greater chessboard of white kinship and descent. Yet even under the harshest and most coercive of historical conditions, enslaved persons were possessed of degrees of agency and sentient intentionality. In significant instances, the enslaved were at times able to influence the overall white-dominated social calculus of human relationships in which they were enmeshed.

This chapter seeks to illustrate these contradictory dynamics through an examination of slavery and kinship in antebellum Newton County, Georgia, with a particular emphasis on Oxford, the town to which Miss Kitty was brought by Bishop Andrew in 1840 and in which she would reside the rest of her life. As we shall see, enslaved persons in Newton County functioned, in significant respects, as exchange objects through which the structures of white kinship were delineated and reproduced over time. Yet they also actively pursued their own kinship strategies, at times under the most difficult of circumstances, seeking to forge and reproduce familial bonds across the generations.

"Her Family, White and Black"

Let us return to the headstone of Mary Rogers, at the northern end of the historically white section of the Oxford City Cemetery. The inscription reads,

> In memory of Mary, wife of Rev. Osborn Rogers. Embraced Religion August 12, 1812. Died 15 Feb. 1856. The morning before her death she called her family, white and black, around her and bade them farewell. From that time as long as she could be understood she continued to praise God.

The phrasing is fairly standard for the mid-nineteenth-century South: slaves and masters were routinely referred to, by slaveowners at least, as members of the same family. The Good Death, it was believed, should take place in the presence of the entire "family," white and black, free and slave. To our modern ears this usage of the term "family" seems baffling. The historical record is clear that enslaved persons in antebellum Georgia were routinely sold or exchanged, that parent-child or conjugal bonds among slaves were often violated, that what we now regard as the elementary principles of family life were repeatedly undercut by the slavery system. Although the moment of the Good Death was idealized as a tableau of white and black "family" unity, death in practice signaled the ultimate separation: persons of color in Oxford were buried across the way from the virtually all-white field in which Mrs. Rogers was laid to rest, yet slaveowners insisted that master and slave were all part of the same "family."

In this chapter I seek to take this assertion seriously. Although we should not accept the slaveholders' claims unquestioningly, we should try to understand the many ways in which slaveowners and the enslaved were kin to one another. While they were manifestly not "kin" in the conventional sense, they were in many senses "distant kin" to one another.

This chapter's title, "Distant Kin," has multiple meanings. Persons enslaved in antebellum Newton County are distant kin to contemporary African Americans, who may have only fleeting recollections of their names and biographies. In their own time, members of families held in slavery were often distant kin to one another, separated by physical distance through arbitrary inheritance assignments or by being sold away from their loved ones. Most important, enslaved African Americans were, in several senses, distant kin to white members of slaveowning families. In many cases, of course, black slaves and white masters were biological kin to one another. The much-discussed case of Thomas Jefferson and his enslaved mistress Sally Hemmings is simply the most celebrated example of a phenomenon that occurred with great regularity throughout the period of slavery. As historian Theodore Davis notes, "The very first indictment issued by the Newton County Grand Jury, in 1822, concerned Moses Brown, who was indicted for cohabiting with his slave, although to the Jury's embarrassment, it was later discovered that such relations were not a crime."[2]

Even when there were no clear biological ties between owners and slaves, the peculiar institution of slavery that bound them must be regarded as a curious structure of "kinship"—in the broadest sense of the term. African Americans often served as wet nurses and childhood companions to white children in the families of masters and employers, in ways that replicated the patterns and emotional contours of conventional familial relations. To say that enslaved persons and white slaveowners were distant kin is not to subscribe to the discredited white sentimental view explored in part 2 of this book that slaves were fully accredited "members of the family," treated with kindness and indulgence by their white masters. On the contrary, the historical record makes clear that the master-slave relationship was often characterized by unspeakable violence, cruelty, and neglect, as well as relations of solidarity, mutual interdependence, kindness, and friendship. My point is that these ambiguous relations, of violence and affection, all took place within the framework of kinship.

For anthropologists, "kinship" has a very particular meaning. Kinship is not simply a matter of biology, pedigree, or blood relations. It is, rather, a "social calculus" through which human relations are classified and organized, usually in the idiom of biological relatedness. Like all seemingly natural idioms, kinship, a human-made construction, has particular power precisely because it naturalizes social and conventional relationships, rendering them seemingly normal and inevitable. In the world's premodern small-scale societies, it is usually the institutions of kinship that make the social world meaningful. In most traditional societies kinship determines a person's chances in life, his or her access to wealth and resources, his or her work and profession, where he or she lives, whom he or she may marry, and what legal rights, duties, and obligations he or she may have. Kinship manifestly establishes the legal and political framework of the entire society. At the same time, within any kinship system, a range of possibilities and potentialities can subtly be stressed, or ignored, according to the political calculus of specific persons or groups. Kinship is thus a political arena in which the operations of interest and calculation are usually rendered invisible or are at least "mystified."[3]

Modern capitalist societies are very different. In modern societies, for all the public rhetoric about the centrality of the family, kinship is only of secondary importance to the overall functioning of the social system. As much as we might cherish and love our families, other factors often exercise much greater influence in determining our profession, residence, wealth, or access to scarce resources. The primary goal of life under capitalism is ever-increasing control over physical things and money, and especially over capital (that is to say, money that is invested to make more money). In contrast, in a kinship-based society the goal of life is not simply control over things or capital, but control over other persons and over the reproduction of social beings. Wealth is measured not in money but in people.

By this reckoning, was the antebellum South a modern or premodern society? In many respects, as a slave-based society within a national and international market economy, the pre–Civil War South was in a transitional era, between being a kinship-based society and a fully rationalized capitalist society. The entire structure of the antebellum agrarian South rested on a vast enslaved population, who were kin in many senses to the white elite. Yet, the internal kinship or family relations of enslaved

African Americans were continually warped and violated by that system, in which slaves were simultaneously assessed as valuable in and of themselves *and* in terms of capitalist monetary classifications. Even those slaveowners and courts that honored a mother-child bond only respected this bond up to the age of five to twelve years at most. After that, most felt a child was in effect an adult and could be legitimately sold away from its mother. Sentiment had its place, but after childhood, "business was business."[4] To a large extent, this hybrid nature of the peculiar institution, which occupied an intermediate position between kinship-based and capital-based forms of social organization, accounted for the unprecedented violence and tenacity of North American chattel slavery.

In his excellent account of Newton County slavery, Davis provides striking testimony of the systematic violations of African American family integrity in antebellum Newton County. He cites the 1844 will of Henry Harper:

> My entire family of negroes (not including Esther) I leave with my beloved Rhoda subject to a division amongst my children.
>
> Unto my son, Edward . . . I give my negro boy, Sam.
>
> I give to my daughter, Margaret Ann, my Negro boy, Franklin, about seven years old.
>
> Unto my son, Uriel, I give my negro boy, Jacob, about five years old.
>
> I give unto my daughter, Sarah, my negro boy, Burrel, about three years old.
>
> I desire that my executors herein appointed shall sell and dispose of Esther, about 30 years old, by public or private sale for the purpose of paying all my just debts.[5]

Undoubtedly, Davis notes, Esther was the mother of these young children, brothers and sisters who were being separated. She alone, also interesting to note, is being sold away outside of the patriarch's white family; in a symbolic sense it is almost as if her status as parent has to be usurped by the supreme white parent.

The division of this enslaved family provided a resonant "social map" of the white family, which would continue, after the death of the white patriarch, to be intimately linked together through the tangible presence of their enslaved property. Each white child was provided with one child of the enslaved family that had been owned and dominated by the late patriarch, who would in this way be able to express both affection for and social control over his white and black families from beyond the grave.

This was the case even as Esther herself, the mother of the enslaved family, was sold out of the extended white family network. Such were the contradictions and tragedies of slavery as a system of human kinship and human property.

Davis also quotes the ex-slave Peter, a resident of Newton County, who when asked if he had married under slavery responded, "Yes, sir. But was seldom a ceremony said at our marriages. There was no law for our marriages except that from above. We went along and lived with such women as we liked. There was no need for any law; for nobody knew when a husband and wife were to be torn asunder from one another."[6] Nonetheless, for all the continuous assaults on African American family integrity that enslavement generated, considerable historical evidence remains that powerful relations of family love, honor, and affection existed among enslaved African Americans in Newton County, and that these bonds provided a firm foundation for many families in the generations that followed emancipation. Such, as we shall see, was dramatically the case for many of the enslaved families held by Bishop Andrew, including the family of Miss Kitty, and the families owned by Bishop Andrew's closest associates at Emory College.

Although Newton County had a substantial manufacturing base before the Civil War, it was a significant slaveholding county. In 1830 the county contained 513 slaveowners; in 1850, 648 slaveowners. In 1860 there were 6,460 slaves held by 756 slaveowners. Thirty-eight free persons of color also resided in the county in 1860 and were required to pay an annual head tax of five dollars.

Intertwined Families across the Color Line: The Case of the Hendrick/Hendrix Family

The intertwined nature of white and black kinship in Newton County is well illustrated by the multiple families of Dr. John B. Hendrick (1817–81). Dr. Hendrick was a prominent member of the white slaveowning elite of Covington during the decade before the Civil War, closely allied to other members of the local ruling stratum by bonds of marriage, business partnerships, and common political interests. (He was the son of General Gustavus Hendrick of Alabama and Butts County, Georgia.) A popular medical doctor and successful planter, Dr. Hendrick helped establish the Southern Masonic Female College in Covington, and was a trustee of the Male Academy, the forerunner of Emory College. He also served as one of Newton County's four representatives to the Georgia Convention of 1850 (at which Georgia's white leaders considered seceding from the United States) and served a two-year term in the Georgia House of Representatives, 1851–52.

Like many members of the southern white slaveowning class, Dr. Hendrick had a white family and a black family. He married his white wife Zalema Williamson (1826–68) in January 1846. Zalema was the daughter of the leading Covington attorney, John N. Williamson (1802–57), who had served as a brigadier general in the Georgia State Militia. General Williamson, one of the wealthiest men in Newton County, owned about seventy slaves when he died, worth over twenty thousand dollars. General Williamson's will bequeathed the following slaves to his daughter Zalema, wife of Dr. John Hendrick: "The negro woman Fanny and her children, also negro girl Flora . . . the negro woman Mary and her child, also Susannah, and her two children." A court inventory compiled in 1857 notes that "Susannah and [her] two children, Eugenia and Susie [?]" were valued at fourteen hundred dollars.

We have no subsequent record of Susie, but African American family lore in Newton County insists that during the 1860s Susannah's daughter Eugenia became the mistress of her master, Dr. John B. Hendrick. She bore him a son, Jesse, in March 1862, about a year into the Civil War. She bore him a second son, William ("Babe") in February 1865, about three months after General Sherman's troops had come through Newton County and declared all African Americans emancipated. Jesse, in other words, was born in slavery, but Babe was born free.

By 1870, five years after emancipation, the only African Americans still residing in Dr. Hendrick's household were Susannah, Eugenia, Jesse, and Babe. Susannah was employed as a laundress, Eugenia as a domestic servant. Around 1874 Eugenia married a freedman, Fredrick Biggers (born in August 1845 in Alabama), who eventually became a minister. In 1877 Susannah, her daughter Eugenia, and grandsons Jesse and Babe purchased, for three hundred dollars, about one acre of property, containing a house within which they had already been living. They purchased this property from William W. Clark (ca. 1818–83), one of the wealthiest white men in Newton County. Clark was a close associate and neighbor of Dr. Hendrick; it is possible that Dr. Hendrick assisted Susannah and her family in making this purchase, or perhaps they raised the three hundred dollars on their own. In any event, this land remained in the African American Hendrick family for generations and became known as Hendrick's Circle (or Hendrix Circle).

With his white wife Zalema Williamson, John Hendrick had two white daughters, Mary Louise ("Loudie"), who married Dr. A. C. Perry in 1898, and Charlotte N. ("Lottie"), who married John Conyers in 1891. (John and Zalema Hendrick had one white son, John Williamson, who died in infancy.) Lottie's marriage may not have lasted long; she seems to have kept the Hendrick name until her death in 1933. She and her sister Mary Louise ("Loudie") ran a dry goods store in Covington for many years and kept up good relations with their African American relatives throughout their lives. As elsewhere in the region, whites acknowledged kinship relations across the color line privately until the era of the civil rights movement. From the 1960s onward, it became much less likely that local whites would overtly acknowledge kinship with African American relations in any context, public or private, except under unusual circumstances. Yet, many older African Americans in the county note, at times of crisis or hardship these largely unspoken family and historical bonds could be mobilized, and white relations could still be called upon to provide assistance, even if the actual kinship relations among the parties were not explicitly referenced. As Anna, an older African American woman residing in rural Newton County, remarks of her white distant kin,

> Well, they'd never say out loud they were kin to us, that their great-grandfather, the old master, fathered my grandmother with a slave woman. That would be, oh, indelicate, I suppose you could say. No, they'll just say, "Oh, Miss Anna's family has worked for our family forever, we've always looked after them." That's what they'll say . . . but everyone always knew, who you'd go to, if you or your children had trouble with the bank, or the sheriff, or what have you. Those are "your" people, and they'd help you out, drop a word here or there, you know. Letting people know that we are all, ah, connected somehow. And eventually the problem would usually settle itself, let's say.

In characterizing these kinds of shifting social fields, it is helpful to draw on anthropologist Michael Herzfeld's concept of cultural intimacy. For Herzfeld, societies are often held together not so much by the overtly acknowledged beliefs and values expressed by their members but rather by a body of knowledge and sensibility that can generally not be publicly articulated. The most powerful social bonds he notes are often only hinted at—through shared glances, seemingly offhand remarks, or humorous asides that tacitly signal an unspoken shared understanding or a hidden common history. (One thinks of Margaret Watkins's gentle jokes and silent looks with J. P. Godfrey at the opening of chapter 1, following Martin Porter's public lecture on Kitty.) Herzfeld's insights are consistent with the classic work on the social dimensions of secrecy developed by the great German social theorist Georg Simmel. For Simmel, secret knowledge has profound social force, establishing and reproducing intense solidarity and distinction even when the actual content of the secret remains unarticulated.

"That Tree'll Talk to You": Revisiting the Old Hendrick Place

The burden of shared historical knowledge can at times be deeply painful, disturbing, and uncanny. Such knowledge is often embedded in landscape features, including trees, which powerfully mediate relations between the present and the past, and between visible and invisible domains of experience.

Consider a hike I once took with a man I'll call James Lawrence, who through his mother is an African American direct descendant of the slaveowner Dr. John B. Hendrick. In his youth, James had been a leader of the civil rights movement in Newton County, where he has lived most of his life.

That day, James was eager to show me a heavily wooded site that he believes is a slave cemetery. He was convinced that his mother's ancestors, held in slavery on the old Hendrick plantation, are buried in unmarked graves under "these old trees." During the hike, James spoke positively of the forest trees, explaining that the trees had guided him to this spot a year earlier, when he had searched on horseback for this long-lost graveyard. "Look at those," he said to me as he pointed to two large sycamores, "I look at trees when I see 'em like that."

"Why is it important to look at trees?" I asked.

He explained, "'Cause that's a different age tree, that's a different age tree. You know, I'm looking at the terrain. Whenever you see things, you know how you see things? You see a chimney out there, they leave a big old tree out there." Finally, we came to a large, gnarled oak, with long twisted limbs radiating out from several interconnected trunks: "See that tree? It's different from anything," said James. This tree, he explained triumphantly, had "told" him that he'd finally found the lost cemetery.

But a few minutes later, after we had emerged from the deep cemetery grove, James began to berate this same old oak:

> That tree'll talk to you if stand out here in the dark. You'll hear that Negro crying out to you, man. Can't you hear? Shoot. Look at that tree, man. That's an ugly tree. You never see limbs like that now-adays. That tree was *bred* for it. They just threw the rope up and pulled it up. Like this here, they just bring 'em here, hang 'em and throw 'em down in that pit. Shoot. You think that tree don't know? Look at them limbs here. You don't see limbs growing down like that. There been some dead folk here.

The same tree that moments earlier had positively revealed to him one set of buried secrets, about an honored slave cemetery, becomes a dark, ominous presence, hinting at nocturnal lynching parties.

Still staring at the tree, James began to speak of his difficult relationship with his late father, a conservative businessman and politician, who had always refused to speak of "old-time" family history, especially "going back to slavery times." Thinking on this, and still looking at the great oak, James reflected on his own deep confusion, a year earlier, when he first learned there was a cemetery on "the Old Hendricks" land: "I thought to myself, amazing, this here was *our* property, it belonged to us Hendricks. But then when I came out here, and looked at all this deep in the woods, I realized, wait, you're a fool, this wasn't *our* property. We *was* the property. [laughs] I got myself confused with *him*!"

The "him" in this statement is his ancestor, Dr. Hendrick, the white master who fathered James's enslaved great-grandfather. The old tree, both admired and feared, seems to be imbued with the complex presence of both the black and the white father figure, a composite Oedipal entity that is simultaneously an impediment to proper family memory and a disturbing link to remembered traumas of the past.

Slavery in Oxford

These tangled relations of cultural intimacy, born of a shared, if rarely publicly acknowledged common history of slavery and its aftermath, are particularly intricate in the small city of Oxford, to which Kitty was brought in 1840. To review: Located just to the north of the county seat of Covington, Oxford emerged in the late 1830s around the newly established campus of Emory College, a Methodist institution founded in 1836 and opened in 1839. The city was, for all intents and purposes, directly under the control of the Methodist Episcopal Church up until 1844, and then after the great national schism, under the newly formed Methodist Episcopal Church, South (MECS). All land in the city was purchased or granted by the college, and legally, only Methodist houses of worship were allowed within the town's precincts. (The city is now an official "shrine" of the United Methodist Church.) Bishop Andrew and his family had been in Newton County since the winter of 1836–37, but only moved to Oxford proper over the course of 1840.

Most of the faculty and officers of the college were slaveowners, as were most of the prominent Methodist clergymen who settled in the town. Most of these men owned farms and divided their enslaved property between their residence in town and their plantations in outlying areas of Newton and Walton counties. The 1860 census lists thirty-eight free people of color in Newton County; none of them resided in Oxford.

In contrast with some prominent Georgia institutions, such as the Georgia Railroad, the Emory College itself never owned slaves. Rather, the college and its predecessor, the Georgia Conference Manual Labor School, at times rented slaves from their owners. For instance, the minutes of the Manual Labor School Board of Trustees for February 9, 1837, state, "Resolved that the Treasurer be instructed to pay the sum of Fifty Dollars for the hire of a negro woman by the name of Sib for 1836 and to give notes for the hire of the negroes ordered to be hired for the present year and the following rates, for Sim: $150, for Charles: $150, for Sib and her children: $75."

The economic fortunes of the men who founded Emory and guided the college in its early years indisputably rested upon the institution of slavery and upon the labor of hundreds of enslaved persons. Most slaves were moved back and forth between farms on the city's outskirts and residences within Oxford itself. Some were rented out as factory laborers and artisans to businesses in Covington or elsewhere in the state.

The nature of slavery has rendered many of these persons anonymous. Yet through diaries, memoirs, letters, probate records, bills of sale, and oral historical research, it has been possible to identify by name some of the slaves owned by the college's antebellum leaders; in some instances, through census records we have been able to determine their years of birth or death and the surnames they assumed after emancipation. Many of the persons of color who had been owned by the college's white faculty and administration were linked by close family ties that often predated emancipation. In 1840, the year he assumed the college presidency, Bishop Andrew's closest friend Augustus Baldwin Longstreet owned at least fifteen slaves in Newton County. In 1850 Longstreet's successor to the college presidency, George Foster Pierce, also a close friend and confidant of Bishop Andrew, owned ten slaves in Oxford. Henry Gaither, an influential member of the board of trustees, owned seventy-three slaves in 1860. Iverson Graves, another important college trustee, owned thirty-seven slaves in 1860, among them Charley, Lawrence, Leniah, and Nick. The latter, known as Nick Graves after emancipation, married Rena, a daughter of one of Bishop Andrew's former slaves, Orlando, also known as Lander. In 1840, the year in which he became one of the college's first faculty members, Alexander Means owned eleven slaves; by 1850, a few years before he assumed the college presidency, he owned twenty slaves, among them Albert (b. 1818), Fanny (b. 1828), Harriet (1852–61), Iveson (b. 1858), Samuel, Henry Robinson (b. 1806), Cornelius Robertson (b. 1836), Ellen Robertson (b. 1835), Millie Robinson (b. 1811), Mildred Robinson Pelham (b. 1836), Thomas Robinson (b. 1850), Troup Robinson (b. 1852), Thaddius, and Anna Tinsely. On the eve of emancipation, Gustavus John Orr, professor of mathematics, owned Charles, Hannah (b. 1833), George W. (b. 1853), Henry, Lizzie, Octavia Hunter (b. ca. 1856–57), Peter, Phil, and Walter. Another professor of mathematics, George W. W. Stone Sr., owned Abner, Anna, Caesar, Clinton, Darcus, Duncan, Frank, Hunter, Isaac Stone (b. 1810), Jake, Lucinda, Mary, Nancy, Phillip, Ruth, Sallie, Silas, Sterling, Tempy, Tony, Victoria [Carter], and Louisa (ca. 1832–82). Louisa was married during "slavery times" to Samuel Means, a slave of President Alexander Means. James R. Thomas, the president of the college before and just after the Civil War, owned eight slaves in 1860, including Charity, Lewis, and Dave; it would appear that Peggy, one of the slaves of Bishop Andrew's second wife, was married to one of President Thomas's male slaves. Professor George W. Lane, who with Augustus Baldwin Longstreet conducted the famous 1841 interview of Kitty, owned at least seven slaves, among them Elleck (or Allick) and Aphy. Professor Luther M. Smith, who succeeded Rev. Thomas as college president, owned over twenty slaves; as we shall see in chapter 9, at least a half dozen of these were evidently acquired from Bishop Andrew through Professor Smith's first wife, Mary Eliza Greenwood, Bishop Andrew's stepdaughter.

The thirteen major African American extended families in present-day Oxford are able to trace their descendants back to these early enslaved families of Oxford, who labored on or near the college in slavery times. J. P. Godfrey Jr., the African American city councilor so troubled in chapter 1 by Martin Porter's tour of Old Church, often points out to college students the campus buildings, including Few Memorial Hall, that his elderly relatives recalled were built by enslaved men. Mr. Godfrey's own grandfather, Israel Godfrey, who was enslaved in Newton County, served in the 1870s as the lead stone mason in the construction of the Emory College chapel.

The web of distant kinship relations binding slaveowners and the enslaved in Oxford are well illustrated by the case of Louisa, a woman born around 1832, held in slavery by the family of G. W. W. Stone Sr., Emory's professor of mathematics during the middle third of the nineteenth century. Stone had purchased Louisa on the occasion of the birth of his daughter Tudie in 1841, when Louisa was about nine years old. Louisa was in a sense already a member of the family, for Professor Stone bought her from his brother John. In this as in so many other instances, enslaved persons functioned as the social glue that held together extended, elite white families in antebellum Georgia.

Louisa worked for the Stone family for the rest of her life, in slavery and in freedom, as nurse, cook, and caregiver. In a memoir dictated in the 1930s, G. W. W. Stone Jr., the son of Professor G. W. W. Stone Sr. (and an important local raconteur of the Kitty-Andrew story), recalls, "[Louisa] became our head nurse, washwoman and mammy. We all thought she was one of the best niggers [*sic*] ever born. And we think so yet. She couldn't have loved her own children any more than she did us. And we loved her just like she was kin to us. She married a man named Sam Means. He was a blacksmith and behaved himself until after the surrender. Then he was unkind to Louisa. He became *too free*. When she died in 1882 Father's children put a tombstone over her grave."[7]

The passage is fascinating. In phrasing reminiscent of the Mammy Memorial movement of the early twentieth century, the white author is sure that Louisa "couldn't have loved her own children any more than she did us," although he makes no mention of her actual children. Louisa was loved "like she was kin to us," but she was buried in the segregated section of the Oxford City Cemetery, hundreds of feet away from the Stone family plot. Although the white author acknowledges that she married Sam Means, he can never bring himself to refer to her as Mrs. Means; a substitute mother figure, she is always "Louisa" to him. The rather ominous figure of Sam Means, whom the white children might have regarded as threatening to alienate the affections of their substitute mother, is dismissed by the telling phrase, "too free."

The 1882 headstone, erected by the adult children of G. W. W. Stone Sr., still stands in the oldest section of the historically African American portion of the Oxford City Cemetery. It is inscribed on its east side, "Louisa. Faithful servant of G. W. W. Stone, Professor of Mathematics. Oxford College." No mention, significantly, is made of her actual children or of her married name; instead she is referred to solely by the name she had in slavery and by which she was known by the white family for the remainder of her life.

Yet Louisa's identity was not exhausted in her relationship as substitute mother to the white children of her master. Even under slavery, her conjugal bond with her husband Sam, a slave of Dr. Alexander Means, was sufficiently strong that Dr. Means had to take it into account when he rented Sam out for a profit. In December 1861 Dr. Means reports in his diary that he had hired out Sam, a skilled carpenter and blacksmith, to a white man in West Point for three hundred dollars a year, "with the privilege of coming home four times per year." (The white renter of Sam was to provide him, as well, with at least three pairs of shoes per annum.) The fact that Dr. Means stipulated these visits home in the contract presumably indicates that he recognized Sam's desire to see his wife and family back in Oxford. (To be sure, Dr. Means did not assign excessive weight to the conjugal bond between Sam and Louisa; he had no qualms about profiting from their enforced separation, which allowed Sam only four conjugal visits home per year.)

As noted, the headstone placed by the white Stones for Louisa did not mention her married name. Yet, as some African American residents wryly note, the white Stone family did not have the final word in this story. On the west side of the headstone is inscribed, in a different, less professional hand, "Louisa Means."[8] According to oral tradition in the Oxford African American community, her own kin surreptitiously inscribed her full name, sometime after the white family had erected the headstone. The diverse facets of her identity—slave and free, unmarried and married, domestic servant and head of family—thus remain juxtaposed on the stone. In death, she is "kin" to at least two families, black and white, entangled in an intimate web of relations that allows for no easy definition.

The ambiguous status of distant kin is further illustrated by internal dynamics in the household of Dr. Alexander Means, the owner of Sam Means, Louisa's husband. Dr. Means, Emory's first professor of natural sciences, briefly served as the college's president. One of Oxford's greatest landowners, by 1850 Dr. Means owned twenty slaves and about five hundred acres in various plots scattered through Newton County.

According to their descendants, two slaves of Dr. Means, Cornelius (b. 1836) and Ellen Robinson (b. 1835), were married to one another, and were allowed to live in a small house behind the Means mansion, Orne Villa, on present-day Emory Street. Cornelius, a Native American who was probably Creek, was Dr. Means's valet. Ellen was the personal maid of Dr. Means's wife. As such, they seemed to have occupied the highest status among all those enslaved in the Means household. After emancipation, Cornelius and Ellen formed an independent household, which by 1870 consisted of their children Cora (b. 1857), George (b. 1859), Sarah (b. 1861), John (b. 1853), and Thaddius (b. 1867). Sarah Robinson married Robert Mitchell, the son of Thomas Mitchell, who, like his father, had been enslaved by Bishop James Andrew. One of the sons of Robert and Sarah was Henry "Billy" Mitchell, who served as chief janitor of Emory-at-Oxford for much of the first half of the twentieth century. In antebellum Georgia, a marriage union between slaves had no force of law, but in this specific case the bond between Cornelius and Ellen lasted through slavery and freedom, and gave rise to an important line that has prospered through at least five generations.

However, not all enslaved couples within the Means household were as secure as Cornelius and Ellen. Dr. Means often sold off plots of land in order to acquire other areas of land, and he similarly would sell off or give away slaves from time to time. Consider, for example, the family of Henry and Millie, who like Cornelius and Ellen took the name Robinson after emancipation. During the first year of the Civil War, Henry was sent off to the front, as a slave to Dr. Means's son, Thomas Alexander Means, who was serving in the Confederate Army. Henry returned home to Oxford in November 1861, having served in the first battle of Manassas (known in the North as the first battle of Bull Run), a Confederate victory, only to discover that three weeks earlier Dr. Means had sold him along with his wife Millie, and their three children, Thomas, Troup, and Mildred. They had been sold to Judge Reynolds in Covington.

A domestic battle ensued between the slaveowner and the enslaved family. Dr. Means writes in his diary, "Henry is much distressed and unwilling to go." Over the course of the argument, Dr. Means became in-

furiated at Milly, Henry's wife. He wrote, "Milly's insolence and angry re-
torts first induced me to think of parting with them." But finally, Means
relented and convinced Judge Reynolds to release him from the contract,
with one exception. Means was so angry with Mildred, the young adult
daughter of Henry and Milly, who had used particularly harsh language
against him, that he insisted on selling her along with her young child.
Means wrote, "Mildred much in fault and therefore I sell Mildred who
expressed a desire that I should [do] so." Mildred, in turn, was given by
Judge Reynolds to his son-in-law Coleman Brown, who had married Fannie Reynolds, as a dowry gift.[9]

Within five years after the Civil War, Henry and Milly's family was
reunited. The 1870 Freedmen's Census for Newton County records as living together in Oxford the family of Henry Robinson, with his wife Milly
and three children, Thomas, Troup, and Mildred, who gives as her last
name "Pelham." Unfortunately, the story may not have had an entirely
happy ending: Mildred's small child, with whom she had been sold in late
1861, seems to have disappeared in the meantime. Perhaps the child died
or was sold off to a different owner.

What lessons can we draw from these events? First, there were close
family bonds among enslaved persons. Second, in spite of the risks, these
bonds were openly expressed at times to the master. Henry and his wife
Milly were visibly outraged that their family was being sold, and seem
to have had enough moral bargaining power that they were able to per-
suade their owner, Dr. Means, not to sell off the bulk of their family.
But there were limits: Henry and Milly were not able to prevent the sale
of their daughter Mildred and their grandchild. Finally, we know that
whatever strains may have been placed on this family, their bonds were
strong enough that after emancipation Mildred returned to live with her
parents, albeit without her lost child.

Slaves as Gifts of Dowry

Inheritance and marriage transfers were key institutions for the reproduction of white kinship relations in slaveowning families. Yet these processes, which depended on the transfer of slaves, were often threatening
to the integrity of the enslaved families. The death of an owner usually led to the distribution of slaves among white heirs. The marriage
of a white daughter, in turn, often led to the splitting up of enslaved kin
groups, as slaves were presented as dowry gifts to the new son-in-law.[10]

Consider several illustrative instances from the Alexander Means household. In late 1858 Dr. Means decided to provide each of his two recently married daughters, Victoria and Mary Elizabeth, with a set of slaves from his household. These gifts can be regarded as a form of dowry, a way of passing on wealth to the next generation before death and thus avoiding inheritance taxes and unpredictable complexities of contested probate judgments.

On December 27, 1858, Dr. Means gave his daughter Victoria and her new husband, George Johnson, "Fanny, a woman about thirty years of age, and Albert a Man about forty years of age. Harriet about six years of age, and Iveson about five months of age (all children of Fanny)." It seems likely that Albert was the husband of Fanny, but there is no proof of this: as I have noted, in most cases, the only kinship relationship recorded by most slaveowners was the mother-child bond.

We know the fate of Harriet, the daughter of Fanny: she died in a coma three years later at age nine after Dr. Gaither, the physician whom Dr. Means had summoned to treat her, had given her oil and spirits of turpentine to revive her. We also know from a later diary entry that Albert was a shoemaker, whom Dr. Means rented out during the Civil War to a local factory, to make boots for the Confederate war effort. "Fanny" was likely Fanny Branham, born around 1830 and employed as a domestic servant. According to the 1870 census, taken five years after emancipation, she lived in Oxford a few doors away from Victoria Johnson as a head of household with five or six children. Of Albert, however, we have no further trace.

Two months before giving away Fanny and Albert, on November 2, 1858, Dr. Means gave to his other married daughter, Mary Elizabeth, the following, for the token price of one dollar: "One negro boy named Thaddius about nineteen years old. Tinsely Anna a negro girl about fifteen years old and a Piano Forte, with the future increase of said negro Tinsely Anna."

How are we to understand these sorts of transfers of human property within white families? There was surely a material dimension to this gift; five slaves represented a significant economic resource, and Dr. Means clearly hoped to improve the material circumstances of his daughters and his new sons-in-law. Yet, as anthropologists have long argued, all gifts also have powerful symbolic dimensions, evoking poetically the social relationship between donor and recipient. The gift, as Marcel Mauss notes, carries the persona and memories of the donor; in giving his newly married daughter a family of slaves, the white patriarch sought, consciously or unconsciously, to pass on memories of his own persona and his own family to the new family. In this regard, the pairing of Tinsely Anna with a pianoforte, a cherished heirloom replete with memories of the family and of cultivated leisure, seems particularly evocative.

In many instances, gifts have what linguists term a "performative" element. That is, they may symbolize the state of affairs they hope to bring about—rather as the speech act by an officiant, "I now pronounce you husband and wife," makes real the event it describes. In this respect the gift of an African American mother and child to the young white newlyweds seems to have had symbolic significance, in effect encouraging the couple to emulate the fruitfulness demonstrated by the gifted enslaved family.

At the same time, Dr. Means, like many other slaveowners, sought to preserve his estate through the changing circumstances of his extended family: his deed of gift stipulated that should early death befall his son-in-law George Johnson, these slaves would revert back to his daughter Victoria, in effect staying within the Means family. This is precisely what happened: George Johnson died during the Civil War, and the widowed Victoria kept the surviving slaves, at least one of whom continued to work for her as a domestic servant after emancipation.

The Stone Families, White and Black

Although the possibilities of such sales or transfers hung perpetually over the heads of all enslaved persons, in some instances we have evidence of many generations being held in slavery within a single household. Through excellent family records provided by Virgil and Louise Eady of Oxford, we have remarkably good information on several such multigenerational enslaved families in the antebellum household of Professor G. W. W. Stone Sr., Emory's famed nineteenth-century professor of mathematics, who was the owner of Louisa Means.

We know, for example, of the enslaved woman Nancy, whose daughter was the Stone's plantation cook Ruth. Ruth in turn was the mother of Lucinda and Tom. Lucinda was the mother of Sterling and Duncan. (Once again, our knowledge of early kinship is limited by the fact that slaveowners tended to record only the mother-child connection, if they noted slave kinship relations at all.) In any case, we do know that at least four generations of this family were held in slavery by the white Stone family.

After emancipation, Duncan and his wife Miriah took the family name of Stone and obtained some land from the white Stone family. Their son, Rev. John Foster Stone, attended Morehouse College and married Luvenia Stone, who lived until 1967. Their descendants, who include parts of the Hamm family, are respected citizens of Newton and Rockdale counties.

We can also trace early genealogical relations in another extended family owned by the white Stones. The slaves Caesar and Sallie had three children: Hunter, Jake, and Mary. Mary married Isaac, also enslaved by the Stones. After emancipation, Isaac and Mary also took the family name "Stone." Isaac and Mary had three children: Eudocia, Laura, and Victoria. (Victoria later took the married name Victoria Carter.)

These three families of Stones, one white and two black, were thus intertwined by slavery for at least four generations. Their stories are a testament to the enduring faith and commitment of enslaved families, who survived not only as individuals but also as coherent family units.

Emancipation and Sharecropping

Having said that, the coming of emancipation in November 1864 may not have made an immediate difference in the material circumstances of many of the African American families of Oxford. Take, for example, the case of those enslaved by Professor Gustavus J. Orr, Emory's other professor of mathematics. In August 1865, five months after the final Union victory, Professor Orr signed a contract with his former slaves:

As slavery has been abolished by the Government of the United States, the undersigned make the following contract. I, G. J. Orr, agree, on my part, to furnish the freedmen whose names appear below, food, clothing, fuel, quarters and medical attention, and pay them one fourth of the corn, fodder, peas, and syrup of sorghum and sweet potatoe . . . for their services for the whole of the present year. . . . I do furthermore agree that, should Phil. and Charles leave me on the first of December, there shall be no abatement as to the part of the crops they are to receive, and if they stay with me longer than that time, I am to pay them such compensation as we may agree upon.

We, the undersigned freedmen, agree on our part to labor faithfully and diligently, for G. J. Orr, to obey him in all things, pertain-

ing to labor and service and to treat him and his family with proper
respect and courtesy.

The document is worth pondering. In many respects, what it offered to
Phillip, Charles, Eliza, and Hannah and her children was not so different than what they had experienced, materially, before emancipation:
hard work without monetary compensation. But they did of course have,
in principle at least, the right to leave Orr's property and to make their
own lives.

In time, they did just that. By 1870 Hannah was living on her own as
head of household under the name of Hannah Hunter; her daughter
Octavia, thirteen years old, was attending the newly founded school for
free children of color near Rust Methodist Chapel. Hannah's seventeen-
year-old son, George, was working as a domestic servant. For all the immediate constraints of their first year of freedom, within five years this
family had at least been able to move out on their own as wage earners,
away from sharecropper status. In this respect, they resembled many
of their neighbors in the new free community of Oxford, employed as
domestic servants and artisans.

Postslavery Marriage and Kinship

What, in turn, became of Louisa and Sam Means during the years that
followed the formal cessation of slavery? Some evidence shows that
Sam and Louisa did not have an easy time of it. The son of their owner,
George G. W. Stone Jr., asserts in his memoirs that after the war, Sam
was "cruel" to Louisa. In 1870 Sam and Louisa are listed as married and
residing in the same house, but the 1880 Census indicates that although
Sam and Louisa were both still in Oxford, they were no longer living together: Sam was with one of their adult children; Louisa was living with
another adult child and her grandchildren, some distance away.

Much about the lives of Sam and Louisa we may never know, but the
surviving evidence indicates they were distant kin, in many senses. During slavery, they were forced to live at a social and physical distance from
one another. They were owned by different white families in Oxford.
Sam, at times rented out to a distant temporary owner who lived many
days' travel away, was allowed to see his wife only four times a year.

As with all the slave men and women explored in this study, we can
only speculate what stresses such circumstances placed upon their mar-

ried life and contributed to their later difficulties. Having seen their kith and kin sold off, their fellow slaves transferred away as dowry or chattel, they must have wondered if such a fate lay in store for them. We do know that Sam, a skilled carpenter and blacksmith, was a man of remarkable abilities and initiative; he was able to earn his master three hundred dollars per year. Legends of his ingenuity have lived on in Oxford for generations. (J. P. Godfrey recalls that as a child in Oxford he would routinely hear a bright young person referred to as being "as clever as Sam Means!") It may be that as Reconstruction ended and the grim era of "Redemption" and Jim Crow segregation set in, the accumulated stresses and indignities of slavery and its aftermath finally broke him, or at least tore asunder the bond between husband and wife.

To be sure, given the mysteries of the human heart, it seems presumptuous to reduce to a single explanation the difficult choices made by family members at any moment in history, past or present. After all, who among us, living in a world far removed from slavery times, does not know of the anguish and heartache that can threaten any close family bond? This very shock of recognition is one of the most important lessons of this history: for all the extraordinary strains and terrors of the peculiar institution, many aspects of this story remain familiar to us. African American family life under slavery was unimaginably hard and was often brutally violated by the slavery system, but many enslaved families somehow endured, and in spite of legal and economic impediments many prospered in slavery's aftermath. In this respect, all of us living today must recognize aspects of ourselves in these struggles to forge and safeguard the bonds of love.

Nearly a century and a half after the legal ending of chattel slavery, our nation still struggles with the political, economic, and moral legacies of the peculiar institution. Yet the ultimate lesson to be drawn from this history, I suggest, is not simply of our radical separation and estrangement from one another, but rather an appreciation of the intimate, enduring, and ambiguous bonds between us all. Although law and custom radically separated the families of master and slave, all these families, black and white, were intimately intertwined by the larger system of enslavement. Kin to one another, often on biological as well as sociological levels, their stories cannot meaningfully be disentangled from one another.

Pondering this history of cultural intimacy and distant kin, I am once again drawn to the haunting line from Ralph Ellison's *Juneteenth*, a novel that contemplates the profound interrelatedness of all Americans, black and white: "There's always the mystery, of the one in the many and many in the one, the you in them and the them in you." Surely, this mystery confronts each of us as we contemplate the curiously linked fates of the white and black members of the multiracial households and extended family of Newton County, Georgia: the "white and black" family of Mary Rogers, drawn around her deathbed; Dr. Alexander Means, who sought to preserve his extended estate by transferring enslaved family units to his newly married daughters; Dr. Means's slaves, Henry and Milly, who so forcefully opposed being sold off that they were able to convince Means to let them and their two sons stay, but were unable to prevent their daughter and grandchild from being sold; Hannah Hunter, who chose to work without wages for her former master during her first autumn of freedom, but who by 1870 was her own head of household and able to afford to send her daughter to school; and Duncan Stone, whose family had been held in slavery for at least three generations by the white Stone family, but whose descendants still farm the land they received from G. W. W. Stone after the Civil War.

For all the differences that divide us, for all the injustices and inequities that still remain, these stories bring us face-to-face with the most fundamental of mysteries, "of the one in the many and many in the one, the you in them and the them in you." The story of our distant kin, in slavery and in freedom, holds up an intimate mirror to each and every one of us.

IN PART 2, we turn from this general portrait of slavery and kinship in nineteenth-century Newton County and Methodist-dominated Oxford to the most famous narrative (or bundles of narrative) generated out of this social matrix, the story of Bishop Andrew and his connections with slavery. At stake in these representations are the multiple ambivalent white orientations toward enslaved distant kin considered in this chapter. The common white assertion that slaveowners and their enslaved constituted a unitary "family," bound by ties of fealty, love, and loyalty, was hedged about with intense white anxiety over sexual traffic across the color line and the ever-present possibility of violent insurrection by the enslaved. The social project of extending and reproducing white families depended in both practical and symbolic ways upon the labor of bondsmen and bondswomen, and this dependence was simultaneously acknowledged and disavowed. Yet while the Kitty-Andrew narrative complex in retrospect may be seen as exemplary of much broader social dynamics, it also has made singular characteristics that have rendered it especially compelling for white tellers and hearers across the generations. Let us now consider in detail how the story evolved over time, and what shifting significance it has had from the mid-nineteenth century to the present.

Part Two

Slavery as a Mythical System

Chapter Three

"The Tenderest Solicitude for Her Welfare"

Founding Texts of the Andrew-Kitty Narrative

W HY DID THE STORY that Martin Porter told in Old Church in 2000 seem so profoundly moving to him and his white compatriots in Oxford and its environs, even as it deeply disturbed many of his African American neighbors? Part of the explanation, as I have tried to suggest, lies in underlying structural features of the narrative, when thought of in the classic terms of myth. Porter's rendition intuitively "feels right" to nearly all of his local white interlocutors in part because it inverts standard racially charged depictions of choice and coercion and poignantly emphasizes Bishop Andrew's predicament in a way that foreshadows the vast national tragedy of the Civil War. The story also resonates for its supporters with present-day racial politics in the South. The narrative emphasizes comity and mutual understanding between the races, in a way that is manifestly inclusive, summoning up the voice of a sympathetic, unthreatening African American character. "Every time I hear Martin tell the story of Kitty," one of his white neighbors, a woman in her sixties, told me, "it just brings tears to my eyes. And frankly, it makes me proud to live here in Oxford."

For all its idiosyncrasies, Porter's version of the narrative did not emerge out of whole cloth. It is the sedimented product of a cultural and political history that stretches back to the mid-nineteenth century, produced through countless tellings and retellings, in speech and written word among white interlocutors. In this chapter and the one that follows, I revisit the story through a process of textual excavation, tracing the history of public narratives about Bishop Andrew and his connections with slavery from the 1840s to the present. I concentrate on close readings of published accounts, teasing out what the story seems to have meant to writers and readers at different historical moments, before the Civil War, during Reconstruction and the rise of Jim Crow, during the struggles in the interwar period over the reunification of the Methodist Church, and during the civil rights movement and its aftermath. For a century and a half, the story of Andrew and Kitty has been retold and transformed in many hundreds of written publications. Nearly all of these published accounts are by white southern authors who treat Bishop Andrew with extreme sympathy, although abolitionist and African American demurrals have been printed from time to time. The variations among these successive retellings are often subtle, but they do illustrate what we might call the "mythological imagination" at work.

This chapter concentrates on the primary sources for the Andrew-Kitty narratives, penned by those who were either personally familiar with the relevant events in Oxford or who lived through the 1844 crisis in the Methodist Episcopal Church. These persons include Bishop James Osgood Andrew himself, the southern Methodist scholar and advocate A. H. Redford, Bishop Andrew's biographer George Gilman Smith, and Bishop Andrew's close friend and passionate defender Bishop George Foster Pierce.

Andrew's May 1844 Letter

The foundational text of what I have termed "the myth of Kitty" is a letter authored by Bishop James Osgood Andrew in May 1844, addressed to his fellow bishops at the General Conference in New York City of the Methodist Episcopal Church. Several northern antislavery members of the Conference had proposed that Andrew refrain from exercising his duties as a bishop as long as he continued to own slaves. The letter was reprinted in scores of newspapers in the North and South, and elicited widespread national discussion and debate:

> Dear Brethren:—In reply to your inquiry, I submit the following statement of all the facts bearing on my connection with slavery. Several years since an old lady in Augusta, Ga., bequeathed to me a mulatto girl, in trust, that I would take care of her until she should be nineteen years of age, and with her consent I should send her to Liberia and that in case of her refusal I should keep her and make her as free as the laws of the State of Georgia would permit. When the time arrived she refused to go to Liberia and of her own choice remains legally my slave, although I derive no pecuniary advantage from her, she continues to live in her own house on my lot, and has been, and still is, at perfect liberty to go to a free State at her

pleasure, but the laws of the State will not permit her emancipation, nor admit such a deed of emancipation to record, and she refuses to leave the State. In her case, therefore, I have been made a slave-holder legally, but not with my own consent.

Second—About five years since, the mother of my former wife left to her daughter—not to me—a negro boy, and as my wife died without a will, more than two years since, by the laws of the State he becomes legally my property. In this case, as in the former, emancipation is impracticable in the State, but he shall be at liberty to leave the State whenever I shall be satisfied that he is prepared to provide for himself, or I can have sufficient security that he will be protected and provided for in the place to which he may go.

Third.—In the month of January last I married my present wife, she being at that time possessed of slaves inherited from her former husband's estate, and belonging to her. Shortly after my marriage, being unwilling to become their owner, regarding them as strictly hers, and the law not permitting their emancipation, I secured them to her by deed of trust.

It will be obvious to you, from the above statement of facts, that I have neither bought nor sold a slave, that in the only circumstances in which I am legally a slave-holder emancipation is impracticable. As to the servants owned by my wife, I have no legal responsibility in the premises, nor could my wife emancipate them if she desired to do so. I have thus plainly stated all the facts in the case and submit the statement for consideration of the General Conference.

Yours Respectfully,
James O. Andrew.

It seems likely that Andrew drafted the letter with the aid of his close friend Longstreet, an accomplished attorney and president of Emory College, who accompanied him on the trip north. The brevity of language, the authoritative tone, the emulation of a tightly argued legal brief are all reminiscent of Longstreet's prose, which is crafted to emphasize the Bishop's blamelessness. He makes use of passive construction—"I . . . have been made a slaveholder"—to foreground his own lack of free will in this matter. In contrast, the slaves are presented as having choice: Kitty could have gone to Liberia and in principle his first wife's slave could choose to go to a free state. Like most of his white southern contemporaries, he characterizes himself through the relatively mild term "slave-holder," not "slave-owner," and speaks of his wife's bondspeople as "servants," not slaves.

Although the letter is framed with reference to objective "facts," it does appear that Andrew stretched the precise details of his case. To begin with, the Bishop avoids all mention of his previous slave ownership; as we shall see in chapter 9, he evidently owned at least two slaves in the early 1830s, one of them the young man Jacob, perhaps inherited from his father, John Andrew, who died in early 1830. It seems likely he was a slaveowner when elected as bishop in 1832, even though many northern electors at the time assumed he was not one.

As we shall see in chapter 8 Andrew's claim that he had secured his second wife's slaves to her by a "deed of trust" was not strictly accurate. In mid-April 1844, a few weeks before the New York Conference, he deeded these fourteen slaves to his close friend Augustus Baldwin Longstreet, then president of Emory College, who immediately deeded them back to the Bishop and his wife for their natural lives. In this way, it would appear, Andrew and Longstreet had hoped to circumvent censure by the northern delegates by claiming that Andrew was not in fact the slaves' legal owner. Andrew also skips over the fact that he from time to time rented out slaves (primarily from the estate of his second wife); that he was trustee for at least one enslaved young woman, Lucy, being held for his nephew, Alexander McFarlane Wynn; and that several other slaves, legally held in trust for his stepchildren, were residing in his household and working his land.

One might also query Andrew's insistence that he planned to offer Kitty and Billy, the second slave mentioned, the option of relocating to a free state in the North. There is no evidence that the Bishop ever made such an offer or seriously pursued the possibility of resettling Billy outside of the South. As we shall see in chapter 9, he almost certainly in 1855 took Billy (acquired from his first wife) with him to Alabama, where Billy remained enslaved until 1865.

The letter's greatest prevarication may be the precise circumstances under which Andrew acquired Kitty, the "mulatto girl" mentioned in the first paragraph. As we shall see in chapter 7, there is no trace in Augusta or Richmond County, Georgia, of any such will or probate records bequeathing a slave to the Bishop. It is possible that Andrew and Longstreet in 1844 concocted the whole story of an Augusta will in order to disguise the precise details of Kitty's origins. (Alternatively, there may be missing documents that would support Andrew's version of events.)

In any event, there is no indication, in the voluminous published minutes of the 1844 General Conference or in any correspondence or memories left by those who attended it, that any Conference participants openly questioned Andrew's claims of fact. All were willing to trust his word, as an ordained minister of gospel and elected bishop, that he had never bought or sold a slave and that he had done everything in his power to limit his legal ownership of the bondsmen and women under his legal authority.

Andrew's letter and the associated debates at the Conference were closely followed in the national press. Numerous newspapers, for instance, printed the following southern response to the northern-backed resolution that Andrew be requested to refrain from exercising the duties of a bishop as long as he remained a slaveholder:

On Wednesday afternoon, the members from the slaveholding States, submitted this protest:

"The delegates of the Conference in the Slaveholding States take leave to declare to the General Conference of the Methodist Episcopal Church, that the continued agitation on the subject of Slavery and Abolition in a portion of the Church; the frequent action of that subject in the General Conference; and especially the extra judicial proceedings against Bishop Andrew which resulted on Saturday last, in the virtual suspension of him from his office as Superintendent, must produce a state of things in the South, which renders a continuance of the jurisdiction of this General Conference over those Conferences, inconsistent with the success of the Ministry in the Slave-holding States."[1]

The *Gazette* of Barre, Massachusetts, reported, "Rev. Bishop Andrew of Georgia has been suspended from the exercise of his office by the late Methodist Conference at New York on the grounds that he is the owner of slaves. This movement is likely to occasion a separation between the northern and Southern portions of the Methodist Church, which may perhaps be regarded as another sign of the times, ominous of a division of the Union."[2] Extensive coverage was also given to follow-up motions throughout southern Methodist networks in support of a break with northern Methodists. The *Pittsfield Sun*, for instance, reported in late June 1844,

Division of the Methodist Church. The Methodists of Raleigh, N.C., met in Convention to consider the action of the General Conference relative to Bishop Andrew, passed the following resolution,

"Resolved, That we believe an immediate division of the Methodist Episcopal Church indispensable to the peace, prosperity and honor of the southern portion thereof, if not essential to her continued existence, and that we earnestly request the southern delegation never to return to their homes until a dissolution is effected."[3]

In the subsequent debate on the schism of the church, Henry Clay is quoted as observing, "I will not say that such a separation would necessarily produce a dissolution of the political union of these States; but the example would be fraught with imminent danger, and in co-operation with other causes unfortunately existing, its tendency on the stability of the confederacy would be perilous and alarming."[4]

Bishop Andrew's letter of self-defense was reprinted in scores of American newspapers, sometimes with considerable editorial commentary. Consider the preamble printed in the *Mississippi Free Trader and Natchez Gazette*:

The following letter explains the Bishop's case. The Methodist General Conference have debated it and the whole slavery question for several weeks, and have just passed a resolution that he can no longer exercise the functions of a Bishop! . . . These are alarming decisions. The R. Mr. Winans, Mr. Drakes and other ministers from the South resisted them with great energy but they were overpowered. These decisions should open our eyes, however, to one thing—the rapid progress of abolition at the north, and the necessity of strengthening ourselves here in the South. Can it be possible that any southern man, in the face of these alarming facts, will longer oppose the immediate annexation of Texas? Shall we silently witness the progress of fanaticism and see it profane the sanctuary, and strike down our venerable bishops and faithful ministers without an effort to save them? And to save ourselves, our wives, children and property? Nay our very liberty? There is now but one remedy—the immediate annexation of Texas. Give us that we have a bulwark forever against oppression. Without it, *the South is lost*.[5]

In these commentaries, north and south, the case of Andrew's slaveholding was quickly linked to the national struggle over the expansion of slavery in the westward territories, the issue that was, ultimately, to precipitate the Civil War seventeen years later.

Bishop Andrew's Obituary of Kitty: 1851

In Andrew's 1844 letter to the Conference, Kitty is unnamed. The first published reference using her name is evidently Bishop Andrew's obituary of her, published in the May 30, 1851, edition of the *Southern Christian Advocate*. Andrew submitted the obituary to the journal, in which he published scores of articles during his career, a few weeks after Kitty's death in April 1851. The full text is fascinating and worth considering in detail:

OBITUARY

Blessed are the dead who die in the Lord

Some years since a lady in Augusta who had formerly been under my pastoral care, being about to die, bequeathed to me a little mulatto girl, named Kitty, requesting that I should keep her in my family till she was twenty-one years of age, and then if she had conducted herself properly, and was willing, I was to send her to Liberia, and if not, I was to keep her and make as free as the laws of Georgia would permit. Now this lady had children, but such was their situation in life that she [believed?] her little pet girl would be peculiarly ex[posed?] if she was left to them, and as she had taken great pains with the child, and she was a [illegible] promising child, she wished to place her in circumstances of less peril, and she had confidence in both myself and wife to believe [that she?] might with safety confide her little [charge?] to us. Such I understood were the re[asons?] she assigned for the bequest. Now there was no motive of profit to induce me to undertake the charge, but when I thought of the little [illeg.] and her probable fate if I declined [illeg.] to accept the trust. I accordingly received her into my family and she grew up with my daughters, and she was almost one of our children. She was smart and intelligent beyond her class; could read very well, and was rather fond of books. I told her of the purpose of her mistress's will and endeavored to [prepare her?] for a home in Liberia. She however profusely expressed her opposition to going there, and when the time specified in her mistress' will arrived, and it became necessary for her to make her final decision, she utterly refused to go, and said she preferred to remain where she knew my family were her [illeg.] whereas in Liberia she would be an utter stranger. I had then only one alternative and that was to retain her in my possession and make her situation as nearly one of freedom as the law would allow. This I did. I gave her a lot in which her husband errected [*sic*] a comfortable house and we fitted her out to housekeeping. She worked for herself, and by her hard work undoubtedly doubtless hastened her dissolution but it was all for herself and I received not a cent for her labour. She had [illeg.] a member of the Church, but did not [illeg.] a very lively Christian, though her conduct was, as far as I know, perfectly [unobjectionable?]. In the course of the last winter she was attacked with something like typhoid fever, which ultimately assumed the form of consumption, and after lingering till some time in April, she left this world for a better. I visited her repeatedly during her illness, and the whole family showered her with all possible kindness, of which in the closing hours of life she [expressed?] the most grateful appreciation. During the earlier period of her illness, when I talked to her as to the prospects beyond the grave, she expressed some dissatisfaction, still mingled, however with earnest prayer and some good measure of confidence in God. She said however that she did not feel as happy as she wished to do before she left the world. One evening just after family worship I was sitting in the room when a messenger came rushing in and said that Kitty wished me and all the family to come to her. We hastened to her bed-side and found her happy and exalting in God. "Oh, Mr. Andrew," said she, "I am so happy, and I wanted to see you all to tell you how happy I am. The devil has been tempting me that God [would cast me off?] but I know Jesus would not do it, and now I have got the victory, now I have got Satan under my feet. Oh, I shall be in Heaven and I shall soon be at home and when I get there, I'll tell Mrs. Andrew (my first wife, to which she was greatly attached) how good you have all been to me." She seemed anxious to depart and expressed great disappointed when informed that her pulse indicated she might live yet several days. We thought, indeed, that she would hardly live beyond a day or two, but she lingered more than a week [persisting] in the [happy state of mind?] not always shouting but her . . . [one line illeg.] a holy, happy calm. Peace [illeg.] [confidence?] in God, seemed to have taken possession of her heart, and she spoke of dying mainly as if she were going to visit a friend. A few hours before her death, she turned to my daughter Sarah, who had nursed her with the [illeg.] and kindness of a sister, "Miss Sarah," said she, "I want you to tell all after I am gone, that I am freighted with grace, and bound for heaven." Thus she passed away from the toils of earth to the rest of heaven. I confess, that as I stood by her happy bedside, and heard her expressions of peace and triumphant confidence, and looked back on all my conduct in reference to her case, I felt thankful that God had made me in any measure instrumental in saving this precious soul; and although you know this effort of mine to save a young and unprotected creature from the snares and evils of a life, such as hers would probably have been, and to make her as free as she could be in this country, was one of the capital sins charged against me in 1844, by men in sacerdotal robes, who profess to be, par excellence, the friends of freedom and of the slaves, yet I can look back with gratitude to God who enabled me to pursue my course conscientiously; and I can humbly look forward to the time when the Eternal will render an impartial verdict between me and those who sought on that occasion to crush me.

James O. Andrew[6]

To my knowledge, this is the only obituary of a slave or person of color published in the *Southern Christian Advocate* during the antebellum period. This privileged position is clearly due to Kitty's celebrated status as having partly occasioned the 1844–45 national schism of the Methodist Episcopal Church. Seven years after the fateful Conference, Andrew clearly remains embittered and looks forward to divine judgment against the northern abolitionist clerics "who sought . . . to crush me."

In this light, it is striking that in this account Andrew implies that Kitty was threatened with sexual predations by the surviving adult children of her late mistress, and that he acted to protect her virtue. Thus, he, and not the so-called northern friends of the slave, was privileged "to save a young and unprotected creature from the snares and evils of a life, such as hers would probably have been."

In many respects, Andrew's account of Kitty's deathbed "triumph" closely follows the structure of his written account of the death in 1842 of his first wife, Ann Amelia, which he had published in the *Southern Christian Advocate* several years earlier. Both women are initially dissatisfied with their personal experience of grace as they face death, and then both are granted, as the hour of their passing approaches, a powerful sensation of calm holiness. Both, according to Andrew, wrestle with Satan, who tempts them with the thought that God will abandon them. Both at the end look forward to their heavenly reward and exit this world triumphant.

(These parallels are to some extent due to the constraints of the genre of the good death scene, but they also seem to hint at Andrew's sense of a profound affinity between the two women, which Andrew's detractors may point to as evidence that Kitty was, in effect, a second wife of the Bishop.)

The obituary makes no mention of Kitty having children, or of her dying request, reported by G. G. Smith in *Life and Letters*, that the Bishop's daughter Elizabeth care for her own little girl. In this text the focus is solely on Kitty and her relationship with Jesus, as mediated through the Bishop. Andrew presents himself, though pilloried for his decision to take responsibility for Kitty as her owner, as an instrument of divine grace, ensuring that she would pass from this world beloved of the Lord.

Amid these theological commentaries, a few puzzling statements of fact emerge in the death notice. Andrew here asserts that the Augusta will specified that Kitty was to be offered the opportunity to go to Liberia when she turned twenty-one. However, in the May 1844 letter to the bishops, Andrew claimed that the age of decision was to be nineteen. Similarly, Smith's 1882 account, quoting Longstreet and Lane's signed account of the 1841 interview, mentions age nineteen. In addition, Bishop Andrew must be mistaken about who nursed Kitty. It cannot possibly have been his daughter Sarah, who had been bereft of reason since her illness of 1841 and who was at that point residing in her parents' household; indeed, elsewhere Andrew writes that the scene of Sarah giving birth without understanding the cause of her agonies was so traumatic to his first wife, Ann Amelia, that it hastened Ann Amelia's illness and death some months later. In his 1882 biography of Andrew, Smith identifies the Bishop's daughter Elizabeth, who was living in Oxford at the time, as nursing Kitty.[7] Perhaps Andrew was simply careless in penning the essay, or perhaps at an unconscious level he hoped to restore the deeply disabled Sarah to reason and competence.

Three years after the obituary, Kitty is mentioned in Bishop Andrew's twenty-four-page biography of his first wife, Ann Amelia McFarlane, in the book, *Miscellanies* (1854), a compilation of his essays.[8] Much of the biographical essay is devoted to Ann Amelia's pious death scene. After describing Ann Amelia's parting words to several young men (presumably Emory College students) boarding in the house, Andrew writes, "She also desired that each one of the servants should be called in, and gave them each a separate and solemn charge to meet her in heaven. To one of them especially—a girl who had nursed her with the affection and assiduity of a daughter, she said 'Kitty you have been very kind to me, and I love you as if you were my own child; be pious: serve God; and promise me now that you will meet me in heaven.' The pledge was given; 'And now,' said she, '. . . come and kiss me.'"[9]

This deeply sentimental passage reiterates the 1851 obituary's assertion that Kitty was like one of the Bishop's "own children" to him. The portrait of the kiss between mistress and bondswoman anticipates, in the style of many mid-Victorian scenes of the "good death," the coming reunion of the linked parties in the afterlife. The sequence reinforces a point that Andrew advanced constantly in his published work during this period: evangelical outreach to negro slaves would not inspire them to rebellion or pretensions beyond their station, but would rather encourage them to deference and affection for their masters and mistresses.

Two years later, Bishop Andrew published a series of letters in a New Orleans newspaper calling for masters to undertake the tender Christian instruction of their slaves. As with the Amelia death scene, he conjured up a reunion in the afterlife, but this time in more ominous hues:

I will suppose you feed them well and clothe them well, and lodge them comfortably; and all that is very well. But this is not enough. Do you not bestow the same care upon your mules? Believe me, though you may ignore this, God will remember it; and, if you neglect your duty in the premises, your remembrance of it in coming time will be bitter. You can not—no, you can not neglect your duty on this subject, and escape. God has a thousand ways even here to bring home the curse of disobedience to you, in your soul and body, in your habitation, in your children; and this curse has very often fallen upon the transgressor in this world. The chain of connection, it may be, has not been noticed; but the woe, the bitter curse, the ruin, has been patent to everybody. But even supposing no such curse to manifest itself here, the day that cometh shall reveal it. The careless master and the neglected slave shall meet and confront each other face to face, and the recollections of that day shall bring out your mutual delinquencies, with the motives, ends, and aims which have actuated you in every instance. Thoughtless, prayerless, godless master, you will, you must meet this responsibility![10]

The image of Kitty's loyal and tender solicitude, in contrast, was set as a positive example, to encourage the redemption of master and slave alike.

Abolitionist Critiques

Not surprisingly, militant abolitionists were unimpressed by this sort of rhetoric. The most prominent dissent from mainstream coverage of the Andrew case was delivered by Frederick Douglass, in an antislavery address in London, England, in 1846. Although southern Methodists had for two years been decrying the great injustices they had suffered at the hands of the northern Methodists, Douglass would have none of it. At heart, he insisted, the northern and southern wings of the church are alike. His witty and impassioned address is worth quoting at length:

> I wish the people of this country to be acquainted with the divisions that have taken place with respect to the Methodist church. It is believed here, that there is an anti-slavery and a pro-slavery Methodist Episcopalian church; that the Methodist church, north and south, differ entirely with regard to that subject; but I wish you to understand that the Methodist church south is no more pro-slavery than the Methodist church north. The former is honest in declaring its adherence to slavery—the former has been governed by expediency, and, in 1844, after the division took place [because] Bishop Andrew became a slaveholder by marriage. He had the power of emancipating his slaves, and, coming to the slave conference, and being called upon to do so, said he would not. (Hear, hear.) A resolution was introduced, to the following effect: "That Bishop Andrew be, and he hereby is requested to suspend his labours till he has got rid of his impediment!" [Laughter and cheers.]
>
> We have various ways of covering slavery. We call it sometimes a peculiar institution—the patriarchal institution—the civil and domestic institution, but it was left for the Methodists to coin a new phrase by which to designate slavery, and it is, "The Impediment!" He was requested to suspend his labour till he had got rid of his impediment. [Laughter and cheers.] One might have thought it was his newly-married wife. [Laughter.]
>
> How long do you think it took the Conference to settle this question? Just three times as long as it took the Evangelical Alliance to settle the compromise—three weeks. They had prayers for the Committee to examine the matter—they had Conferences that they might be brought to an harmonious resolution. They fasted and prayed, and had communion and prayed, and had love-feasts and prayed. They held class-meetings and prayed, and held all kinds of meet-

ings for three weeks, and came to the determination that Bishop Andrews be, and hereby is—what?—suspended? No; but requested to suspend himself till he got rid of his impediments,—only requested! He was left to determine how he should get rid of the slaves. Had the bishop become a sheep-stealer instead of a man-stealer, he would have been cut off at once. Had the Evangelical Alliance the other day had to do with sheep-stealing, had they known how much better a man is than a sheep, they would at once have declared against the slaveholders. [Loud cheers.][11]

Douglass's humorous polemic targets the timidity of northern antislavery critics, with whom he was increasingly frustrated. His address is one of the very few published commentaries on the Andrew slavery affair that directly acknowledges that the fate of actual enslaved human beings was at stake. The vast majority of the extensive published discussion of the matter concentrates on narrow matters of canon law, especially whether the General Conference had the right to unseat a settled bishop, and how precisely the material assets of the Methodist Episcopal Church should be divided up between the northern and southern wings. (The matter eventually reached the U.S. Supreme Court, which largely decided for the southern church.)

From time to time, other abolitionist writers alluded to Andrew's case. On the eve of the Civil War, an extraordinary reference to Bishop Andrew was published in an abolitionist essay titled "The Negro," which argued, in a fascinating mixture of humor and insight, that the Negro was at the heart of every major issue being debated in the United States:

It was a negro that formed the rock upon which the Methodist Episcopal Church split. Bishop Andrew had married a gang of negroes with a wife annexed, and wished, like other patriarchs, to drive slaves, and to be considered a good Christian too. But Sambo invoked the shade of Wesley and of Freeborn Garrison, and the church divided. And because the line of separation did not suit him, and the Church North did not break the yoke, every Conference, Annual and General, is converted into a debating society, to discuss questions which will never aim until his claims as a man and brother are recognized.

The essay concludes,

If we belonged to his proscribed people, and felt the iron of slavery enter into our soul, in the midst of our degradation of ruin, we should feel proud and defiant at the thought that, by an eternal decree of the Almighty God, the Politics, the Religion, the Literature and the Jurisprudence of this guilty nation were inseparably interwoven with the destiny of the American slave.[12]

Like Douglass, the abolitionist author jokingly conflates the Bishop's second wife with her slaves: Andrew had "married a gang of slaves with a wife annexed." Rhetorically, he thus inverts the usual southern claim that slavery was incidental to the domestic affairs of the Bishop. Rather, slavery in their retellings is brought back to the fore as the motivating force in the entire narrative.

After the Civil War

Post–Civil War coverage in the white southern press tended to present Bishop Andrew as an enduring victim of northern fanaticism. A commentary in the *Atlanta Constitution* reported on a gathering of the Methodist Episcopal Church, South (MECS), and noted continuing opposition to reunification with the northern church, in sarcastic terms, alluding to legislation by the Reconstruction-era Congress:

> It is evident from the Address of the Bishops, and from a significant prayer by Bishop Andrew, that the Church cannot be reconstructed. I supposed Congress will take hold of the matter, depose Bishop Andrew, and set up Bullock or some Northern knave and adventurer in the venerable Bishop's stead.[13]

Aspects of Bishop Andrew's slaveholding were widely recalled in the public press when he passed away in March 1871 in Mobile, Alabama. The *Georgia Weekly Telegraph* (March 7, 1871) reported,

> An action of his led to the division of the Methodist Church. He married a lady who owned slaves. At a session of the Conference in New York, Bishop Andrew was requested to resign by many of the Northern ministers on this account. The Southern men deeming the request an insult to them, submitted a proposal for a christian parting and division of property, which was accepted. A separation was effected. A year elapsed and it was found the North wanted all the property. Suit was commenced by the South for her share, and both the Court below and the Supreme Court of the United States decided in favor of the Southern church. It was at this time Henry Clay, a warm friend of Bishop Andrew, remarked with a spirit of

prophecy that the Northern fanaticism of that church was the entering wedge to the dissolution of the Union.[11]

Similarly, the *Daily Evening Bulletin* of San Francisco noted, "The late
Bishop Andrew of the Methodist Church South came into possession
of slaves by his marriage and was suspended from this office on that account in 1844. This was what sundered the great Methodist body and led
to the organization of the Southern Methodists, who continued Bishop
Andrew in his office."[15]

Several months later the *Atlanta Constitution* printed a memorial sermon preached for Bishop Andrew by Bishop George F. Pierce at the
Emory College commencement held in the Old Church at Oxford: "The
dignity and grandeur of this noble man was conspicuous before the General Conference in New York in 1844 when the members of that body
conspired to make him the victim of their fanaticisms, in ousting him
without accusation and convicting him without trial."

In another memorial sermon, Bishop Pierce had nothing but scorn for
Andrew's opponents: "The man, on trial without accusation in 1844 . . .
wronged in his rights and outraged in his feelings by a foul conspiracy."[16]
In a similar vein, the Minutes of Annual Conference for the MECS in 1871
published a *Memoir of Bishop Andrew*:

> He was united to his second wife, an excellent Christian lady of
> Georgia—a little while before the session of the General Confer-
> ence of 1844. Mrs. Andrew was the owner of slaves, and though
> the Bishop had no pecuniary interest in them, and could not have
> liberated them had he wished to do, yet the Northern majority in
> the General Conference virtually deposed him from his office as
> Bishop, against the dearest protestation of the Southern delegates,
> the Southern church and many in the North. He would gladly have
> resigned his office to preserve the union and peace of the Church;
> but as such a step would have been fatal to Methodism in the South,
> and would have sanctioned a false, fanatical, and an unconstitutional
> principle, he maintained his position with dignity, humility and pa-
> tience, though the trial through which he passed was exceedingly
> severe. A Plan of Separation was agreed upon between the Northern
> and Southern sections of the Church.[17]

In all these obituaries, no mention was made of the slaves Kitty and Billy,
whom Bishop Andrew had acquired through the mother of his late first
wife; only the slaves of his second wife, Ann Leonora, are alluded to. The

frequent assertion that the Bishop had no "pecuniary interest" in these slaves goes unchallenged, even thought these enslaved people clearly labored in the Bishop's household and fields for many years.

A. H. Redford's Account (1871)

In 1871, the year of Bishop Andrew's passing, Rev. Albert Henry Redford published a detailed, influential discussion of the schism of the Methodist Church. Like his predecessors the author is at pains to demonstrate that Andrew cannot be held responsible for the events of the 1844 General Conference in New York, which led to the virtual expulsion of Andrew from the episcopacy, guaranteeing that the southern wing of the church would separate from the northern wing. Redford insists that the Bishop was a relative latecomer to the growing tension between the northern and southern branches of the church, and was simply caught in a political storm not of his own making. Andrew and his fellow southern Methodists were ultimately victims of northern intolerance.

Redford builds slowly to this defense. After detailing the growing dispute over slavery within the Methodist Church in the 1830s and early 1840s, he writes,

> Frequent efforts have been made to impress the public mind with the conviction that the connection with slavery, by marriage, of the Rev. James O. Andrew, D.D., one of the Bishops of the Methodist Episcopal Church, had led to the division of the Church, and no pains have been spared to devolve on this distinguished minister of the gospel the responsibility of the separation.
>
> It will be seen, however, that up to this period the name of Bishop Andrew, as connected with slavery, had not been referred to in the official proceedings of the General Conference. . . . The clouds of disunion were rolling up from the horizon of the Church in every direction, previous to the arrest of the official character of Bishop Andrew. Unwilling as the southern delegates were to entertain the idea of the division of the Church, they were, nevertheless, forced to apprehend such a result.
>
> Bishop Andrew, however, had become connected with slavery several years previous to General conference, without his consent. A lady in Augusta, Georgia, had bequeathed to him a mulatto girl, in trust until she should be nineteen years of age; the will provided

that he should then send her to Liberia, if she was willing to go. If, however, she would not consent, then he should retain her and make her as free as the laws [of] Georgia would admit. When the time arrived, she refused to go to Liberia, and was consequently *legally* [emphasis in original] the slave of Bishop Andrew. She continued to reside in her own house, on a lot owned by the Bishop—he deriving no pecuniary benefit from her services—and having the privilege of going to Liberia at any time. She, however, steadily refused to leave the state of Georgia, and as the laws of that State would not permit her emancipation, nor admit to record any deed of emancipation, Bishop Andrew was legally her master.

Bishop Andrew also inherited, by the death of his former wife, a colored boy, whom he could not liberate in the State of Georgia, but whom he proposed to set free as soon as he prepared to earn his own living, provided he would leave the State.

He had also married a lady in January, 1844, who held certain slaves, inherited from her former husband, and belonging solely to her. Unwilling to become their owner, and the law not permitting their emancipation, he secured them to his wife by deed of trust.

It will be seen by the above statement, that Bishop Andrew's connection with slavery was accidental, and not in violation of any law of the Church.[18]

In many respects, Redford follows the structure of Bishop Andrew's letter to the bishops at the 1844 Conference. Rhetorically he offers a legalistic consideration of Andrew's slaveholding. Note that he mirrors the contrast drawn in Andrew's 1844 letter: Andrew, the master, is deprived of volition, while Kitty, the slave, is free to choose. Andrew is made a slaveholder "without his consent," while Kitty will "not consent" to be free.

Note, as well, that Redford makes no specific mention of any of the names of the enslaved persons and refrains from any affective imagery. Andrew is simply a victim of the growing breach between North and South. These legal arguments and this factual tone were to be echoed in many subsequent white defenses of Andrew: the Bishop was only an "accidental" slaveholder, whose slaveholding was principally the result of his marriages and external legal constraints.

Redford does interpolate several elements that would be reiterated in subsequent accounts. He insists, for example, that the unnamed Kitty "steadily refused to leave the state of Georgia," even though there is no evidence at all that she was offered this choice at any other point than the December 1841 interview with professors Longstreet and Lane. In characterizing Bishop Andrew's relationship to slavery, Redford also introduces the term "accidental," which resurfaces in many later retellings.

"Merely in Name a Slave": G. G. Smith's 1882 Account

In contrast to Redford's rather dry factual defense, Rev. George Gilman Smith's lengthy 1883 biography, *The Life and Letters of James Osgood Andrew*, offers a deeply affecting portrait of the relationship between Kitty and the Bishop's family. This literary portrait has been extensively cited and developed, as we shall see, in subsequent representations.

Smith (1836–1913), a southern Methodist minister and prolific writer, grew up in Oxford, Georgia. He was around four years old when the Andrews (including Kitty) moved to Oxford and around fourteen when Kitty died. His father, a physician, tended to members of the Bishop's white family as well as a number of his slaves. Smith thus presumably witnessed many of the events he describes in the 1840s.[19] In the biography, Smith, who writes that Bishop Andrew was "like a father to him," is an impassioned defender of the Bishop at great pains to demonstrate Andrew's noble conduct in the Methodist schism of 1844.

Smith's discussion of Kitty must largely be understood in this context; he wishes to absolve Andrew of the charge of self-interested slaveholding and to demonstrate Kitty's deep loyalty to the Bishop and his family. In so doing, Smith seeks to prove that the northern delegates who sought to expel Andrew from the Episcopal office were unfairly interfering in a personal domestic matter. In these respects, Smith largely follows Redford's portrayal of the case, published a decade earlier, while rendering a much more sentimental portrait of Kitty, who becomes a central player in the drama.

Smith's first mention of Kitty is in a reproduced letter written by Andrew to his wife Amelia in late 1840. Andrew at this point was traveling to Mississippi, while his wife had moved their household, including slaves, to the city of Oxford, which would serve as Andrew's base for the next decade. Toward the letter's end, Andrew complains of the cold weather and writes, "Tell Kitty I wish I could drink a cup of her best coffee this morning. I hope she is doing well and will preserve herself chaste in Oxford. She will be greatly exposed to temptations, and I hope will be carefully guarded in her conduct."[20]

To most white readers in Oxford with whom I have discussed the letter, the passage provides clear evidence of Andrew's high-mindedness and his commitment to preserving Kitty's virginity. Conversely, for some African American readers the wording demonstrates at the very least that Andrew was well aware of Kitty's new sexual maturity and that she was very much on his mind during his travels as a provider of physical comfort. One African American man wryly remarked, "It's just the typical black mammy complex that white people have; they're always thinking of black women suckling them or giving them something warm to drink!" Many other African American interlocutors in Newton County find the passage hilarious, inferring a sexual innuendo in the Bishop's professed desire, in their words, "to drink some of Kitty's strong *black* coffee." Nonetheless the theme of Kitty as beneficent provider of nourishment and comfort has continued in more recent white representations.

Kitty next appears, five pages later, in Smith's description of the death of Andrew's first wife, Amelia, in early 1842, developing Andrew's 1854 account in *Miscellanies*. As in many nineteenth-century literary representations of a "good death," Amelia is depicted giving a careful farewell in turn to each person close to her. Toward the end of the death scene, Smith presents the following vignette:

> Calling to Kitty, who had nursed her with the affection of a daughter, she said: "Kitty, you have been very kind to me, and I love you as if you were my own child. Be pious, serve God, and promise me that you will meet me in heaven." The pledge was given now she said, "Come kiss me," and the negro slave placed her ardent kiss upon the lips of her dying mistress.

Suggestively, Smith has added to Andrew's account a description of Kitty's "ardent kiss upon the lips" of her dying mistress. Through this interpolation Smith presumably wishes to stress even further the affection felt by Kitty for the Andrew family, an important point in the subsequent story. Smith's phrasing might also be read as an act of literary displacement, simultaneously evoking and disavowing images of Kitty's emergent sexuality by transferring her "ardor" from the Bishop to his wife and recasting physical affection into a nonerotic register. He has also excised Andrew's mention in the 1854 account of the other servants of the household, each called to bid farewell to their mistress, evidently in order to emphasize the unique position Kitty occupied in the Andrew household.

Several pages later, following an account of Amelia's final moments and her funeral, Smith embarks on a three-page account of Kitty. After describing the surviving members of the Andrew family, from the adult Elizabeth to the baby James Jr., he adds the following passage: "There was however, another—Kitty, the servant-girl. We have seen the Bishop's message to her, and her dying mistress' injunction and caress, and if there was a faithful, loving servant it was Kitty. Jacob and herself were the only slaves Bishop Andrew ever really owned."[21]

How are we to read the opening phrase of this passage, "There was another"? In a manifest sense, Smith seems to mean there was another remaining "child" of Bishop Andrew, in a moral, nonbiological sense. But the phrase may be more revealing than intended by the author: Kitty occupied a very special status, clearly different from the other enslaved members of the household. She was a virtual member of the immediate family circle, although not quite the same as the white children. In what sense was she "an other"—unusually loyal slave, covert mistress of Bishop Andrew, or even Andrew's illegitimate daughter?

In any event, Smith continues,

A good woman in Augusta left him in her will this negro—a mulatto child. He was to bring her up and educate her as far as he could, and when she reached the age of nineteen she was to be free to go to Liberia or remain with him as a slave. Kitty was a model girl, brought up by a mistress who loved her, watched by a master who felt the tenderest solicitude for her welfare, she grew up a pure, good young woman. She married a colored man named Nathan, and Bishop Andrew had a neat little house built for her on his own lot, and she lived here merely in a name a slave.

As in Bishop Andrew's 1851 obituary of Kitty, the unstated problem of sex hovers over this carefully crafted passage, which culminates in the story of Kitty's marriage to "Nathan." Smith mentions that Kitty is a "mulatto," that Andrew "felt the tenderest solicitude for her welfare," and that she was "pure" up until her marriage.

As we shall see, both Kitty's house and her marriage have proved rather nettlesome subjects for subsequent white tellers of the tale. In the above passage, Smith indicates that only once Kitty was married to "Nathan" did the Bishop have a house built for her on his property, a point he reiterates several paragraphs later.[22] Curiously, later accounts usually present Andrew building the house the moment Kitty refused manumission, so as to indicate that she was no longer, in his mind at least, a slave of his household. Nathan, in fact, seems at best a shadowy (if necessary) presence in the later accounts: the house is never referred to in white versions as belonging to Nathan, but only as "Kitty's Cottage." (Some later accounts insist that once Kitty married, she moved out of the cottage.)

In the most famous passage ever published in reference to Kitty, Smith next recounts in detail her "decision" to remain in slavery:

Before her mistress' death in 1842 she reached her maturity, and the question of what she would choose was submitted to her. Judge Longstreet and George Lane were selected to lay the matter before her. The document, in Judge Longstreet's hand, says:

"This day, Kitty, a woman of color, left in charge of the Rev. James O. Andrew by the will of Mrs. Power, came before us, when, in the absence of anyone but herself and the undersigned, the following conversation occurred:

"A. B. Longstreet—'Kitty, your mistress directed in her will that you should remain with Bishop Andrew until you reached the age of nineteen, when it was to be left to your choice go to Liberia or remain with the Bishop. The time has now come when you are to make your choice, and you will do well to think seriously of the matter. If you go to Liberia you will be perfectly free, as free as I am now. You will be under laws, to be sure, just as I am, to prevent you from doing anything very bad, but you will have no master, no mistress; you will be in all respects just like white women in this country; you will have to work for your living, as all must, but what you make will be your own. The climate is not as healthy as this, particularly to persons going there for the first time, but after you get used to it you would probably live as long there as you will here. If you conclude to go the Bishop will send you at his expense. It is a long voyage by water. If you stay with the Bishop the will directs that he is to grant you all the privileges of a free woman that the law will allow, but you will have to depend upon his character for that, and you will still be a slave. Now, think of this matter and make your choice for all time to come. If you have had any stories told you about that country that have alarmed you, disregard them. I have told you the truth, so far as I know it. Now, make your choice.'

"Kitty—'I don't want to go to that country. I know nobody there. It is a long ways and I might die before I get there.'

"A. B. Longstreet—'This, then, is your choice?'

"Kitty—'Yes, sir.'

"A. B. Longstreet—'Then I may write it down as your final choice that you remain with Bishop Andrew?'

"Kitty—'Yes, sir. I don't want to go there.'

"We certify that the above is as nearly a literal report of our interview with Kitty as we can make. Not a word was said that could influence her decision which is not here recorded.

"A. B. Longstreet,
"George W. Lane.
"December 4, 1841."

We can approach this document with respect to its internal rhetorical construction, in term of its legal functions, and in terms of its function within Smith's overall text. To begin with, Longstreet, an accomplished short story writer, newspaper publisher, and attorney, clearly took great care with the report's rhetorical construction, crafting his prose to emphasize, by his own lights at least, his fairness to Kitty. In a paternalist register, he urges her to "think seriously" on her choice. He first gives her a minor disquisition on the meaning of freedom: all of us are bound by laws and by the necessity to work, but in Liberia (a land named, after all, for liberty) she would be as free as anyone else. Significantly, in laying out the terms of her choice, Longstreet draws parallels between the position of whites in America and those of blacks such as Kitty in Liberia: she would be "as free as I am here," and "will be in all respects just like white women in this country." Whiteness here is posited as the central, anchored position from which all analogies are extended, as Kitty is asked to contemplate the unknown conditions of distant Africa.

The most fascinating aspect of the text is the way in which it allows for the possibility of a slave's informed consent and subjectivity, within a highly constrained arena that is exclusively authorized and constituted through white male authority, knowledge, and discursive action. Longstreet's background as a magistrate is telling here; like a judge giving instructions to a jury, he is the source of all knowledge about Liberia, explicitly telling Kitty to disregard everything else she may have heard on the topic. He thus, as the prime speaker, establishes the framework within which Kitty is to make her decision, concluding with the commanding imperative, "Now, make your choice." She is, for a single moment, constituted as the jury deciding her own fate.

As Longstreet would have known, the background legal issue concerned the "right of election," that is to say, the slave's right, if mandated by a duly constituted bequest, to elect to go to Liberia. As Thomas Cobb explains in his authoritative 1858 volume, *An Inquiry into the Law of Negro Slavery in the United States*, such a right was highly constrained. If, for example, the negro slave named in such a will had been sold between the writing of the will and the testator's death, that section of the will was held to be retroactively revoked and invalid.[23] By 1844 there was a good deal of complex case law addressing the extent of the right of election. In the case of infants, their slave mothers were at times granted the right to decide on their behalf whether to accept manumission and go to Liberia. Yet such a right might not be extended to infant slaves born after the death of the testator, since their mothers were still slaves at the time of their birth. Also of concern to the court was whether the deceased's estate or some other body, such as a colonization society, was ready and able to fund transportation to Liberia.[24] An Alabama Supreme Court 1848 decision in the *Carroll v. Brumby* case held that even if a testator willed that his slaves be given the right to choose to leave the state or be colonized to Liberia, such a provision was invalid: slaves, as property of the heirs, had no right to make such decisions. In 1855 Justice Lumpkin of the Georgia Supreme Court opined that all postmortem manumissions should be disallowed, as they would encourage disaffected slaves to engage in insurrection.[25]

Although Smith presents Kitty's response as signifying her full and free volition, the fundamental fact is that the "choice" offered her was highly constrained. Rather than signifying a state of freedom, the Longstreet contract exemplifies Kitty's enslaved status. A free woman, after all, could change her mind and not be bound forever by the decision of an instant. Longstreet, however, commands her: "make your choice for all time to come." The legal document, masquerading as a charter of freedom, may equally be regarded as a bond of perpetual servitude.

Nonetheless, Longstreet's text and Smith's elaboration of it do develop the fascinating ideological inversion that Redford had emphasized. In their accounts, Kitty, the slave, is free to make a choice, whereas Bishop Andrew, the master, is represented as a slave of duty, bound to fulfill the terms of Mrs. Power's bequest. This paradox is key to the enduring appeal of the narrative to white audiences through the generations: the slave was free to choose and, having made her choice, was allowed to live in virtual freedom. In contrast, the white bishop was constrained by his sense of honor to follow a certain course of action, and then was unjustly victimized by northern abolitionists for acting in such a manner. Kitty and Andrew are thus positioned as mirror images of one another; by extension, for many southern white readers, the white South is rendered relatively blameless in the grand national narrative of crisis and separation.

In any event, the provenance of this celebrated text is not entirely clear. Smith asserts that it is written "in Judge Longstreet's hand," which indicates that he personally viewed and consulted the original document. If it was stored among Andrew's or Longstreet's papers, the original text has not survived; all we have is Smith's transcription of it. There is no evidence that any white person other than Longstreet, Lane, and Andrew attested to seeing it prior to Smith's publication of the text. Although Kitty was literate, she was not invited to sign the document; only Lane's and Longstreet's names are listed.

We should therefore acknowledge the possibility that some or all of the document is fictitious. Perhaps Longstreet drafted the document not in December 1841, immediately after the alleged interview with Kitty, but rather in the spring of 1844, on the eve of the New York Conference, the same time that he and Andrew created the somewhat deceptive deeds that seemed to transfer the Greenwood slaves out of the Bishop's ownership. Longstreet, it should be noted, was a renowned practical joker who took great pleasure in playful hoaxes, pranks, and deception. Indeed, his first published work of writing was a fraudulent newspaper letter, which purported to be authored by two escaped convicts under sentence of death.[26] Might he have done something comparable in this case, in the interest of sewing confusion among the northern Methodist abolitionist delegates?

At the very least, the reference to "the will of Mrs. Power" in Longstreet's opening sentence is questionable. As we shall see in chapter 7, no will or associated probate record bequeathing a slave to James Andrew exists in the Richmond County, Georgia, court records, and the only two women named Power or Powers to die in Augusta in the 1830s made no such bequest. Longstreet may thus have been engaging in willful deception or misdirection in this instance.

To be sure, the possibility that some or all of the interview document was fraudulent never seems to have occurred to Rev. Smith. His decision to include this quasi-legal document in its entirety is presumably due to his desire to establish that Kitty had made the voluntary decision to remain in slavery and that Andrew should thus be absolved of all responsibility for her status. This written exchange has been frequently cited in subsequent published and oral accounts as providing factual anchoring for the claim that Kitty chose to remain a slave of her own free will. (As will be discussed in chap. 5, the above passage from Smith was also reproduced on a wall of the Kitty's Cottage Museum in Salem Campground from 1939 onward.)

Smith conveniently neglects to mention that Longstreet was a substantial slaveholder and avid defender of the institution of slavery, or that Longstreet would "purchase" fourteen slaves from Andrew in 1844 as a strategy for deflecting attention from the Bishop's slaveowning status. Nor does Smith discuss the option available to Andrew (followed by some Georgia slaveholders of the period) of manumitting Kitty by settling her in a free state, such as Ohio or New York.

In any event, having established the voluntary nature of Kitty's "choice" to remain in slavery, Smith then briefly goes on to summarize Kitty's remaining years: "Kitty's decision was final, and she remained as before, the faithful friend and dutiful servant, until her marriage, when she went to housekeeping near by, and her house was the resort of the children, and Mammy Kitty (as the baby called her) was one to who, in hours of childish grief or perplexity, all the troubles were carried."[27]

In this passage, Smith negotiates a standard problem in white southern images of the black mammy: is she an adult being, linked to the potentially threatening figures of the white or black adult male, or a source of unconditional, singular affection for white children? Kitty's marriage is briefly alluded to, but in the softest terms—"when she went to housekeeping nearby"—and the reader is reassured that her new house was entirely open to the white children of the Andrew family. Kitty's house, in other words, is carefully classified as a space of white childhood delight and indulgence.[28]

As we shall see in chapter 6, Smith's literary maneuver anticipates subsequent white ritual management of "Kitty's Cottage," which remains to this day a space in which whites are encouraged to feel warmth and acceptance, and from which the troubling presence of male sexuality, white or black, has been evacuated.

Continuing his testimonial to Kitty's selfless (and asexual) benevolence, Smith then moves back in time, to Amelia Andrew's terminal illness of 1842:

During Mrs. Andrew's illness, which was some time previous to Kitty's marriage, she was tireless in her attentions. Watching by her bedside through the night, and reading the Scriptures and singing the sweet songs of Zion to her dear Miss Amelia, was her delight. Her love seemed more like that of a child than a servant. Toward the close of that long illness, when the nurses were being exhausted, Kitty still clung to her post, and could only with difficulty be prevailed to retire for rest.[29]

As Smith structures the narrative, Amelia's own good death anticipates the passing of Kitty, described three lines later:

She was universally respected in the community of Oxford, and loved by the members of the Bishop's family as a true and faithful friend. In her last hours, when she felt she must die, she sent for the Bishop and thanked him for kind care and for the religious training of her earliest years. She said, "I shall soon see Miss Amelia in the better land," and after commending her little girl to the Bishop's daughter, she passed with triumphant shouts from this scene of toil and conflict to the world of brightness and glory above.[30]

Note that this passage reconstitutes a unified family, transcending the divisions of race and servitude in heaven and on earth, within an entirely female frame of fictive, sentimental kinship. Kitty would be reunited with Amelia above, just as Kitty's daughter would be cared for by Amelia's daughter in this world.

Smith's account of Kitty "commending her little girl to the Bishop's daughter" is his first indication that she had children. The question of Kitty's progeny becomes even more intriguing at the bottom of the page, for at the close of his account of Kitty, Smith inserts the following footnote, which Martin Porter was later to cite in his oral accounts of the story:

In 1877 I went to Washington, and in company with Judge McCallister visited the Department of State. The Judge conversed for a moment with an intelligent, well-dressed colored man, who was the messenger. Calling to me he said, "Mr. Smith, here is a Georgian." Giving the young man my hand cordially, I said, "You are a Georgian?" "Yes, sir," "Where from?" "Oxford, sir." "Why, Oxford, my old home. Who was your master?" "Bishop Andrew." "Is it possible? You were one of his second wife's slaves?" "Oh, no, sir, I was Kitty's son." He spoke very lovingly of the Bishop and his care for him.[31]

In chapter 8 we return to this passage, which provides hints to the identity of Kitty's second son. For our purposes here it is striking that Smith makes no mention of the black man's first name or family name, nor does he indicate who the man's father was. (Smith, normally obsessed with genealogical detail, must have inquired as to these particulars, after all.) Is Smith negotiating here an issue that he (consciously or unconsciously) recognizes as difficult? Since he grew up as a neighbor of the Andrews in Oxford, he might well have heard rumors of a sexual liaison between Kitty and the Bishop. Does the absence of detail imply that he knew, but found it expedient not to mention names or the question of paternity?[32] Or is the name of a free man of color simply not worthy of mention in Smith's mind?

Kitty reappears briefly, without being mentioned by name, in Smith's detailed account of the Methodist Conference that led to the split of the northern and southern branches of the church. Smith quotes in its entirety Andrew's 1844 letter to his fellow bishops explaining his ownership of slaves. Andrew's letter, as we have seen, is the basis of Redford's commentary and many subsequent defenses of Andrew.[33]

The theme of Andrew's innocence and symbolic martyrdom seems to have been well established in southern Methodist circles by the time Smith published Andrew's biography in 1882. An unpublished section of his original manuscript for the biography contains the following 1882 testimonial letter from a Tennessee Methodist minister, who like many believes that Andrew never actually owned slaves:

In the great conflict of 1844 [Bishop Andrew] showed himself more the man and the Christian than ever. He had never owned a slave, but had married an excellent Christian woman, a widow with children, to whose family there were attached several slaves. Over these he had no control, had no power or [illegible] position to interfere with the relations of his family and their domestics: but his conviction brought [illeg.] trouble upon the church, because of the anti-slavery sentiments that predominated in the general Conference. To the Bishop this was matter of inexpressible grief. He would willingly have resigned his position rather than disturb the [illeg.] of the church which he so much loved and for which he had spent many years of toil and ministerial labor, but a principle was involved and his brethren from the south protesting against the idea of his yielding under the pressure brought to bear on him and the whole of the southern conference, so he willingly made himself the scapegoat to bear away what was a considered a great sin of his people. Noble man! He suffered himself accursed for the sake of his brethren and his kinsmen. He was never heard to utter a word of complaint.[34]

The image of the martyred Andrew was repeatedly invoked in the years that followed, as leading southern Methodists drew close connections between the Andrew story and the policies and legacies of Reconstruction, which they deeply opposed. In a revealing 1884 interview in the *Atlanta Constitution*, published just before his death, Bishop Pierce, then the leading figure in the MECS, emphasized that the antebellum southern church had unflinchingly evangelized among the enslaved:

> The church never was responsible for the existence of slavery. It was recognized as an existing fact in the constitution of the country and in the discipline of the church. She had to deal with it as she found it, carrying the gospel to the utmost of her ability on the rice and cotton plantations, through her missionaries, and by the blessing of God, through her labors gathered a great multitude into her membership, and made a great impression for the good upon the entire negro population, as demonstrated by the subordination and quiet of the colored population during the war. The peaceful demeanor and faithful service of the colored race during the war is one of the most remarkable facts in the history of mankind. The solution of it is to be found, not the constitutional traits of the negro, but in the wonderful influence of Christianity upon his untutored mind, as he has been taught to receive and understand it. The chains of slavery were softened and lightened by the influences of churches and religion, and the relation of master and slave, though positive and real, were nevertheless kind and full of domestic affection. These attachments have largely survived both slavery and emancipation and are elements of control and order down to the present day.

Pierce continues in this vein in his defense of his late friend and mentor Bishop Andrew, who had ordained him as a bishop:

> Slavery was the occasion but not the cause of the division of the Methodist church. The real provoking cause was the extra judicial action of the dominant majority in the general conference of 1844 with regard to Bishop Andrew on account of his incidental connection with slavery. Andrew was never a slave-holder although he had

legal connection with it. He had violated no law of the church. The discipline fully attempted him in its authority, but to carry out a sectional partisan purpose the majority overrode the provisions of the discipline by an arbitrary resolution and virtually deposed him without crime and without trial. This outrage upon his personal legal rights, involving as it did all the rest of us, the south resented, and demanded separation.

Pierce draws an immediate connection between this history and the continuing unacceptable interference of northern Methodists in the conduct of Christianity in the South. The presence of northern clerics is, he insists, "an insult to us, as it implies that we are either incompetent or not preaching a pure gospel." This point leads into Pierce's call for limitations on black education and enfranchisement:

In my judgment higher education, so called, would be a positive calamity to the negroes. It would increase the friction between the races, produce endless strife, elevate negro aspirations far above the station he was created to fill and resolve the whole race into a political faction, full of strife, mischief and turbulence. My conviction is that negroes have no right in juries, legislatures or in public office. The appointment of any colored man to office by the government is an insult to the southern people, and provokes conflict and dissatisfaction, when, if left as they ought to be, in their natural sphere, there be quiet and good order.[35]

Pierce's 1884 interview established the tone of most white versions of the Andrew-Kitty narrative up until the 1950s. The story was increasingly framed as a morality tale foregrounding the best of the Old South and legitimating the emerging institutions of segregation. Kitty's warm regard for her master was presented as emblematic of the real nature of hierarchical white-black relations in the South, which should be allowed to continue free of northern censure and interference.

The Loyal and Grateful Slave

As these post-1865 texts indicate, the meanings of the Kitty-Andrew story for white southern audiences altered in the wake of the Civil War. In his magisterial *Race and Reunion: The Civil War in American Memory*, David Blight demonstrates that even as the guns of the Civil War ceased firing, the ideological battle over the meanings of the war raged intensely.[36] At the war's end, a substantial section of northern opinion held that the war's principal significance was the liberation of 4 million slaves. Yet gradually this liberationist reading of the war was displaced by a reconciliationist reading that emphasized, above all else, noble struggle and sacrifice by soldiers north and south, warriors in blue and gray who were overwhelmingly represented as white "brothers." In the course of this shift, the political and economic predicaments of African American freedpeople rapidly faded from the eyes of the white majority, north and south. Through a vast profusion of sentimental images and narratives, the Civil War was increasingly depoliticized in public discourse. As that happened, the nation's attention was diverted from major civil rights debates for nearly a century.

Even when freedpersons were acknowledged in the public sphere, these representations tended to efface their political agency. In *Standing Soldiers, Kneeling Slaves*, Kirk Savage explores the political and racial iconography of post–Civil War public statuary, building on Mikhail Bakhtin's distinction between the upright and self-contained "canonical body" and the open and misshapen "grotesque body."[37] Freedmen were generally depicted as bent and kneeling at the feet of Abraham Lincoln and the other white liberators, grateful, passive recipients of the gift of freedom. These images tended to portray African Americans as eternal children, to be guided by white parental figures.

The longevity and robustness of the mainstream Kitty-Andrew narrative must be situated within this larger ideological trajectory. Through hundreds of such stories, partisans of the Lost Cause argued for the benign nature of chattel slavery and for the innate honesty and decency of the slaveholding class. Kitty typifies this image of the grateful, loyal, and submissive slave, childlike in her innocence and dependence on a powerful white male. Appropriately, as we shall see in chapter 6, her former slave quarters were refurbished in 1939 as a Lost Cause museum within a segregated Methodist campground, celebrating the romance of the Confederacy.

In any event, with the deaths of both Bishop Pierce and Rev. A. H. Redford in 1884, the last major eyewitness southern chroniclers of the 1844 General Conference passed from the scene. Longstreet had died in 1870, and Bishop Andrew in 1871. Rev. G. G. Smith, who knew these men intimately, remained productive until his death in 1913. Although he repeatedly referenced the schism and the Andrew story in his later writings, he did not introduce any new material into these accounts. The subsequent textual retellings of the Andrew-Kitty narrative would increasingly come from those who did not personally know the principal parties, but who would rely on the major published accounts considered in this chapter, embellished by oral accounts and their own imaginations. We turn in chapter 4 to these twentieth-century texts.

Chapter Four

"As Free as I Am"

Retelling the Narrative

B Y 1900 THE foundational texts of the Andrew-Kitty narrative—
especially those by Andrew, Redford, and Smith—were familiar to all those steeped in southern Methodist history and lore.
Subsequent accounts of the tale would draw on these texts with varying degree of fidelity. In reading through the hundreds of accounts of
the Andrew-Kitty story from the early twentieth century, one is again
reminded of Franz Boas's famous characterization of Northwest Coast
Native American mythology, adopted by Claude Lévi-Strauss in his development of the concept of "bricolage," the endless breaking apart and
recombination of a fixed set of mythic elements. Pondering hundreds
of myths from the region, Boas is left with the following impression:
"It would seem that mythological worlds have been built up only to be
shattered again, and that new worlds were built from the fragments."[1]
In Lévi-Strauss's terms, the teller of myth does not invent an entire story
out of whole cloth, but draws on his or her "treasury," selecting and re-
combining elements that are aesthetically appealing. No single version of
the myth is "correct," in his view, since myth is generated by underlying
cultural instability and necessarily produces variable transformations.

During the early twentieth century, southern newspaper articles would
from time to time review the outlines of the story, picking and choosing among various elements from the foundational texts, which came to
function rather like Lévi-Strauss's mythic treasury. Kitty is usually the
only slave specifically referenced in these pieces, although at times she
is referred to simply as a "slave girl" or a "mulatto girl." For instance, in
1904 the *Atlanta Constitution* reviewed the well-established outlines of the
story. The mildly sardonic account, under the subtitle "Bishop Andrew's
Slaves," relies heavily on Bishop Andrew's 1844 letter, Redford's 1871
account, and Smith's 1882 text:

In 1844 the general conference, held at New York, regarded it a very grave offense that Bishop Andrews [sic] had become the owner of a few slaves, and passed resolutions deposing him from his office, unless he would abandon his connection with what they were pleased to call "the great evil."

The fact [sic] were these: Many years since, an old lady of Augusta, Ga, bequeathed to the bishop a mulatto girl in trust, that he should take care of her until she should be 19 years of age. Provided she was willing she should then be sent to Liberia, otherwise he should keep her and make her as free as the laws of Georgia would permit. When the time arrived, the girl refused to go to Liberia and of her own choice remained legally his slave, although he derived no pecuniary benefit from her services. She continued to live in her own house and was at liberty to go to a free state whenever she thought proper. The mother of Bishop Andrew's first wife left to her a negro boy slave and, dying without a will, he became by the laws of Georgia, the bishop's property. In January 1844, Mr. Andrew married a lady possessed of slaves, but secured them to her by a deed of trust.

This act of the general conference was initiative [sic] to the seceding of the Methodist churches from Maryland to Louisiana. . . . These good people formed "The Methodist Episcopal Church, South", which is at present one of the most efficient Christian denominations of the whole world.

Now that Bishop Andrew sleeps amidst the classic shades of his beloved Oxford, he deserves a monument to be erected, not by any single conference, but by the joint contributions of southern Methodism from California to Florida.[2]

This call to erect a memorial to Andrew would often be echoed in the years to come, although no serious effort to building such a monument was undertaken until the late 1930s.

Wrightman Melton (1916)

The Kitty story had its next public revival in 1916, when it appeared for a time that the reunification of the northern and southern branches of Methodism was imminent. The fiftieth anniversary of the end of the Civil War, 1915, had seen a great deal of public discourse about "sectional reconciliation," and in that spirit many assumed that the long schism between the churches would soon be healed.[3] The *Atlanta Consti-tution*, among others, confidently predicted that by 1920, the northern and southern wings of the Methodist Episcopal Church would be fully reunited and amalgamated with a third church, the Methodist Protestant Church.

In this context, Emory's professor of English and journalism, Wight-man F. Melton (1867–1944), published a lengthy article in the *Atlanta Con-stitution*, "How Mulatto Kitty, Slave Girl Who Refused Freedom, Brought about Division of Methodist Church in 1844." Melton, who served as the *Constitution*'s local correspondent and who was Georgia's poet laureate in 1943, often published on Emory and Oxford lore. Among other things, in a 1939 article he was to claim that Emory's president Alexander Means was the probable inventor of the electric light, well in advance of Thomas Edison.

In his 1916 piece, written while he was mayor of Oxford (1912–18), Melton is at pains to demonstrate that Kitty, and not the other slaves owned by Bishop Andrew, was the major cause behind the 1844 schism. To my knowledge, Melton's article is the first published allusion, follow-ing Smith's account itself, to Kitty's dwelling place and the first that refers to it as a "cottage." Significantly, he begins the story with a description of the cabin:

> Of the seven million Methodists in the United States, few have seen or will see, the humble cottage of Kitty, the mulatto girl, who figured so prominently in the division of the Methodist church in 1844.
>
> In the quiet college town of Oxford, Ga., forty-one miles east of Atlanta there still stands—in a fair state of preservation—Kitty's two-roomed cottage, built specially for her, the basement kitchen in which she cooked, and the house of her master and mistress.

Melton's account draws heavily on Smith's book, quoting his various passages on Kitty, including his transcription of Longstreet and Lane's interview with Kitty and his account of meeting Kitty's son in 1877. He concludes with an elegiac commentary on death and reconciliation that recalls the *Constitution*'s 1904 imagery of the pastoral village graveyard:

> Almost a half century—since the first Sunday in March 1871—Bishop Andrew has been sleeping, among the sumach bushes in the village cemetery of Oxford, Ga, his memory revered by half a continent and respected by the whole of it.

Kitty's dust reposes in some unmarked grave not far from the simple, moss covered tomb of her former master. Her life was humble
and obscure, but doubtless she was largely instrumental, in the
hands of an All-Wise Providence, in bringing freedom to the people
of her race.

Note how Melton carefully contrasts the two figures whose remains rest
close by one another in the Oxford cemetery. The white man is nation-
ally renown; the black woman is "obscure." Both, however, are blessed
and taken together are metonymic of all the contrasts that are to be
reconciled in reunion (a reunion of the church and of the entire nation).
He concludes with a vision of future regeneration:

The old hurts and heartaches occasioned by the breach in the
Methodist church are now largely forgotten. These two branches of
American Methodism with a combined strength of more than five
and a quarter millions, are now unanimous in rejoicing that slavery
in America is a thing of the past; and they are working with every
increasing harmony—now seemingly approaching organic union—to
the end that humanity may be liberated from the bondage, supersti-
tion and other and grosser forms of iniquity.[4]

The article is noteworthy for the way in which it plays with a series of bi-
nary oppositions: it begins with the contrast between the house of Kitty
and the house of her own owners and concludes with the contrast between the (unmarked) grave of Kitty and the venerable "moss-covered"
tomb of Bishop Andrew. Along the way, Melton successively contrasts
white and black, famous and obscure, south and north. All of these oppositions are ultimately transcended, in the dream vision of "organic
union" enabled by the cemetery and reverence for the honored dead.
Although the precise details of Civil War and emancipation are skirted
over, the long trial of national disunion and reunification are framed as
providential, so that Kitty plays a part in bringing about the "freedom
of her race." The ideological maneuver is a familiar one, well charted
by historian Blight in *Race and Reunion*: sectional division is overcome
by an appeal to the great and small figures of yesteryear, in eternal rest
underground.

In a form of what Lévi-Strauss termed "bricolage," numerous writers
pick and choose various elements from the Kitty-Andrew treasury, re-
arranging components with at times scant concern for fidelity to the

major published sources, such as G. G. Smith. Thus, the segregationist author Rebecca Latimer Felton, in her 1919 book *Country Life in Georgia in the Days of My Youth*, summarizes the story in these terms: "I was a small girl when I became acquainted with Bishop James O. Andrew and I was only nine years old when the Methodist church split over a negro girl owned by Bishop Andrew's second wife in 1844. The story of the split has been so often discussed—abused and defended—that I am not inclined to say any more on that line, at this time. From the hour when the Methodist brethren separated at a General Conference, until Georgia seceded in January, 1861, this slavery question was kept to the front."[5] Notably, Felton conflates the story of Kitty, acquired by the Bishop during his first marriage, with the slaves that came into his possession through his second marriage. The most interesting point here is not Felton's carelessness with the facts, but the way in which she confidently signals this well-known tale and uses it as a springboard for a longer discussion of the theological defenses of slavery.

John Donald Wade on Longstreet (1924)

A few years latter, the Andrew-Kitty story reappears in John Donald Wade's 1924 biographical study, *Augustus Baldwin Longstreet: A Study of the Development of Culture in the South*. The book extensively addresses theological debates over slavery within the antebellum Methodist Church, emphasizing Longstreet's leading role as defender of the southern pro-slavery position. In this context, Wade touches on the Kitty story, as illustrative of the bonds of mutual understanding and affection existing between masters and slaves in the Old South:

> Bishop Andrew's connection with slavery, Longstreet knew like a book. The Bishop owned a negro boy, named Jacob, whom he had inherited from his first wife, and a negro girl, named Kitty, who had been left to him for rearing by a lady who lived in Augusta. The slave property that had come to him through his marriage with his second wife he had secured to her by deed of trust immediately after the marriage.
>
> Having come into the Andrew home when she was a young girl, Kitty had been reared by her guardians with tenderness which she soon grew ardently to reciprocate. When the first Mrs. Andrew lay

dying, she sent for Kitty, and after kissing her affectionately, extracted
from the girl a promise to live righteously and strive for Heaven—
held out to her guerdon the possibility of meeting there at last her
beloved mistress. The scene had been most affecting. Longstreet
himself had witnessed it. Another episode concerning Kitty he had
witnessed in a capacity that was official. Upon Bishop Andrew's request he and another member of the Emory faculty had undertaken
to explain to the girl the provisions relative to the Will of her original
owner. With his own hand, Longstreet had written down everything
that had happened at this meeting. According to the specifications
of the Will, Kitty was to be offered the opportunity, when she was
nineteen years old, either of going to Liberia, free, or of remaining
a slave with Bishop Andrew. When the matter was explained to the
child, she was naturally afraid. "I don't want to go to that country."
She had said, "I know nobody there. It is a long way and I might
die before I get there." In a special sense, then, Longstreet was personally responsible in the matter of the Bishop's connection with
slavery.[6]

Although Wade discusses Longstreet's views on slavery and African
Americans at many points throughout the book, the portrait of Kitty is
the only instance in which a person of color is introduced as an actual
character. Equally of interest is the way in which Wade balances Longstreet's sentimental and "official" encounters with Kitty, contrasting the
affecting death scene with the legalistic interview. In this way, the Kitty
saga serves a metonymic function for Wade's overall point in the book,
that the southern literary culture brought to fruition by Longstreet was a
novel synthesis of the legal and the affective, the rational and emotional,
a blend missing from the more materialistic and profit-oriented culture
of the North.

Wade's account largely follows Smith with a few interpolations. He errs
in confusing Jacob, a slave Bishop Andrew owned in the early 1830s, with
"Billy," inherited by Ann Amelia from her mother in 1840. The scene
of the dying Amelia holding out to Kitty the promise of meeting her in
heaven seems to be Wade's own elaboration or invention, as it does not
appear in Longstreet's account of Amelia's death that Wade cites. From
Wade's account onward, however, future narrators, including Martin
Porter, would echo this detail.

The Church Reunification Controversy in the 1930s

The pivotal figure in the emergence of the Kitty story in the twentieth century is Warren Akin Candler (1857–1941), who in his time served as president of Emory College, senior bishop of the Methodist Episcopal Church, South, and the first chancellor of Emory University. Candler had long prevented the national reunification of the church, but in 1934 he was forced to retire from the office of bishop and reunification became inevitable. The next year, in 1935, he authored a column in the *Atlanta Journal* titled "Forgotten History," arguing that the North preceded the South in its involvement with slavery and the slave trade, and that "in New England today there are fortunes which began to be made with wealth derived from the sale of negroes." A section of this column, along with Candler's public lectures on the topic, served to establish the modern mainstream narrative of Kitty:

> In 1844 proceedings in the General Conference of undivided Methodist Episcopal Church on the case of Bishop James O. Andrew led to the division of the church into the northern and southern branches, but it is known to all who knew Bishop Andrew that his very kindness to negroes bought him unwillingly into the possession of slaves, for which possession he was virtually deposed by a majority of the General Conference of 1844. His second wife owned slaves inherited from her first husband and Bishop Andrew had no authority or power to emancipate them. A lady in Augusta willed to him a negro girl named Kitty, and when Kitty was 19 years of age the Bishop sent Judge Longstreet to her, offering to send her to Liberia and give her money enough to live after she reached that country, but Kitty declined to go, preferring to remain in the possession of Bishop Andrew, to whom she was deeply devoted. Not being able to emancipate Kitty under the laws then existing, he built for her a cottage in his yard and gave it to her for her absolute possession, requiring no service as a slave from her. In that cottage Kitty lived for many years. It is significant that when the house in which Bishop Andrew lived in Oxford was burned a few years ago, Kitty's cottage, which was still standing, escaped the fire, and it is standing there at this time. No more interesting building in Georgia can be found than Kitty's cottage, which is a monument to Bishop Andrew's tenderness and Kitty's responsive affection.[7]

Although Candler follows previous white commentators in most respects, this text adds several key points that resurface in subsequent retellings. He plays on the concept of "possession"; Bishop Andrew was "unwillingly" brought into the "possession" of slaves, yet Kitty in time is given "absolute possession" of her cottage. He emphasizes, in a manner that previous writers had not, that Andrew's status as a slaveholder was due to his "kindness to negroes." At a historic moment when, in Candler's eyes, the national reunification of the church threatened the integrity of the Methodist Episcopal Church, South, Candler's rhetoric emphasizes a deeper unity—that between master and slave in the Old South—exemplified by Andrew and Kitty's relationship and by the enduring monument of the cottage.

In the years immediately following this editorial, Candler's close friend, Harry Y. McCord, a powerful Emory University trustee, purchased the grounds of the old Bishop Andrew estate and arranged for the cottage to be transported to segregated Salem Campground, twelve miles away. He also organized the placement of a large Kitty memorial stone tablet in the Oxford cemetery.

To understand why these events took place in the latter half of the 1930s, it is helpful to consider the background of these two men and the larger political and cultural context in which they operated. Warren Akin Candler was born into a slaveowning household in Villa Rica, in Carroll County, Georgia, four years before the start of the Civil War. Family lore recounts that his father Samuel Candler and his fourteen-year-old bride Martha Beall began their married life in 1833 with only two possessions, received as dowry from Martha's father Noble P. Beall: an Indian pony and an enslaved woman named Mary. In 1860, when Candler was three years old, his father owned eighteen slaves, which placed him among the leading slaveowning families in the county.

Later in life, Warren fondly recalled one of these enslaved people. One of the original commissioners of the Paine Institute in Augusta, Georgia, the principal college of the Colored Methodist Episcopal Church (CME), Candler remained a dedicated supporter and fund-raiser for Paine throughout his career. Significantly, in an 1885 editorial he justified his support for black higher education, as a cause even more worthy of support than foreign mission work, with reference to his enslaved African American childhood nurse:

I do not hesitate to say I love the Negroes better than any other people except my own. There is no use to lecture me about not loving a Chinaman as much as I do the race to which my old nurse belongs. I can't do it, and I won't do it and I am not going to reach clear over the heads of faithful old "Nan" and her people to build Anglo-Chinese Universities and Rio Colleges while Paine Institute languishes.[8]

The Candler family's ties to Emory are deep and extensive; when Warren's father Samuel was a boy, his own father died, and the youth was looked after by Ignatius Few, who would serve as Emory College's first president in 1836. (The Candler family converted to Methodism during Warren's boyhood.) Warren attended Emory College (1873–75) and later played a pivotal role in the creation of Emory University, encouraging his wealthy brother Asa, whose fortune was anchored in The Coca-Cola Company, to fund the university's establishment with a million-dollar gift and the donation of a substantial tract of land in Druid Hills, one of Atlanta's eastern suburbs. Warren served as the university's first chancellor, based at the Atlanta campus, but remained a champion of "Old Emory" at Oxford throughout his life. In the depths of the Great Depression, he embarked on a campaign to raise funds from Oxford alumni, the "Old Emory boys," to fund the restoration of Old Church, the famous structure in which Bishops Andrew and Pierce had preached and in which Emory commencements had been held since the 1840s.

As undergraduates at Emory College in the 1880s Warren Candler and his close friend H. Y. McCord were surely socialized into the Kitty-Andrew legend by George Washington Stone Jr., the blind son of Emory professor of mathematics George Washington Stone Sr., who in the time of slavery had owned Louisa Means, discussed in chapter 2. Candler and "Mr. George" remained close correspondents for decades, and at times George Jr. dictated reminiscences of Oxford and Emory history at Candler's request.

Stone's oral version of the Kitty narrative was recalled in the 1986 book *The Blessed Town*, authored by his niece, Polly Stone Buck:

Another tale was of the famous Kitty, a slave girl belonging to the wife of a bishop living in Oxford. The Church forbade a bishop owning slaves but Kitty refused to be set free and leave her beloved mistress. As a result, the Methodist Church had split into northern and southern segments in the years when the issue of slavery divided the nation. Kitty stirred up as much of a turmoil in her little puddle as Martin Luther once had in a larger Catholic one. Kitty had her way; she stayed with the white family until death, when she was buried in their lot in the Oxford cemetery—the only black person ever interred there.[9]

As in so many white accounts of the story within Oxford, Kitty is the only slave mentioned; she is assigned to the Bishop's wife, not to James Osgood Andrew himself. Her decision alone is foregrounded; she "had her way" and stayed with her "white family" in life and death. As in many white accounts, Kitty's historic impact is treated in a rather humorous vein; an innocent slave girl, she has little inkling of the momentous events she has unwittingly precipitated.

Although he had reportedly loved the story since his time as an undergraduate, Candler became particularly concerned with the Kitty narrative over the course of 1935, a significant year in his life. The previous year he had been finally eased out of his office as senior bishop of the Methodist Episcopal Church, South, thus rendering inevitable the reunification of the Methodist Episcopal Church, South with the Methodist Episcopal Church (the northern church), a move he had long and strenuously opposed.

Race was at the heart of this struggle. As we have seen, the split dated back to the 1844 Conference at which northern abolitionist delegates had sought to compel Andrew, as a slaveowner, to resign the episcopacy. During the post–Civil War era, many white southern Methodist leaders feared they and their congregations would be "subordinated" to northern black bishops if reunification occurred. Some, like Bishop Candler, prophesied that reunification would lead to the abolition of the color line itself.[10]

Candler's views on race were distinctly paternalistic. Insisting that the "governing power in the South will remain forever in the white hands," he strongly supported racial segregation in the public sphere. For decades he led the struggle against the reunification of the Methodist Episcopal Church, South and the (northern) Methodist Episcopal Church, largely because he opposed the prospect of African American bishops being assigned to districts in the South. He denounced women's suffrage, in part because it would lead to, in his words, "the enfranchisement of the negro women of the South, and with it the inevitable consequences of evil."

Nonetheless, Candler emerged as a stalwart opponent of lynching, following the coerced resignation of his son-in-law Andrew Sledd from

Emory College for publishing antilynching views in 1902 in the *Atlantic*. Candler also published an important denunciation of white violence following the Atlanta white riot in 1906. In the face of substantial white opposition, Candler helped bring about the desegregation of the Paine faculty and supported a liberal arts education program for African Americans. He was viewed ambivalently by leading African American figures in Georgia during this period, and was a fierce opponent of any trend toward what he termed "modernism" within Methodism.

In this light, I am struck by a particular line with which Candler commented on the role he reluctantly played in the church's reunification. When one white church in 1938 sought to secede from the Methodist Episcopal Church, South rather than be party to reunion, Candler intervened to prevent the secession. Afterward, he remarked on the irony, "It is strange thing that my name would be used to tear up the church which has been a nursing mother to me." Given that Candler's own "nursing mother" had in fact been an African American woman, "Nan," might we infer that for Candler, the Methodist Episcopal Church, South and the figure of the loyal black mammy were intimately intertwined? How appropriate, then, that his response to the demise of the southern church after his forced retirement from the episcopacy in 1934 was to promote the story of the mammy figure Kitty and the preservation of her "cottage."

Candler had long been a passionate defender of Bishop Andrew's conduct in the 1844 case. He famously stated, "Bishop Andrew was practically deposed from his office for having in his possession a slave he did not purchase and could not, under the laws of Georgia, emancipate." For all the wealth of his brother Asa, however, Warren Candler was of distinctly limited financial means, and was incapable of memorializing Andrew's heroism on his own. That task would fall primarily on his close friend and colleague, H. Y. McCord Sr., a prominent member of the Emory University Board of Trustees who, like Warren Candler, felt strong loyalty to "Old Emory," as the Oxford campus was often termed.

The McCord Tablet: 1939

Candler's and McCord's initial intention seems to have been to place a marker in front of Kitty's Cottage, leaving it on the property where it had stood for a century. As early as 1935 Candler was in correspondence about placing a bronze tablet, to be written by a Dr. Haynes, at the cottage.[11] However, as the likelihood of church reunification increased, McCord became convinced that a better course of action would be to transport the cottage to Salem Campground, a move we discuss in chapter 6. He also drafted, in consultation with Candler, a detailed account of the Kitty story, and arranged to have it inscribed on a stone tablet, erected in the white section of the Oxford City Cemetery.[12] About ten yards east of the Andrew family plot, at the base of the western side of the great water oaks that marked the entrance to the white cemetery, the four-foot tablet reads:

SACRED

To the Memory of

Kitty ANDREW SHELL

Kitty was a slave girl bequeathed to Bishop James O. Andrew by a Mrs. Powers of Augusta, Georgia in her will when Kitty was 12 years of age, with the stipulation that when she was 19 years of age she was to be given her freedom and sent to Liberia.

When she reached the age of 19, Bishop Andrew had Dr. A.B. Longstreet, who was then President of Emory College, and Professor George W. Lane, to interview Kitty. They did. Kitty declined to go to Liberia, saying she preferred to remain with Mrs. Andrew at Oxford, Georgia.

Under the laws of the Georgia at that time, Bishop Andrew could not free Kitty unless she would agree to leave the state. So he built for her a cottage in his back yard and told her "You are as free as I am."

Kitty lived in that cottage—a free woman—until she married a man named Nathan Shell, and went to her own home.

The ownership of this slave was the cause of the division of the Methodist Episcopal Church in 1844.

For a full history, see:

"The Life and Letter of James O. Andrew" by Rev. George G. Smith, D.D.

"Miscellanies" by Bishop James O. Andrew

"History of the Organization of the Methodist Episcopal Church South," by A. H. Redford, D.D.

Kitty's Cottage was purchased by H. Y. McCord and moved to Salem Camp Ground in 1938.

Interpreting the Text of the Tablet

In a little under 250 words, the text inscribed on the tablet skillfully compresses the now-familiar story in authoritative language, emulating the clipped style of regional Civil War and other historical markers. While largely following the three cited accounts, the text takes what might be termed "poetic license" with some of the standard features of the case as presented in previous white-authored versions. First, the title "Sacred to the Memory of . . ." assigns a full name to Kitty, which to my knowledge had not been done before in white representations, which generally used only her first name. "Andrew," the name of her master, is used as her middle name, and "Shell," which McCord maintains was the surname of her husband, is used as her surname. The name is consistent with the way married white women would be referred to, their Christian name followed by their father's last name, follow by their husband's last name. However, in the first line of text the naming practices revert to the standard racial hierarchy; Kitty is a "slave girl," not a woman, and is referenced only by her first name, while Bishop and "Mrs. Powers" are referred to through their surnames and courtesy titles. Similarly, the white figures of Augustus Longstreet and George Lane are referred to respectively as "Dr." and "Professor."

The final line of the second paragraph contains an interesting interpolation. McCord has Kitty state she declines to go to Liberia, not because of her fear she might die there, but because of her loyalty to "Mrs. Andrew," meaning the Bishop's first wife, Ann Amelia. This novel assertion, in keeping with the motif of the loyal slave, motivates the next line's implication that she also refused to be sent to a free state in the North. (In fact, there is no evidence that the Bishop ever offered to set her up in Ohio, Pennsylvania, or any other free state.)

McCord also evidently coins the phrase "You are as free as I am," a telling variation on the Bishop's utterance, "Here you may live as free as the laws of Georgia may permit," and on Longstreet's statement that in Liberia Kitty would be as "free as I am now." He also introduces the idea of two different houses occupied by Kitty, the first a "cottage" and the other "her own home," in which, the text implies, she resided with her husband. (The actual residences that Miss Kitty occupied have long been debated.) McCord, unlike Andrew, Smith, and other previous white commentators, assigns a last name, "Shell," to Kitty's husband, whose legal status, as free or enslaved, is conveniently not mentioned in the text.

McCord affixed to the name of the enslaved man Nathan the surname of his owner, not the surname "Boyd," which Nathan himself used. The term "free" is repeated in the next sentence, in which Kitty is said in the cottage to have been a "free woman," an exaggeration of her actual legal status.

The narrative concludes with an even more striking exaggeration, the claim that "the ownership of this slave was the cause of the division of the Methodist Episcopal Church in 1844." Kitty was in fact only one of at least sixteen slaves owned by the Bishop in 1844 whose enslaved status was at issue in the fateful New York Conference. This line also occasions an interesting rhetorical shift as the narrative frame expands from the personal to the level of national history: Kitty is no longer referred to by name but is instead only "this slave."

The inscribed text concludes, it is fascinating to note, with three bibliographical references—to Smith, Andrew, and Redford—evidently given to bolster the authority and legitimacy of its claims. Only in the final line does McCord mention himself, as having purchased the slave cabin ("the Cottage") and moved it to Salem.

Since its erection in 1939 the tablet has been viewed by many thousands of visitors, and written about in hundreds of publications. Along with the Cottage itself, it has helped to fix the Andrew-Kitty narrative in white Methodist memory throughout the region.

Stubbs's *Family Album* (1943)

Several years later, another version of the Andrew-Kitty narrative surfaced in Thomas Stubbs's book, *Family Album*, a history of his family, the Moods of Charleston, collateral relatives of James Osgood Andrew. After quoting Wade, Augustus B. Longstreet's biographer, on Kitty's loyalty to the Andrews, Stubbs writes,

> In May, 1844, Bishop Andrew met with other bishops of the Methodist Episcopal Church in general conference at the Green Street Methodist Church in New York City. He then owned the slave, Kitty, and negro boy, Jacob, who was left by his first wife, Anne Amelia, who in turn, had received the boy from her mother, Catherine Stattler McFarlane. He had married as his second wife Mrs. Leonora Greenwood, of Greensboro, Georgia, who also owned slaves. The Bishop refused to set Kitty free when she declined, upon the questions

propounded to her by Judge Longstreet, to accept freedom. This resulted in the division of the Methodist Episcopal Church into the Northern and Southern parts—a breach which lasted for ninety two years.[13]

Like Wade, Stubbs confuses the slave "Jacob," whom Andrew owned in the early 1830s, with "Billy," whom Ann Amelia McFarlane Andrew inherited from her mother in 1840 and whom Bishop Andrew subsequently inherited. Following McCord, Stubbs attributes the schism of the church entirely to the dispute over Kitty. Stubbs further emphasizes that the principal agent of choice in the whole matter was Kitty, who had "declined . . . to accept freedom," representing Bishop Andrew as simply bowing to her wishes.

A few years later, in 1948, an essay in the Emory University *Bulletin* referred to the Andrew-Kitty story as "a story that is full of drama, pathos, and of tragedy."[14] In 1952 the *Covington News* ran a story by Oxford faculty member Wilbur A. "Squire" Carlton on the history of Oxford's Old Church: "The slave girl Kitty attended services in the Old church and lived in her own cottage nearby. Not far from the Andrew lot stands an impressive marble marker to Kitty, the slave girl who through no fault of her own or her master's caused the division of the Methodist Church."[15]

The Andrew-Kitty Narrative in the Civil Rights Era

The Kitty narrative was next revived in spring 1954 by Rev. Charles Crawford Jarrell, nephew of the Methodist historian George G. Smith, who had authored the 1883 biography of Bishop Andrew explored in the previous chapter. Jarrell, an Emory College professor, emerged as a leading chronicler of the history of Emory University and its birthplace of Oxford, Georgia, and wrote a regular column in the *Wesleyan Christian Advocate*. On the eve of the Supreme Court's *Brown v. Board of Education* decision, Jarrell wrote a series of columns decrying what seemed to him a new and unwarranted tension in race relations. His evocation of Kitty was in this spirit, as he called for a return to a previous era of amity and mutual understanding and a brake on precipitous action.

Following previous white commentators, Jarrell asserts that Kitty had voluntarily remained in slavery when offered manumission and transport to Liberia in 1841, and been allowed by the Bishop to reside in de facto freedom on his estate, a loyal "servant" of the family:

Kitty, the servant girl, "willed" to him by an Augusta friend, grew to womanhood on the Andrew place. Then she married Nathan Shell and settled in Oxford. She and her husband were respected by all as worthy members of that old Oxford colony of colored people. Her triumphant, dying words were spoken to Bishop Andrew at her bedside, "I shall soon see Miss Amelia (Mrs. Andrew) in the better land."[16]

As in the many other white accounts, the enslaved status of the African American figure is glossed over; she is the "servant girl." Even the disquieting term "willed" is placed in quotation marks. Kitty and her alleged husband are presented as emblematic of "that old Oxford colony of colored people" nostalgically memorialized by Jarrell. Like McCord, he assigns Kitty's husband Nathan a surname, "Shell." In this rendition, the story is not tragic but rather joyous, as her final words are "triumphant," a sign of a life well lived under the tutelage of her benevolent white master and mistress, whom she will rejoin in heaven.

Two months later, following national controversy over the *Brown* decision, the image of a loyal slave resurfaces in another column by Jarrell, which begins with these telling lines: "On September 29, 1848 a neatly dressed, courtly old colored house servant could be seen going from house to house in the village of Oxford. He is holding in his hand a scroll, beautifully embossed and mounted at the top with black ribbon. It carried a manifesto to the citizens of Oxford, summoning them to the funeral of their beloved fellow citizen, professor George W. Lane."[17]

Jarrell's mythic antebellum landscape typifies representations of African Americans in the standard historiography of white Oxford before the civil rights era. The black presence is not entirely erased, but when mentioned, it usually sets the scene and then fades out, as white figures move to the forefront of the historical stage. The unidentified "house servant" (the term "slave" is carefully avoided) exists for Jarrell eternally in the present tense, like a figure frozen in an old photograph, a benevolent silent guardian marking the passing of great men and the passage of time. African Americans, when introduced, are almost always situated firmly in the bourgeois domestic realm, subordinated to the wider public sphere: the perambulating slave is referred to as a "house servant," well attired, and "courtly." As in other such representations, the black figure is linked to a written text that he himself does not control. In this opening vignette, the African American herald is seen but not heard; he simply carries a scroll, a text that functions as prelude to Jarrell's own written account of Emory's early history. Like the courtly herald in Jarrell's June 1954 column, "going from house to house," Kitty is frequently represented in an interstitial role, as a bridge between white actors. In her death scene she reassures the earthbound bishop, her master, that she will soon be reunited with his late wife, her mistress, in heaven.

Through the tumultuous 1950s, "old style" African American figures periodically appear in Jarrell's history column. Three years after his "Kitty" column, Jarrell republished a laudatory obituary of Samuel Wade, a "negro handyman" and longtime Oxford resident who had helped construct the house of the college's famed president, Atticus Haygood, and the great college edifice that Haygood had overseen, Seney Hall. The obituary praises Wade's honesty, humility, and deference. Welcomed in all the white households of the village, "Uncle Sam" is recalled as a comforting, humorous, self-deprecating figure. Referring obliquely to the contemporary atmosphere of political struggle, Jarrell concludes the column with a rhetorical question, "Will we see any more like him in these days of confusion and conflict?"[18]

Although these passages were written on the eve of Emory University's move toward desegregation, they emerge out of a long literary tradition at the institution, dating long before the Civil War. In these texts, African Americans tend to play a necessary, if muted, ideological function. Represented as respectful caretakers of the institution and of successive generations of students and faculty, they tend to move between the domestic sphere and the more public landscapes of the campus and village, linking together the various locales of the extended Emory community, past and present. Whether working as laundry women, carpenters, domestics, chauffeurs, valets, janitors, or cooks, persons of color enable the college's history yet are rarely directly credited with the institution's accomplishments. Interstitial figures, they are *of* Emory, but not fully *at* Emory. Inhabiting the liminal space between the lines of Emory's official history, they are perpetually, in Jarrell's telling phrase, "going from house to house."

Around the same time, the *Covington News* began running periodic stories on the Kitty story, often around the time of the annual camp meeting at Salem. In 1952, for instance, the paper noted, "Kitty's Cottage, the original building which was erected by Bishop Andrews for his slave girl, Kitty, is now located on the grounds. It was moved intact by H. Y. McCord Sr. just prior to his death. 'Kitty's Cottage' was the cottage which caused the split between Northern and Southern Methodist Church which occurred in 1844 and lasted until 1937 [*sic*] when the Northern and Southern Methodists were united in one church."[19] Suggestively, in these pieces, the cause of the split is not Kitty or the Bishop but the cottage itself.

Rev. Webb B. Garrison (1960)

Emory and Methodist texts throughout the 1960s continued to take up the Andrew-Kitty story. During this period, by and large, the story ceased to function as an instrument of overt white resistance to desegregation and instead tended to be retold in support of white moderate and liberal calls for "mutual understanding" between the races. The narrative was, for example, recalled by Rev. Webb B. Garrison (1919–2000) in 1960, as part of a series in Emory publications associated with the Civil War centennial. Garrison, a Methodist minister and associate dean at Emory, was a prolific author who published extensively on the Civil War. Having served for a year as pastor of the Salem circuit, immediately adjacent to the Kitty's Cottage Museum, he was intimately familiar with the story of Kitty. His 1960 article in the *Emory Alumnus* is titled "Emory's Role in the Methodist Civil War," and bears the subtitle "Bishop Andrew's Ownership of the Slave Kitty Precipitated the First North-South Split." Most of Garrison's article is a detailed account of the political intricacies of the 1844 Conference, drawing heavily on G. G. Smith and other southern Methodist authors. Like his predecessors, he emphasizes the fanaticism of Andrew's northern critics: "Men who would have hesitated to let others call them abolitionists were ready and eager to correct the ways of their brethren from slave states. They came to New York with blood in their eyes, armed with antislavery materials whose number tended to obscure the fact that they spoke for a relatively small segment of Methodism."[20]

In most respects, his account of Kitty echoes the earlier texts: "No one knows what Bishop Andrew asked of God in the next troubled days. But history has preserved the explanation and petition he presented to his brethren. An old lady of Augusta, Georgia by her will left a mulatto girl in trust to him, he explained. She provided that at 19 this slave, Kitty, was to be offered an opportunity to go to Liberia and freedom. Offered her freedom and refusing to accept it, the girl remained his property under the laws of Georgia but actually was as free as the social order permitted."

After quoting from Longstreet's 1841 interview, Garrison then shifts to Kitty's loyal nursing of her mistress Ann Amelia Andrew: "Only a few months after she moved into [the cottage] Kitty was called to the big house to stand beside the deathbed of Mrs. Andrew. They exchanged promises of love, says biographer Smith, and made plans to meet in Heaven. Mrs. Andrew signaled for a parting token of affection and Kitty 'Placed her ardent kiss upon the lips of her dying mistress.' This was the girl who was to have a focal role in debate that led to the division of Methodism."

Garrison's rhetoric elegantly contrasts the symbolism of joining and division. Mrs. Andrew and Amelia exchange their hopes of a heavenly reunion and are conjoined in a kiss, even as the gathering storm will tear asunder the church and, in time, the nation itself. Note that in Garrison's retelling the kiss is not commanded by Ann Amelia, as it had been in Smith's version, but instead seems to be a spontaneous act by Kitty, signifying her complete, even childlike, devotion.

Like many chroniclers Garrison seems uncertain as to precisely when Kitty moved into which house. My sense is that these variations over the question of just when the cottage was built are instances of the mythic imagination at work, as successive white chroniclers have negotiated the thorny problems of affinity, sexuality, and reproduction that swirl around the narrative. Garrison, perhaps vaguely aware of the possible appearance of impropriety, seems uncomfortable with the thought of Kitty residing alone in the Cottage.

"The Tragic Issue": The Emotional Economy of the 1966 Dedication Speech

The story of Kitty was again given local prominence in 1966, in the wake of the Civil Rights and Voting Rights Acts. A plaque was dedicated at Bishop Andrew's grave in Oxford, by representatives of Andrew College—an institution originally dedicated by Bishop Andrew 110 years earlier—members of the Oxford Historical Cemetery Foundation, and representatives of Oxford College. The virtually all-white cemetery foundation had been established a year earlier to ensure the "perpetual care" of graves in the historically white section of the city cemetery.

Mrs. Emilio Suarez, alumna of Andrew College, delivered an address

about Andrew titled "James Osgood Andrew: Memory of a Great Man."
The address concluded with the following retelling of the Kitty story:

Here, in Oxford [Bishop Andrew's] family lived and here his wife,
Ann Amelia died. The family included Kitty, the mulatto slave girl,
given to the Bishop by a friend when she was a child—given with
the request and instructions that he raise and educate her, until she
became of age. Then she was to be free to go to Liberia. The time
came and he gave Kitty the privilege of going free but she refused.

We all know that it was Kitty who became the tragic issue in 1844.
Kitty, a slave within the ranks of Methodism, was the *property* of a
Bishop.

On the one side were those staunch non-believers in slavery and
the political abolitionists of the north. On the other side, the Methodist leaders of the south who, knowing and loving Bishop Andrew,
refused to allow him to resign from the Episcopacy. This reason
for resigning was that his human feeling for and loyalty to Kitty
and the slaves of his second wife prohibited him from freeing them
from slavery and so be without protection. He offered his conference friends his resignation. It was refused.

So, it became a question: resign, or be deposed. When brought to
a vote in the General Conference of 1844 the vote 111 for deposing
him and 69 against. If he resigned, that would not satisfy the northern conference. If he was deposed the Southern Conference would
withdraw. All felt it was division or death to the Methodist denomination. The division became inevitable. But fairness and love for the
Church was evidenced by *all*.

The Reverend George Smith says, "Without schism or secession, but joint consent it was agreed to hold a convention of those
Southern Conference and then to organize the Southern Methodist church. . . . No doctrines were changed, not usages, rites, nor
customs modified. . . . And Bishop Andrew came through it all,
unscathed and unembittered, with his loyalty to the church and to
God unflinching and feeling no powers, but from God's hand."

We of Andrew today want to thank the Oxford Historical Cemetery Foundation for their interest in permanent care of this sacred
spot—for the pleasure and privilege you give us to be here today,
and to wish you God-speed and God's blessings upon your loyal
undertaking.

At one level, the address reiterates the familiar themes of the standard white narrative of Kitty, seen in the Redford and Smith accounts. The Bishop's ownership of Kitty was a technical legal matter, not driven by pecuniary (or sexual) interest. Kitty possessed free will, and voluntarily chose to stay with Andrew. Andrew's course of action was driven by a principled sense of responsibility for Kitty and her fellow slaves. Andrew was himself blameless, caught in the midst of a great historical and political struggle raging around him. The church endured.

One particular feature of the speech, however, distinguishes it from Redford and from the text of McCord's historical marker, which stands about twenty yards from the site of the 1966 dedication ceremony. Rather like G. G. Smith, Mrs. Suarez presents the tale as a morality tale of the emotions. Andrew was motivated by "his human feeling for and loyalty to Kitty" and the other slaves, by his fatherly desire to protect them, and so wished to resign. But Andrew's fellow southern bishops loved him and would not permit his resignation. There were strong feelings on both sides of the church debate. "But fairness and love for the Church was evidenced by all." This emotional purity of feeling was exemplified by the Bishop, as the quote from Smith emphasizes: "Andrew came through it all, unscathed and unembittered," feeling only the power of God. The dedication of the plaque is thus a reconsecration of the timeless covenant between the Lord and his loyal people.

The Kitty tale functions as the immediate stepping-stone to Suarez's conclusion, the Andrew College alumni's heartfelt expression of gratitude to the foundation for their "loyal undertaking." The myth of Kitty, in other words, is being ritually reenacted by the dedication ceremony and the foundation's perpetual care of Andrew's resting place. The eternal bonds of loyalty that are exemplified by the filial (nonromantic) affection between slave and master serve as the mythic foundation for subsequent sentiments and acts of loyalty—among the college alumni, the foundation members, and the sons and daughters of the South.

The underlying emotional economy of the narrative helps explain why the speaker and so many other nonblack tellers of the tale concentrate on the figure of Kitty in their accounts of the Methodist division, and so rarely emphasize the existence of black male slaves. As a black female, Kitty is the appropriate embodiment of positive affect, of (nonsexual) love and loyalty.

That same year, 1966, the Georgia State Historical Commission erected a large metal plaque to the immediate north of the Emory at

Oxford campus, detailing twenty-one historical sites in the city. The text marking the map site for the original location of Kitty's Cottage reads,

#18. "Kitty's Cottage" location. Kitty was a mulatto slave girl willed to Bishop James O. Andrew, President of the Board of Trustees of Emory College, with the stipulation that at age nineteen she was either to go to Liberia or remain as free as the law and society of Georgia would permit; her decision to remain in Oxford, technically the slave of a Methodist Bishop, partly brought about the organization in 1845 of the Methodist Episcopal Church, South. Kitty's Cottage was moved in 1938 to Salem Campground near Covington.

The wording remains galling to many African Americans in Oxford. They are distressed over the use of the term "girl" in reference to Kitty, and query the use of the "technically" in characterizing Kitty's slave status.

Several years later, on the eve of the Methodist Episcopal Church's merger with another wing of the Methodist movement to create the United Methodist Church, the prominent Methodist minister Rev. John Marvin Rast, who as an Emory college student in 1916 had gazed out at Kitty's Cottage from his boarding-room window, published an essay, "The Slave Girl Who Divided a Church." Rast was especially well known as the writer of Emory's subsequently controversial alma mater, "In the heart of dear old Dixie, where the sun doth shine, that is where our hearts are turning, round old Emory's shrine."[21] In the essay, he emphasized Kitty's ignorance of the historical events swirling around her:

How could a slave girl, Kitty Andrew, in the obscure village of Oxford, Georgia in the mid 19th century know that she was to be the issue provoking the major division of the Methodist Episcopal Church? How could she in her wildest conjecture dream she would be buried in Oxford Cemetery, called the "Westminster of Georgia Methodism" and that the inscription on her cenotaph, in another part of the cemetery, would be the longest there, far longer than the epitaph of her master, Bishop James O. Andrew on whose lot she was buried?[22]

Around the same time, the newly established United Methodist Church's *Book of Discipline* settled on this wording to explain the 1844–1939 schism:

The slavery issue was generally put aside by The Methodist Episcopal Church until its General Conference in 1844, when the pro-slavery and anti-slavery factions clashed. Their most serious conflict concerned one of the church's five bishops, James O. Andrew, who had acquired slaves through marriage. After acrimonious debate the General Conference voted to suspend Bishop Andrew from the exercise of his episcopal office so long as he could not, or would not, free his slaves. A few days later dissidents drafted a Plan of Separation, which permitted the annual conferences in slaveholding states to separate from The Methodist Episcopal Church in order to organize their own ecclesiastical structure. The Plan of Separation was adopted, and the groundwork was prepared for the creation of The Methodist Episcopal Church, South.[23]

As in the 1871 Andrew obituaries, the entire controversy was reduced to the slaves of the Bishop's second wife. In deference to both southern and northern opinion this carefully crafted conciliatory passage ambiguously states that the Bishop "could not, or would not, free his slaves."

John Jakes's *The Furies* (1976)

In addition to the regular round of articles about the story in Newton County newspapers, Methodist periodicals, and Emory-related publications, the Andrew-Kitty tale from time to time finds its way into national publications. The narrative even makes a brief appearance in modern popular historical fiction. Book 1 of John Jakes's *The Furies* (1976), the fourth volume of his best-selling *American Bicentennial* series (also known as *The Kent Chronicles*), concludes with a set of fictional journal entries by his hero Rev. Jeptha Kent. Jakes, it should be noted, was educated at Indiana's DePauw University, a Methodist institution founded in 1837 (one year after Emory College). He presumably encountered the story of Bishop Andrew in the course of his religious upbringing or education at DePauw.

The relevant sequence is titled "The Journal of Jeptha Kent, 1844: Bishop Andrew's Sin."[24] Kent, torn between abolitionist sympathies and loyalties to his slaveowning Virginia congregation and in-laws, attends the 1844 Methodist Conference in New York, which Jakes presents as a veritable dress rehearsal for the looming Civil War. Kent is agonized by the choice of whether to compel Andrew to relinquish the episcopacy. In the end he decides to vote with the southern minority, in the hopes of gradually convincing the southerners to see the error of their ways. The passage in which Jakes introduces the Andrew case is telling: "The anti-slavery delegates are operating according to a plan drawn long before we assembled. The ultimate target of the strategy is the worthy and well-regarded Bishop James Andrew of Georgia, whose sin is this: he is the unhappy possessor of a mulatto girl and a Negro boy, neither of which he purchased. Both were bequeathed to him in the estate of his first wife. His second wife is also the inheritor of slaves. Under Georgia law, neither the bishop nor his spouse can manumit the slaves."[25]

Like many chroniclers, Jakes makes a minor historical mistake, asserting that Kitty was bequeathed to Andrew by his first wife. Otherwise his presentation follows G. G. Smith in the details and tone of his account. Andrew is presented as virtuous and blameless, a victim of circumstances and of northern abolitionist fanaticism. The title phrase, "Bishop Andrew's Sin," repeated in the above passage, is used ironically to imply that Andrew is himself in fact innocent of wrongdoing. This framing is all the more interesting given that later in the series, as Jeptha Kent's abolitionist commitments deepen, he becomes a conductor on the Underground Railroad and dramatically breaks with his wife's family, in a foreshadowing of the coming fratricide of war. For Jakes, the story of the Bishop, rooted in the domestic scenario of a marriage, effectively anticipates the strains in the hero's own marriage and the looming division in the national house.

History of Newton County (1988)

The 1988 volume *History of Newton County*, written by members of the Newton County Historical Society, contains several retellings of the Kitty story, not all of them consistent. Like many southern county histories the volume consists of scores of essays. The majority of the contributions are written by local white authors, who tend to reproduce standard white versions of southern history. Like John Jakes, they see in the Andrew-Kitty story a foreshadowing of the War between the States. For instance, in her essay on "Emory College," Hanna Aiken-Burnett writes,

> The tranquil atmosphere of Old Oxford was shaken in 1844 when the General Conference of the Methodist Episcopal Church, to which President Longstreet was delegate, refused to continue to rec-

ognize the position of Bishop James Osgood Andrew. Along with his high position in the church, Bishop Andrew was President of the Board of Trustees of Emory College and a friend of and neighbor of Longstreet's in Oxford. The issue was over a slave girl named Kitty, who had been willed to the Andrew family. She had been offered her freedom at the age of nineteen and, according to Georgia Law, would be transported to Liberia had she accepted freedom.

Kitty chose to remain with the Andrew family, and the Bishop would not force her to leave. The Conference did not condone this, and so the break was made some sixteen years before the Civil War, and the Methodist Episcopal Church, South was organized.[26]

In her essay on the town of Oxford, Margaret Stephenson similarly reduces the 1844 split to the story of Kitty:

Kitty's Cottage, the home of the slave girl who refused her freedom in 1840, and thus caused the historic split in the Methodist Church, was moved from its location on the grounds of Bishop Andrew's home in 1938 to the grounds of Salem Camp Ground west of Covington.[27]

The more scholarly James Waterson devotes the first two pages of his essay on the Civil War in Newton County to a detailed, careful discussion of the Kitty story. He largely follows Smith, with a few additions. He notes that in 1844, "Andrew, suspecting trouble in New York, deeded all his slaves to [Emory College President] Longstreet for $10.00 just before they left for New York." He asserts that the year after the 1845 separation conference, "Kitty married Nathan Shell, a free person of color and continued to live in her small house after Bishop Andrew's wife Ann Amelia died." Although it is not clear what source Waterson had for asserting that Nathan was a freeman, this claim in subsequent years became part of the standard white narrative.

Describing the current appearance of the old Andrew homestead in Oxford, Waterson (who now resides on this site) writes, "The only visible sign of the bishop's house . . . in Oxford is the basement pit. The original site of Kitty's cottage can be located only by a small mound of bricks where the chimney stood, marking the place where perhaps the greatest story of antebellum Newton County occurred."[28]

"Just as innocent as she could be":
Martin Porter and the Kitty Story

Having considered this history of narrative texts, let us return to Martin Porter and his oral version of the tale, with which chapter 1 began. From the early 1990s up until his death in the late 2000s, Porter was the principal white guardian of the Andrew-Kitty narrative. He retold his version of the Kitty story hundreds of times to friends, acquaintances, visiting schoolchildren, journalists, and researchers. His version of the story took on canonical qualities: even liberal white and African American residents of the town, who complained about Porter's "racial insensitivity" in other contexts, initially referred me to him when I inquired about Kitty.

Porter's interest in the Kitty story was triggered as plans were made to return her small house to Oxford in the early 1990s, a process discussed in chapter 6. He began to read the primary sources and chatted with several elderly members of the Oxford African American community, and then reported on the story to the town historical society.

Porter came from a long line of Georgians but was not a native of Oxford, having moving there soon after the Second World War. He taught at Oxford College, where he also worked for some time as an administrator. He occupied many leadership positions in local civic organizations and was the town's most widely respected white amateur historian. Not insignificantly, Porter was a leader of the Oxford Historical Cemetery Foundation, a private foundation that cared for the (virtually all-white) southeastern portion of the Oxford City Cemetery, within which Kitty is buried. He was also prominent in the Oxford Historical Shrine Society, a private organization founded in 1974. As we shall, during the late 1990s the historical society restored Kitty's Cottage on the grounds of Old Church. Porter gave frequent tours to schoolchildren from all over the region of the Oxford cemetery and of the Old Church and often conducted college students and other visitors on walking tours through the cemetery. In all of these tours, as in the vignette given at the start of chapter 1, the story of Kitty occupied pride of place.

As we can now appreciate, in his skillful oral renditions of the story Porter largely followed Smith's account and the McCord historical marker of the late 1930s, with several imaginative interpolations and additions. Unlike Smith or the marker's author, Porter was perfectly willing to entertain the possibility of miscegenation in the Kitty story, inasmuch as he raised the possibility (for adult audiences) that Kitty was a relative of the white Mrs. Powers family. However, he never raised the possibility that Kitty was the lover of James Andrew or the Bishop's illegitimate daughter.

Porter's command of the historical sources was variable. He regularly insisted that Kitty was actually the property of Amelia, Bishop Andrew's first wife, and not really of the Bishop. In fact, as we have seen, Smith specifically states that Kitty was willed to Bishop Andrew by Mrs. Powers of Augusta. Porter may have confused Kitty in this respect with the enslaved young man, Billy. According to the 1844 letter by Andrew reproduced in Smith's volume, Billy was inherited by Ann Amelia, several years after Bishop Andrew inherited Kitty.

Like Smith and the other white narrators, Porter conveniently skipped over Andrew's legal sale to President Longstreet of the fourteen slaves he acquired by his second marriage. (In contrast, Porter's friend James Waterson in his 1988 history of the story, was, as we have seen, careful to cite the deed.) Following the McCord historical marker, Porter insisted that Kitty married a free black man named "Nathan Shell." As we have seen, Smith never refers to Kitty's supposed husband by the family name of "Shell," but only identifies him as "Nathan" and never actually states that he was a free man of color.

Reiterating a theme in Rev. Rast's 1968 account, Porter frequently asserted that Kitty was ignorant of the split in the Methodist Church. He liked to say that back in Oxford, as these great historical events unfolded, "She was just as innocent as could be." In interviews he often remarked, "Kitty had nothing to do with this in that she was just being Kitty."

In private conversations, many African Americans quietly objected to Porter's characterizations of Kitty as "ignorant" of the national debates occasioned by the Bishop's slave ownership. The issue of the church division must have been extensively discussed in the Andrew household, since the Bishop wrote his second wife letters detailing the 1844 Conference, and these events must have been closely followed in the town of Oxford, an exclusively Methodist enclave during this period. They suggested Porter's phrase, "She was just as innocent as could be," reflects the widespread white tendency to infantilize Kitty as a bystander ignorant of the historical events swirling around her.

Nonetheless, Porter's version of the story became so widely accepted in Oxford and Emory circles that it found its way into the quasi-official history of Emory University, *A Legacy of Heart and Mind*, written by then-secretary of the university Gary Hauk. Normally an impeccable scholar, Hauk reproduces Porter's incorrect claim that Bishop Andrew's first wife inherited Kitty.[29] Elsewhere in his book, Hauk is careful to explore the discordant and dissident notes in Emory's past, devoting an entire chapter to the vicissitudes of political protest in the school's history. He notes that Emory has often shown a penchant for compromise, preserving an outward face of propriety while allowing a degree of tolerance and diversity internally. He casts the Kitty-Andrew story within this larger implicit narrative: "Caught in a nineteenth-century 'Catch-22,' Bishop Andrew allowed Kitty to exercise virtual freedom while she continued to live in a cottage on his property and work for his family." In contrast to earlier accounts, Hauk's version does not use the figure of Kitty to defend the institution of slavery; instead, he places it within his wider account of tolerance and diversity at Emory.

For all the novel qualities of Hauk's use of Kitty, his account shares with previous versions an emphasis on her cottage, which Bishop Warren Candler in the 1930s termed the most "interesting" building in Georgia. Hauk's sidebar on Kitty features a photograph of this small, restored house, with the caption,

> The cottage built for Kitty by Bishop Andrew was moved from its original spot to Salem Camp Ground, where it remained until being returned to Oxford in 1994. Now owned by the town of Oxford, it stands near Old Church, some fifty yards from its original location. At one point the cottage was used as a carriage house.[30]

A version of the story was published in Emory University's alumni magazine in 1997, quoting Porter extensively:

> Far away from the tumult in New York, Kitty Andrew lived quietly in her cottage in Oxford. "She was just as innocent as she could be," says [Martin Porter] Oxford history buff. She eventually left her home on the bishop's property when she married a free man named Nathan Shell. The couple had two sons and a daughter before Kitty's death sometime in the 1850s.[31]

The same year, Kitty appears in *Touring the Backroads of North and South Georgia* by Victoria and Frank Logue, who add a few touches of their own. They assert, for example, "When the General Conference of the Methodist Episcopal Church met in 1844, Kitty was living [in] her cottage as a free woman." They further claim, "Kitty continued to live in

her cottage until she married Nathan Shell and moved to his home."[32]
Along similar lines, also in 1997, the *Atlanta Journal-Constitution* referred
to Kitty and her cottage in a story on a fund-raising drive to repair Old
Church: "In 1844, the Methodist Church was split over the issue of the
ownership of a slave by Bishop James O. Andrew, who lived next to the
church. The cabin of the slave Kitty, who was passed to Andrew by inheritance and who did not want to leave the family, has been preserved and
stands adjacent to the church building."[33]

Scores of comparable brief accounts continue to appear in Georgia
newspapers, magazines, and Web sites each year, generally emphasizing
Kitty's loyalty to the Andrew family and her special role in triggering
the Methodist schism. Many of these pieces unintentionally illustrate
the mythic imagination, as members of the local historical society freely
improvised in their interviews. One account based on an interview with
several senior members of the society went as follows:

> The wife of Bishop Andrew inherited Kitty in 1834 from an Augusta
> woman, Augusta Power, who did not want her to be a slave. Local
> historians said Power willed the girl to the bishop's wife, hoping the
> bishop would love, guard, and educate and set her free from slavery
> when she reached the age of 19. The bishop's wife died in 1842, and
> Kitty is believed to have served as a wet nurse for one of the bishop's
> children following his wife's death, living both in the house with the
> bishop and in her own cottage. Kitty lived as a free woman and in
> 1842 married a free man, Nathan Shell.[34]

The interviewees appear to have invented a number of details freely:
the year 1834, the first name of Mrs. Powers (perhaps inspired by the
first name of Augustus Baldwin Longstreet), the insistence that Kitty was
willed to Ann Amelia, the unsupported claim that Kitty was a wet nurse,
and the year of Kitty's marriage.

Reflections

In sum, the Andrew-Kitty story appears to have served different political
and cultural functions at different historical junctures. In the antebellum
period it was key to southern slaveholding defenses against northern abolitionism, and also a powerful moral tale aimed at convincing southern
slaveholders to allow for Christian evangelism among the enslaved. In
the 1880s Smith and his colleagues saw in the history a charter for the

moral legitimacy of the M. E. Church, South and as a demonstration of the errors of Reconstruction. In the 1930s Candler, McCord, and others retold the story in order to argue against the coming reunification of the two branches of the church, and to help safeguard the theological and social foundations of racial segregation. In the 1950s and 1960s the story was recirculated by whites in a rather nostalgic vein, pointedly in contrast to the "confusion" of the civil rights era. The resurgence of the story in the 1990s was partly triggered by the return of Kitty's Cottage to Oxford in 1994, as well as tacit struggles over race and justice in the county.

IN THE NEXT TWO chapters I consider how these memories and contests have been embedded not only in written texts but also in landscape and architectural sites. I begin with the Oxford cemetery, and then turn to Kitty's restored and perambulating "cottage." These elaborated spatial sites have helped to reproduce and extend the dominant white narrative of Kitty. In many respects this political geography has made it difficult for alternate, African American tellings of the story to circulate publicly. Yet in other ways, these same mythologized geographical sites have also put the dominant narrative at risk, opening it up to questioning and critique by those who have long felt excluded from the mainstream story.

Chapter Five

"The Other Side of Paradise"

Mythos and Memory in the Cemetery

IN CHAPTERS 5 and 6, we turn from textual analysis to the emplacement of remembrance and mythos in lived social space. We consider the elaborated spatial sites that have helped to reproduce and extend the dominant white narratives of Bishop Andrew, Miss Kitty, and Andrew's other slaves, even as they opened up fissures in the mainstream structures of remembrance. My point of departure is Jessica Adams's fascinating argument in her study of a postslavery plantation that "careful readings of plantation images suggest that slavery's physical and psychic violence is always active within scenes of nostalgia."[1] To what extent might this be the case in the deeply nostalgic and lovingly tended locales of Oxford, Georgia?

This chapter's title, "The Other Side of Paradise," is taken from a commentary by Ms. Emogene Williams, one of the matriarchs of the African American community of Newton County, Georgia, as she led my students and me in late 1999 across the historically white section of the Oxford City Cemetery. She pointed out the gleaming marble headstones marking the final resting places of the Methodist leaders associated with the early years of nearby Emory College. She called our attention to the beautifully maintained lawns on the "white" side of the cemetery, in striking contrast to the long-neglected gravesites in the historically African American family plots, overgrown with weeds and privet: "So you see, for the white founders the college was a kind of paradise, their vision of what heaven was supposed to look like. But never forget, there were many others living and toiling in this county, who lived on the other side of paradise. They built this town and this college, going all the way back to slavery times. . . . They are just as much as part of this place as anybody else. You just have to learn how to look, learn to see what they left behind, learn to hear what they are still telling you, after all these years."

This chapter is a meditation on Ms. Williams's admonition: How do we learn how to see traces of the peculiar institution on college and university campuses and their surrounding neighborhoods many generations after emancipation? How do we learn to hear the echoes of those who labored without acknowledgment or recompense to erect and maintain these academies in their early years?

The story of Miss Kitty and Bishop Andrew is a particularly evocative and potent instance of this widespread phenomenon. Yet it is worth noting at the outset that the broader trope to which Ms. Williams alluded has a long and rich history in North America: for centuries, many have wryly juxtaposed the utopian promise embodied by the academy with the hidden underside of coerced, exploited labor upon which such institutions of higher learning inevitably rest.

Such observations, it should be emphasized, are hardly confined to the South. In her famous poem, "To the University of Cambridge, in New-England" (1773), Phillis Wheatley addresses herself, from the position of the enslaved, to those who study the great mysteries of the universe at Harvard College: "Students, to you 'tis giv'n to scan the heights / Above, to traverse the ethereal space / And mark the systems of revolving worlds." Yet, while these privileged students occupy an exalted space that approaches the heavens, it is given to the ostensibly subordinate slave to remind them of the temptations of sin that threaten to return them to earthly bounds: "An Ethiop tells you 'tis your greatest foe / Its transient sweetness turns to endless pain / And in immense perdition sinks the soul."[2]

Slavery's Legacies in Oxford, Georgia

Six decades after the publication of Wheatley's poem, the white Methodist founders of Emory College in 1836 laid out another terrestrial evocation of the celestial kingdom. They designed the newly incorporated town of Oxford, Georgia, to radiate out along broad geometrical avenues from the planned campus, itself organized around a stately oval drive. Devoted in large measure to preparing young men for the clergy, the new college aimed to provide its students with disciplined routines and surroundings that would incline its pupils toward thought of "higher spheres."

A strong case can be made that the problem of slavery was central to the creation of the college in the 1830s. The institution's founders were, without exception, slaveholders. In seeking to develop a prominent Methodist educational institution in the South, they took it for granted that their students would largely be drawn from southern white families that owned slaves, or for whom slaveowning was considered normal and desirable. At a time when the struggle over slavery was taking on increasing national importance, those involved in the early years of the college would often find themselves called upon to legitimate the "peculiar institution" of chattel slavery.

In a proximate sense, the decision to name the new college for the recently deceased Methodist bishop John Emory (1789–1835) was owing to his important contributions as an educator and the role he played presiding over the Washington, Georgia, Conference at which the development of a Methodist college in Georgia was proposed. Yet in a more nuanced sense, the naming of the college for Bishop Emory was embedded in the fact that for its white founders, John Emory was emphatically one of their own. He had recently published a powerful tract against "radical abolitionism" and came from a prominent Maryland slaveowning family. A slaveowner who believed the institution would gradually fade away, he had arranged for the manumission of several of his slaves after his death.[3]

College officials publicly defended the institution of slavery, often asserting it would help lead to the Christian conversion and spiritual elevation of Africans in America. College president Augustus Baldwin Longstreet, who played a central role in the great national schism of the Methodist Episcopal Church in the mid-1840s over the issue of slavery, published several impassioned defenses of involuntary servitude, including an 1845 commentary on the scriptural foundations of slavery—*Letters on the Epistle of Paul to Philemon* and *Letters from Georgia to Massachusetts* (1848) —in which he denounced the hypocrisy of northern abolitionists for not attending to the plight of exploited New England mill girls.

Without access to the archives or to oral historical records, a casual visitor to the bucolic campus of Oxford College of Emory University (as the original Emory College campus is now known) would remain oblivious to the long history of slavery at and around the institution. The only visible memorial to African Americans on the college grounds is a tree on the central quadrangle in front of Pierce Hall. Planted in 1966 by representatives of the class of 1913 in honor of two of Emory's most celebrated African American employees, the tree is marked at its base by a small plaque:

The members of the class of 1913
in loving appreciation
Dedicate this tree to the memory of
Bob Hammond
1858 to 1923
and
Billy Mitchell
1886 to 1958
Who together contributed 95 years
Of faithful and efficient service to "Old Emory"
Dedicated June 12, 1966

The 1943 Emory-at-Oxford yearbook was dedicated to Henry "Billy" Mitchell. At his 1958 funeral, eight years before the tree planting, he was eulogized by College Dean Virgil Eady, who stated, "Billy Mitchell's friends included people in many stations of life—congressmen, U.S. senators, Methodist bishops, great and influential business and professional men and women." Other white speakers referred to his family's "long service" to Emory. Yet, as had long been openly discussed in Oxford African American families, this service stretched far back into "slavery times." As we shall see in chapter 9, Billy Mitchell's paternal grandfather was enslaved by Bishop Andrew. His maternal grandparents were enslaved, respectively, as valet and maid, by Emory Professor Alexander Means, who briefly served as the college's president. The last time I looked at the tree with Ms. Williams, she sighed and quietly remarked, "How they loved Billy, their 'best friend,' they called him. But 1966, you know, that was *two years* before they even admitted the first black student to study on this campus. They'd happily plant a tree dedicated to us. They just wouldn't let us in the front door."

The Oxford City Cemetery

The ironic status of the academic earthly paradise is especially pronounced one mile north of campus in the Oxford City Cemetery. Here are buried hundreds of persons, slave and free, closely connected with Emory College from its founding onward. Over the course of the nineteenth century, on both sides of the Atlantic, the dead were increasingly resettled in pastoral, gardenlike settings, often in suburban locales; these carefully sculpted landscapes, replete with foliage, running and still bodies of water, and neoclassical architecture, reflected emerging visual conceptions of heaven and helped to solidify these visions. There is in this respect a potent elective affinity between the pastoral cemeteries and college campuses of the Victorian era, which similarly offered earthly visions of utopian tranquility as they honored the lives and wisdom of idealized progenitors.

Like many southern graveyards the Oxford cemetery has long been a political flashpoint. From 1965 until 2000 a wealthy, all-white foundation cared for the white half of the graveyard, drawing on public funds covertly funneled to it by the white-majority city council. The city government tended to ignore the historically African American two acres of the cemetery, containing many graves dating back to the 1840s and 1850s. For decades, the white cemetery's lawns were neatly mowed, its marble headstones carefully mapped and lovingly restored. For most local whites the older markers evoke a nostalgic era of antebellum amity among the races. White-led tours of the cemetery often point approvingly to the Mary Rogers marker (discussed in chap. 2), one of the few direct allusions to slavery in the cemetery.

After 1965, in contrast to the well-kept white cemetery, the unfunded adjacent African American sections became densely overgrown, many plots inaccessible to living family members.[1] Yet many white Oxford residents spoke of the carefully tended white cemetery as affording visions of the celestial kingdom. During struggles in the late 1990s to desegregate the cemetery, a local white man confided in me, "I truly don't understand why they are making such a ruckus. Don't they understand all the love and care that has gone into this cemetery? This is where we honor the story of Emory and southern Methodism. It is our Westminster Abbey. It is just our little plot of heaven." Indeed, the two great water oaks that for decades stood side by side at the entrance to the white cemetery were sometimes jokingly referred to by white residents as the "pearly gates," welcoming the deceased to their just reward.

The Kitty Gravesite: Comparative Reflections on Burying the Loyal Slave

In certain respects, the burial site of Kitty within the "white" cemetery zone would seem to be consistent with the social imagining of the cemetery as a virtual celestial space. The decision to bury Kitty close by the white Andrew family resonates with the sentimental white narrative, discussed in chapters 3 and 4, that she longed to be reunited with her late mistress, Ann Amelia, "in the better land."

At least two accounts of Kitty's gravesite have been reported. In the 1930s H. Y. McCord claimed to be told by a black woman named "Katy Mitchell" that Kitty had been buried at the base of one of the great water oaks that marked the entrance to the white cemetery. In the 1990s Martin Porter claimed to have been told by an African American matriarch that Kitty was buried within the Andrew family plot, next to Elizabeth Andrew Lovett, one of Bishop Andrew's married daughters, who died in 1856. Several of my elderly African American informants maintain they had been told by their elders that Miss Kitty was buried somewhere within the Andrew family plot, and that the black community had been bemused when McCord erected the tablet next to the water oaks. (They also insisted that they had no idea who "Katy Mitchell" might have been.) Others assert that no one was ever quite sure where Kitty was buried. "You have to understand," said Margaret Watkins, "she really wasn't kin to anyone here in Oxford. The white folks sort of took her over for themselves, in life and in death. That's why we always felt so sorry for her, my mother used to say."

Although racial segregation in death was the norm in antebellum cemeteries, there are multiple instances across the Atlantic world in which enslaved persons were buried in close proximity to their owners. At times, such burial practices signified intimate liaisons between the interred parties. For example, a prominent Virginia planter, John Eppes, chose to be buried next to his enslaved lover, Betsy Hemmings, whose grave is marked with an elaborate marker. Betsy is widely believed to be the illegitimate daughter of his father-in-law, Thomas Jefferson. Betsy Hemmings as a fourteen-year-old had been given to Eppes as a dowry present. Family lore holds that John Eppes's legal wife "was buried at her daughter's home in nearby Chellowe instead of beside her husband at Millbrook. Anecdotal evidence suggests that Patsy Eppes would not be buried near her husband's mistress, Betsy Hemmings."[5]

The practice of burying slaves with masters appears to be an ancient one in the northern European world. There are archaeological accounts of Anglo-Saxon burial sites in which a female slave appears to have been killed in order to be buried beside a high-ranking woman, presumably in order to serve her in the afterlife. I know of no such accounts in slave plantations in the New World. Rather the practice of burying slaves with their masters seems to have been conceived by slaveowners as a mark of privilege granted to favored slaves. To this day, many whites point to this practice of burying African American slaves in white family plots as evidence of the relatively benign nature of slavery and of the close sentimental ties between masters and bondservants. This white reading has a long history. George Washington's grandmother, Mildred Gale, for example, is reported to have chosen to have a favored slave, Jane, buried beside her. Her headstone in Whitehaven, England, reads,

> Died 1700, Mildred Gale nee Warner of Warner Hall Virginia, wife of George Gale merchant of Whitehaven. Here also lie with her, her baby daughter and her African slave Jane.
>
> Mildred Gale was the widow of Major Laurence Washington and mother of their three children: John, Augustine and Mildred.
>
> Her grandson, Major George Washington, showed great courage in 1781 when he promised slaves their freedom if they would fight for him against the British.
>
> A lot of them did and he won the battle of Yorktown 1781.
>
> He was the first president of America, eight years later in 1789.

Yet, if white masters generally presented such burials as marks of favor, African Americans have long wryly remarked that the practice signifies a continuing desire by whites to continue to enslave their human property, even in death. Consider, for example, a revealing passage from Harriet Jacobs's *Incidents in a Life of a Slave Girl*, in which she recounts the death of her beloved Aunt Nancy, a death she attributes to the white mistress, Mrs. Flint, who always insisted Nancy sleep on the floor by her bedroom's door, to attend to her at night; after Nancy's death Mrs. Flint decided she wanted Nancy buried in the white family plot:

> Mrs. Flint had rendered her poor foster-sister childless, apparently without any compunction; and with cruel selfishness had ruined her health by years of incessant, unrequited toil, and broken rest. But now she became very sentimental. I suppose she thought it would be a beautiful illustration of the attachment existing between slaveholder and slave, if the body of her old worn-out servant was buried at her feet. She sent for the clergyman and asked if he had any objection to burying aunt Nancy in the doctor's family burial-place. No colored person had ever been allowed interment in the white people's burying-ground, and the minister knew that all the deceased of our

family reposed together in the old graveyard of the slaves. He therefore replied, "I have no objection to complying with your wish; but perhaps aunt Nancy's mother may have some choice as to where her remains shall be deposited."

It had never occurred to Mrs. Flint that slaves could have any feelings. When my grandmother was consulted, she at once said she wanted Nancy to lie with all the rest of her family, and where her own old body would be buried. Mrs. Flint graciously complied with her wish, though she said it was painful to her to have Nancy buried away from her. She might have added with touching pathos, "I was so long used to sleep with her lying near me, on the entry floor."[6]

Perhaps the most suggestive disquisition on the practice of burying slaves in the master's plot was penned by Henry Wadsworth Longfellow. A popular story holds that Madame Vassal, the original owner of Craigie House in Cambridge, Massachusetts, chose to be buried with two slaves in the graveyard next to Christ Church. Longfellow, who subsequently acquired Craigie House, composed a poem, "In the Churchyard at Cambridge" (1858), meditating on this tableau:

In the village churchyard she lies,
Dust is in her beautiful eyes,
　　No more she breathes, nor feels, nor stirs;
At her feet and at her head
Lies a slave to attend the dead,
　　But their dust is white as hers.

Was she a lady of high degree,
So much in love with the vanity
　　And foolish pomp of this world of ours?
Or was it Christian charity,
And lowliness and humility,
　　The richest and rarest of all dowers?

Who shall tell us? No one speaks;
No color shoots into those cheeks,
　　Either of anger or of pride,
At the rude question we have asked;
Nor will the mystery be unmasked
　　By those who are sleeping at her side.

Hereafter?—And do you think to look
On the terrible pages of that Book
To find her failings, faults, and errors?
Ah, you will then have other cares,
In your own short-comings and despairs,
In your own secret sins and terrors![7]

In the initial stanzas, the vignette of African slaves buried alongside their white mistress is compelling precisely because it evokes the enigmatic status of death; the dead cannot answer the question of the dead woman's motivations, of "vanity" or "Christian charity." The scenario is contradictory. On the one hand, the poet presents the scene as hierarchical, as the slaves still "attend" their mistress. On the other hand, the grave renders master and slave coequal in their silence and their corporeal decay—"their dust is as white as hers." The dead slaves are as silent and mysterious as the woman who commanded their fates in life: "Nor will the mystery be unmasked / By those who are sleeping at her side." Yet in the poem's final stanza a significant shift occurs, as the poet's voice becomes a channel not of any individual dead person, free or slave, but of the dead in their terrifying collective and oracular form. The dead, silent at the poem's outset, do ultimately speak in a way that holds up an uncanny mirror to the reader's private soul. Paradoxically, the silence of the graveyard renders possible the most forceful of all voices: the Book of Life that speaks, on behalf of the Dead, from the Hereafter.

My point, then, is not simply that the Andrews' decision to bury Miss Kitty in their family plot had many precedents. As Longfellow alerts us, the paradoxical tableau of slave and master buried together evokes in the living a deep longing to hear the dead speak, to reveal the mysteries of life and death. As we shall see, such has been the case with the Kitty burial site. Successive visitors to the Oxford cemetery have felt compelled to speak for the dead, to merge their own narrative with the authoritative voice of the lost.

The McCord Marker

H. Y. McCord's 1939 tablet may be fruitfully approached in this light, as a ritual attempt to speak for and through the dead. Significantly, the inscription on the tablet does not literally quote Kitty, but only cites the (apocryphal) performative utterance of the late Bishop Andrew, "You are as free as I am." Yet paradoxically, Kitty does speak, in her mute testimony, through the spatial positioning of the marker. McCord was careful to plant the detailed stone tablet at the base of a vigorous young oak tree; one of his descendants told me that McCord hoped that as the tree grew to provide shade over this oldest part of the cemetery, it would demonstrate the "deep roots" of Oxford's families, and remind everyone of the valued position of Kitty in the city's proud history. Kitty, in effect, was grafted onto the collective white family tree. She is situated, albeit in a transitional and subordinate position, within the heavenly landscape of the white cemetery. Incorporated into the eternal as a loyal retainer, she shows fidelity beyond death itself. The McCord marker is placed in a line about twenty-five yards due east of the Bishop Andrew obelisk, which is itself close by the markers for Elizabeth Mason Andrew Lovett, the Bishop's daughter, and his wife Ann Amelia.

The white spatial positioning of Kitty is consistent with the most famous white stories about her. As we have seen, she is said to have nursed Bishop Andrew's first wife Amelia on her deathbed and to have kissed Amelia on the lips as she passed away. Several years later, it is said in numerous white-authored accounts, Kitty herself died in a pious Christian manner, declaring on her deathbed, "I will soon see Miss Amelia in the better land." In the Oxford cemetery, the Kitty marker serves a comparable function, mediating white transitions between the realms of life and the afterlife.

In physical and ideological senses these Kitty substitutes served to greet whites entering into sacred spaces that evoke the celestial kingdom. Just as a relatively privileged house slave once stood as a welcoming presence at the door of the big house, she serves through the medium of the memorial to welcome whites back to their eternal home. In turn, just as field slaves were located in outlying cabins, so other people of color are buried in the peripheral fields well outside of the gateway oaks of the cemetery. In these respects, the entire cemetery—and the celestial topography it evokes—may be regarded as an enduring projection of the idealized white vision of the social structure of the antebellum plantation.

Meanwhile, the oak tree, stone marker, and the more recent headstone to Kitty are enclosed within a section of the city cemetery that remains segregated, and that has become more markedly segregated in recent years in the face of the periodic campaigns for the ceremony's reunification. A paved street, named for the great Methodist Bishop Asbury, has even been constructed by the city between the "white" and "black" sections of the cemetery. The virtually all-white private foundation that long cared for the white section (largely with funds obtained from the city treasury) had refused to extend care to any African American grave but Kitty's. For decades, Kitty's inclusion into the white family tree functioned markedly to exclude the rest of the African American citizenry from that family. In McCord's cosmology, Kitty is forever conscripted into the naturalized landscape of segregation and taken-for-granted white domination.

The 2000 Marker

Over the course of the late 1990s Martin Porter and his colleagues in the Oxford Shrine Historical Society became increasingly concerned that McCord had made a "mistake" in implying that Kitty had been buried at the base of the water oak, and not in Bishop Andrew's family plot. During this period, the city was deeply polarized by struggles to desegregate the city cemetery, and over the related question of whether the city government would honor its responsibility to provide perpetual care for African American gravesites in the cemetery. Porter, who also presided over the all-white Oxford Historical Cemetery Foundation, was deeply stung by accusations from African American residents that he was insensitive to the feelings of African Americans in this matter. In his mind, he explained to me, he was simply demonstrating fidelity to his "fiduciary responsibilities"; the foundation had been established in 1965 solely to care for the white cemetery, and it was unfair for others in town to seek to benefit from its resources. African Americans, including Porter's neighbor J. P. Godfrey, responded that the foundation had been established precisely to circumvent the public accommodations provision of the Civil Rights Act, and that it was "high time" that perpetual care be guaranteed to all those buried in the cemetery, regardless of race.

In 2000 Porter and several other members decided to place a modest headstone in Kitty's memory on the location in the Andrew family plot that they were convinced was her most likely burial spot, between the grave marker of Catherine McFarlane, the mother of Ann Amelia, the Bishop's first wife, and Amelia, one of the Bishop's granddaughters. (As noted above Porter claimed that an elderly African American woman had pointed him to this locale, although she later denied having done so.) The headstone bore the simple inscription, "Kitty Andrew Shell,

1822–c. 1850."[8] At the time, Porter explained that he hoped this gesture would "restore good feelings between the races in Oxford." He was genuinely perplexed, he told me, that African American protests over the state of the cemetery intensified after the new Kitty marker was erected.

Counternarratives in the Oxford Cemetery

Thus far, our discussion has been largely consistent with the model sketched out by Emile Durkheim and Marcel Mauss in their classic anthropological study *Primitive Classification*: the basic principles of social organization structure visions of the cosmos as well as how those cosmological schemes are realized in lived social space.[9] Yet in practice the picture is more complex. The objectification of these schemes in tangible concrete form also puts these ideological systems potentially at risk, or at least subject to critical interrogation.

Among local African Americans, the cemetery and Kitty's gravesite have not so much reinforced the dominant narrative as opened up fissures in it. Tending family graves or walking through the cemetery, a number of African American women have rolled their eyes at the white city fathers' repeated insistence that Kitty is the only person of color buried in the "white" half of the cemetery. "Why, she's in good company, that's all I'll say," one woman remarked with a quick, enigmatic smile. The burial of Miss Kitty near Bishop Andrew was often interpreted as a sign that she was in fact the Bishop's lover. As Janet Simmons, an African American Oxford resident in her fifties, laughingly remarked of the white slaveholding elite, "Well, they figured they'd take it all with them. So why not make sure the old Bishop could have Kitty right there next to him in the afterlife?" She took great delight in Countee Cullen's poem, "To a Lady I Know," when I shared it with her:

> She even thinks that up in heaven
> Her class sleeps late and snores
> While colored cherubs rise at seven
> To do celestial chores.

"Yes," laughed Janet ruefully, "that's just the way they thought. There was slavery in heaven, and they just knew that favorite slaves would be waiting up there for them, doing everything for them in the Great Beyond that they used to do here!"

Divergences and Convergences

During spring semester 2000, students in my Sociology 101 course were given two tours of the Oxford cemetery, the first by Martin Porter, the second, about a month later, by J. P. Godfrey Jr. Not surprisingly, the tours were very different; Porter confined himself to the southeastern ("white" section) of the cemetery, taking the students through the many memorials in honor of Emory's presidents, faculty members, and Methodist bishops, as well as the unmarked mass grave of Union soldiers. Porter made no mention of the African American sections of the cemetery, and it only occurred to most of my students afterward that they had not visited at least half of the graveyard during the tour. Godfrey, in contrast, concentrated on the African American sections. He talked to the students about the many, interrelated black families of Oxford and shared his own memories of segregation and the civil rights movement.

Yet both tours, as it happened, ended in precisely the same spot, the grave of Kitty, just south of the frontier between the historically white cemetery and the oldest, nineteenth-century section of the African American cemetery. To be sure, the two men drew very different conclusions from this site. For Porter, Kitty's was a heart-warming and redemptive story of traditional southern honor that cuts across racial lines. Andrew's solicitude and Kitty's loyalty, for Porter, challenge conventional northern accounts of slavery and of southern white racial prejudice.

Godfrey, in turn, read the dominant Kitty tale as a product of southern white confusion and self-deception; he noted, "No black family can recall anyone named Nathan Shell." He shared with the students the line he and his cousins used to hear from their elders: "What did white people think we were doing in the kitchen all the time? Cooking?" Rather, he explained to the students, we were listening: we knew the truth of who fathered Kitty, just as we know the truth that interracial liaisons have long been commonplace in the South. The "true story" of Kitty, for J.P., was that the color line is ultimately illusory, that everyone in Oxford, in the final analysis, is part of the same "family."

At the time, the two men, former friends who had long opposed one another over the enduring segregation of the cemetery, were hardly on speaking terms. Yet their tours ended at Kitty's final resting place. Both sensed that the "true" history of Oxford, and perhaps more broadly of the American South, is exemplified in Kitty's story and in her gravesite.

All agreed, in effect, that the long-dead woman was saying something, but just what was she trying to say and who had the right to speak for her?

Going by the Trees: Arboreal Symbolism in the Cemetery

The local struggle over the meaning of Miss Kitty's gravesite was embedded in a larger contest revolving over the status of the dead in Oxford. In the late twentieth century, the Oxford City Cemetery, so beloved by white residents, was in many respects a site of anguish for the city's African American residents. In 1990 disaster struck the oldest section of the African American cemetery. An unscrupulous pulpwood dealer allied with members of the city council cleared the pine forest that had grown up over this one-acre site. Backhoes buried, displaced, or fractured scores of headstones, and disturbed hundreds of graves.

As I listened to African American residents try to characterize the nearly indescribable pain this episode caused them and their families, I was struck by subtle yet persistent differences in women's and men's accounts. One middle-aged African American woman, whose father's grave had been destroyed, was confined to bed for three weeks, an experience she later likened to "going to my deathbed." In later years, she spoke in a wistful tone of driving to work each morning past the nearly empty meadow of the old cemetery: "I guess I just miss the trees. I used to know those trees, you know."

When my students and I undertook our restoration and documentation project in this cemetery, I often heard women speak in similar terms about the absence of the trees. I recall, in particular, a conversation with an African American woman in her seventies, Mrs. Anna Neumann, the community's informal authority on the cemetery. She led a group of us through the grassy field, punctuated by occasional shattered headstones and unmarked patches of sunken ground. As well as she could, she recalled for us the location of the destroyed gravesites, "My aunt, Altheria, she's right here. Over there, that's the plot of our neighbor family, old Mr. Jim Benton and Miss Sadie, you remember, I told you all about them." But then Mrs. Neumann stopped in mid-sentence, her arm half-raised, and said softly, "I can't, I just can't remember where they're buried. I used to be going by the trees, you know, I went by the trees."

For Mrs. Neumann, trees evoke proper family remembrance and continuity, signaling productive linkages to ascendant generations. Cemetery trees, in particular, remind her of her mother, mother's sisters, grand-mothers, and great-aunts, the women who taught her how to "go by the trees" in finding grave sites. Like many other women in the community, she often refers to respected, deceased female relatives as people who "really knew the trees," meaning either that they were root workers (tra-ditional healers) or that they could find their way to grave sites by reading the landscape.

In this connection, it is striking that at a Family Day Celebration at Rust Chapel United Methodist Church, the oldest African American congregation in Oxford, the program featured a cover drawn by one of Anna's cousins, Laura. The cover depicted a large oak tree containing fourteen branches springing from a common root, each branch bearing the name of one of the fourteen African American families of the town, who are all interrelated through multiple bonds of marriage and descent. Anna approvingly told me in church as she stared intensely at the cover, "That tree says it all. We're all just tied up together here. Can't go talking about one family's roots without running into another branch of some other family!"

In contrast, men's references to trees in comparable contexts tend to deploy more traumatic imagery of violation and dismemberment. Wil-liam Arnold, an African American man in his sixties, recalled the 1990 clear-cutting:

> That morning, when I saw all the trees gone, and the earth torn open like that, it was as if we were back there, you know. Everything we got, the houses, the cars, all that "progress," doesn't mean anything. Can you tell me what's changed, since those days, you tell me? You think it matters if they don't have manacles and whips and aren't sell-ing families apart anymore? Right now, right now, every tree that's gone, that's every black family in town, with a hole in its heart.

Suggestively, men sometimes relate the problem of cemetery trees to fraught memories of their fathers. J. P. Godfrey, for instance, has main-tained that, as much as possible, trees in the more recent parts of the black cemetery should be pruned or taken down. "It is terrible the old trees were mowed down in the old section, I know that as well as anyone, but now we just need to clear things out, open things up. . . . Let's clear out all these trees and brush . . . so these plots can all be out in the light, for every family. Why, you can't even get to my father's grave this way."

One day, as he and I worked together to clear foliage from his father's and grandfather's graves, J.P. spoke explicitly of his father, who died twenty years before at the age of ninety-two:

> He never told me anything about our family history, no matter how hard I tried. Proud man, would never say a single word about slavery. That's what we "came up from," you know, that's how they thought then. Except right before he died, he told me something, for the first and only time. He told that his father, my grandfather, had been born and grew up in slavery just here in this county, and that he and his full brother Stephen came off the old Cody place. But my grandfather hated old man Cody so he took the name Godfrey. But Stephen kept the name Cody. So all these Cody buried here [gesturing to the adjacent graves] they are all my cousins. But I only found that out from my father at the end.

Looking into the thick patch of trees that still covered this section of the cemetery, J.P. softly murmured, "So many secrets, you know, so many secrets."

Some of these long-term "hidden transcripts" have come into visibility over the past decade. In late 1999, largely inspired by conversations with Ms. Williams and Mr. Godfrey, my students at Oxford College partnered with local African American and white community members to restore the historically black sections of the cemetery. On our second weekend of work, we uncovered the elaborate carved grave marker of J.P.'s paternal grandfather, Israel Godfrey, who had lived as a slave the first seventeen years of his life, and who had, postemancipation, worked as the head stone mason in the construction of the Emory College Chapel. The Godfrey monument is carved in the form of an open Bible. J.P. remarked, "Just look at this marker. And look over there at that [pointing over to the Kitty marker]. . . . I have lost count trying to reckon all the lies inscribed on that Kitty tablet. And the way some of our neighbors go on and on about it, quoting it at every possible occasion, you'd think it was one of the tablets Moses himself brought down from Mount Sinai." He ran his fingers along the weathered top of his grandfather's memorial, on the pages of the open stone Bible: "My grandfather was born a slave and kept his Christian faith all his life. If some people are looking for the Rock of Ages, it wouldn't hurt them to come on over here to this side of the cemetery and look at this particular Good Book right now. That book is still open for all to see, after all those years in the wilderness." He smiled ruefully, "But somehow, I don't think they'll be taking that walk anytime soon!"

As interracial groups of students and community members labored in the cemetery, more white families came to support efforts to excavate the history of slavery at the college. Virgil Eady, a descendant of Professor George Washington Stone, for example, generously shared a manuscript that revealed, among other things, that the core area of the "historically white" cemetery was in fact built upon land occupied up until the Civil War by an African American church in which enslaved African Americans worshipped for two decades. The church building was gifted to the black community in the late 1840s by the Emory College Board of Trustees; at the Civil War's end the white leaders of the town took the building down so that the white cemetery could expand.

The news of this historical discovery had an electrifying effect among local families of color. As one respected Baptist deacon remarked, "All these years they told us this was the 'Historic Cemetery,' which meant the white cemetery. But now we find out this was black land. More than that, consecrated land, which they just took from us when it suited them. I don't know what to think, but one thing I do think, some things have got to change in this town, and change now."

In the months that followed, the enduring segregation of the cemetery, as well as continued white efforts to memorialize Kitty in architectural form, became increasingly bitter flashpoints in the town. Struggles to integrate the cemetery, to restore its historically African American sections, and to prevent schoolchildren's tours of the slave quarters known as Kitty's Cottage, discussed in the next chapter, helped catalyze a series of far-reaching political struggles, leading to voter registration drives, the breaking of the color bar in the town's police force, and campaigns against environmental racism. A space that had once been held up as an earthly instantiation of heaven on earth came to function as an important medium of social remapping that proved, in Lévi-Strauss's terms, "good to think" with about a wide range of social and cultural contradictions. In W. E. B. Du Bois's terms, the cemetery and the college campus to which it was so intimately connected had long functioned as evocative sites of double consciousness, foregrounding the ways in which persons of color were simultaneously included in and excluded from the promise of redemption. Yet, in time, this charged space also made possible the progressive articulation of double consciousness as an explicit predicament, helping to trigger transformative social action.

Slavery in Heaven: Summerfield, Alabama

The catalyzing power of concretized double consciousness is illustrated even more potently by another segregated cemetery, in another southern Methodist college town. Two hundred fifty miles east of Oxford lies the town of Summerfield, Alabama, a little north of Selma, the seat of Dallas County. In 1855 Bishop Andrew moved to this beautiful small community with his slaves, including the enslaved children of Miss Kitty, who had died in 1851. In Summerfield Bishop Andrew served on the board of the town's Methodist college, the Centenary Institute, just as he had served on the Emory College board in Oxford. He worshiped regularly at Summerfield Methodist Church, an institution that like the Old Oxford Methodist Church numbered among its congregants many enslaved persons.

No traces of the Centenary Institute survive in today's Summerfield, other than its weathered and worn front steps, which can be just glimpsed along the curving road that meanders through the town. When I visited Summerfield in 2008 in search of evidence of what became of Kitty's children and the other persons enslaved by Bishop Andrew, I was directed by white residents to the venerable Childers Chapel Cemetery, in which are buried many of the white citizens who played a leading role in the college and the town over the course of the nineteenth century. As in Oxford, the carefully maintained white cemetery is adjacent to a historically African American cemetery, a burial ground that is structurally "invisible" to most of its white neighbors. In the white cemetery is buried the Bishop's third wife, Emily Sims Woolsey Heard Childers Andrew; in the adjacent black cemetery, I was repeatedly told, many of Bishop Andrew's former slaves rest in unmarked graves.

Like the Oxford City Cemetery, Childers Chapel Cemetery to this day subtly evokes enduring, albeit subtle, racial divisions in how the past is recalled, affording starkly opposing visions of the afterlife. Consider, for example, the variable reactions to the large stone monument that visually dominates the center of the cemetery. Dedicated to Mrs. Carrie M. Cleveland, the memorial consists of a large pillar on which are inscribed the words, "Carrie Maude Pinson, Wife of Morgan S. Cleveland, was born Sept, 5, 1834 and died May 10, 1860." Atop the base is carved a statue of a beautiful young woman dressed in a long robe, her flowing hair coursing down to the shrouded urn on which her head rests. Whenever I asked white Summerfield residents about Bishop Andrew I was invariably pointed to this statue; as many noted, Bishop Andrew had married this couple soon after he came to Summerfield, and he was, through his third wife, kin to the young bride, Carrie Maude Pinson.

In 1860, the year Carrie died, her husband Morgan, age twenty-five, owned forty-three slaves; she left behind a two-year-old daughter, and, local whites recall, a deeply distraught husband. In classic mid-Victorian style, recalling the influences of the Greek revival, Mrs. Cleveland slumbers for eternity upon a shrouded urn, a standard Victorian signifier of mourning. Several members of the Summerfield white community note that the statue exemplifies the genteel romanticism of the Old South. It serves, they explain, as a touching celebration of a husband's deep love for his beautiful young wife and typifies the abiding Christian faith of the era. "You can see how much he loved her," Lucy Jameson, an older white woman, told me, adding, "In those days, you know, death wasn't really something to be feared. It was a long slumber, a just reward for the virtuous; that's how they saw it back then." She added (a little mischievously for the benefit of the professor conversing with her), "You know, that's what they taught at the college in those days. Not like what they teach in, ah, some schools nowadays." The statue, she noted, reminded her of a story passed down in her husband's family, who were longtime Summerfield residents: "Bishop Andrew, you know, always wanted to free his slaves but his wife kept on telling him, 'Well, James, if you free them, you'll need to start doing some work around here!'"

Rebecca Anders, another white woman in her seventies, remarked of the Pinson Cleveland statue, "She is just the most beautiful angel, isn't she? She looks out over all of us, we're all her family here in Summerfield, really. They do say that angels watch over us, don't they?" Another white woman, Elizabeth Fenton, added, "It is not given to us to know everything that awaits us, but when I look at that statue, resting in this beautiful place, I do feel, well, that we are given a glimpse of our just reward. That's what a college town was, after all: a little glimpse of heaven." She recalled the story of Bishop Andrew, who had to her mind been cruelly deposed by the northern delegates in 1844: "You need to understand that by his lights he was working hard for all the slaves, trying his utmost to guarantee them salvation. The monument reminds us of that, that the old Methodist preachers really were committed to everyone's just reward, regardless of race."

YET, AS SEVERAL local elderly African Americans have told me, the Summerfield black community has long interpreted the statue in a quite different way. They insist that the sculptor depicted Mrs. Cleveland with a long bullwhip draped over her, its handle near her hand, the better to beat her slaves with. Alicia Fenton, an elderly African American woman about ten years older than Lucy and Rebecca, noted that from her pedestal "the old mistress" looks over the wrought-iron fence into the old slave cemetery behind the white cemetery. "Even in death, white people still wanted to intimidate black folks," she sighed. The humiliation inflicted by the statue, she recalls, deepened each time a black funeral was held; mourners would have to carry the casket directly through the white cemetery under the old mistress' ever-ready whip.

Mrs. Smithson specifically noted, "The way I see it, that old mistress is still looking over the slave's burying ground, keeping an eye over them."

Mrs. Fenton sighed in agreement. "They really believed, still do I think, that they could bring all their slaves to heaven with them. Just like Pharaoh in the days of old!"

Mrs. Smithson nodded emphatically, "Now I ask you, is that Christian?"

Having spent a good deal of time perusing the statue up close, it seems to me that the African American vision of a whip is a creative (re)reading of the carved cloth that adorns the statue. The cord dropping down from the urn's shroud is read as the handle of the whip; the folds in the figure's robes are seen as a whipcord that encircles the figure. This reading is presumably aided by the fact that few African Americans spent much time contemplating the statue in close proximity; as far as I can tell, it was only glanced at during funerals. Black pallbearers passed directly by it going to the burial site, as they prepared to lift a casket over the rear iron fence for easier access to the black burial ground. Most black mourners did not enter into the white cemetery, but only saw the statue from afar, outside the iron fence. Since the statue faces away from the road, and since the woods behind the cemetery are thickly overgrown, the only way nowadays to see the front of the statue would be to enter into the actual confines of the white cemetery. To this day many local African Americans do not feel comfortable entering this space. The older reading of the statue in the local black community thus endures.

Mrs. Fenton describes with pride the more recent all-black Summerfield community cemetery (established around 1920), located on the slope of a beautiful hill three miles north of the white cemetery:

> You can understand why as soon as we got the land up the hill we started burying our people up there. That's our land, given to the community by a strong black woman. No white mistress with a whip carved in stone looking over them up there! Every one of those headstones is resting on *our* land.

She and her sisters note proudly that soon after the Civil War the Summerfield black community broke from the white-dominated Summerfield Methodist church and established an African Methodist Episcopal congregation. "We might not have been welcome at Centenary," Mrs. Fenton's sister Violet remarks with a laugh, "but we've been sending our children to AME colleges ever since!" Once again, a college community's segregated cemetery has made painfully apparent the incomplete promise of education under Jim Crow. Once again, a scarred final resting place has inspired an independent course of action.

Reflections: Double Consciousness and the College Campus

The cemeteries of Oxford, Georgia, and Summerfield, Alabama, so closely linked to college campuses and the Bishop Andrew story, are thus sites of both deep emotional attachments and political struggle. In these respects, they are illustrative of a broader set of dynamics that characterize multiple university-related landscapes. As noted in chapter 1, in recent years more and more institutions of higher learning east of the Mississippi, North and South, have been exploring their historical entanglements with the Atlantic slave trade and the operations of slavery. Important work has been done on the pro- and antislavery ideological functions of antebellum colleges, on the sources of early college bequests, on slave ownership by colleges, on the labor by enslaved persons in building and maintaining campus structures, and the educational and labor trajectories of new freedpersons at institutions where they and their foreparents had worked in involuntary servitude. University files, probate records, deeds, bills of sale, correspondence, and even antebellum textbooks are being read in increasingly original and insightful ways.

As we pursue this vital research in the archives, we must remain sensitive to Ms. Williams's admonition to observe the traces of hidden histories, of slavery and antislavery struggles, embedded in the material architecture and landscapes of present-day colleges and their environs. We must learn to see anew the face of ideological repression that for generations has rendered nearly invisible the legacies of enslavement and that has cast the campus as an earthly anticipation of heaven. In this work we need to remain especially sensitive to charged sites on the land where the living and the dead intersect, at times uneasily; to memorial trees and monuments; to headstone and plaques; and to the places that call forth quiet stories of those who have passed on.

In these acts of witnessing let us honor the fact that in slavery and freedom many African Americans who were long excluded from these virtual enactments of the afterlife did not necessarily reject the promise that these spaces embodied. Like Phillis Wheatley many persons of color have rejoiced in the calling to "scan the heights above" and "to traverse the ethereal space," even as they have denounced efforts to limit these aspirations to a single race or gender. It is worth noting that Ms. Williams, who pointedly reminded us that so many persons of color were relegated to "the other side of paradise," is a retired educator and a passionate advocate of higher education. She is devoted to Oxford College, even as she remains a pointed critic of much of its history during slavery times and Jim Crow. Her daughter, Rev. Avis Williams, one of the first African Americans to matriculate at Oxford, holds undergraduate and postgraduate degrees from Emory University. Ms. Emogene and her daughter Avis have lectured to Emory students and faculty on numerous occasions.

Let us honor as well the strategies through which persons of color, while formally excluded from matriculating on segregated white campuses, often managed to educate themselves in the face of extraordinary odds, even while working at these institutions under conditions not entirely of their own choosing. Significantly, J. P. Godfrey recalls that during 1955–56, when forced to leave Clark University for a year due to his father's illness, he was tacitly allowed by Oxford College Dean Virgil Eady Sr. to audit classes on the still-segregated Oxford campus—while technically employed as a "janitor"—so as not to fall behind in his studies.

Let us remain attentive, then, to the coercive underside of universities' utopian claims, even as we honor the promise immanent in the extraordinary ritual space of every campus—the promise long ago penned by Phillis Wheatley, that all may someday, in this lifetime and on this terrestrial plane, look heavenward to "mark the systems of revolving worlds."

IN CHAPTER 6 we turn from the cemeteries to another important spatial site of concretized double consciousness entangled in the Kitty-Andrew story. Like these hallowed burial grounds, the slave cabin known as Kitty's Cottage has elicited powerful positive and negative reactions since the mid-nineteenth century. For many whites, this small building has remained sentimentally imbued with Kitty's presence, a reassuring reminder of a nobler, simpler era. For many African Americans in turn, the cottage has become a critical flashpoint as they have tried to reinterpret regional history and the relevance of that past for a contested present. As in the cemetery, many have strained at the cottage to hear the dead speak, even as they have struggled over what they might be saying and how their words are to be interpreted.

Chapter Six

"The Most Interesting Building in Georgia"

The Strange Career of Kitty's Cottage

T HE EARLY HISTORY of the building that came to be known as Kitty's Cottage is rather obscure. Presumably, from the time of the Andrew family move in Oxford in autumn 1840 up until the time of her fateful interview with Professors Longstreet and Lane in December 1841, Miss Kitty resided in the Andrews' new house in Oxford. From spring 1840 onward, at least two other slaves, Billy and Lucy, were living in the Andrew household; it is not clear if Kitty shared a room or a cabin with them on the Andrews' lot.[1]

Once she moved out of the Andrews' house or the regular slave quarters, Kitty may have resided in one or two different buildings on the Andrew property in Oxford. As we have seen, some sources suggest Kitty initially resided after the December 1841 interview in a building adjacent to Bishop Andrew's house and then at some point moved to a different house some distance away, where she resided with her husband. In contrast, G. G. Smith writes in 1882, "[Kitty] married a colored man named Nathan, and Bishop Andrew had a neat little house built for her on his own lot, and she lived here merely in name a slave." In his 1851 obituary of Kitty, published a month or so after her death, Bishop Andrew writes, "I gave her a lot in which her husband errected [*sic*] a comfortable house and we fitted her out to housekeeping." The obituary implies that this second house was not immediately adjacent to the Bishop's own dwelling. When Kitty becomes grievously ill, a "messenger" was dispatched to inform the Bishop and his family, so clearly Kitty was no longer living a few yards away from the Andrews' Big House. In an unpublished letter, Bishop Andrew's son-in-law Robert Lovett, whose wife Elizabeth had nursed Kitty on her deathbed, implies that Kitty only moved out of the Andrews' house after her marriage:

> As a master, whether considered in his treatment of his servants, or
> those belonging to his family, [Bishop Andrew] was most human. In-
> deed religiously, they were considered part of the household. They
> were protected from harsh treatment from others. This can be veri-
> fied by the Court records in Covington. Again, after the marriage
> of the colored woman whom he raised, when she refused to go to a
> free state, she was allowed a house on his lot, and she and her family
> enjoyed the [illegible—perhaps extra] benefit of her time and labor.[2]

Since Lovett resided a few doors from the Andrews' house and is likely to
have been in the Andrew household nearly every day, he is presumably
a reliable witness. He alludes to only one special slave house for Kitty,
constructed after her marriage. Nonetheless, numerous subsequent commentators assert there were two houses, one behind the main Andrew
house and another one in which she lived with her husband.

Although white accounts usually assert that Bishop Andrew built the
cottage after 1841, after Kitty expressed her desire to not be sent to Liberia, some evidence exists that the building may have predated the
Longstreet-Lane interview. James Waterson, a conscientious amateur historian who has owned the Andrew property since the 1970s, notes that
the building now called Kitty's Cottage was originally a carriage house
and surmises that the house was not in fact originally built for Kitty.
A photograph in Waterson's possession, marked "Kitty's Cottage, circa
1930," shows a ramshackle building with a porch area containing several
rocking chairs, sheltered by an overhanging slanting roof. It is possible
that this is an outbuilding that Kitty initially resided in after 1841 and
that her enslaved husband Nathan later built her a different house, some
distance away, in a location that has not been recorded or remembered.
Waterson has located traces of a cabin's footprint about ten yards behind
the remaining foundation of the old Andrew house; this, he infers, was
the original location of the building that came to be known as Kitty's
Cottage.

When the term "Kitty's Cottage" was first used for this structure is not
exactly clear. The first published reference may be in Wrightman Melton's
elegiac essay in the *Atlanta Constitution* in 1916, discussed in chapter 3:

> Of the seven million Methodists in the United States, few have seen
> or will see, the humble cottage of Kitty, the mulatto girl, who figured
> so prominently in the division of the Methodist church in 1844.

Such residences are normally termed "slave cabins" or "slave quarters." Melton's preference for the more pastoral, bucolic term "cottage" is consistent with his romantic softening of the story.

Whether this house is really the one in which Miss Kitty resided with her children, the structure was warmly remembered by generations of college alumni, who accepted the story that Kitty had in fact resided there "as a free woman" after 1841. Consider, for example, alumnus J. Martin Rast, who authored the 1968 article "The Slave Girl Who Divided a Church" discussed in chapter 3. Rast recalled, "Kitty's cottage stood outside my window in the James O. Andrew house in Oxford when I was a student at Emory College in 1916."[3] At some point after 1916 the Andrew house burned down. The Kitty slave cabin survived the fire, and was evidently inhabited for some time by a white family. It seems to have been periodically visited by members of the Emory University and Oxford communities, and stories about it were passed down in college and town lore.

Moving the Cottage to Salem Campground: 1935–38

As noted in chapter 4, on August 18, 1935, retired Methodist Bishop Warren Candler, former Emory president and chancellor, wrote an article in the *Atlanta Journal* titled "Forgotten History." He wrote, "No more interesting building in Georgia can be found than Kitty's Cottage, which is a monument to Bishop Andrew's tenderness and Kitty's responsive affection." In an unpublished handwritten version of the essay, the basis of his spoken lectures about Kitty, Candler noted that the cottage "is a monument to the tender kindness of Bishop Andrew and the faithful affection of Kitty for him and his dear wife. It is a historic building that deserves preservation until the end of time. . . . It is a visible and conclusive refutation of all the censure ever visited upon Bishop Andrew on account of his connection with slavery."[4]

As we have seen, Candler's growing public interest in the cottage was directly related to his anxiety over the coming reunification of the northern and southern wings of the Methodist Church, a merger he believed would ultimately undercut segregation in the South. In this light, Candler's conclusion to the editorial is particularly striking: "No man, north or south, was ever more kind and considerate of Negroes; and no man was ever more beloved by them."

Candler's original plan seems to have been to keep the cottage in Oxford on its original site on the main Andrew plot. Four months after the publication of his column, he received a letter from "Dolly" at Burge Plantation in southeastern Newton County, indicating that a Dr. Haynes was working on the text of a plaque to be placed at Kitty's Cottage.[5] As noted above, although a brother of the Coca-Cola magnate, Warren Candler was of modest financial means. He thus depended on his wealthy friend, H. Y. McCord Sr.—a prominent grocery store owner, Coca-Cola stockholder, and Emory trustee—to resolve the status of the cottage. McCord purchased the old Andrew grounds, including the cottage, in late 1938, evidently benefiting from a recent foreclosure of the property.

A revealing interview with McCord was published in the *Atlanta Constitution* on Sunday, June 4, 1939: "Kitty's Cottage—A Shrine of Southern Methodism: Historic Cottage now Permanently Located on Salem Camp Ground." The piece was written by Louie D. Newton (1892–1986), a prominent Baptist clergyman who, from 1929 until his retirement in 1968, was the pastor of the important Druid Hills Baptist Church in Atlanta, near the main campus of Emory University. From 1936 onward he wrote the "Good Morning" column in the *Atlanta Constitution*. Although known as "Mr. Baptist," he was close to many prominent Georgia Methodists.

Newton begins his story six months earlier during the winter of 1938–39:

"I bought a house today that I want you to see" said H. Y. McCord Sr. one night last winter while I sat with him before the open fire at his home. "Did you ever hear of Kitty's Cottage?" he continued.

I had not.

"The house in which Bishop Andrew lived was burned, but Kitty's Cottage was left, and I bought the tract of several acres today in order to preserve this historic little house, which is a symbol of cherished tradition for all who understand and appreciate the relationship of the races in the south," said Mr. McCord.

"Kitty lived and loved and served," said Mr. McCord as we stood next to the yard, ". . . and I propose to perpetuate the little cottage that those who come after our generation may share in the blessing of one of the finest traditions of those pioneer days when noble men and women laid the foundation of our Georgia civilization."

"What are you going to do with it?"

"I haven't decided yet," he said, "but I will either put it in good repair and keep it here on this tract of land which I bought, or, if agreeable to the trustees of Salem Camp Ground, I will move it to Salem where it can take its place on that spot so dear to many Georgians."[6]

During the early months of 1939 McCord and Bishop Candler became increasingly taken with the idea of moving the cottage out of Oxford. Both men were deeply opposed to the pending reunification of the Methodist Church's northern and southern branches, which Candler had devoted much of his career to preventing. Several relatives and friends recall that McCord was particularly anxious that the "Yankees" not damage the cottage after reunification, allow it fall into greater disrepair, or spread false rumors about Andrew and Kitty. McCord thus arranged for Kitty's Cottage to be transported twelve miles on the back of a large truck to Salem Campground, an important religious revival meeting area established in 1828. Here, the cottage would not come under the direct control over the reunified church, and would thus, he felt, escape the disrespect or interference of northern interlopers.

It would be hard to overstate the spiritual and emotional importance of Salem Camp Meeting to white Georgia Methodists. Since 1828, with few interruptions, families have gathered there for a weeklong revival each summer. To this day, they reside in simple cabins still known as "tents" and are often referred to as "tenters." Camp meeting is a vast, multilayered reunion in which multigenerational families reconvene, eat together, play together, and worship together under the great tabernacle at the camp's center. Many worship at the spring across the main road, returning each year to partake of its waters and of the "sweet, sweet spirit" of the Lord's blessings and collective fellowship.[7]

McCord and Candler's efforts to bring the cottage to Salem, strongly supported by their close friend and fellow Salem trustee Colonel Robert Guinn, closely coincided with efforts to renovate the campgrounds, which they had long felt were in need of improvements. The 1939 camp meeting opened with a dedication of three buildings, one of them Kitty's Cottage. Not coincidentally, a few months earlier, on May 10, 1939, the Methodist Conference in Kansas City had made official the reunification of the northern and southern branches of the church. For the trustees, whatever errors were being committed at the national level, the rejuvenated campground at Salem was a veritable shrine to the integrity and endurance of southern Methodism.

The moving of Kitty's Cottage in early 1939 also seems to have, in part, been in response to internal controversies in the new Emory University Board of Trustees, following the founding of the university in 1917–18. McCord and Candler were troubled that many members of the board were openly distressed by the weight of Emory's southern history, which they considered an impediment to the new university achieving serious national status. Both men wished to emphasize, in contrast, that the strength of the new university was anchored in its southern heritage, which they wished to promote as a positive asset.

In a symbolic sense, I speculate that McCord, Candler, Guinn, and others were attempting to locate Kitty within the overarching ritual dynamic of Salem, a powerful site of regeneration and ancestral remembrance that had been of vital importance to their families for generations. Moving the cottage to Salem allowed Kitty, in effect, to live again, and through her, allowed for a rebirth of the values upon which they believed Emory and southern Methodism to have been founded. Their decision to open the Kitty Cottage Museum on Independence Day, July 4, 1939, reinforced the motif of returning to a moment of mythic origins, celebrating a foundational spirit of autonomy and spiritual freedom.

An essay penned in the 1980s by Mary Fleming, the wife of Oxford College's Emeritus Dean Bond Fleming, nicely summarized the prevailing local white thinking about the cottage. It concludes with this evocative paragraph: "In 1939, the year before the Methodist Church was finally reunited, Kitty's Cottage was purchased by Mr. H. L. McCord, a Methodist layman, and was moved from Oxford to the Salem Camp Ground near Covington, where Methodists have held Camp Meetings since 1828. It is kept there, filled with interesting Southern Methodist memorabilia, as a reminder both of the gentler side of the Old South's master-slave relationship, and of the bitterness that once existed within the Church."[8]

As with the other events we have considered, local African American reflections on the 1938 relocation are strikingly different from those of their white counterparts. "They wanted to take the cottage somewhere segregated," Margaret Watkins recalled, noting that the Campgrounds were segregated at that time. "They were worried it would be open to everybody once the church got reunited." She continued, "Now, I ask you, is that Christian?"

Arthur Freeman, an African American man, notes the irony that local African Americans had very little interest in the cottage at the time, and would have been unlikely to visit it even if it had been opened generally to the public. He remarked with a wry laugh, "Of course, considering who always did all the work at Salem, it sure struck mother as appropriate that they'd get so excited about taking a slave cabin there!"

Along similar lines, Jane Callaway, an elderly African American woman, whose mother had regularly cleaned the museum at Salem, sardonically commented on the spectacle of the cottage being transported from Oxford to Salem on a truck in the late 1930s: "Mother used to joke that white folks just enjoyed carrying black people all over the county, without asking their say-so. One day they just decided Miss Kitty's place was gonna move, and they just took her, just like that!" Jane also recalled her mother's ambivalence over her time at Salem: "It kept us going during the Depression. All that extra food that the white folks didn't eat, she canned and that got us through the winters. . . . She said she felt safe working right in Salem, but the neighborhood could be downright frightening. The Klan use to hold their rallies, driving right up and down the street in front of the campground. You never quite knew what might happen." To this day, the annual closing ceremony at Salem featuring illuminated crosses still arouses disturbing memories among some of the camp's African American neighbors.

The Kitty's Cottage Museum at Salem: 1938–94

After being transported from Oxford in 1938 the Cottage itself was positioned by McCord, Guinn, and Candler at the right-side entrance to the campground, in preparation for its grand opening in July 1939. Just as the Kitty memorial tablet (also positioned to the right) welcomed visitors into the white cemetery at Oxford, where they might commune with and honor their ancestors, so too did the cottage welcome whites upon their annual return to Salem, where the living similarly entered into intimate and proximate relations with antecedent generations. (Later, in the mid-1990s, immediately after its return to Oxford, the cottage would be positioned for several years to the right of Old Church.)

McCord conceived of the cottage at Salem as a museum, in which he would document the history of southern Methodism and the Confederacy, with which the Kitty story was, in his mind, so intimately intertwined. Many of my white informants recalled that upon entering the cottage their eyes were first drawn to General T. J. "Stonewall" Jackson's portrait, hanging above an elaborate engraving titled "The Note Memorial." For many years, the cottage also housed the desk of Emory College President Atticus Haygood, upon which he is believed to have written his famous Thanksgiving Day "New South" sermon, an important ideological document of the post-Reconstruction South. (The desk was evidently given by Haygood's daughter to the Kitty's Cottage Museum.) Also in the cottage were engravings of Bishop James Osgood Andrew, Bishop Warren Candler, and General Robert E. Lee; a gavel said to be used at nineteenth-century Methodist Conferences, made from the wood taken from the house of Congressman Tait, in which Bishop Asbury held the first Georgia Methodist Conference; a photograph of the 1934 dedication ceremony, presided over by Bishop Warren A. Candler, marking the site of the first Georgia Methodist Conference; an engraving of the 1858 General Conference of the Methodist Episcopal Church, South; a 1914 photograph of the trustees of Emory College, including H. Y. McCord, Robert J. Guinn, Bishop Warren Candler, and Bishop Candler's brother, the Coca-Cola magnate Asa Candler, patron of Emory University; a painting of a late-nineteenth-century couple that regularly attended Salem, known as "tenters"; and a color lithograph of the Battle of Atlanta. A handwritten account of the Kitty-Andrew story, composed by Robert Guinn, was displayed, along with a copy of Longstreet's famous account of his December 1841 interview with Kitty, in which she declined manumission.

The Confederate Note Memorial: Loss and Regeneration

Several elderly white Salem tenters recalled that their favorite object in the museum was a large framed color engraving, "The Confederate Note Memorial." "In my mind," Edna Jameson, a woman in her seventies, states, "Kitty's Cottage and that old print just went together beautifully. . . . They took you back in history, to a time when people sacrificed everything for their beliefs."

Thomas Lazar agreed: "If you want to understand what we call the 'Lost Cause,' you just need to look at that old print and read those poems. That's what the story of Kitty and Bishop Andrew is about—honor, truth, decency. All commodities which are, I'm afraid, in rather short supply these days."

His distant cousin Natalie Rabson, also in her eighties, elaborated, "I don't really know why I always thought of them together, since now that I think on it, I realize they were about separate historical events. But they just always seemed to fit, the Cottage and the Note memorial. As a girl,

I would just weep reading those lines on the wall of the cottage. I suppose you had to grow up in that time period. . . . We felt we had a duty to remember, as southern women especially. That's what the cottage meant to me."

In many respects, the engraving was the most ideologically intriguing of all the displayed elements in the museum. The print, produced in Washington, D.C., by lithographer Gray Ellis in 1902, depicts various currencies along with pictures of Civil War battles and fragments of two sentimental poems. The print is centered on the image of a grave, marked by a half-furled Battle Flag, a cross in which is inscribed "unknown," and a headstone reading "C.S.A." (Confederate States of America, or Confederate States Army), overlooking a calm sea reflecting the setting sun. Below this image are the lines:

> On fame's eternal camping ground
> Their silent tents are spread:
> While glory guards with solemn round
> The bivouac of the dead.

These lines, although not identified in the print, are adopted from Colonel Theodore O'Hara's poem "The Bivouac of the Dead," written in honor of Kentucky soldiers who died in the Battle of Buena Vista during the Mexican-American War. The stanza is inscribed on numerous memorials across the South and also appears in Arlington National Cemetery.

The central image is flanked, on the left and right columns, by a sentimental poem authored by a Confederate veteran titled "State's Money":

> Representing nothing on God's earth now
> And naught in the waters below it
> As the pledge of a nation that passed away
> Keep it dear friend and show it
> Show to those who will lend an ear
> To the tale this trifle will tell
> Of liberty born of a patriot's dream
> Of a storm cradled nation that fell
>
> Too poor to possess the precious ores
> And too much of a stranger to borrow
> We issued to-day our "promise to pay"
> And hope to redeem on the morrow
> The days rolled on and weeks became years,

But our coffers were empty still
Coin was so scare the Treasury quaked
If a dollar should drop in the till

That the faith that was in us was strong, indeed
Though our poverty well we discerned
And this little check represents the pay
That our suffering veterans earned
They knew it had hardly a value in gold
Yet as gold our soldiers received it
It gazed in our eyes with a promise to pay
And every true soldier believed it

But our boys thought little of price or pay
Or of bills that were ever due
We knew if it bought our bread today
Twas the best our poor country could do
Keep it, it tells all our history over
From the birth of the dream to its last
Modest and born of the Angel Hope
Like our hope of success it PASSED

The poem was authored by Major Samuel Alroy Jonas (ca. 1840–1915) of Aberdeen, Mississippi, who served after the war as editor of the *Aberdeen Examiner*. Often reprinted under the title "Lines on the Back of a Note," the poem is familiar to those steeped in Confederate lore. Jonas himself insisted that he wrote the poem on the back of a five-hundred-dollar note soon after he had been paroled, following the surrender of Lieutenant General Johnston's troops in North Carolina. He claimed to have written it spontaneously at the request of a visiting northern actress as a keepsake.

Although the chromolithograph was mass reproduced, and not specifically made for the Cottage Museum, the decision by McCord and others to hang and preserve it in the museum is suggestive. In Jonas's poem, the monetary value of the old notes paradoxically signals the ethical worth of the soldiers who accepted them, who were uncorrupted by mere material concerns. Loss, in terms of both the loss of a nation and of its soldiers, centers on the flag emblem, organized to produce an enduring memory picture. The currency notes, worthless in themselves, occasion the noble labor of southern white memory, through which the honored dead are allowed, in a poignant fashion, to speak once from beyond the grave.

To external observers, this pastiche of poetry and images might seem to conform to the classic definition of kitsch: exaggerated sentimentality in word and picture oriented toward a cult of heroic death. As such they might seem rather removed from the details of the story of Kitty, which took place well before the Civil War. Yet it should be noted that for many tenters at Salem, the print and the other memorabilia assembled in the cottage were considered of a piece with the noble story of the Lost Cause of the Confederacy and the subsequent struggle to forge a "New South" in the face of northern occupation and interference. Inasmuch as the Kitty gravesite and cottage opened up channels between this world and the hereafter, they were considered appropriate sites through which other honored dead might, from time to time, commune with the living.

Symbolic Reproduction in the Cottage

These images and artifacts, primarily associated with prominent southern white males, were in keeping with the gender politics of the mainstream white Andrew-Kitty narrative. Andrew, a powerful white man, is celebrated for having kept Kitty from sexual promiscuity or from indiscriminate breeding with male slaves, preserving her within a safe house. At Salem, for decades a segregated institution, Kitty was similarly reserved for the white community, her cottage filled with the visible accoutrement of white masculinity.

The net effect of all these elements seems to have been to transform the cottage into a site of regenerative, sentimental remembrance, consistent with the overall ritual functions of Salem Campground. Anthropologist Bradd Shore terms Salem Campground a "theater of family memory," through which the structurally entropic and dispersive features of the family unit are overcome (within the ritual domain at least) so that the family may be experienced as eternal and perpetually regenerative. To his analysis I would add that Salem has for nearly two centuries also been oriented toward the reproduction of whiteness, establishing an inclusive space through which white families may experience their own solidarity across time, binding the living and the dead.

To be sure, this symbolic reproduction of whiteness across the generations depended upon the constant labor of African Americans, in slavery and freedom. White antebellum tenters brought along their slaves to cook and clean for them during the weeklong annual camp meeting. To this day, African American cooks and maintenance staff are essential to the functioning of the Salem hotel and camp activities. The "recruitment" of the spirit of Kitty into Salem was in a curious way consistent with this long history of white dependence on an African American presence, a presence that the white worshippers rarely explicitly acknowledged.

Through the Kitty Cottage's Museum this reproductive schema of white regeneration was grafted onto the extended family of the Confederacy and southern Methodism, so that the honored military dead and Methodist worthies commingled, in effect, with the antecedents of the Salem tenting families. Hence, the ancestral images on display on the museum's walls, including the martyred General T. J. "Stonewall" Jackson, the painting of Bishop Warren Candler, the great engraving of the 1854 Conference of the Methodist Episcopal Church, South, and the photograph of the memorial ceremony to the first Georgia Conference.

Subsequent gifts to the cottage were consistent with this overarching theme of genealogical continuity. As late as 1986 an Andrew descendant donated the Andrew family Bible and a spinning wheel said to be used by Mary Cosby Andrew, the mother of Bishop Andrew.[9] The Bible was promptly transferred to Oxford College's special collections library for safekeeping, but the spinning wheel stayed in the cottage when the building and its contents were moved back to Oxford.

The motif of ancestral veneration and generational succession is nicely illustrated by a framed sign placed in the museum at its opening on July 4, 1939, by H. Y. McCord:

REV. JOEL STANSELL

Rev. Joel Stansell licensed to preach by Bishop J. O. Andrew at Prospect Church, this circuit in 1848. Was one of the Original tenters at Salem Camp Ground. He was the grandfather of R. J. Guinn. This militia district was named for him.

H. Y. McCord
July 4th, 1939

The Kitty's Cottage Museum can thus be thought of as a complex instrument for the intensification and reproduction of white kinship and descent lines, charting an intertwined biological and spiritual genealogy. Methodist lines of connectedness and biogenetic kinship are here grafted together. As elderly tenters recalled, Bishop Andrew himself had ordained Rev. Stansell, an honored ancestor of Mr. Guinn, then a trustee of Salem and close friend and relation of McCord. Thomas Lazar—whose family, he joked, had been attending Salem "since the dawn of creation" —remarked, "As a boy, it was just remarkable seeing all those old documents and all those artifacts together. It just reminded you that you were part of something bigger than yourself, that you were, as they say, a son of the South." Unstated by Lazar, of course, is that the ritual instrument of white social reproduction depended on the shadowy presence of a benevolent African American female figure. The cottage was known to generations of local whites as the place built by Bishop Andrew for Kitty, where she lived and raised her own children, while simultaneously looking after the white children of Oxford. White lineal continuity depends on the constant ministrations of the mammy figure, brought into careful calibration with the white patriarchal figures: Generals Robert E. Lee and Stonewall Jackson along with Bishop Andrew, Bishop Warren Candler, President Atticus Haygood, and other Methodist worthies.

Although there was no figurative representation of Kitty on display in the cottage, her presence clearly imbued the place. Many white informants recall that in the old museum they were reminded of Kitty's kind and welcoming presence, and felt protected and comforted within its confines. A number of elderly white couples have confided that they shared their first kiss or embrace inside the cottage. "Well, partly," one octogenarian woman recalls. "It was the only place you could get a moment's privacy at the campground. But also I always felt the whole story was so beautiful, so reassuring. It really was the romance of the Old South, I always thought."

Thomas Lazar remarked, "I think for a lot of folks, their cares just melted away at Salem, and especially in the cottage. It was a soothing place, kind of romantic even, not a bad place for a little courting." Indeed, the Kitty Cottage Museum seems to have been figured as a kind of nurturing womb, within which white kinship bonds could, in effect, be protected and reproduced.

The Mammy Memorial Movement (ca. 1900–1939)

In this respect, the cottage at Salem was consistent with the trajectory of what has been sometimes termed the Mammy Memorial Movement, a social movement by southern whites that aimed to honor African American women who had served as nannies, cooks, and domestic servants in white households from the time of slavery onward. The narrative of the loyal slave, as historian Micki McElya notes, rose to increasing prominence in the first decade of the twentieth century, expressed in movement to raise memorials to "faithful slaves."[10] As in the standard Kitty narrative, white commentators emphasized that the love for their masters kept the enslaved from seeking freedom. In 1910, funds were raised for a Black Mammy Memorial Institute in Athens, Georgia. The fund-raising pamphlet for the institute stated, "Did you not have an 'Old Black Mammy' who loved and cared for you in the days of your youth whose memory and spirit you want perpetuated?"[11] In its rhetoric and iconography, the institute's founders strove to preserve the remembered or fantasized relations of love and unconditional affection associated by whites with their African American caretaker.

A decade later, the Mammy Memorial Movement would lead to the unsuccessful attempt, backed by the United Daughters of the Confederacy, to pass federal legislation mandating the construction of a physical monument to the southern black mammy in Washington, D.C. The measure ultimately died in the Senate but not before it had attracted extensive attention in the white and black press, along with numerous detailed designs from hopeful sculptors and architects. One of the proposed designs depicts a large black woman holding a white baby near her bosom, while a white boy and a white girl flank her, holding onto her skirts.

Senator John Sharp Williams (D.-Miss.) introduced the bill, with the intention that it would be his last legislative act in his thirty-year congressional career. In turn, a decade later, H. Y. McCord Sr., in his eighties, built the Kitty memorial just before his death. Is it entirely coincidental that two elderly white men, both arch-segregationists, conceived of their final acts in public life as being memorials to the southern mammy? In both cases, Mammy seems to have been a sanctified guardian spirit for white men facing the end of life, promising them a warm forgiving embrace in the great beyond. Once again we are reminded of the haunting scene that frames Ellison's *Juneteenth*: as the segregationist white senator, who may be of African American parentage, lays dying, his final wish is to enter into the forgiving embrace of the "old negroes" who secretly raised him to be a black man.

The Mammy Memorial Movement, one might argue, culminated in the publication of Margaret Mitchell's novel *Gone with the Wind* in 1936 and the celebrated premiere in Atlanta of the film on December 15,

1939, after three days of festivities. Mitchell famously describes Mammy in *Gone with the Wind* in the following terms:

> She was shining black, pure African, devoted to her last drop of blood to the O'Haras, Ellen's mainstay, the despair of her three daughters, the terror of the other house servants. Mammy was black, but her code of conduct and her sense of pride were as high as or higher than that of her owners. She had been raised in the bedroom of So-lange Robillard, Ellen O'Hara's mother, a dainty, cold, high-nosed Frenchwoman. She had been Ellen's mammy and had come with her from Savannah to the up-country when she married. Whom Mammy loved, she chastened. And, as her love for Scarlett and her pride in her were enormous, the chastening process was practically continuous.[12]

In the film, the character of Mammy (played by Hattie McDaniel) is un-remittingly loyal to Scarlett. (At one point in the film, the McDaniel character famously glowers at Yankees in Atlanta who promise other African Americans forty acres and a mule.) The standard white Kitty narrative, the Mitchell novel, and the film all share a familiar racial politics, drawing a sharp distinction between the trusted domestic and the less-trusted fieldhands. In a sense it is hardly coincidental that six months after the opening of Kitty's Cottage in Salem, white Atlanta poured forth at the *Gone with the Wind* premiere, an event Jimmy Carter was later to recall as the "biggest event to happen in the South in my lifetime." Three hundred thousand people lined the city's streets to catch a glimpse of the stars and other luminaries en route to Loew's Theater. In an irony scarcely lost on Atlanta's African American residents, excluded from the festivities was Hattie McDaniel, whose brilliant performance marked the apogee of the white Mammy fantasy.

Bringing the Cottage Back to Oxford: 1993–97

Around 1991, members of the Salem Trustees began discussing the idea of sending Kitty's Cottage back to Oxford. The pivotal figure in these conversations was the then-mayor of Covington and chairman of the board of trustees at Salem, Sam Ramsey. A fifth-generation Salem tenter and Emory alumnus, Mayor Ramsey was deeply steeped in Methodist and Emory history and strongly felt that the cottage should be preserved in Oxford itself, where the Kitty-Andrew story had unfolded. By 1993 an agreement was entered into by the Campground and the city of Oxford that the city would transport the cottage back to Oxford and take ownership of the structure, with the stipulation that it would remain on public property.[13] The city paid for most of the transportation costs, around six thousand dollars, of bringing the building the twelve miles from Salem back to Oxford.

A little in advance of the move, in July 1993 the mayor of Oxford, Jack Atkinson, asked a group of prominent white citizens (but no African Americans) to serve on an ad hoc Mayor's Committee to Move Kitty's Cottage. The committee was chaired by a white woman deeply committed to historical preservation in Oxford; she was married to a well-known journalist who had covered the civil rights movement in the South. The mayor also brought into the committee a former dean of Oxford College, as well as Martin Porter. All of these persons had long been involved in the Oxford Historical Shrine Society, a nonprofit founded in 1974. Notes from the committee's meeting of September 14, 1993, contain the handwritten annotation, "Can we involve blacks, and if so, who?" but it would appear that no African Americans were in fact consulted during the planning process.

Mayor Atkinson initially arranged to have the cottage dropped off in the city cemetery. There he hoped it might serve as a business office for the all-white historical cemetery foundation, and perhaps a reception space for out-of-town visitors. After some time, however, the decision was made to move the cottage several blocks south, next to Old Church. The Historical Society was already engaged in a much-needed restoration of Old Church, and the two projects quickly became closely linked.

Restoring Kitty's Cottage in Oxford (1994–2009)

Most members of the Shrine Society were familiar with the old interior of the Kitty's Cottage Museum; all agreed that in Oxford, the renovated cottage needed to look very different. The Shrine Society members were committed to principles of historical verisimilitude, and sought to gather the kinds of objects that would have been present in an antebellum slave cabin. No such effort had ever been mounted at Salem. Admittedly, the committee did not consult with African American historians on this project, nor did they talk to any elderly local African Americans. Yet they did make what they regarded as good-faith efforts to research the likely contents of a slave quarters. For a time they hoped the cottage would become the society's principal interpretive center, which would attract African American residents as well as local whites. These efforts coincided with extensive work around the greater Atlanta area in preparation for the 1996 Olympic Games, and with a general sentiment in the region that Georgia's multicultural tapestry should be broadcast to the world.

In January 1995 the Historical Society voted to take responsibility for the restoration and preservation of Kitty's Cottage. The initial restoration was partly paid for out of funds paid by the television show *In the Heat of the Night*, which had shot footage in Old Church, supplemented by a grant from the Georgia Heritage program of the state's Department of Natural Resources.[14] Funds were also raised by a Christmastime tour of ten of Oxford's historic houses, including Kitty's Cottage. The tour itself, which did not include any African American–owned houses, caused considerable consternation in the local African American community. Several African Americans were quick to note the irony in itself that a local newspaper story on the Christmas tour began with the line, "Ironically an issue that split the Methodist community around the country in the 1840s is bringing the little town of Oxford together."[15] Rereading this article some years later, Rebecca Lawson, an African American woman in her forties, sighed to me, "Well, it's a lot more ironic than that. Can't say I've seen much bringing us all together. Our people certainly have plenty of history to tell them, if they ever showed the least interest."

The society quickly learned that the cottage had been damaged by the stress and strains of being moved back from Salem. The cottage had separated from its sill or foundation. White volunteers worked together with contractors to restore the structure, leveling the floor, resetting and stabilizing the sill or foundation, rebricking the hearth, and trying to eliminate termites and beetles.

There was considerable uncertainty as to whether the city of Oxford or the society was ultimately responsible for the cottage. In 1997 the city attorney determined that the cottage was in fact the property of the Historical Society, resting on land leased from the city of Oxford, in a manner akin to the adjacent Old Church.

As they worked on the project, many local whites expressed deep affection for Kitty's Cottage. Many have told me they find it a comforting place to enter. Plans centered on restoring the kitchen area around the large fireplace to make it seem as realistic as possible. It was at this fireplace, I have often been told, Kitty kindly fed "treats" to the Andrew children and to her own children, and comforted them. Since the late

1990s the society has held regular celebratory meals—black-eyed peas, collards, and so forth—served in Kitty's Cottage.

To this day, Shrine Society members offer periodic tours of the cottage. Significantly, no African American interpreters or docents have been involved in these events. Nor were any African Americans consulted in developing the wording of the plaque in front of the cottage, placed in 2000:

KITTY'S COTTAGE
1842

Kitty's cottage was built in 1842 by Bishop James O. Andrew for an inherited slave who could not be freed and still live in Georgia; Kitty preferred to remain with the Andrew family rather be sent to Africa. In 1938 Kitty's Cottage was bought and moved to Salem Campground for safe-keeping. In 1994 the Board of Salem Campground offered to help move Kitty's Cottage back to Oxford. The City and the Oxford Historical Shrine Society worked together to help bring this sacred treasure back home. It was placed behind Old Church, near its original site. It is now a museum.

Placed by Landmarks Committee

Newton County Historical Site 20   June 1, 2000

Old Church and Kitty's Cottage: Post-1994

Since the mid-1990s the cottage has been intimately paired with Oxford's and Emory's historically oldest white house of worship, Old Church, where Bishop Andrew once preached and where his portrait hung for many decades. For a time, the cottage was placed on the north side of Old Church, abutting Bishop Andrew's old property, so it was visible from Wesley and Fletcher streets. Finally, in 1997 the decision was made to move the cottage behind Old Church, where it rests to this day.

The unsolved dynamics of kinship, blood, and law that we have considered in the mythic narratives loom large in the composite architecture of the Old Church / Kitty's Cottage assemblage in the center of Oxford. This architectural configuration reproduces the white paternalist motif of loyal black servants encompassed within the framework of white supervision. This mythic image was centered up the hill on the vignette of Andrew's Big House, in front, and Kitty's Cottage, behind.

This hierarchical pairing is reduplicated nowadays in the standard tour of this historic landscape, which begins in Old Church, the large restored white Methodist building where Bishop Haygood preached his famous 1880 "New South" Thanksgiving sermon, and then behind to the small restored cottage where Kitty is said to have resided. A comforting domestic space, imbued with the spirit of the loyal black house servant, the cottage becomes emblematic of the university's enduring commitment to tolerance and social justice. Kitty is eternally lodged in her house and yet she transcends any given moment. Entering the cottage, the visitor is transported, through Kitty and her story, back in time to the era of Emory's origins. Once again, the black domestic servant serves as a perambulating operator, bridging the gap between the university's past and present. Like Jarrell's unnamed house servant, who sets the stage for the unfolding historical pageant, the domestic Kitty makes it possible for the visitor to move back and forward in time, traveling between the varied "houses" of Emory and Oxford's history.

In contrast to the warm and nurturing domesticity of the cottage, the restored Old Church is characterized by formality. Many people mention the stern nature of the Methodist sermons preached there since the 1840s, and refer rather approvingly to the hardness of the benches, the simplicity of the décor, and the lack of modern conveniences such as a public address system. While Kitty's Cottage is envisioned as a living museum, with friendly costumed interpreters serving as guides, the side room of Old Church is envisioned as a real museum, with important historical artifacts in cases with captions.

Without the conscious intention of local white actors, the church/cottage assemblage has emerged as a ritualized "compromise formation," attempting to give tangible form to two largely incompatible images of the American family. In Old Church, one sees the principle of the stern law of the father; in Kitty's Cottage, one sees the principle of unconditional acceptance associated with the maternal principle, detached from what psychoanalytic thinkers would term the Oedipal scenario. Taken together, then, Old Church and Kitty's Cottage can be seen as a ritual attempt to resolve, if only momentarily, an irresolvable tension in American models of the family.

The church/cottage assemblage may also be understood as an ongoing attempt by white families to manage the enduring blood/law conundrum discussed in chapter 1. Once again, these categories, so complexly

conflated and intertwined by the historical dynamics of slavery, are seemingly disambiguated. Old Church, at least for the purpose of elementary
school tours, embodies the masculine realms of law and positive history.
When Marvin Porter spoke in the church, he emphasized the legal particulars of the case and the large historical picture, details that he insists
Kitty was ignorant of. In his words,

> Meanwhile, back in Oxford in her little cottage, Kitty was just as
> innocent as she could be. She had no idea that events of national
> importance were swirling around her, that she was actually being
> talked about way up in New York City.

In turn, the white women in period dress who lead the visitors through
Kitty's Cottage talk neither of the legal case nor of the approaching national crisis. Rather, they stress the great love that Kitty had for her children, a love that she shared with the white Andrew family members. One
female tour guide observed to a group of schoolchildren, "You know,
Miss Kitty was loved by Mrs. Andrew as if she were her own flesh and
blood. And Kitty felt the same way about the Andrew children. That's
the way it was in those days, people just took care of children your age,
they could just go in and out of people's houses like they were in their
own, and be fed, and loved, and looked after. That's the way things are
supposed to be." She then asked them rhetorically, "But is that how we
live now?"

In a similar vein, a white woman in her seventies explained why she
freely gave of her time and effort to help restore Kitty's Cottage: "I really
feel this is a place of love, where we can really do something for the community, for everybody, to bring us all together. These days, we need some
place like that." Many of her white friends emphasized that the cottage
epitomized the "mutual deference and understanding" that had characterized antebellum race relations. Many recalled stories passed down
through their families of the kindness that Kitty had shown in the cottage to local white children, comforting them and feeding them treats.
Janet, a white woman in her sixties, told me, "I always feel so peaceful
whenever I'm in Kitty's Cottage. The world has grown so confusing with
so much hatred since those days. But being close to Kitty reminds me of
a better times. . . . I feel she's still looking out for me, after all this time."
Another woman member of the Shrine Society explained, "We realized
what a historical gem it is for Oxford. . . . We wanted to bring it back."[16]

African American Perspectives on the Cottage

Nearly every aspect of this standard white narrative about Kitty's Cottage is disputed or dismissed by older African Americans in Oxford. As we have seen, many recall learning from their elders a very different history: Kitty was the coerced mistress of Bishop Andrew, and the Bishop was the father of her children. Hardly any adult African Americans have consented to enter the building. Annette, an African American woman in her late fifties, told me, "I just go in a rage every time I drive by that place. They might say it is a place of kindness and affection, but for me, it is such a reminder of the way so many thousands of black women were mistreated and abused across the years."

J. P. Godfrey notes, "For us, it is a place of violation, not of love." He elaborates, "Lord knows, I've tried to extend the olive branch over the years to our white citizens. I've gone in all sorts of houses I never thought I could tolerate. I've been proudly told by my white neighbors I'm the first colored person to enter their house by the front door, and I've just put up with that. But something in that place just won't let me enter. I just can't do it."

Rebecca, an African American woman in her mid-eighties, recalls her grandmother's stories of Miss Kitty and of the slave quarters: "That was always an unhappy place. You could just feel the sorrow. Can feel it still. . . . And we felt sorry for Miss Kitty, always. It seemed so lonely, her being kept up like that, behind the Big House. The rest of us, you know, we had our families, but she was locked up there. You can feel all that if you get too close to that place. I try to avoid it myself."

In the wake of the 1990 clear-cutting of the Oxford cemetery, white fascination with the Kitty gravesite and the cottage struck many elderly black residents as particular distasteful. Remarked Peter, a man in his sixties, "They did this to us, to our people, to our land. And still all they can talk about is 'Kitty this, Kitty that,' as if none of it, none of it, ever even mattered!"

His cousin Samuel concurred, noting, "A hundred years ago, the majority of the land in this town was black-owned. And it was stolen away, piece by piece. Now they want to take our children on tours through that cottage to hear about how everything's always been so warm and fuzzy in this county. I've had just about enough of this. How can they say this sort of thing, this kind of 'history' brings families together? This is what tore our families apart."

A number of local African American women have told me privately that they regard the cottage as a likely site of rape, where Kitty was repeatedly forced to submit to James Andrew's sexual assaults, and are repulsed by the thought of entering it. Many others have told me they would prefer not to discuss the Kitty story or the house. "Really," one middle-aged woman remarked, "don't we have more important issues to talk about: education, gerrymandering, violence, pollution? How are we even wasting time on this subject?"

Among those African Americans who are willing to speculate about Kitty, most insist that she would have been accepted by her fellow African Americans in Oxford. "This wasn't unusual, bearing a white man's child," one man told me, citing numerous other incidents in local history. "White families often repudiated their black relatives, but black people didn't do that to one another." Many people compare Kitty to Sally Hemmings, Thomas Jefferson's enslaved mistress. An older black woman told me, "This was so common, nobody would have been surprised." However, she added, "Just because it was common doesn't mean we need to go to places where it happened."

To return to the structuralist model of myth proposed in chapter 1, African American reactions to the cottage emphasize the violation of the blood/law distinction. Nearly all adult Oxford African Americans refuse to enter Kitty's restored house, to the disappointment or bafflement of their white neighbors, many who have worked long and hard to restore the structure. "Why should I go to see a place where a sister was raped and nobody will even talk about it?" one African American woman in her twenties asked me rhetorically. "I can't believe that in the year 2000 that place is still standing!"

Samantha, a middle-aged black woman, remarked that the cottage has been "making me think long and hard on a lot of things in this town." She privately questioned the motives of white neighbors who have worked to renovate the cottage. "It almost seems like they want to 'know' us, without talking to us," she commented. She was troubled by a tendency by many whites to try to enter into a sanitized version of slavery and the black experience on white-governed terms. In one conversation she attributed her recent interest in "getting more active in local concerns," including a voter registration drive that aims to increase local African American political participation, to this growing disquiet over the cottage. "I don't know, but like I say, the cottage just got me thinking about the way things are here."

Jason, an older African American man, told me that he'd "never really thought much about the Kitty thing" before the placement and restoration of the cottage in the mid-1990s. But after the cottage rose to prominence, and was exhibited weekly to Georgia schoolchildren, including African American children, he began to ask older relatives about the "true facts of the case." Now, he ponders more and more the injustices of the story:

> You know, every time I drive by that place, I can feel my blood pressure rising. A lawfully married man owned a grown woman, he *owned* her, and every law in this state supported that fact. So what did that law let him do? Have his way with her, outside of marriage, have children by her, children that he legally owns, and then leave those kids to fend on their own. Lord knows where. His own flesh and blood, and he's a pillar of virtue? And our own children are getting marched through every Friday, to learn about the proud traditions of the great state of Georgia. I don't know whether to laugh or cry.

Blood and law are impossibly, painfully confounded. A legal institution enables rape and the abandonment of one's natural offspring. Significantly, the spatial realization of the white myth variant has inspired the speaker to come to this formulation: only once he started seeing the restored cottage every day did Jason begin to inquire into the historical story critically.

Reflections: Space, Race, Remembrance

Taken together, the city cemetery and the cottage suggest that the social organization of landscape is never simply the externalized projection of a preestablished narrative script or mythic text. Rather, ritualized spaces, like myths, are often generated by cultural paradoxes, by conceptual tension and social contradiction. Spatial realizations or enactments of mythic scenarios at one level may suppress these contradictions, rendering certain orientations to the world seemingly self-evident, automatic, or natural. Yet these spatial or architectural forms, by virtue of their tangible presence, may also place dominant mythic narratives at risk, or at least open to interrogation and debate. Having to see the cottage "every day" as they drive by it inspires some African American women and men to articulate a wide range of long-term injustices. Encountering the Kitty memorials within the cemetery triggers mildly subversive commentaries on the fictive nature of the color bar. It has often been remarked that systems of racial apartheid, in South Africa, North America, or elsewhere, depend on the structural invisibility of oppressed persons and communities. Patterns of residential and commercial development, in Johannesburg or Atlanta, tend to obscure most underclass neighborhoods inhabited by persons of color, while providing occasional glimpses of impoverishment that reinforce dominant assumptions about the underclass.

In one sense, the Kitty memorials may be understood as components of this larger spatial and ideological apparatus. In foregrounding a deeply nostalgic narrative of tranquil antebellum race relations, they tend to deflect attention away from contemporary dynamics of race and class. White meditations on the cottage, as we have seen, are so often delivered with an elegiac sense, accompanied by observations about how "we don't live that way anymore," bemoaning the fact that neighbors don't look after each other, that people don't trust one another, that crime is rampant in America's cities. These not-so-coded embedded racial commentaries seem to flow quite naturally from white conversations about the Kitty story, just as modern-day conversations about contemporary families seem to turn quite naturally to retellings of the Kitty narrative. As I have suggested, these dynamics have partly motivated and structured well-meaning white efforts to restore the cottage and memorialize Kitty in the graveyard. The cottage offers white residents a way of entering into a sanitized version of the African American experience, solving the moral and cultural conundrums about family and community historically generated by slavery, without directly encountering most of their working-class and underclass black neighbors.

Yet once concretized in material form, ideological projects have a way of escaping the control of their architects and builders. The myth of Kitty and its architectural dramatizations, which have so long been associated with the silencing of African American histories and memories, may, unexpectedly, prove "good to think" with, generating new local insights and initiatives by those who have long felt themselves excluded from the dominant historical narrative. The mysterious figure of Kitty, so long held up as an exemplary guest within an idealized white family, may inspire creative reexamination of the bonds of history and obligation that link all American families.

The Juneteenth "Ancestral Walk"
to Kitty's Cottage: June 2007

In the spring of 2007, members of First Afrikan Presbyterian Church, an Afrocentric congregation in the Atlanta suburb of Lithonia, came across an online essay I had written six years earlier on the Andrew-Kitty story. On June 19, 2007, "Juneteenth," a delegation of about forty worshippers from the church drove about twenty minutes to Oxford, parked in the college parking lot, and then undertook an "ancestral walk" to Kitty's Cottage.

Many clad in white robes, the group walked along tree-lined Wesley Street and then headed behind Old Church to gather in front of the cottage. There they poured out libations, danced, and sang hymns. The pastor then gave Miss Kitty a new name in the West African Ewe language, "Na-Yahm-ka" meaning "gift of God." Several members of the congregation insisted during prayer that Miss Kitty had spoken to them, telling them that she been kept as a sexual slave by the Bishop to be shared with his "minister friends" for their "sexual release." As a senior woman in the church told me, "For a hundred years she's been trying to speak, to tell her story, and no one's listened to her. Well, let me tell you, we heard her, we heard her loud and clear!" The church's pastor explained, "She might not have seen herself as anyone's gift but her mama's, but we want her to know that she was 'God's gift.'" The group then walked back to their cars in the college parking lot and drove back to Lithonia.

When the story was printed a few days later in the county newspaper, local whites were of course outraged. But perhaps more surprisingly, African American residents of Oxford seemed nearly as upset as their white neighbors. J. P. Godfrey, who has often spoken of his refusal to enter the cottage, said dismissively, "Well, I don't know who these people from Lithonia were. They didn't ever contact us, and we don't know them. You know, we just don't do things like, barging into another church's area and not even visiting." Rebecca, the woman in her eighties who serves as the local black community's informal historian, was even more annoyed, alluding to the widespread perception among the county's African American residents that the new black bourgeoisie of Lithonia have little common cause with their less well-off brethren:

> The way I heard it, they just drove down [interstate highway] I-20 in their Lexuses and BMWs, did their thing, and turned around and drove right back home. . . . Who *are* these people from Lithonia,

anyway, so high and mighty? This is our land, we worked this land, and my grandfather and grandmother worked this land. We know Miss Kitty's story. How can they say she just talked to them? They don't know what they're talking about, just a lot of nonsense.

Annette, the African American woman in her fifties, sighed, "It seems like everybody has some use for Miss Kitty, to make some point or another. Slavery was good, slavery was terrible. The South was good, the South was bad. But nobody seems to care about Miss Kitty herself. She's still getting used, one way or another. Everybody feels like they can speak for her!"

While from time to time white residents of the town have placed flowers on Kitty's headstone within the Andrew family plot, I have never seen, or heard of, local African Americans doing so. I had never really thought about this, until the Juneteenth ceremony by the Lithonia Afrocentric church. I then asked many of my African American friends and informants in Oxford why they've never conducted any sort of memorial ceremony for Miss Kitty themselves and don't even visit her grave. Several expressed some annoyance at the question. James, a civil rights movement veteran in his fifties, remarked,

> Why does it always come down to Miss Kitty? Thousands and thousands of black people were held in bondage in this county. Thousands of black women and girls were raped. Black men were lynched for sport. And all anyone wants to talk about is Miss Kitty. There are simply other stories we need to tell first, other souls that need tending to.

But a number of older women expressed more nuanced positions. Rebecca's cousin Natalie thought about the question and then said quietly,

> Oh, I wouldn't say Kitty is unremembered in the community. We just have our own way of doing things here, for one of our own, you know. . . . As a girl, I remember being out in the cemetery many times with my mother and grandmother when we were cleaning up those old graves, on Mother's Day or at Christmas, you know. Sometimes I'd catch them just looking out at Miss Kitty's grave, over there way over on the white side. They'd get a quiet, serious look and would just give a little nod. Wouldn't ever walk over there to the white side, unless some white man made them come over to "pay their respects to Kitty," which nobody liked to do. . . . Miss Kitty didn't have any kin

here, you know, we don't think so at least. Her children were taken off as slaves by the Bishop after she died . . . but we have our own ways of remembering.

Alice, in her seventies, told me,

I can't see any of us going in for that whole "Afrika" thing with a "K," marching over to the cottage, talking up a storm, and getting in the newspaper and all that. But I do think on her sometimes, when I'm at my mother's grave in the cemetery or just walking quietly through the slope. I think what a lonely life she had, she and all those strong black women who had to endure the unendurable, all for the sake of their children and the ones they loved. I think on her, I really do.

Significantly, in these accounts, the historically African American side of the cemetery—not the cottage or Kitty's actual resting place (on the white side of the cemetery)—is understood as the appropriate site of remembrance. Rather than formal or marked ritual action, quieter practices of gazing, walking, and "thinking on" seem much more fitting. For all its painful recent history, the black half of the city cemetery remains "our place," encompassing all who were once part of the community, even those, like Miss Kitty, who were for so long under intimate white encompassment, in life and in death.

Reflections on Sound and Silence

For all their differences in these commentaries across the "color line," these varied accounts of the cottage and graveyard do seem to share an intimate relationship between kinship and landscape. For many local whites, the restoration and sanctification of the cottage is a noble cause, a tangible way of countering what they regard as a long history of northern slurs against their ancestors and of honoring their kin who fought in the War Between the States or the War against Northern Aggression. Many speak of the physical labor of restoring the cottage as a way of "becoming close" to their long-dead family members, who worked so hard to "make the county what it is today." A number specifically contrast the "beauty" and "serenity" of the cottage with the scars inflicted on the local landscape during General Sherman's march to the sea during the final months of the Civil War. As one member of the historical society told me, "Up this street, that's where the boys in blue came marching and pillaging, taking everything that wasn't nailed down from my great-grandfather's place. When we fix up the cottage, we're honoring our heritage, remembering just what it was our people fought and died for."

The restored cottage, in these white accounts, helps heal breaches in the local landscape and in local descent lines. In a curious way, as I have suggested, the project of reproducing whiteness demands the collaborative, if hierarchical, material and symbolic labor of white and black women. Recall that many elderly white couples in Newton County have confided that their first kiss took place within the Kitty's Cottage Museum at the entrance of Salem Campground, and that the Kitty marker marks the transition into the white cemetery, where the city's white ancestors are honored.

In contrast, for many local African Americans, the cottage bears mute testimony to enduring inequity, viscerally embedded in the proximate landscape, which in turn bears traces of a long history of white dispossession of black-owned land. The site epitomizes white refusal to admit to the horrors of slavery, Jim Crow, histories of sexual assault and coercion, and the enduring legacies of white privilege. The cottage and cemetery, in African American eyes, specifically call attention to white denial of the tangled lines of descent that cut across putative lines of racial difference. Consider, for example, an encounter between retired African American schoolteacher Emogene Williams and my students as she guided them through the white cemetery, moving back and forth between her version of the Kitty story and detailed accounts of prominent Oxford white family genealogy. When a white student asked how she knew so much white genealogy, she laughed and responded, "Honey, what you need to understand is that when we're visiting this side of the cemetery, we're just visiting our kin!"

The range in the audibility of these memorial practices is especially suggestive. I am struck by how the voluble normative white accounts of Kitty were, strangely enough, paralleled by the public reclamations of Kitty's narrative by the Afrocentric visitors from Lithonia. Each side forcibly claims Kitty's story for their own; she either is classified entirely as part of white history or part of black history. In contrast, local African American women in Oxford have tended to memorialize Kitty in much quieter, less public ways, through almost imperceptible moments of "thinking upon" her or glancing across the spatial lines of segregation at her distant final resting place. Such acts would seem to allow a positioning of Miss Kitty, and of so many other women of color, in ambiguous enduring contact zones that cross-cut conventional racial distinctions. They allow for a solidarity that transcends normative categories of distinction, for forms of embodied and spatialized kinship beyond the spectrum of visible difference. They make possible, across local landscapes that have been violently and painfully interrupted, the reinstitution of alternate forms of lineage and the reemergence of new pulses of life and historical continuity.

The Question of Choice: Structure and Agency

In the standard white mythic representation of the cottage, both Andrew and Kitty are presented as making fateful choices that paralleled one another: Bishop Andrew chooses to remain loyal to his duties to his wife and to the wishes of the unnamed Augusta white woman, while Kitty chooses to remain in slavery. No suggestion is ever given that any other enslaved person in the story, such as his second wife's slaves, made any choices at all, for they are merely pawns in the larger narrative. Volition is reserved in the myth to the two central protagonists, master and slave, in a way that inverts the standard configuration of structure and agency: Kitty is allowed to live in virtual freedom in her cottage, while the Bishop is rendered a slave of duty. In a precise inversion of this classic myth, in the recent mythic narrative propounded by the Afrocentric First Afrikan Church of Lithonia, Kitty is entirely deprived of agency, and is figured as a passive object of sexual exploitation passed among white clergymen. For the First Afrikan congregants, the cottage was, quite literally, a "prison," an enduring signifier of Kitty's lack of choice throughout her life.

In part 3 we attempt a process of historical reconstruction to portray a more nuanced picture of structure and agency for slaveowners and the enslaved. The logic of kinship relations within the context of agrarian capitalism was highly restrictive for virtually all actors, across lines of race, gender, and class, but did at times allow for strategic manipulation in the pursuit of goals and life possibilities. As we shall see, Kitty, her close family members, and the forty or so other enslaved persons owned by Bishop Andrew were unquestionably embedded within a wider calculus of white-dominated kinship relations. The difficult life choices they made took place under constraints generated by overarching structures of white affinity, filiation, and property relations, which rendered them in white eyes "members of Bishop Andrew's family," even as they were systematically marginalized by centers of economic and political power. They were forced to operate within structures of paternalist dependence and patron-client relations, even as they strove for degrees of autonomy and independence.

With these thoughts in mind, let us turn in the next chapter to the most puzzling aspects of the Andrew slavery drama, the stories of Miss Kitty and her children. What kinds of choice, precisely, did Miss Kitty make, and under what specific restrictions and circumstances? What, in time, were the consequences of these decisions, for herself, her offspring, and their posterity?

Oxford cemetery. Bishop Andrew obelisk in foreground; Kitty memorial at base of water oak (Ellen Schattschneider).

Kitty's Cottage, ca. 1930. Special Collections, Oxford College Library, Manuscript, Archives, and Rare Book Library, Emory University.

Kitty's Cottage in Salem Campground, 1948 (*Covington News*).

Kitty's Cottage, 2010 (Ellen Schattschneider).

Oxford African American community, early twentieth century. Courtesy of John P. Godfrey Jr.

First Afrikan Presbyterian (Lithonia, Ga.) performs Ancestral Walk and African Naming Ceremony, Kitty's Cottage, June 19, 2008 (*Covington News*).

Cynthia (left) and Darcel Caldwell, presented by Oxford Mayor Jerry Roseberry with a proclamation for descendants of Nathan and Catherine "Kitty" Boyd Day. Old Church, Oxford, Ga., February 6, 2011 (Ellen Schattschneider).

Oxford College students and community members read names of enslaved Oxford residents at the unveiling of Lynn Marshall-Linnemeier's *Unraveling Miss Kitty's Cloak*, in Old Church, Oxford, Ga., February 6, 2011 (Bradd Shore).

Darcel (left) and Cynthia Caldwell, with historical documents on the Miss Kitty story. Manuscript, Archives and Rare Book Library, Emory University, February 3, 2011 (Maureen McGavin/ Emory University).

Dr. Joe Pierce Jr. and Aaronetta Pierce next to *Unraveling Miss Kitty's Cloak*.
To their left is a photograph of Dr. Pierce's father, Joe Pierce Sr., an African
American mathematician and president of Texas Southern University. Dr.
Pierce was the great-grandson of the white Methodist Bishop George Foster
Pierce, third president of Emory College (Ellen Schattschneider).

Detail from Lynn Marshall-
Linnemeier's artwork
Unraveling Miss Kitty's Cloak.
Bottom left surrounded by
doves are Miss Kitty's eldest
son, Rev. Alford Boyd, and
his wife Malvina. Top left:
John Pliny Godfrey Sr. in
his World War I uniform.
Bottom right, the names
of enslaved antebellum
residents of Oxford, Ga.
(Ellen Schattschneider).

Part Three

Families Lost and Found

Chapter Seven

Enigmas of Kinship

Miss Kitty and Her Family

IN PART 3 we turn from the mythological elaborations of the story of Bishop Andrew and his relationship to slavery to a rereading of the historical record. We begin with the many puzzles involving the story of Miss Kitty (ca. 1822–51). Who were her parents? How did Bishop Andrew acquire her? What was the precise nature of her relationship with the Bishop? What was her life in Oxford in the Andrew household like? Was the Bishop in fact the father of her children?

In this chapter I review and sift through the available evidence, and attempt to reconstruct what we can of Miss Kitty's life in Augusta and Oxford, and then consider the lives of her children, who were taken away from Oxford after her death.

Kitty's Origins

Kitty's parentage and her childhood before coming into James Andrew's possession remain puzzling. As noted in chapter 3, Bishop Andrew in his May 1851 obituary of Kitty states, "Some years since a lady in Augusta who had formerly been under my pastoral care, being about to die, bequeathed to me a little mulatto girl, named Kitty, requesting that I should keep her in my family till she was twenty-one years of age, and then if she had conducted herself properly, and was willing, I was to send her to Liberia, and if not, I was to keep her and make her as free as the laws of Georgia would permit." Augustus Baldwin Longstreet asserted in the 1841 interview, reproduced in G. G. Smith's 1883 biography of Bishop Andrew, "This day, Kitty, a woman of color, left in charge of the Rev. James O. Andrew by the will of Mrs. Power, came before us." In the interview, Longstreet tells her, "Kitty, your mistress directed in her will that you should remain with Bishop Andrew until you reached the age of nineteen, when it was to be left to your choice to go to Liberia or remain with the Bishop."[1] The original 1841 document quoted by Rev. Smith does not exist in Smith's or Andrew's papers at Emory or in other known repositories. We must thus rely entirely on Smith's reproduction of the text.

The Andrew obituary and Longstreet interview do differ on the question of Kitty's age. Longstreet in 1841 states that Kitty was to be given the choice to go to Liberia when she turned nineteen; ten years later in 1851 Andrew states this choice was to be presented to her at age nineteen. Since Longstreet was writing closer to the original events, it would seem that his account is more trustworthy and that Kitty was nineteen in 1841, and thus born around 1822.

It is not clear precisely when Andrew acquired Kitty. All published accounts assert that this took place after Andrew became a bishop in 1832. Some accounts state Kitty was twelve years old when she came into the Bishop's household, which would probably have been around 1834. In a letter to his friend Rev. Wightman in 1844, in reference to the New York Conference controversy, Bishop Andrew asserts, "I have been eight years a slaveholder," which would suggest he acquired Kitty around 1836, just around the time he departed for Newton County, about one hundred miles west of Augusta.[2] The first direct mention of Kitty that I know of is in a letter dated December 5, 1840, by Bishop Andrew to his wife, Ann Amelia. All we can say in confidence is that Bishop Andrew acquired Kitty at some point between mid-1836 and late 1840.

Bishop Andrew in his obituary asserts that Kitty could read and write, and that she was "rather fond of books." Since the Bishop evidently acquired Kitty when she was at least twelve, it seems likely that she had learned to read before she came into the Bishop's household. This would make it likely that she spent her childhood in a Methodist household, as Andrew himself implies by his statement that her former mistress had been one of his congregants. Although teaching slaves to read was illegal in the antebellum Deep South, there are a number of accounts of white Methodists in the region teaching favored slaves to read and write. No less a figure than the great Methodist Bishop Francis Asbury is reported, after a prayer meeting in Charleston, South Carolina, to have vowed in secret with Rev. John Mood (Bishop Andrew's brother-in-law) to help teach negro preachers to read the gospel.[3]

Who were Kitty's parents, and how precisely did she come into Andrew's possession? She is listed in the 1850 census as "M" for "mulatta," so it seems likely that her father was a white man and her mother an enslaved African American woman. (It is, of course, conceivable, although much less likely, that her mother was white and her father African American.) Longstreet, Andrew, and Smith insist that she was willed by a woman in Augusta to the Bishop. However, I have reviewed every last will and testament by a woman recorded in Augusta or Richmond County, Georgia, in the first half of the nineteenth century, and worked carefully through all estate inventories in Augusta during this period. None mention Kitty or James Andrew; nor do any wills refer to Liberia.

We are thus left to speculate on a number of different scenarios to account for how Andrew acquired Kitty. I consider two of these scenarios below, and review several others in Appendix 3, leaving the reader to weigh the direct and indirect evidence in support of them.

Lovey Powers (ca. 1777–1832)

The only woman of the period to leave a will in Augusta or Richmond County, Georgia, with a name similar to "Power" was a Lovey Powers, who was buried in Augusta's city cemetery on April 13, 1832, at the age of fifty-five.[4] She appears never to have been married, and to have come, like so many residents of Augusta, from South Carolina. Her will, recorded in the Richmond County Ordinary Court in 1832, makes no mention of Kitty or of James Andrew; the deceased woman simply leaves her estate to be held in trust for her daughter, Eliza Olivia Collins; Eliza's daughter, Emma Bracket Hartford; and any future children of her daughter Eliza, with a modest provision for her own (unnamed) "aged mother," who is to live with Eliza.[5]

Kitty's original mistress is invariably described in published accounts as a "wealthy woman," but according to the county's evaluation, Lovey Powers's estate at the time of her death amounted only to $1,161.62, hardly a fortune by the standards of the day. The majority of her estate lay in her five slaves, "Lucy and her three children, viz. [Liam or Louis?], Zelda and Dennis," valued at $800, and "Fanny," valued at $352.[6] No other slaves are listed. No document among her probate records mentions James Andrew, Kitty, Liberia, or any intentions regarding her slaves. On January 14, 1833, Joseph Collins, the son-in-law of Lovey Powers and coexecutor of her estate, applied for leave "to sell two negro slaves" from the Powers estate; no records survive of the disposition of the other three inventoried slaves.

In the 1830 census, two years before her death, Lovey Powers is listed as having nine slaves: two male slaves under ten years old, one male slave between thirty-six and fifty-four, one female slave under ten, two female slaves between ten and twenty-four, and three female slaves between ages twenty-four and thirty-six. Of these, it is possible that Kitty, born around 1822, could have been the female slave under ten years old, although, as noted above, there is no mention of a Kitty in the court inventory or legal papers regarding the Powers estate.

I know of only one other piece of evidence in regards to slaves in the Powers household. Five years before Lovey Powers's death, a legal document refers to her holding a slave girl named "Maria" on behalf of her minor ward, a young white woman named Mary Susan Johnson. This young woman was the great-granddaughter of Nathaniel Hall, a planter in Emmanuel County, about forty miles from Augusta, who in 1813 had deeded eight slaves ("Mary, Nell, Joe, Prince, Sophia, Hannah, Paddy, Jacob") to John Course in trust from his daughter Mary, married to an Andrew MacLean. These slaves in time passed to the daughter of Andrew and Mary MacLean, Catherine MacLean, who married a Robert Johnson. The slaves seem to have been subjected to considerable contestation since several relatives were paid by Andrew MacLean to relinquish all claims to them. On October 27, 1827, John Course made an agreement with Lovey Powers that Powers would maintain the slave girl "Maria, about eleven years," the daughter of the slave Mary, one of the original eight slaves deeded by Nathaniel Hall, for the use of Mary Susan Johnson, who was then living with Lovey Powers.

I have not been able to trace the subsequent fate of Mary Susan Johnson or her slave Maria. Maria, if eleven years old in 1827, would have been born around 1816, so would have been about six years older than the usual age assumed for Kitty; she thus seems an unlikely candidate to be Kitty.[7]

On balance, the case for Kitty coming out of the Lovey Powers household appears weak. Lovey Powers was often in financial straits. Augusta newspapers report at least one sale of her possessions by the sheriff to settle her debts. Given her concerns over looking after her mother, daughter, and granddaughter out of her very limited estate, it seems quite unlikely she would have been willing to relinquish the financial value of a slave girl in her possession by transferring her to Bishop Andrew. It should be recalled that Lovey Powers died in 1832, but that as late as 1836 Bishop Andrew still is not listed in the county tax records as owning any slaves; it seems most unlikely that it would have taken four years for a slave to be transferred from the Powers estate to the Bishop.

Richard and Emily Tubman

Alternately, perhaps Kitty was connected to one of the most prominent couples in Augusta antebellum society, Richard and Emily Tubman. There is no positive evidence for such a connection, but there is a good deal of intriguing circumstantial evidence to consider.

Recall that both Andrew and Longstreet insisted (in the 1841 legal document and in the 1851 obituary) that Kitty's mistress had specified that Kitty was to be offered the opportunity to be transported to Liberia. The Liberia connection in this case is a little surprising, given that in the mid- to late 1830s, when Kitty was apparently given or bequeathed to James Osgood Andrew, colonization to Liberia was not an especially popular concept in Georgia. To take but one example, a newspaper editorial in the *Augusta Chronicle* in January 1836 denounces colonization in these strident terms: "We have always maintained [the Colonization society] is much worse than the Abolition society, as that it is a secret and insidious enemy, under the pretense of friendship, and consequently the more dangerous one."[8] The editorial approvingly quotes a recent opinion piece in the *New York Herald*, "Colonization is the mother of Abolition—and they are both vagrants, and ought to be put in Bridewell [prison]."[9]

The principal pioneer of colonization in the state of Georgia, flying in the face of powerful white anticolonization sentiment, was the wealthy Emily Tubman. In seeking to fulfill her husband's will to manumit his slaves, Emily Tubman arranged in spring 1837 for over forty freed slaves to be shipped to Liberia.

The outlines of the famous Tubman case are worth reviewing. Richard Tubman, originally from a wealthy slaveowning family in Maryland, moved to the Augusta area with his brother in the early nineteenth century and established himself as one of the wealthiest planters in the region. He seems to have resided for some years in relative isolation on his plantations in Columbia County, just north of Augusta, until he met the young beauty Emily Harvie Thomas, recently arrived in Augusta from Frankfort, Kentucky. After the couple were married in 1818 Emily proved a brilliant financial and social partner for Richard, establishing their residence in Augusta as a glittering hub of Augusta high society.

Emily was highly involved in the management of the plantation, on which about sixty-five slaves on average are recorded in the tax records of the 1820s. Richard died in the summer of 1836. His will declared his intention of freeing all of the slaves then in his possession. Since emancipation was at that point illegal in Georgia, he sought to convince the George Legislature to pass a bill legalizing this massive manumission. By way of inducement, his will specified that if the legislature was to free his slaves, a bequest from his estate of ten thousand dollars would be made to the then-struggling University of Georgia in Athens. A committee of the legislature in Milledgeville, however, refused to support this course of action.

Emily was thus forced to pursue other options. She wrote to both the American Colonization Society (ACS) and the more recently established Maryland State Colonization Society (MSCS), the two major organizations arranging for slaves and free persons of color to be transported to West Africa for resettlement. In March 1837 she wrote to R. R. Gurley of the American Colonization Society: "My late husband desires me in his will to emancipate 48 of our slaves and remove them to one of the U. States in which I may deem the Laws calculated to give them the most protection and liberty. I have thought it not departing from the spirit of the will (the happiness and comfort of these people), to lay before them such information with regard to Liberia as I could collect, and let them choose a home for themselves."[10]

Since the ACS's rival, the MSCS, responded more quickly to her inquiries, she contracted with them to relocate her husband's slaves. She quickly arranged to transport them to Baltimore, where they were outfitted for the expedition across the Atlantic. On May 17, 1837, the brig *Baltimore* sailed from Maryland with about forty-six slaves, forty-two of whom had belonged to Richard Tubman and four others who were spouses or children of the Tubman slaves, freed by "benevolent individuals," in Augusta. Some of Richard Tubman's slaves whose kin in Augusta were not freed elected to stay behind in slavery to remain close to their relatives.

The forty-six or so freedpeople who traveled to Liberia founded the community known as Mound Tubman in the state of "Maryland in Africa," in Liberia, named in honor of their former master and mistress. Among their descendants were many of the leading citizens of Liberia, including President James Tubman. They remained in contact with Emily Tubman, who sent them occasional gifts. One member of the Mound

Tubman community, Caesar, undertook a return voyage to Baltimore to
meet with Emily Tubman the following year to collect from her the ten
thousand dollars provided for in Richard Tubman's will to support his
former slaves.

Although Emily conscientiously honored her husband's wishes to
manumit his slaves, she continued to own, buy, and sell slaves of her own
across the subsequent decades. In 1850 she owned four slaves in Augusta,
and twenty-eight in Columbia County; in 1860 she owned one slave in
Augusta and forty-one slaves in Columbia. As late as 1858, on the eve
of the Civil War, she purchased three slaves. She remained one of the
wealthiest and most respected figures in Augusta society until her death
in 1885; ironically she is commemorated to this day with monuments and
exhibits in Augusta as an antislavery heroine.

There is no mention in any of the voluminous Tubman legal documentation and correspondence of a child named Kitty. However, there
is circumstantial evidence that Richard Tubman fathered a number of
his slaves through sexual relations with enslaved women in his possession. Indeed, cases of mass emancipation in the antebellum South were
often motivated by close kinship relations between owners and slaves.
The most famous instance is George Washington's decision to manumit
posthumously his slaves, among whom seem to have numbered many of
his collateral relatives.[11]

In this connection, a highly suggestive incident took place three years
after the resettlement of the Richard Tubman slaves. On January 30,
1841, Emily Tubman sold to a Milton Brown of Houston County, Georgia, halfway across the state from Augusta,

> a certain negro woman named Frances and her child Mary with the
> express understanding and agreement that neither he nor his execu-
> tors . . . will ever permit the said Frances to come within seventy five
> miles of the city of Augusta in the state of Georgia or of the Planta-
> tion of the said Emily H Tubman in Columbia County in the state
> of Georgia and immediately to remove her to at least that distance
> from both the said places if the said Frances should ever without
> their permission come within that distance of the same.[12]

The most plausible explanation of this provision is that Mary was the
daughter of Richard Tubman. Frances, Richard Tubman's likely former
mistress, would have been a painful reminder to Emily of her late husband's infidelities. Emily thus wished to ensure that she would never

again see Frances and thus sold her and her daughter off at a great distance.

We could thus envision the following scenario. The mulatta Kitty, an illegitimate daughter of Richard Tubman and one of his female slaves, had been particularly favored by him. Before his death, Richard indicated to Emily Tubman he wished Kitty to be well looked after. It was impossible, however, to send Kitty on the original expedition in April 1837 to Liberia, perhaps because her mother was no longer alive and none of the slaves leaving on the voyage were willing to assume responsibility for her. Emily herself could not tolerate the thought of having to see Kitty, her husband's mulatta daughter, ever again. She thus prevailed upon Bishop Andrew to take Kitty with him as he relocated to Newton County, a significant distance from Richmond and Columbia County. Consistent with her husband's desires, she specified that Kitty be given the choice of going to Liberia, the same choice she had presented the rest of her husband's slaves in late 1836 and early 1837.

I have not seen any direct evidence of friendship between Emily Tubman and Bishop Andrew, but they lived several streets away from one another and certainly would have encountered one another in Augusta's white elite society. Richard Tubman had been a leading member of St. Paul's Episcopal Church in Augusta. Emily does not appear ever to have been a member of St. John Methodist Church, where James Andrew had served as pastor, but she had broad religious interests and was a great patron of various Christian denominations in Augusta. We do know that Bishop Andrew's closest friend, Augustus Baldwin Longstreet, did some business with Richard Tubman. In spring 1834, two years before Richard Tubman's death, Longstreet transferred five of his slaves to Richard Tubman to settle a debt of $1,160. It seems likely that Emily knew Bishop Andrew and would have trusted him with a discreet request of this kind. Since, according to county tax records, Andrew still had not acquired Kitty as late as mid-1836 the time frame works. Emily Tubman would presumably have started to consider how to place an unaccompanied minor child among her late husband's slaves in late 1836, after the state legislature rejected her petition to manumit them.

If, in fact, Emily Tubman transferred Kitty to Bishop Andrew in this way, it would be understandable that Andrew and Longstreet took special care to preserve the reputation of Emily Tubman and her late husband Richard, two of the most powerful figures in Augusta. They might thus have concocted the fiction that Kitty had been willed by a lady in

Augusta upon her death, to conceal the precise circumstances of Kitty's parentage. It should be noted that Andrew and Longstreet were not above a little creative misdirection in matters concerning slavery: in April 1844, as we have seen, they produced an elaborate deed transaction so as to project the legal fiction that Andrew was not the actual owner of the fourteen Greenwood slaves.[13]

Kitty in Newton County

In any event, it is difficult to say how long Kitty resided in Augusta in the Andrew household. She must have worshipped with the Andrews in St. John Methodist Episcopal Church, where the Bishop had previously served as senior pastor. In the 1830s the African American membership of St. John's numbered 323 out of 610 members. In 1840, 125 African American members of St. John's famously processed bearing torchlights to a new spiritual home, a brush arbor, at Eighth and Taylor streets in Augusta, to establish the congregation that after the Civil War would become known as Trinity Colored Methodist Episcopal Church. It is quite possible that Kitty's kin were members of this congregation. By 1840, however, Kitty was residing in Newton County, and may have lost touch with family and friends in the Augusta African American community.

Bishop Andrew had settled his household near Covington, the county seat of Newton County, during the winter of 1836–37. He purchased a plot of land he named Chestnut Grove, where he seems to have settled his family until autumn 1840. It seems likely that Kitty was already part of the household when the Andrews moved to Newton County in late 1836, although there is no direct proof. G. G. Smith, Andrew's biographer, notes that from 1836 to 1839 there is a striking absence of surviving correspondence by the Bishop, and Smith himself has few details on this period in Andrew's life. From real estate and tax records, we know that Bishop Andrew was joined at some point in the late 1830s by his mother, Mary Cosby Andrew, who acquired property nearby and resided there with her slaves.

By the summer of 1840, when the federal census was enumerated, a female slave who must be Kitty is recorded as part of the Andrew household in "town" (which must mean Covington). Also in the household is a male slave who must have been Billy, inherited by Ann Amelia from her mother, Catherine Stattler McFarlane, who had been visiting the Andrew family in Covington when she died several months earlier, on

April 1, 1840. (Presumably, Billy accompanied her during this visit.) The Andrews during summer 1840 appear to have made plans to relocate to the nearby new town of Oxford, site of the recently established Emory College, where Bishop Andrew served as the first president of its board of trustees. Andrew had been instrumental in the founding of the college in 1836. The college officially opened in 1839.

In November 1840 Bishop Andrew traveled west on church business. On November 21 he wrote to his daughter Elizabeth, whom he believed was still living at Chestnut Grove. He jokingly mentions, "Your mother has transferred her headquarters to Oxford," and notes that he is unsure which household members have been moved to the new home in Oxford. He concludes, "My love to all at home, white and black."[14] Two weeks later, on December 5, the Bishop wrote to his wife, Ann Amelia, the oft-quoted passage, "Tell Kitty I wish I could drink a cup of her best coffee this morning. I hope she is doing well and will preserve herself chaste in Oxford. She will be greatly exposed to temptations, and I hope will be carefully guarded in her conduct."[15]

By this point, then, Kitty was residing in Oxford, the newly established college town a mile north of Covington. The Bishop was evidently concerned about the sexual attention that Kitty, now about eighteen years old, would attract from college students, faculty, and other men, now that the household had moved out of the country.

How precisely are we to read the Bishop's phrasing? As we have seen, African Americans in present-day Oxford are inclined to interpret Andrew's reference to drinking Kitty's "coffee" as a sexual innuendo. Some suggest that the Bishop was expressing the hope that Kitty would preserve herself sexually for him alone. White readers in Oxford are much more inclined to read the letter as an innocent expression of sentimental concern for Kitty's virtue.

Three weeks later, on December 31, Ann Amelia Andrew wrote to her nephew John Amos Mood in Charleston that she, Kitty, and Henry (Rev. Henry Bass Jr.) had painted the inside of the new house in Oxford.[16] The following spring, the Bishop's daughter Sarah, who was the wife of John O. Lamar, contracted rheumatic fever; she survived but was left "bereft of reason," and was returned to her parents' home in Oxford to be cared for. It would seem likely that one of Kitty's duties, in addition to preparing coffee each morning, would have been looking after Sarah.

The next record of Kitty is her famous interview with Augustus Baldwin Longstreet and Professor George Lane, on December 4, 1841. In chapter 3, we considered the rhetorical structure of Longstreet's account. What can be inferred about what the interview was actually like from Kitty's perspective? What were her motivations for staying in Oxford and refusing transport to Liberia? Longstreet quotes her as saying she was fearful she might die in Africa. But perhaps she had other concerns. One possibility is that she was already romantically involved with the man known as Nathan, whom she would evidently marry at some point in the early 1840s. As early as December 1841, she may not have been willing to leave him even at the cost of her own freedom.

Nathan Boyd and Stephen Shell

As we have seen, white lore in Oxford, commemorated in the 1939 McCord cemetery tablet to Kitty, has long maintained that Kitty's husband was a free man of color named "Nathan Shell." Local African Americans, noting that no African American family named "Shell" ever resided in Oxford, have long doubted this claim, and at times cited the story of a "Nathan Shell" as evidence that their white neighbors have been in denial about the facts of Miss Kitty's life. Indeed, when I began my research some local African Americans jokingly referred to the search for Nathan as "a 'shell' game."

The documentary record lends credence to aspects of the respective white and African American accounts. On the one hand, there does not appear to have been a free man of color named Nathan living in antebellum Newton County. No such person is listed in the surviving county tax digests or the records of the ordinary court, where free men and women of color were legally required to register themselves. The 1860 census, which lists twenty-one free men of color in the county, does not record a Nathan or a Shell.

On the other hand, strong evidence exists that there was in fact an African American man in antebellum Oxford named Nathan who had children with Kitty and who considered himself married to her. However, he was almost certainly a slave.

The chain of evidence is as follows: One of the few white men in antebellum Newton County named Shell was a "Stephen Shell" (ca. 1800–1885). He grew up in Newberry, South Carolina, and was the son of a prominent Methodist minister, Rev. Stephen Shell. When Rev. Shell died in Newberry on December 11, 1822, he willed his slaves, including a male named Nathan, to his children. Rev. Shell's will specifically mentions that

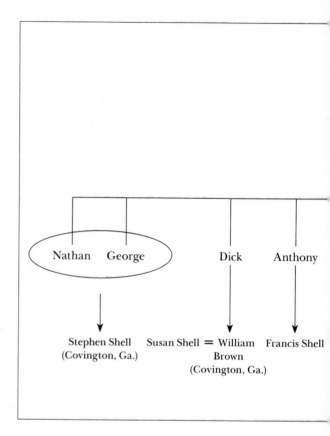

FIGURE 7.1. Distribution of Nathan Boyd's enslaved family from Rev. Stephen Shell to his sons and sons-in-law (broken lines are speculative)

Nathan   George   Dick   Anthony

Stephen Shell   Susan Shell = William   Francis Shell
(Covington, Ga.)   Brown
                        (Covington, Ga.)

he wills to his son Stephen Shell, "my negro boy Nathan"; to his daughter Mary E. Lofton, "one negro girl Delsey"; to his son George Shell, the "negro Isaac"; to his son Ira Shell, "one negro boy Joseph (which said negro he hath parted with since I gave him possession)"; and to his daughter Permelia "Milly" Yeargain, one "negro boy named Peter." Anthony was distributed to Francis Shell. The eldest slave in the group appears to be Richard, who had been purchased by Rev. Stephen Shell in August 1803 from Hibbert (Harbert) Tucker in Newberry, South Carolina.[17] By 1824 Richard had been distributed to Deverick or Deveraux Yeargain, Milly's husband. A negro woman Judi and her child Isaac had been delivered to Rev. Shell's son, Lemuon Shell, who later relocated to Mississippi.[18] A slave "boy" named "Dick" was distributed to Rev. Shell's daughter Susanna and her husband William Brown. A "boy named

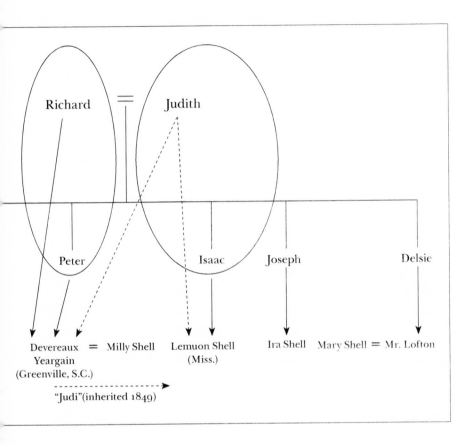

George" was distributed to Stephen Shell the younger, who also received Nathan (see Fig. 7.1).

These names precisely correspond with the family members that an African American man named "Nathan Boyd" was to list, two decades later, in his 1871 Freedman's Bank application in Atlanta. His siblings were his brothers Isaac, George, Joseph, Anthony, and Peter, and his sister "Delsie." He lists his parents as Richard and Judith, both dead. He lists his wife as "Catherine, dead." ("Kitty" is the diminutive form of Catherine.) His three children are recorded as "Alfred, Nathan, and Emma L." Nathan Boyd further writes that he was born in Newberry, South Carolina, and was brought up in Newton County, Georgia (see Fig. 7.2).

At some point after he inherited Nathan in 1822, Stephen Shell the younger moved to Covington, Georgia. Before 1840 his older sister,

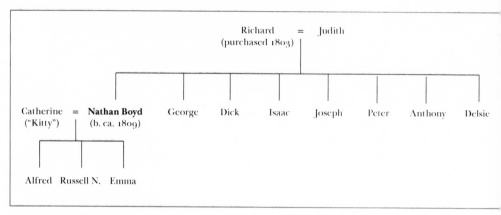

FIGURE 7.2. Nathan Boyd's family

Susanna Shell Brown, who had inherited from their father Rev. Shell the slaves "John Wesley" and "Dick" (the latter a brother of Nathan Boyd), had also moved to Covington with her husband, William Brown. Their relative Lenmere Shell, born around 1834, resided with them.[19]

By 1837 Nathan Boyd's owner Stephen Shell appears to have been well established in Covington, Georgia, and in acquaintance with Bishop Andrew, who had moved there the previous year. On May 1, 1837, Stephen Shell cowitnessed Bishop Andrew's purchase of two lots of land south of Covington. (Evidently this was the land where Bishop Andrew's mother Mary would reside for several years.) Stephen Shell subsequently appears in the county's legal records from time to time, buying and selling land, and serving after 1851 with Nathan Turner as coadministrator for the estate of the late Rev. Charles Haney Sanders. Charles H. Sanders, a close confidant of Bishop Andrew, was one of the founding trustees of Emory College and served as the first treasurer of the institution's board of trustees. Among their duties, Shell and Turner managed the slaves in the Sanders estate; for example, in 1856, they rented out a "negro man named Jim" in the estate to a local white man for $110. In the 1860 census Stephen Shell and Nathan Turner are recorded as living together in the home of a local widow Penelope Glass. The 1860 slave schedule indicates that Shell and Turner are listed as holding ten slaves on behalf of the Charles H. Sanders estate.

Shell evidently also had a small mercantile business and eventually served as a court recorder, but never married. He resided as a bachelor in Covington until the early 1880s, living in a series of boardinghouses.

Then, facing health and financial crises, he moved to Houston, Chicka-saw County, Mississippi, to reside with one of his brother's sons, and died there on January 27, 1885, aged around eighty-five.[20]

It would appear that, while residing in Covington before the Civil War, Stephen Shell the younger rented out his slave Nathan to local planters. In the 1849 and 1851 tax digests for Newton County (among the very few antebellum tax records from the county that have survived), Stephen Shell is listed as owning one slave, unnamed. However, in the 1850 and 1860 federal census records, he is not listed as owning any slaves. (As noted above, the 1860 slave schedule only records that he is coadminis-trator for the ten slaves of the Charles H. Sanders estate.) I infer that the census enumerator recorded the slave Nathan as residing elsewhere than with Stephen Shell; this is hardly surprising, given that Shell, a bachelor, was residing in boardinghouses in 1850 and 1860. It thus seems likely that Nathan was regularly rented out, and that Stephen Shell received an income for Nathan's services. Perhaps Nathan was rented out to Stephen Shell's sister, Susan Brown, and her husband, William Brown, who like him lived in Covington and who are listed as slaveowners during this period.

If Nathan was the property of Stephen Shell, this would explain why in local white memory, Nathan was referred to as "Nathan Shell," even though Nathan himself referred to himself as "Nathan Boyd," and passed the Boyd surname onto his sons, who referred to themselves through their lives as Alfred (or Alford) Boyd and Russell Nathan Boyd.

Where might Nathan have acquired the surname Boyd? It seems likely that he starting using "Boyd" before 1855, when his children were taken away from Newton County, since, as we shall see in the next chapter, that is the surname that his two sons used throughout their lives. Perhaps he had even been using the name before 1844 or so, when his eldest child, Alfred, later Alford Boyd, was born. Nathan might have been born with the last name Boyd. It should be noted that many enslaved people used surnames, even if these were rarely recognized in white-authored legal documents. In Newberry District, South Carolina, the place of Nathan's birth, there was a white Methodist minister, Rev. Nathan Boyd, who was born in Ireland in 1768 and who died on May 13, 1826. The court in-ventory of his estate lists five slaves. Both Rev. Stephen Shell, the slave Nathan's original owner, and Rev. Nathan Boyd were traveling Methodist preachers in the Carolinas together as early as 1805; they presumably knew each other extremely well. Perhaps the slave Richard admired Rev.

Boyd and took his family name, and named one of his sons after the Methodist worthy. Richard himself, as we have seen, was purchased by Rev. Shell from Harbert Tucker in 1803; we do not know if he lived to see emancipation or if he ever used the surname Tucker, Shell, or Boyd.

What became of Nathan Boyd's brother George, who was also distributed to Stephen Shell the younger around 1823? Presumably he was also brought to Newton County by Stephen Shell, who may have subsequently sold him. The only African American man named "George" from South Carolina born before 1824 (the year George was assigned to Stephen Shell) in the 1870 Freedmen's Census for Newton County, Georgia, is Rev. George Ansley, born about 1820. Rev. Ansley was a Methodist minister who in 1868 chaired the board of Richards Chapel, a Methodist church in the Bethany Community in the southwestern part of Newton County. He had evidently been owned by the Newton County white planter Thomas Ansley, one of the most prominent white pioneers of Newton County. The 1857 inventory of Thomas Ansley's estate lists among its slaves, "George a negro man 37 years of age, $1300," which is consistent with a birth year of 1820. Rev. George Ansley and his wife Nancy subsequently moved to Henry County, south of Newton County. His children settled in the Starrsville and Brick Store communities in eastern Newton County.

It is not clear how precisely Thomas Ansley might have acquired the slave George. Thomas Ansley was a close friend of Charles Haney Sanders, whose estate Stephen Shell coadministered after Sanders's death in 1851. Thomas Ansley's daughter Rebecca married Charles C. Shell, who may have been a kinsman of Stephen Shell. It is thus likely Stephen Shell and Thomas Ansley knew one another well; perhaps Ansley purchased George at some point before his death.

Less clear is what might have happened to the enslaved man "Dick," Nathan and George's brother, who was inherited by William and Susan Shell Brown, who like Stephen Shell resided in Covington. William Brown's will in 1856 enumerates the slaves Milly, Eli, Letty, and "Nancy and her children" but makes no reference to a Dick, who may have died, or been sold or transferred in the interim.

Kitty's Adult Life

As we have seen, Bishop Andrew does report that Kitty read well and was "rather fond of books." Was she allowed to borrow and read from

Bishop Andrew's library, reportedly the largest collection of books in Oxford? Was she able to read newspaper reports of the 1844 New York conference, in which the Methodist Episcopal Church was torn asunder by the question of Bishop Andrew's ownership of slaves, including Kitty herself? She may have written letters or even kept a diary, but if so, no such documents have survived the passage of time.

During the spring of 1842 Ann Amelia Andrew became extremely ill, dying on April 24. As Andrew and Smith report, Kitty tended her attentively during this period. Invited by Ann Amelia to kiss her on her lips on her deathbed, she complied. Bishop Andrew writes that Ann Amelia's final decline was brought on by her witnessing the traumatic scene of her mentally retarded daughter Sarah delivering a baby without understanding what was happening to her. We can presume that Kitty was intimately involved in all these events, helping attend to Sarah during her birth giving, and nursing Ann Amelia in her final weeks.

Recall that in Kitty's 1851 obituary, the Bishop writes that after Kitty refused to go to Liberia in 1841, "I gave her a lot in which her husband errected [sic] a comfortable house and we fitted her out to housekeeping." Similarly, in an undated letter, Andrew's son-in-law, Dr. Robert W. Lovett, asserted, "When she refused to go to a free state, she was allowed a house on his lot, and she and her family enjoyed the [illegible—perhaps extra] benefit of her time and labor."[21] As noted in chapter 5, the precise location of this house, which became such an abiding object of white sentimental memory after the Civil War, remains unclear. It seems likely it was at some distance from the Bishop's main house, since in the same obituary he recalls that a messenger had to come to his home to inform him that Kitty was grievously ill.

In the 1851 death notice, Bishop Andrew asserts that after she moved into her own house, Kitty worked for herself and he received "not a cent" from her labors. It seems quite possible that she worked as a seamstress during this period. In May 1842, about six months after her interview with Professors Longstreet and Lane, and about one month after Ann Amelia's death, Kitty appears three times in the account book of Iverson Graves, who owned a dry goods shop in Oxford:

May 26. 1 Br thimble and spool white thread .16

1 oz camphor .12

27th James O Andrew for Kitty

1 1/2 yrds blue (?) homespun for lining .15

28th J.O. Andrew for Kitty on
Cathy Windsor Soap .13

It seems most likely that the sewing instruments and cloth were purchased for the small sewing jobs through which Kitty supported herself. But I should note that Ms. Emogene Williams, one of the leading
African American community historians in Newton County, suggested
upon reading these records that Kitty was preparing to give birth or to
assist another woman in giving birth. Camphor, she notes, was tradition-
ally used by African American women to aid them during the birthing
process. Homespun and thimbles were used to make a "belly band" for
a newborn.

In any event, the 1850 census suggests that Kitty had three children, an
eldest son born around 1844, a second son born in 1846, and a daughter
born in 1848. Of course, we cannot know if Kitty gave birth to other children that did not survive until the 1850 enumeration. This record of two
sons and a daughter is consistent with the Freedman's Bank application
filed by Nathan Boyd, Kitty's husband, in 1871, two decades after Kitty's
death. He lists his wife as "Catherine, Dead," and lists three children as
"Alfred, Nathan and Emma L." It is possible, of course, that Kitty gave
birth to other children who did not survive (or that were not considered
by Nathan to have been his children.)

It seems possible that during the period when Kitty conceived and
bore her children, roughly 1843 to 1848, Nathan was rented out as a slave
in or around Oxford, perhaps to Stephen Shell's relatives, the Middle-
brooks, or to a white farmer in the area, Nancy Boyd, from whom he may
have adopted the family name "Boyd." In some instances in elite Georgia
families, marriages between favored enslaved persons were solemnized
by white clerics, although they were not legally registered as such. Bishop
Andrew might have performed a wedding ceremony between Kitty and
Nathan, but if so, no record of such an event has been preserved in the
many documents I have consulted. Nor is it clear if Nathan was able to
see Kitty and their children frequently. Since he was not a slave of Bishop
Andrew, they presumably could not live together in the house that Nathan had built, so perhaps Kitty and Nathan only cohabited infrequently.

However, Kitty's children must have in their early lives been on familiar terms with the white children of the Andrew family. Bishop Andrew's
biographer, Rev. George G. Smith, who himself grew up in Oxford during these years, recalls, "Her house was the resort of the children, and

'Mammy Kitty' as the baby called her, was the one to whom, in hours of childish grief or perplexity, all the troubles were carried." (The "children" and "the baby" in this passage surely refer to the white Andrew children, not to Kitty's own children.)

Kitty's life must have changed significantly after Bishop Andrew married his second wife, Ann Leonora Greenwood, in January 1844, bringing at least twelve enslaved people into the Oxford household. Would the new arrivals have resented Kitty because of her position of relative privilege, being exempted from domestic or field labor? Would they have feared her because of her unusual access to the master?

I put this question to Margaret Watkins, an elderly African American woman in Oxford, now deceased, who was descended from at least one of the slaves in the Andrew household. She responded, "Well, my grandmother told me, we were never angry with Miss Kitty. We just felt sorry for her, being his mistress like she was. She didn't have any say in all that, nobody did back then. She just seemed so lonely, so separated from all the other black people in town. That was what he did, you know, try to keep her apart from us, that's how they tried to break your spirit. She was a strong black woman, so she endured that, endured everything. But we still felt sorry for her. I feel sorry for her still, buried like she is on the white part of the cemetery. Like he's still trying to keep her away from her people."

It is probably not possible to determine the veracity of the persistent belief in the local African American community that Kitty was the coerced mistress of Bishop Andrew. The fact that Nathan Boyd in 1871 listed himself as the father of Kitty's three children would seem to establish that Bishop Andrew was not their biological father. Thus, even DNA tests of the descendants of Kitty and Bishop Andrew would not be able to settle the question of whether or not a sexual relationship existed between them.

To be sure, the likelihood that Nathan fathered Kitty's three known children does not preclude the possibility of a sexual liaison between Bishop Andrew and Kitty. As a slave Nathan would, of course, not have had the capacity to intervene to stop a liaison if one was indeed occurring. On balance, I am inclined to trust the oral historical accounts that have been passed down in the Oxford black community across a century and a half, that Kitty was sexually involved with Bishop Andrew under conditions that were not of her own choosing. This would hardly have been an unusual predicament; untold thousands of enslaved African

American women were subjected to sexual predation by their owners and other white men.

As in many mid-Victorian obituaries, Bishop Andrew devotes much of his account of Kitty's life to the story of her dying. He is at pains to emphasize that she died beloved in the Lord as a good Christian. The Bishop's enduring anger at his northern abolitionist accusers, those "who sought to crush me," is evident through the essay, and he presents Kitty's deathbed conversion as the ultimate reproach against his critics. All this would tend to cast some doubt on the veracity of his reports. It seems likely that Kitty died as a person of faith, but perhaps the Bishop exaggerates the intensity of her piety. Having said that, her final plea, that Bishop Andrew's daughter take care of her little girl, does ring true. She must have realized that her daughter Emma, two or three at the time, would have been highly vulnerable without close kin nearby.

What might Miss Kitty's funeral have been like? It seems likely that Rev. Potter, a "colored minister" in Oxford who died about six months after her and who was buried in the Oxford cemetery, may have preached at her funeral. One wonders if in addition to a service in the black Oxford church, adjacent to the cemetery, a white-directed funeral service was also held for her in Old Church, presided over by Bishop Andrew. All the stone markers placed for Bishop Andrew and his white family members have survived in the Oxford cemetery, but if there was an initial headstone marking the grave of Kitty it has not survived the passage of time. Perhaps only a simple wooden cross marked her grave.

It must have been traumatic for the children to observe closely the long illness of their mother starting in the winter of 1850–51, leading up to her death in April 1851. At the same time, her deathbed protestations of religious faith may have had a profound impact on the children. As we shall see, her eldest son Alfred (or "Alford") became a lifelong minister in the African Methodist Episcopal Church, and her younger son Russell Nathan served as senior deacon in a prominent Washington, D.C., Presbyterian church.

After Miss Kitty's Death

Evidently, whatever special quasi-legal status Bishop Andrew afforded to Miss Kitty did not in his mind extend to her children, beyond perhaps the expectation that they would be house slaves and not field hands. He certainly made no provisions to free them then or in the future. Presumably as soon as their mother died the three children were moved away from the cabin in which they had resided with her into the Andrews' general slave quarters, close to the main residence. There, they would have resided with about twenty-one other slaves, ranging in ages from two to sixty-five. With the exception of "Black Billy" and Lucy from Charleston, whom the Bishop had acquired from the mother of his first wife, the other slaves were, it appears, all part of the Greenwood estate from Greene County, either owned by the Bishop's second wife, Ann Leonora, or being held in trust for the children of her late husband, Thomas Greenwood.

At the time of their mother's passing, Alfred/Alford would have been about seven years old, Russell Nathan about five, and Emma about three. It is possible, in light of Kitty's dying request, that Emma for a time would have been taken into the household of Bishop Andrew's daughter, Elizabeth Mason Andrew Lovett, who was married to Dr. Robert Watkins Lovett and resided near the Bishop's household in Oxford. (Elizabeth herself died in 1856.) However, since there were at this time seven adult enslaved women in the Andrew household it seems most likely that one or more of these women was assigned the responsibility for looking after the three children, including the toddler Emma.

Nathan may have been allowed to visit the children in Oxford from time to time. Nathan's brother Richard seems to have been owned by William and Susanna Brown in Covington and may have also been allowed to visit Kitty and his niece and nephews as well. (As noted above, Nathan's brother George, who had also been conveyed to Stephen Shell Jr. in 1824, may have been owned by Thomas Ansley and thus resided within potential visiting distance of the children.)

One thing we can infer about the childhoods of Alford and Russell Nathan is that at some point they learned to read. Both men would prove themselves highly literate in their future careers. Perhaps Kitty herself began to teach them to read before her death, when Alford was seven and Russell Nathan about five. (Since their father Nathan Boyd signed his Freedman's Bank application in 1871 with an "X," we infer that he could not read or write.) Perhaps Bishop Andrew, his second wife Ann Leonora, or the Bishop's daughter Elizabeth continued to teach the boys or allowed them to continue to learn after Kitty's death—even though it was, technically, from 1829 onward illegal to teach slaves to read or write in Georgia. In contrast to her brothers, Emma, only two or three years old when her mother died, was evidently not taught even the elements of literacy. The 1880 and 1920 census entries for her state that she could neither read nor write.

The period after their mother's death must have been a tumultuous one for the children. Ann Leonora Greenwood, the second wife of Bishop Andrew, was an invalid during these years, and it is possible that the children would have been detailed to care for her, just as their mother had nursed the Bishop's dying first wife, Ann Amelia.

During the years immediately after Kitty's death, some of the slaves in the Andrew household in Oxford were coming and going. We know, for instance, that in March 1853, Bishop Andrew rented out two of the male slaves of the household, Aleck and Allen, for one hundred dollars to his brother Hardy Andrew, and that they continued to toil for his estate even after Hardy died. As we shall see in the next chapter, a set of continuing legal transactions governed the disposition of the Greenwood slaves, some of whom were reassigned to the adult white Greenwood children during these years, and may have been thus moved away from Oxford to Greene County.

Would the children have known of the publication of Bishop Andrew's *Miscellanies* in 1854, in which he described how their mother Kitty nursed Ann Amelia during her final illness and gave her a final kiss on her deathbed? Would they have ever come across the Bishop's 1851 obituary detailing Kitty's passing? Presumably, from time to time the children were allowed to visit their mother's grave in the Andrew family plot, near the colored church where they would have been taken for worship services on Sunday. They may also have accompanied on occasion the white Andrew family to Old Church, immediately adjacent to the Bishop's house.

There was surely considerable anxiety in the Andrew slave quarters around the time of the death of Ann Leonora Greenwood, the Bishop's second wife, who passed away in Oxford on June 10, 1854. The Greenwood slaves in the household must have been aware of the Bishop's intention to divide up most of them among the white Greenwood children, and realized that they were facing impending separation from close kin and comrades. They may have feared that some of them would be sold, and the profits realized distributed to the Greenwood heirs.

Within a matter of months after Ann Leonora's death, the children must have learned they were leaving Oxford, the only home they had ever known. Bishop Andrew had decided to marry a third time to a childhood friend, Emily Sims Woolsey Heard Childers, who had nearly three decades earlier been a member of his congregation in Augusta. After the death of her second husband Mr. A. B. Woolsey, Emily (often referred to as "Aunt Emma" in the family circle) married George Childers, a prominent farmer and Methodist lay leader residing in Summerfield, Alabama, just north of Selma. George Childers died in early 1853, and bequeathed to his wife considerable tracts of land and twelve slaves. On November 24, 1854, about half a year after the death of his second wife Ann Leonora Greenwood, Bishop Andrews married Emily in Dallas County, Alabama, presumably in the Summerfield Methodist Church.

When Bishop Andrew moved his household and slaves to Summerfield, Alabama, is not entirely clear. Early in 1855 Bishop Andrew and his new wife Emily traveled together to California on church business; it seems likely that upon his return he arranged for his slaves to be transported to Summerfield. He must have been relocated by January 1856, when he sold his residential property in Oxford, Georgia, to Joseph Griffin. However, he clearly made frequent return visits to Oxford up until the outbreak of the Civil War, since his presence there is often mentioned in contemporary letters and newspaper accounts.

Did the children have a chance to say good-bye to their father Nathan in 1855 as they were taken away from Newton County? Was the farewell tearful or stoic? There is no evidence that any of the children ever saw Nathan again or ever had contact with him. Yet, clearly, the eldest boy Alford remembered his father, since he named his second son, born in 1873, "Nathan." Alford also correctly asserted in the 1900 census that his father was born in "South Carolina," which suggests that he, perhaps unlike his younger siblings, had a clear memory of conversations with his father. We do know that Bishop Andrew passed through Oxford from time to time, and that Methodist clergy did at times travel between Oxford and Summerfield, so Nathan might have had some word of the children, although that is by no means certain.

We do know that by 1870, five years after emancipation, Nathan Boyd was residing in downtown Atlanta on Ivy Street in a boardinghouse. A year later, when he applied for a Freedman's Bank account, he was working as a cook, the same profession his eldest son Alfred would pursue when attached to the Union Army in 1865. Clearly Nathan never remarried or had subsequent children since he only lists "Catherine, Dead" as his spouse and only records "Alfred, Nathan and Emma L." as his children. The same day in 1871, Nathan Boyd is also listed in the Freedman's Bank records as a member of the financial committee of an African American fraternal organization, "The Grand Order of the Brothers of Love and Charity."[22] In 1873 he is briefly mentioned in an Atlanta newspaper as receiving from the city council five dollars for caring for a pauper, who must have been living with him.[23] Yet two years later he was to die indigent himself. He was buried on June 6, 1875, in the Colored Paupers section of Atlanta's Oakland Cemetery.[24]

Nathan Boyd's final years strike me as deeply poignant. He must not have had any contact with his sons, who by 1875 had sufficient means that they surely would have given him financial assistance if they had known of his whereabouts.[25] One senses that he must have still mourned his late wife Kitty, whom he lists as "Catherine, Dead," and worried over the fate of their three children.

Traveling West, ca. 1855

Returning to the children in the mid-1850s, we can only imagine what the trip 250 miles to the west must have been like for Kitty's three offspring, as they were taken from Oxford, Georgia, to Summerfield, Alabama, in 1855. They would have passed by the vast cotton plantations that had developed along the Black Belt, helping to make the region one of the most wealthy and influential in the nation. They would probably have witnessed hundreds, even thousands, of slaves working under brutally difficult conditions and been exposed to a harsher regimen of labor control and surveillance than they would have known in Oxford. During the trip west, they were probably accompanied by a few of the older Andrew slaves, such as Billy. As noted above, most of the other black members of the household would have been distributed to the white Greenwoods, some staying in Oxford, others taken to Greene County or elsewhere in Georgia.

Arriving in Summerfield in the mid-1850s, the children would have encountered a community not so different from the one they had left in Oxford. Summerfield was a quiet, tree-lined Methodist college village about twelve miles up the road from the booming river town of Selma. The antebellum records of the Summerfield Methodist Church list among its members a number of enslaved people. Although the relevant post-1855 church records have not survived, it seems a fair assumption that Kitty's children would have worshipped at the church, a few blocks away from the Andrew house, with the white Andrew family.[26] There was an active Methodist presence among enslaved African Americans in Dallas

County, Alabama; a Colored Methodist Episcopal Church in Cahawba recorded members from 1848 onward.

Perhaps the most striking difference from Oxford would have been the higher level of white anxiety over slave insurrection. Periodic rumors of planned uprisings circulated through the rural Alabama country-side during the late antebellum period. In Summerfield, a white militia routinely drilled on the village grounds, a tangible demonstration of white military power in the face of presumed local threats from African Americans.

In Summerfield, the children would have resided with, at the very least, the twelve other slaves who had been inherited by Bishop Andrew's wife Emily Sims Woolsey Childers upon the death of her husband George Childers in 1853. Among these enslaved persons were Loy, Rose, Sal, Martin, Hasly, Nancy, Selvy, Eliza, Jim, William, Wilson, and Louise. We do not know of the relative status of Kitty's children among this larger group of enslaved people. It seems likely that the children were assigned domestic responsibilities. Since Alfred was to serve as a cook when attached to the Union Army in 1865 he probably had experience around the kitchen and may have been the "dining room boy" referred to by Smith.[27]

The 1860 slave schedule for the Andrew household in Summerfield lists a fifteen-year-old mulatto male (presumably Alford/Alfred), a fourteen-year-old black male (presumably Russell Nathan), and a twelve-year-old black female (presumably Emma). The remaining group of slaves is unusual in that it contains no males over the age of fifteen; all adult slaves listed are female. Perhaps the adult male slaves had been rented out or placed out of Summerfield on a plantation, or perhaps the Bishop simply owned no adult male slaves during this period.

In Summerfield, the children would have seen some familiar white faces, including Bishop Andrew's daughter Octavia and her husband John Wesley Rush, who had married in Oxford in April 1854, and moved to Alabama. By February 1857 they were living in Summerfield, where Octavia gave birth to a little girl, Emily. Many prominent Methodists who had attended Emory College and who knew Oxford well seem to have passed through Summerfield and visited the Bishop, so the children may have been able to glean some news of friends and family still in Newton County.

The children's world would have changed dramatically in 1861, around the start of the Civil War. Bishop Andrew decided to try his hand at farming on a commercial scale and acquired a plantation in western Dal-

las County that he named Tranquilla. This experiment seems to have
ended unsuccessfully in 1864, when Bishop Andrew and his household
returned to Summerfield, according to Smith.

The purchase of the property was facilitated by Bishop Andrew's new
stepson, "Colonel" Benjamin M. Woolsey, the son of the Bishop's third
wife, Emily, by her second husband. Woolsey had been educated at Emory
College in Oxford and presumably knew Bishop Andrew well during that
period. His own plantation was quite near Tranquilla.

It is hard to know much about the life of Kitty's children on the Tranquilla plantation. Presumably their share of agricultural labor increased
during this time, and they likely had firsthand experience in the cotton
fields. It seems likely during this time that the Bishop continued to see
to their religious instruction and that they would have participated in
regular religious services.

In Andrew's biography, G. G. Smith offers two different explanations
as to why Andrew gave up on residing at Tranquilla after two years or so.
He refers to drought and crop failures, but he also asserts that Andrew
was a poor manager of negro slaves. He implies that his principal weak-
ness was his failure to use corporal punishment. Smith's wording, as
usual, is revealing:

> During the period of 1862 to 1863 he lived on a plantation he had
> bought eight miles west of Selma. This place was called "Tranquilla."
> Like almost every other man he thought he could make a living by
> farming, and went there for this purpose. But a poorer farmer never
> put foot in a field. The mental constitution and moral principles of
> the negro require a kind of authority in the management of such
> business which it was simply impossible for Bishop Andrew to exert.
> It is told in his family that once he did slap the jaws of a dining room
> boy about sixteen years old, and that when the boy told the other
> servants about it they could not believe a story so strange; and that
> on another occasion he made another sixteen year old fellow stand
> on a stump in the yard, so that the rest of the negroes could see
> and laugh at him. These two cases make the sum total of his harsh
> discipline over servants. It soon appeared to Colonel Woolsey, Mrs.
> Andrew's son, who lived near by, that things would be ruined if the
> Bishop did not go back to Summerfield—which he cheerfully did,
> turning the management over to the Colonel. It was while living at
> Tranquilla that he fell, for the first time, by a stroke of vertigo (or

it may have been a slight attack of paralysis) which followed him thenceforward to the end of life.[28]

Who were the two sixteen-year-old young men chastised in this way? One wonders if they might have been Alford and Russell Nathan, who as Kitty's sons might have been afforded special privileges yet also stood on a dangerous threshold of familiarity with the master.

When Bishop Andrew returned to Summerfield in 1864, he may have left some of his slaves at Tranquilla, to be supervised by Colonel Woolsey's overseers. It seems probable, however, that he would have taken the house slaves, which were likely to have included Kitty's children, back to Summerfield with him. There they would have resided during the final year or so of the Civil War. If so, the three would have remained together, until they were separated near the end of the war, amid the tumultuous events associated with Wilson's Raid and the fall of Selma to Union forces.

Emma's Story

When Emancipation came to Dallas County in the spring of 1865 Emma would have been about seventeen years old. Five years later, the 1870 census for Summerfield, Alabama, only lists one black woman born in Georgia in the mid- or late 1840s. This was "Emma Sanders," age twenty-four, born around 1846, married to a James Sanders, age twenty-five. Suggestively, Emma and James Sanders resided two doors away from Bishop Andrew, in the same household as a "Martin Andrews," who appears to have been a former slave of Bishop Andrew. He was presumably the "Martin" listed in the 1853 will of George Childers bequeathing his slaves to his wife Emily Sims Childers, whom Bishop Andrew married in 1855. James Sanders might be the "Jim" listed in the same Childers will or he may have been one of the freedpeople associated with the E. W. Saunders plantation in Union district, near Tranquilla plantation, where the Andrew slaves resided in 1862 and 1863.[29]

The approximately 439,000 freedpeople in Alabama faced staggering challenges following Emancipation. Early promises of land redistribution were never fulfilled, and many African Americans found themselves laboring under their former masters for minimal remuneration. Droughts, crop failures, and epidemics compounded the poverty faced by nearly all former slaves. Forced labor and coercive "apprenticeships" were deployed by local whites to continue slavery in all but name. In 1867, white planters in Summerfield formed a compact to control black labor, preventing freemen from shifting from one white-owned farm to another.[30] Various forms of sharecropping were quickly implemented, and many black families found themselves increasingly trapped in cycles of debt and deepening impoverishment amid backbreaking agrarian labor.

Living in Summerfield during Reconstruction, James and Emma would have been aware of, and perhaps even involved in, a series of dramatic civil rights struggles. The Ku Klux Klan operated extensively through northern and western Alabama, and federal troops were during 1867–69 repeatedly dispatched to Summerfield to suppress the Klan's activities.[31] In 1867 the Centenary Institute gave permission to the local African American community to build a black church and school on the college's grounds, on condition that the community remain under the authority of the Methodist Episcopal Church, South. Presumably Emma and her family worshipped in the new church. However, white Methodist authorities became infuriated when they learned that these facilities were being used for meetings of the Loyal League, a northern-based organization that sought to safeguard African American political and civic rights, and insisted that no such meetings be held on church-controlled land.[32] The minutes of the board of trustees of the Centenary Institute for July 6, 1867, record: "Dr. Mitchell stated that the Trustees had authorized the negroes to build on the land belonging to the Board, for the purpose of a school and a church, but that it is now used for the accommodation of the Loyal Leaguers alone. The executive Committee were instructed to require that the terms be complied with, or the privilege of occupying the land be withdrawn."[33]

On the eve of the climactic 1876 national election that heralded the end of Reconstruction, the Union League, which like the Loyal League sought to secure the suffrage and related civil liberties for African Americans, attempted to hold a voter registration drive on church-owned land. The white church leaders prohibited the Union League from operating the church; this event, several elderly African Americans in the community recall, led to local blacks leaving the church and establishing an African Methodist Episcopal congregation nearby. (I do not know if James and Emma Sanders were among the early members of this new church, which later became known as Wayman Chapel AME, and which still operates today.)

It seems quite likely that in 1870, when they were residing next door to Bishop Andrew, James and Emma Sanders were working for their former master, as farm laborers for wages. In February 1871 Bishop Andrew had a major stroke in New Orleans, where he had gone on church business; he was transported to Mobile, Alabama, to the home of his daughter Octavia and his son-in-law Rev. J. W. Rush in the Franklin Street Parsonage. There he passed away on March 1, 1871. His widow, the invalid Emily, returned to Dallas County. She passed away less than a year later in the Selma home of her only son, Colonel Benjamin Woolsey, on January 24, 1872.

After the death of their former masters, it is likely that James and Emma found themselves in an increasingly precarious position. Nine years later, in the 1880 census, an Emma Sanders is listed as residing in Union Beat, the Dallas County precinct next to Summerfield. She is listed as thirty-five years old, that is to say, born around 1845, residing without a husband but with four children, Mary, age nine, Mark, age five, Ina, age four, and William, age two. This Emma is listed as born in Alabama, whereas "our" Emma was in fact born in Georgia, but this simply may be an error of the census enumerator; there is no other plausible Emma Sanders residing in Alabama during this time period, and no Emma Sanders is listed in the colored marriage records for the county during the 1870s.

In 1880 the family of this Emma Sanders (whom I strongly suspect was Miss Kitty's daughter) resided on the land of John Emerson, a local white planter, whose father, Henry Emerson, had been a prominent slaveowner in the area. If this is "our" Emma, her husband James Sanders must have died in the interim. On June 30, 1880, two weeks after the enumeration of the 1880 census in Union, Emma Sanders is listed as marrying an "Abe Neil"; the ceremony was performed by a Rev. Ward on the "Emmerson" [sic] plantation. After that, the records are less clear, although there does seem to be a report of her residing in 1920 in the city of Pine Bluff, Arkansas. (Emma's possible later life is discussed in Appendix 3, and her likely family relations are summarized in Figure 7.3.)

Russell Nathan Boyd

The life and legacies of Kitty's second son are easier to reconstruct. Rev. G. G. Smith's 1883 footnote about meeting Kitty's son, a "well dressed, intelligent colored man" from Georgia serving as a messenger at the U.S. Department of State in 1877, makes identification rather straightforward.

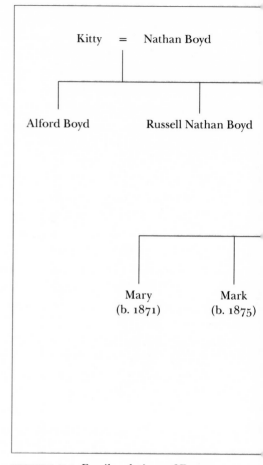

FIGURE 7.3. Family relations of Emma

Among the many African American men employed by the State Department in the late nineteenth century the only one born in Georgia was Russell Nathan Boyd (c.1844–1921). Boyd began his career at the State Department as a laborer in 1875, and was in time promoted to the status of assistant messenger and messenger. For decades he served as a librarian in the Department's library.

A positive identification is also suggested by the fact that Russell Nathan Boyd's passport application, filed in 1903, lists him as born in "Ocward, Georgia," presumably a clerk's mistaken transcription of "Oxford, Georgia." His middle name, "Nathan," suggests that he was named in part for his father, Nathan Boyd.

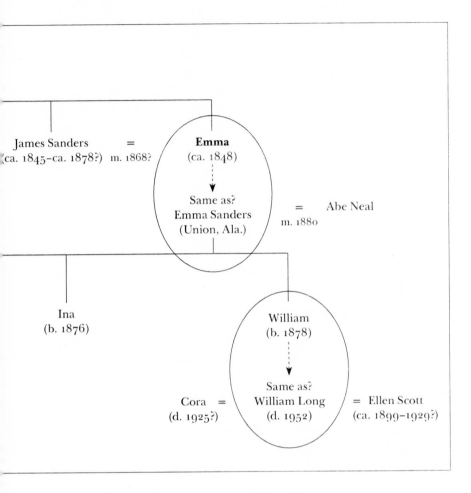

In any event, a **Russell Boyd** first appears in the Washington, D.C., city directory, listed as a servant (colored) living at 402 L St. North. This was, the same directory indicates, the home of Rear Admiral John A. Dahlgren, a prominent figure in the U.S. Navy, and his well-known wife, the socialite Madeleine Vinson Dahlgren.

How did **Russell Nathan** get from Summerfield, Alabama, to Washington, D.C.? How did he come to be employed by one of the most distinguished white couples in the nation's capital? Perhaps he accompanied his older brother **Alford**, who, as we shall see, attached himself to the Union Army near the end of the Civil War. Perhaps Russell Nathan made his way with Sherman's Army north to Washington, D.C., for the Grand

Review of the Armies during May 23–24, 1865, and decided to stay on in Washington.

There is no mention of Boyd in the District of Columbia city directory prior to 1869, so he may have been making his way slowly north or living in Freedman's Village, across the Potomac on the old grounds of the Robert E. Lee estate, where thousands of freedpeople resided during and after the Civil War. In the same year he is first listed in the city directory, on June 29, 1869, Russell Nathan Boyd made a bank deposit at Riggs and Company Bank in Washington, D.C., for $12.23, presumably banking his wages for work at the Dahlgrens.

Working for Admiral John Dahlgren, Russell Nathan would have been exposed to one of the most fascinating and controversial figures in the U.S. Navy. The ingenious designer of the "Dahlgren guns," which revolutionized naval warfare in the mid-nineteenth century, Dahlgren had many avid supporters in the U.S. Congress during the 1850s, as well as many enemies in the senior ranks of the navy. His career during the Civil War was mixed. He was seen as a hero by many in the North at the start of the war. Every other officer at the Washington Navy Yard, including the yard's commandant, was a southern sympathizer who abandoned their post to join the newly formed Confederate Navy. Dahlgren made his way to the White House to inform President Lincoln that Washington lay undefended, and was promptly appointed commander of the navy yard. He retained a close personal relationship with Lincoln, who throughout the war relied on his technological advice, often over that of high-ranking Navy Department officials.

Largely thanks to Lincoln's enthusiastic backing, Dahlgren headed up the South Atlantic blockade squadron and presided over the naval component of the long Union siege of Charleston, South Carolina. The campaign was marred by miscommunication and feuding between Union Army and Navy commanders. According to Dahlgren's critics his poor tactical judgments prolonged the length of the siege unnecessarily. Dahlgren's name was further impugned in some quarters by the rather murky "Dahlgren Raid," led by his son in the midst of the war. Colonel Ulric Dahlgren led a raid aimed at freeing Union prisoners of war held near Richmond, Virginia; after he was killed in action, it appears that Confederate agents placed seemingly incriminating documents on his corpse, suggesting that he was engaged in an assassination effort directed against Confederate President Jefferson Davis. This incident had long and painful ramifications; indeed, some historians assert that

John Wilkes Booth's assassination of Abraham Lincoln was conceived of as retaliation for the Dahlgren Raid. Finally, the failure of Dahlgren's guns against the Confederate ironclad warship the *Virginia* (the former *Merrimack*) cast a cloud over his reputation in some quarters.

Dahlgren had a famously rocky relationship with Secretary of the Navy Gideon Welles and with the navy high command, who resented his close relationship with President Lincoln. Welles's published wartime diaries contain a number of digs at Dahlgren, whom he implies was a technological specialist unsuited to decisive command; we know from Mrs. Dahlgren's letters that these attacks deeply wounded her husband. Immediately after the Union victory in 1865, Dahlgren expected a promotion but was instead assigned to the South Pacific squadron, a peripheral mission at best. He was forced to endure the further indignity of transporting his pregnant wife and family to Peru at his own expense, since the Navy Department refused to authorize their transport on navy vessels. In 1869, when Russell Nathan Boyd is first listed as working for the admiral, the Dahlgrens had just returned from South America and Admiral Dahlgren was resuming his old position at the navy yard, and the Dahlgrens were contemplating how to restore their status in Washington society.

How did Russell Nathan come to serve as a house servant for the admiral? The standard inference would be that Russell Nathan had served with Admiral Dahlgren at sea, since nineteenth-century flag officers tended only to trust servants who had served under them in the military. To date, however, I have found no records of Russell Nathan serving in the navy or receiving a military pension.

No mention of Boyd appears in the voluminous collection of Admiral Dahlgren's private and official papers at the Library of Congress. It is possible that Boyd had a prior connection with the admiral. When Dahlgren commanded the U.S. Navy's South Atlantic Blockade Squadron (1863–65), laying siege to Charleston, South Carolina, the squadron employed a great number of African Americans, including many fugitive slaves, generally known as "contraband." These were employed in all manner of service, as cooks and pilots, all the way up to the rank of petty officer, although they were not always formally enlisted. Admiral Dahlgren collaborated closely with General Sherman in the capture of Savannah, where many more newly liberated slaves joined the Union military. Perhaps Boyd somehow made his way from Summerfield, Alabama, to the South Carolina or Georgia coast, worked for the navy in some capacity, and came to Admiral Dahlgren's attention. Alternately, it is possible that after Russell Nathan had found his way to Washington after the Civil War, a prominent white person introduced him to the admiral and recommended him.

What can we surmise about Boyd's time with the Dahlgrens? Mrs. Sarah Madeleine Vinton Dahlgren, the daughter of a prominent congressman, was a novelist, as well as a famous and exacting hostess. In 1873 she published the authoritative book, *Etiquette of Social Life in Washington*. A contemporary newspaper records, "She was one of the leaders in the most exclusive society circles in the Capital. An invitation to her house was considered the greatest good fortune that could befall a person anxious to climb up socially."[34]

Since Mrs. Dahlgren threw elegant dinner parties for the Washington elite, Russell Nathan would have probably seen the leading figures in Washington society, including a number of cabinet secretaries. In March 1870 Madeleine's daughter by a previous marriage was married in Washington in an elaborate ceremony attended by the president, the chief justice, and the cabinet. It is likely that Boyd would have at least seen Secretary of State Hamilton Fish (in office 1868–77) at this and perhaps other functions. Five years later Secretary Fish would hire Russell Nathan at the Department of State.

Although she came from Ohio, Madeleine Dahlgren's sympathies rested largely with the white southern planter class. Her attitudes toward African American servants are suggested in her fiction. Her novel *Lights and Shadows of a Life* emphasizes the dangers of miscegenation. In her first novel, *A Washington Winter*, a depiction of Washington high society, black servants appear from time to time, invariably caricatured and speaking in dialect. At the home of the secretary of state, "an immense negro with a voice like a Corliss Engine comically mangles the names of the white visitors he introduces at a reception."[35]

At the same time, Madeleine Dahlgren, who had spent some time in the antebellum South, remained conscious of the great prestige attached to employing a black servant. It is intriguing that in describing her protagonists entering the house of the secretary of state the novelist embarks on a description of the figure of the "old Negro Servant":

> In the days now numbered with an effete past, of the old slave aristocracy, the negro, or as he was called, the *nigger boy*, was everywhere seen in his glory. . . . There is a rich raciness of manner, an

identification of himself with the grandeur of the family he serves, a disdain of all upstarts, an accurate measuring of true claims of social prestige, in the old negro family-servant, that is as indescribable as the vintage of certain fruity wines. Wherever he still lingers, the venerable head of snow-crowned wool and the mingling of deference with a kind of affectionate familiarity of manner, invariably marks the old retainer, who still clings to the family that his fathers before him served; and his presence in turn confers upon his master a surer patent of respectability than could be gained by any number of liveried English lackeys or French *garçons*.[36]

In keeping with this emphasis on the discernment of black family retainers, at the novel's conclusion, when the hero, an Italian nobleman, appears at last to propose to the woman he loves, the black servants of the house are duly impressed:

The family servants, with their wonted instinct, knew that *quality* was coming. Dinah declared that she "nowed it in dis old bones. De bootiful young misses to tote back, and go fixing up like mad! Po chile! De massa's to cum." . . . [The Chevalier] had an indefinable bearing which the old negro at once knew never belonged to "de po' white trash." So with many a smirk and courtesy they welcomed him, with the uniform, "De Lor' bress dis massa."[37]

Madeleine Dahlgren's attitudes toward African Americans in Washington, D.C., are also hinted at in an undated passage written in her hand, describing her African American laundress:

The colored laundress I brought from the country with me says, "They tell me some of the cull'd persons here is getting right up right smart and well to do, and some of 'em is Senecas. Can you tell me ole miss what that is? They say, they is Senecas. But the most of 'em I see is wusseraff than where I kin from. Caus' they both starve and freeze. Now when I was littler an a slave we live in a cabin—we could see daylight all thro' the cracks was so big—it was pleasant enuf in Summer time, but when cole we atter kim, mother she jess went out and threw direct in the chinks to fill em up—while Father he was work.[38]

Presumably, working for the Dahlgrens gave Russell Nathan intimate insights into the racial attitudes of the white Washington elite, building on all he had learned as a youth in Bishop Andrew's household. It would seem likely that these insights stood him in good stead over the subsequent half century of his career, serving this privileged class.

During the period that Boyd worked for him, Admiral John A. Dahlgren was largely preoccupied with rehabilitating his reputation as well as that of his late son, Ulric, who some still held indirectly responsible for inspiring John Wilkes Booth's killing of President Lincoln. Dahlgren also was occupied in defending himself against accusations that he had not prosecuted the campaign against Charleston with sufficient vigor or skill. During the siege of Charleston, his relationship with his army counterpart, General Gilmore, had rapidly deteriorated, and the struggle continued to be waged in the postwar public press and drawing rooms of the capital. We cannot know if the admiral confided any of these concerns in Russell Nathan Boyd, during a very trying period in his life, but Boyd must have been conscious of them.

In the midst of all these struggles, the admiral died unexpectedly at home on July 12, 1870, from what seems to have been a massive stroke. By this point the Dahlgrens were residing at 14th and L streets. In her memoir, Madeleine only states that a "servant" informed her that her husband had lost consciousness. It seems likely that it was in fact Russell Nathan who discovered his employer's dead body.

At this point, Madeleine Dahlgren was in severe financial straits, from which she only recovered after she successfully lobbied Congress to vote her husband a posthumous pension and as she began to publish her sentimental novels set in Washington high society. She must have quickly cut the household staff when her husband died, and Russell Nathan would have found himself out of work.

Boyd is not enumerated in the 1870 census for Washington, D.C., nor listed for that year in the District of Columbia City Directory. However, he did make at least one bank deposit at Riggs in 1870. He is next listed in the 1871 Washington City Directory, in which he is recorded as a waiter residing at 1525 H Street, NW, just about four blocks away from the Dahlgren residence. He clearly was not destitute during this period; on March 27, 1871, he withdrew from Riggs Bank in Washington $210 and then on the same day opened a Freedman's Bank account with a deposit of $225. (It may be entirely coincidental, but two months later on May 23, Russell Nathan's father, Nathan Boyd, also opened a Freedman's Bank account in Atlanta.) The 1874 city directory lists Russell Boyd as a waiter, now residing at 1210 E Street, NW.

When the Freedman's Bank failed catastrophically in June 1874, it is likely that Russell Nathan's savings, like those of thousands of other African Americans, were wiped out in the collapse.[39] He may have faced a difficult year, but on July 1, 1875, he was hired as a laborer at the Department of State by Secretary of State Hamilton Fish. The hiring coincided with the State Department's move into the new State, Navy, and War Building, and the reorganization of the State Department, which necessitated bringing in new service staff. Although the hiring was surely of momentous importance for Boyd, it does not appear to have made much of an impact on Secretary Fish himself. The only entry in Hamilton Fish's diary for that day is: "Chevalier de Tavera (the Austro-Hungarian ambassador) calls to take leave, as he expects to be absent for the summer."[40]

Two years later, in 1877, the meeting with Rev. G. G. Smith took place in the State Department. As we have seen, Smith describes the encounter in an evocative footnote:

In 1877 I went to Washington, and in company with Judge McCallister visited the Department of State. The Judge conversed for a moment with an intelligent, well-dressed colored man, who was the messenger. Calling to me he said, "Mr. Smith, here is a Georgian." Giving the young man my hand cordially, I said, "You are a Georgian?" "Yes, sir." "Where from?" "Oxford, sir." "Why, Oxford, my old home. Who was your master?" "Bishop Andrew." "Is it possible? You were one of his second wife's slaves?" "Oh, no, sir, I was Kitty's son." He spoke very lovingly of the Bishop and his care for him.[41]

The "Judge McCallister" who "discovered" Boyd as a Georgian must have been Samuel Ward McCallister, the famous self-appointed arbiter of New York high society who invented the idea of the "Four Hundred," the only four hundred people "worth knowing" in high society. (Legend has it that this number was based on the number of people who could be accommodated in Lady Astor's ballroom.) The term "Judge" was simply an honorific since McCallister never served on the bench, but he was a wealthy attorney from a prominent Savannah, Georgia, family, whom Rev. Smith would have long known. Secretary of State Hamilton Fish of New York was a friend and correspondent of McCallister; perhaps McCallister was paying Fish a visit or perhaps McCallister was visiting Fish's successor, the new Secretary of State William Evarts, who took office as the administration of President Benjamin Hayes assumed control, heralding the end of Reconstruction. Rev. Smith took a trip north during the summer of 1877, and McCallister must have volunteered to show him the sights.

We do not know if the meeting with Smith and McCallister had any lasting impact on Russell Nathan, but Smith's account does at least indicate that the young man (about thirty years old at this point) had the social intelligence to interact fluidly and confidently with prominent whites. We may also infer that he was conscious and proud of his lineage, which distinguished him from the other slaves of Bishop Andrew. To the question of whether he was one of the second wife's slaves he replied, "Oh, no, sir, I was Kitty's son." He pointedly did not use the word "slave" in his response.

During his decades at the State Department, Russell Nathan gradually ascended the social ladder within black Washington. From 1879 until 1883 he boarded with William Gwin, an African American man from Virginia who was the State Department's chief messenger from 1871 to 1901, at Gwin's house at 1110 18th Street in northwest Washington, D.C. Gwin was a substantial figure in the city's African American society; in 1881 he helped lead a breakaway group from the Metropolitan African American Episcopal Church to create Plymouth Congregational Church, where many of the city's African American elite worshipped. Through his connection with Gwin, Russell Nathan presumably came to know many prominent black families in the city.

These connections were extended when Russell Nathan was married, on October 3, 1883, to Tulip Victoria Cook, of the long-established Cook family of Washington. An African American newspaper published a charming account of their nuptials:

THE BOYD-COOK WEDDING

One of the most fashionable weddings of the season took place Wednesday evening at the 19th Street Baptist Church. Russell M. [sic] Boyd, of Georgia, and Miss Tulip Cook, of this city, were joined in the bonds of holy wedlock, the Rev. Walter H. Brooks, officiating.

The elite of Washington were out donned in the paraphernalia of fashion, and every available space in the beautiful church was occupied.

Promptly at 7:00 o'clock the bridal party entered preceded by the ushers, Mr. A. S. Jones of Tenn., H. H. Abrams, Va., George Cook, D.C., and George W. Jackson, Ind. while the grand old organ pealed forth Mendelssohn's "Wedding March."

The bride wore a beautiful white satin dress, that for artistic finish could not be surpassed; tuile over-dress en train. At her throat gleamed with sparkling brilliancy a gold pin studded with diamonds. Her beautiful veil that hung in graceful folds was caught back just enough to expose her beautiful face and form, a more lovely bride never was seen.

Miss Sadie Jones, bridesmaid, wore a beautiful grossgrain silk, French pointed lace and satin basque.

The happy groom wore the conventional black.

After the ceremony the bridal party were driven to the residence of the bride's parents, No. 1532 L st, where from 7:30 until 10 o'clock a brilliant reception was held. Time and space will not allow us to do justice to the feast we saw upon the swaying tables, the succulency of the viands or the rich sparkling wine. Nor can a graphic description do justice to the wealth of presents.

Among the distinguished guests we noticed Prof and Mrs. R. T. Greener, Mr. Jno. F Cook, Asst Secy Davis, Chief Clerk Breven and Mr. Hill of the State Dept., Mr. and Mrs. Leonidas A. Lewis, Miss Wilson, Mr. J. G. Hutchins, Mr. R. S. Smith of "New York Globe," Dr. and Mrs. Augusta, Mrs. and Mr. Spencer Murray, Mr. and Mrs. H. H. Smith, Rev. and Mrs. A. W. Upshaw.

G.W.J.[42]

The couple had one child, George Russell Boyd, born July 25, 1885, a year and a half after their wedding. George was presumably named for his mother's father, George Cook, and for his father Russell Nathan Boyd.

George's mother, Tulip Victoria, died at some point between 1885 and 1895. Russell Nathan Boyd remarried in 1895 to Cordelia Syphax, a member of the socially prominent Syphax family of Alexandria and Washington D.C., who traced their descent back to Martha Custis Washington. Among her siblings and cousins numbered some of the leading intellectuals and educators in the region's African American community.

In 1896 Russell Nathan Boyd applied successfully to become his son's legal guardian, so as to hold in trust for him a modest legacy of Tulip Victoria's share of a house at 1424 L Street, NW, the home of her parents George and Marcelina Cook; the legacy of $373.85 was transferred to George Russell Boyd when the young man reached twenty-one in July 1906.

In 1894, a year before his marriage to Cordelia Syphax, Russell Nathan was received into Fifteenth Street Presbyterian, arguably the

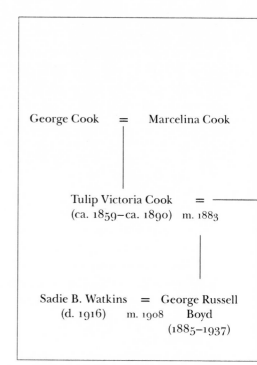

George Cook   =   Marcelina Cook

Tulip Victoria Cook   =   ———————
(ca. 1859–ca. 1890) m. 1883

Sadie B. Watkins = George Russell
(d. 1916)   m. 1908   Boyd
(1885–1937)

FIGURE 7.4. Family of
Russell Nathan Boyd, in
Washington, D.C.

most socially prominent African American church in the District. He
and Cordelia were married in Fifteenth Street Presbyterian by its famous pastor, Rev. Francis Grimke. (Ten years later, his wife Cordelia
was fully received into Fifteenth Street.) The couple had one child, a
daughter, Edna Syphax Boyd, born in January 1896, the year following
their marriage. (The family of Russell Nathan Boyd is summarized in
Figure 7.4.)

Like many African Americans in the civil service during the era, Russell Nathan's formal title and pay scale in the State Department did not
fully reflect his actual assignments. For many years, while he was assigned
to messenger duties, his official job listing was "laborer" (1875–93). He
then worked for many years as a librarian in the department, but he
was listed only as "Assistant Messenger" (1893–1915) and "Messenger"
(1915–21). The occasional lists of library staff in the State Department
records of the period make no mention of him. I surmise that Boyd was
informally seconded to the library for decades, but that he was never of-

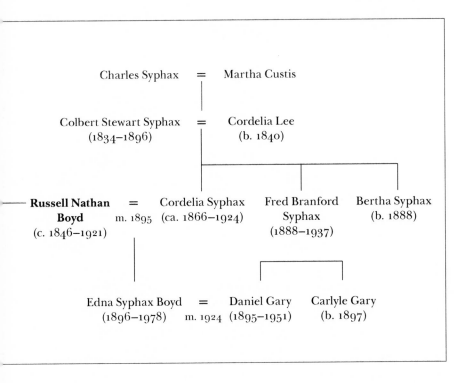

ficially hired within the library itself, which was officially known as the "Bureau of Rolls and Library."

What would Boyd's work experience have been like? The library itself was housed in one of the most splendid rooms of old Washington, the great four-story open atrium in the State, War, and Navy Building, a glorious Beaux Arts structure (now known as the Eisenhower Old Executive Office Building), which the Department of State occupied from 1875, the year Boyd was hired, until 1961. Open balconies looked down on the elegant floor of the library, covered in encaustic tile, a colorful Victorian imitation of Renaissance tiles. From 1877 until 1894 the Declaration of Independence was on display at the library, and it is possible that caring for the document may have been among Boyd's duties.

As noted above, for his first quarter century at the State Department, Boyd worked under William Gwin, an African American man, also a former slave, who served as chief messenger in the department. Boyd roomed with the Gwins starting in 1875, at their home at 1110 18th St.

NW in Washington, D.C., until Boyd married his first wife, Tulip Cook, in 1884. William Gwin's 1901 obituary notes

> He affixed the great seal of the United States to all important treaties and conventions negotiated over the last 30 years. . . . His death is deeply regretted by all officials of the department, who always implicitly trusted him with secrets of State.[13]

Perhaps the high point of Russell Nathan's career in the State Department came two years after the death of his friend and mentor William Gwin. This was the opportunity to travel to England in the fall of 1903, accompanying the U.S. delegation negotiating the demarcation of the Alaska boundary at the "London Tribunal." I suspect he was brought along by John Watson Foster, the Americans' general counsel for these negotiations, who had served as U.S. secretary of state from 1892 to 1893. The two men must have come to know one another while Foster ran the State Department, and it is possible that, as a trusted library staff member, Boyd was brought along on the expedition to safeguard the maps and charts consulted during the negotiations.

Boyd applied for a U.S. passport in August 1903. The only record of his transatlantic passage is the ship's manifest of the return voyage, indicating that he embarked for the United States from Southampton, England, on the S.S. *Philadelphia* on October 24 and arrived home on October 31. Also on the manifest was Otto Hilgard Tittman, then head of the Coast and Geodetic Survey. Tittman published an article on these negotiations in the *Proceedings of the American Philosophical Society* in 1903. A detailed travel diary by Dr. Tittman's wife Kate Tittman (1856–1938), chronicling in day-to-day detail the entire trip, is preserved in the George Washington University Library Special Collections. Like the article by her husband, the diary makes no mention of Russell Nathan Boyd or any person of color.[14] One surmises that Boyd was in the Tittmans' eyes socially invisible.

Yet if Russell Nathan Boyd was marginalized within white society and white-dominated institutions, in the world of the black church he was a highly respected figure. As a deacon at 15th Street Presbyterian, Russell Nathan would have worked closely with Rev. Francis Grimke, one of the most eloquent and visionary African American intellectuals of the period, who played an important role in the founding of the NAACP. Grimke routinely delivered brilliant, progressive sermons on the major issues of the day, including lynching, the evils of imperialism, and black self-betterment. He famously denounced World War I as a war designed not to make the world safe for democracy but rather to divide the world up between the white powers.[15]

Russell Nathan was also active in various African American fraternal organizations in the city, including the Banneker Relief Association, which provided relief to its members during illness and assisted with their burial fees. In 1902 the relief association held a charity ball at Convention Hall, attended by nearly four thousand people, to raise money for the "Day Nursery, the Sojourner Truth Home and the Home for Friendless Girls."[16] Like many black fraternal organizations, the association increasingly began to take on civil rights functions in the early twentieth century; in October 1906, for example, the Banneker Relief Association, "composed of 300 residents, asked President Roosevelt to stop screening of Thomas Dixon's play, the Clansman, at the Columbia Theater next week." The petition specifically pointed to the recent Atlanta race riots.[17]

At home, Russell Nathan would have been at the center of a circle of well-educated and ambitious family members. From 1908 until the early 1920s his brother-in-law and sister-in-law, Fred Syphax and Bertha Syphax, resided with Russell and Cordelia in their home at 1742 K Street, NW. Several years after Russell Nathan Boyd's death, Fred took up a teaching position at Tuskegee in Alabama. Many of his wife's brothers and cousins among the Syphax clan were federal employees, working as messengers and clerks in various cabinet departments and teachers and administrators in the city's school system.

Russell Nathan continued to work in the State Department library up until his final illness. After an operation and twelve days of hospitalization he passed away on February 1, 1921, at Freedman's Hospital. His last will and testament offers some insights into the enduring challenges of his blended family. He specified that the plates belonging to his first wife, Tulip Victoria, should go to her son George Russell. He willed the rest of his estate to his wife Cordelia for her natural life. The estate was then to be divided as follows: two-thirds to his daughter Edna and one-third to George Russell Boyd. He may have been expressing gratitude to Edna for staying at home to care for her aging parents, or he may have been expressing disappointment in George Russell, a manual laborer, for not entering a profession. Alternately, he may simply have been following the common practice of bequeathing more to an unmarried daughter than to a son.

So far as can be determined, the two children of Russell Nathan Boyd, George Russell Boyd (1885–1937) and Edna Syphax Boyd Gary (1895–1978), died without issue. George Russell worked for most of his life as a janitor; Edna was an elementary schoolteacher in the Washington, D.C., public school system. Their lives are reviewed in Appendix 4.

Rev. Alford Boyd and His Posterity

In contrast to Emma and Russell Nathan, Kitty's eldest son Alfred (or Alford) Boyd founded a line that continues to this day. Alfred Boyd first appears by name in the historical record in April 4, 1866, when he married Mrs. Malvina Banks in the town of Keosauqua in Van Buren County, Iowa, where he and Malvina would continue to reside for several years.

How did Alfred get from Summerfield, where he appears to have been a slave through most of the Civil War, to southeastern Iowa? A clue is provided by Alfred's descendants (who insist that his name was "Alford," not Alfred). His great-great-granddaughters, Darcel and Cynthia, recall learning from their grandmother Bertha Caldwell, Alford's granddaughter, that he had been a cook attached to the Union Army. To his great regret, he explained, he had never enlisted although he had been offered the chance to do so. In later years, he would often mention this as a "life lesson," that one should always seize an opportunity when offered.

This family story is consistent with the historical record. In early 1865 the Union command conceived of a major cavalry operation through Alabama and Georgia, striking at the Confederacy's manufacturing and transport capacity. Led by Brigadier General James H. Wilson, the operation became known as "Wilson's Raid." Its most important target was Selma, Alabama, which contained railroad yards and repair shops, military stores and factories, a naval foundry and an arsenal. Wilson was opposed by Confederate General Nathan Bedford Forrest, who would long be associated in African American memory with the Fort Pillow massacre of African American Union soldiers and with serving as the first Grand Wizard of the Ku Klux Klan after the war. Wilson overwhelmed Forrest's forces in the Battle of Selma on April 2 and occupied the city.

My best guess is that Alford joined up with Union forces two days after the battle of Selma on April 4. The Third Iowa Cavalry was dispatched north of Selma to Summerfield to locate Chalmers's confederate forces; they then circled back to Selma. As it happens, the Third Iowa's Company G had been mustered in Van Buren County, Iowa; many of its

members came from Keosauqua, where Alford would settle. I thus surmise that Alford, then about twenty years old, must have joined up with
Company G as a cook at this point, and remained with his new comrades
when they returned north to Keosauqua, Iowa, after the war's end.

The family's recollection that Alford missed a chance to enlist makes
sense. On April 7 at General Wilson's order, a final regiment of the
United States Colored Troops, the 137th United States Colored Infantry,
was organized by Major Martin R. Arches in Selma. Initially consisting of
five hundred black men, the regiment grew to fourteen hundred men by
the conclusion of the war. This presumably was the regiment that Alford
failed to enlist in. I assume that he accompanied the Third Iowa in his
new position as cook when they departed Selma on April 12, heading
toward Montgomery.[48]

Before leaving Selma, General Wilson ordered all black women and
children to be turned back from his military columns. It is possible
that Alford's sister Emma, then about sixteen years old, had tried to
leave Summerfield with Alford, but that she was prevented from leaving
Selma. As we have seen, by 1870 she was once again living in Summerfield. I do not know if Alford's younger brother, Russell Nathan, then
about eighteen years old, also left Summerfield with the Third Iowa or if
he came north to Washington, D.C., at a later date.

Among his new Iowa comrades in the regiment, Alford would have
encountered many white men deeply sympathetic to African Americans.
Many Iowa volunteers had been committed abolitionists before the war,
and many of them wrote home of how deeply shocked they had been,
seeing directly the conditions of enslaved people encountered during
the war. These attitudes are represented by a letter penned by a member
of Company G, the unit to which Alford was evidently attached. Private
Jacob R. Peterson wrote to his wife, Tryphena, on July 22, 1865, describing a visit to Stone Mountain. He notes,

> You want to know what (letter torn) . . . Well you know that I am an
> abolitionist and now I go in for giving their rights and that they will
> never have until they are allowed all the privileges of a freeman and
> surely they are capable of voting as those copperheads that have
> been traitors to their country while they have been as loyal as any
> body they knew enough to be right in this case and I think they will
> know enough to vote right at least I had rather trust to them than
> their former masters and if my vote can give them a vote they will

get it and they will get it in the course of time as they are bound to win in the end.[49]

The regiment spent much of the summer of 1865 stationed on picket duty in Atlanta. On August 9 the Third Iowa was formally mustered out of service and began the long trip home by rail. On August 20 the *Keosauqua Republican* reported that the men of the Third Iowa Cavalry had returned home earlier in the week. Alford presumably rode on the train with his new friends and settled into their hometown.

In Keosauqua Alford would have encountered a small but thriving African American community that was welcomed, or at least tolerated, by the majority white populace. The town, just north of the border with Missouri, had been an important stop on the Underground Railroad prior to the Civil War. Escaped slaves making their way along the Missouri River at times took the river to its northernmost bend and then headed due north across open territory toward Iowa, a free state. Keosauqua was the first free town they would have encountered on this route. While many escaped slaves continued across southeastern Iowa into Illinois and toward Canada, many decided to stay in Keosauqua, a pleasant town nestled in the "big bend" of the Des Moines River.

Among the so-called contraband (as escaped slaves were termed) were Alford's wife Malvina and her siblings; originally from Kentucky, they had escaped from slavery during the Civil War from the slaveholding part of Missouri. They were discovered hiding in a barn by sympathetic Union soldiers, who help them reach Quaker conductors on the Underground Railroad, who in turn escorted them into Keosauqua. There, they may have initially been sheltered in the Pearson home, which has been preserved to this day as an Underground Railroad museum. Malvina, who was previously married, came into the marriage with Alford with two daughters (or perhaps nieces), Millie Banks, born around 1863, and Sarah Banks, born around 1858.

In 1867 Alford is mentioned in the *Recorder*, the national organ of the African Methodist Episcopal (AME) Church, as having donated the sizable sum of $1.25 to the church in Keosauqua, Iowa. Within two decades he would be listed as a pastor in the AME.

Why would Alford, raised within the Methodist Episcopal Church, South, have joined the AME?[50] He might have been exposed to the church's teachings while attached to the Union Army, since AME was the only chaplaincy service authorized for African Americans within the

U.S. military. He presumably was inspired by the church's emphasis on liberation, discipline, and social justice. In this regard, he would seem to have had inclinations similar to his younger brother Russell Nathan in Washington, D.C., who was to find his spiritual home in a church led by the militant theologian and activist Rev. Francis Grimke.

Alford and Malvina's first child, born in 1867, was named Mary Catherine; her second name was presumably in memory of Alford's mother Catherine Boyd (Kitty).[51] She was followed by Russell (b. ca. 1869), Barbara (b. ca. 1871), Nathan (b. ca. 1873), Morris or Maurice (b. ca. 1875), and Shorter (b. ca. 1879).

In post–Civil War Iowa, the Boyds would have found a reasonably tolerant atmosphere. Iowa in 1868 eliminated its infamous "black codes," excised the term "free whites" from its Constitution, and legally enfranchised its black male adults, among the first northern states to do so. Incidents of antiblack violence in the state seem to have been rare, in striking contrast to the terrors increasingly inflicted on African Americans in the South, especially after federal military occupation of the region ended following the 1876 presidential election of Rutherford Hayes.

In 1884 Alford was appointed pastor for the AME congregations in Newton and Marshalltown, Iowa. This appears to have been his first ministerial appointment. For the next four decades he was relocated by the church's General Conference, usually every year or two, among parishes in eastern Iowa and western Illinois. From time to time brief reports appear from him in AME publications. For instance, the February 1889 *Christian Recorder* contains this report from A. Boyd in Moline, Illinois: "Church spiritually and financially in a fair condition, and the outlook for the future bright." Appointments followed in Washington, Iowa; Muscatine, Iowa (1895); Burlington, Iowa (1897); Ottumwa, Iowa (1900–1901); Cedar Rapids, Iowa (1902–3); Oskaloosa, Iowa (1905); Clinton, Iowa (1906); Rockford, Illinois (1908–12); Moline, Illinois (1913–15), and Rock Island, Illinois (1916).

Occasionally, local newspapers would comment favorably on his sermons: The *Cedar Rapids Evening Gazette,* for instance, reported, "St. Paul District of the Iowa Annual Conference of the AME convened. The annual sermon was preached by Rev. Alfred Boyd, a commendable effort from the subject, 'For it pleased the Father that in Him should all fullness dwell.' First Corinthians first chapter nineteenth verse."[52] Like his fellow African American pastors in the region, Alford was deeply concerned with the state of the race during this tumultuous period, as lynchings and other crimes against persons of color reached unparalleled ferocity. A local paper reports in 1902: "Previous Thursday: Rev Boyd in Cedar Rapids one of the judges of a youth debate, 'The Epigram of the Negro from the South to the Western Territories and some portions of the North—Were they could be more protected.'"[53] He also presided regularly over gospel temperance meetings.

Although nowhere near as incendiary as southern newspapers of the period, the Iowa papers did at times engage in racial stereotyping at Rev. Boyd's expense. For instance, in 1906 the *Sioux County Herald* carried the following dispatch: "Trusting the public in general to overcome temptation, Rev. A Boyd, a colored minister in Clinton, left the door of his chicken coop unlocked, and in the morning when he visited the coop all his chickens had mysteriously disappeared."[54]

After the early death of their eldest child Catherine, Alford and Malvina raised Catherine's daughter, Bertha. Bertha was extremely close to them, and was careful, her granddaughters Cynthia and Darcel explain, to pass on to them as much family lore as she could. These women, the great-great-granddaughters of Rev. Alford and Malvina Boyd, were familiar with the fact that Rev. Boyd had been born in Georgia in slavery and that he had been attached to the Union Army. They were unfamiliar with the story of Miss Kitty and Bishop Andrew until I contacted them and their parents in summer 2009. When I met the Rev. Boyd's great-great-granddaughters they shared a surviving photograph of Rev. Alford and Malvina Boyd, which shows he was a distinguished and handsome man, with ramrod straight posture.

Rev. Boyd and Malvina spent their final years in Aurora, Illinois, living close to their son Nathan Boyd, a successful businessman. Alford was in an automobile accident in the mid-1920s; he eventually died of these injuries in May 1926. Malvina passed away four years later, in August 1930. Alford and Malvina were buried together in an Aurora cemetery, near the final resting place of their son Maurice. No markers for them survive in the cemetery. (The family of Alford and Malvina is shown in Figure 7.5.)

Bertha, Alford and Malvina's granddaughter, married and settled in Rockford, Illinois, where Alford had pastored for a number of years. Her sons and grandchildren grew up there. Her son Lee Caldwell continued to live in the city; he worked in the city's water department and remained a proud member of Allen Chapel AME church, the institution that Alford pastored, until his death in November 2010. I attended the very moving "homegoing" service held for him at Allen Chapel, and had the honor of speaking about him and his remarkable family history, which spans seven generations of Methodism. His adult daughters, Darcel and Cynthia, now reside in a metropolitan area on the East Coast and are upper-middle-class professionals. Cynthia, the younger daughter, is married with two young adult sons. These two men are the great-great-great-great-grandsons of Catherine "Miss Kitty" and Nathan Boyd.

Cultural Capital and the Legacies of Slavery

What lessons about the long-term legacies of slavery in general, and Miss Kitty's unusual predicament in particular, may be inferred from these intertwined family narratives? First of all, it is striking that the relative degree of privilege extended to Miss Kitty during her life in slavery by her owner Bishop Andrew only partly translated into increased opportunities for her children postemancipation. The two male children, Alford and Russell Nathan, somehow acquired literacy, presumably either from their mother or from members of the Bishop's household. This capacity clearly opened up life chances for them that seem to have been closed to Emma, who evidently never learned to read or write. More intangibly, growing up in the Andrew household may have provided the two young men with a degree of cultural capital that would aid them in navigating white-dominated worlds. Gender was a clearly determinant variable: whatever social skills Emma may have acquired in the Bishop's household did not ultimately protect her and her family from rural poverty, especially after the end of Reconstruction.

Russell Nathan Boyd's story recalls a common pattern; a relatively privileged background under slavery translates into employment within a white-dominated patron-client network. In certain respects, he seems of the three children to have most closely reproduced his mother's predicament, dependent on the whims of powerful whites. He was afforded glimpses of white centers of national and international power and privilege, without ever being fully welcomed into these precincts. As in many other instances, this pattern does not necessarily confer benefits to the subsequent generations. All of his father's social connections did not seem to provide much help to George; lacking higher education, George never seems to have progressed beyond manual and service jobs. His half-sister Edna's career as a teacher, in contrast, depended on her pursuing postsecondary education, which was to prove more pivotal than patronage per se for African Americans across the twentieth century.

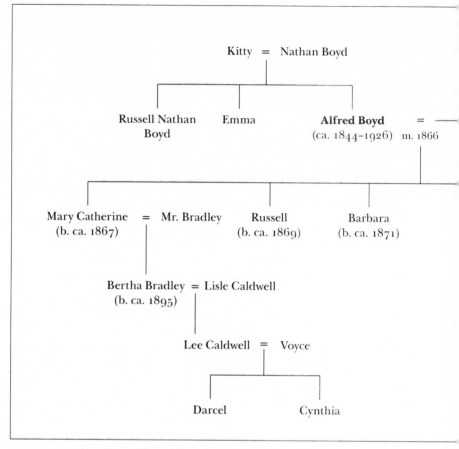

FIGURE 7.5. Family of Alford (Alfred) Boyd in Iowa

In contrast to his brother Russell Nathan, Alford opted for a career path that insulated him from the whims of powerful whites. As a pastor within the African Methodist Episcopal Church, he was responsible to an entirely black leadership. Thus, even though he resided for much of his life within a state that had only a 2 or 3 percent black population, he was significantly buffered from the indignities of white domination.

It is hard to know what psychological impact childhood experiences of enslavement had on the three children. Did Bishop Andrew continue to serve as a powerful father figure in their psyches? Did the two male children deeply identify with the Bishop, as they pursued positions of leadership within their respective faith traditions? Was their considerable personal dignity and their allegiance to autonomous African American

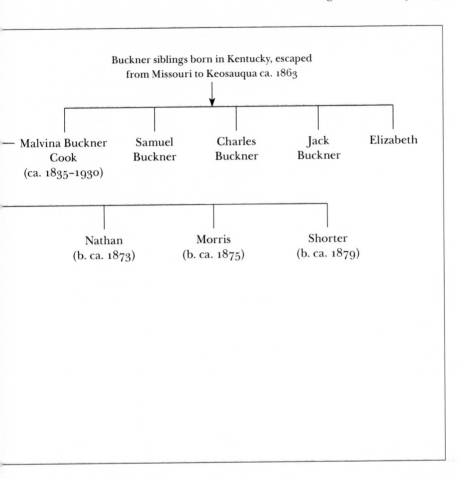

fraternal and religious organizations in any respects a reaction against the indignities of having been dependent on a powerful white man in their youth?

Finally, how much of a sense of family solidarity was engendered through their challenging and rather unusual family background? As of this writing, I know of no evidence that the three children of Catherine and Nathan Boyd were ever in touch with one another, or with their father Nathan, after emancipation. I have not found advertisements placed by any of them in African American newspapers seeking lost family members. It is perfectly possible, of course, that they were in correspondence with one another, and perhaps even visited one another, but if so, no traces of these contacts have survived.

It is not clear if any stories of Miss Kitty were ever passed down through the generations. As is well known, many African Americans born in slavery were reluctant to discuss the nature of slavery with children and grandchildren. In the case of Rev. Alford Boyd, his descendants knew a great deal of family history tracing back to 1865, beginning with his experience as a cook attached to the Union Army. Until I contacted them in July 2009, they knew no family history prior to that, and had not heard of Bishop Andrew or of Kitty.

However, Kitty's great-great-great-granddaughters have embraced this deeper family history and have developed a profound sense of kinship with Catherine/Kitty and Nathan Boyd and with all their descendants. The story outlined in this book now belongs, in large measure, to them and their family. It has been deeply fulfilling for me as a scholar to give, in effect, this gift of historical knowledge to Miss Kitty's descendants, and to collaborate with them as we seek to extend our understanding of the details and significance of this remarkable "developing story."

Chapter Eight

"Out of the Shadows"

The Andrew Family Slaves

MY INSPIRATION for this chapter and its title is an admonition to me from community historian Emogene Williams as we sat in her kitchen in late July 2009, as I excitedly reported to her on my successful quest to locate the living descendants of Miss Kitty's eldest son Alford Boyd: "I'm so pleased you've worked so hard on the story of Miss Kitty and have been led to her children. But just as important is the story of all those other slaves of Bishop Andrew, the ones no one ever talks about. Nobody ever built a house for them, or built a stone monument to them. Isn't it high time we bring them out of the shadows?"

Having explored the lives and legacies of Miss Kitty/Catherine Andrew Boyd and her children, let us thus turn to the wider circle of enslaved persons connected, in one way or another, to Bishop Andrew. Such a consideration is vital if we are to revisit the powerful tendency in white antebellum and postbellum representations to focus only on the image of the mammy and loyal slave, and if we are to dispel the taken-for-granted assumption in many white-authored representations that the enslaved are important only inasmuch as they relate to white elite history.

Most published accounts assert that Bishop Andrew's connection to slavery, the proximate source of the great controversy at the 1844 Methodist Conference in New York City, came about either through his "unwilling" ownership of Kitty or through his marriage to his second wife. The historical picture is considerably more complicated. Evidence tells us that at least forty-two enslaved persons, probably more, were in the possession of Bishop Andrew at one point or another during the course of his lifetime. Only about half of these persons were directly associated with Ann Leonora Mounger Greenwood (ca. 1802–54), his second wife. From wills, deeds, memoirs, and other documents, we can determine the names of about thirty-four of this total group of slaves. In many cases we can determine their likely sources through bequests, marriages, and gifts. In some instances we can determine, or make reasonable inferences about, their identities and fates after emancipation.

My best estimate of these enslaved persons is as follows. They are listed in the apparent chronological order that James Osgood Andrew acquired them from about 1830 onward:

Jacob and an unidentified female slave, both owned as early as 1830, possibly inherited from James Osgood Andrew's father John Andrew.

Kitty, and her three children, Alfred (or "Alford"), Russell Nathan, and Emma. (As we have seen, Bishop Andrew claims to have acquired Kitty in a bequest from one of his former Augusta congregants at some point between 1832 and 36, although no such will exists.)

In 1840, through the will of Catherine McFarlane of Charleston, South Carolina, the mother of the Bishop's first wife Ann Amelia McFarlane: the slaves Billy and Lucy, the latter held in trust for the Bishop's nephew Alexander McFarlane Wynn.

Ben, given in 1843 by James Andrew's mother Mary Andrew to her sons and grandchildren.

In 1844, by marrying his second wife, Ann Leonora Mounger Greenwood, Bishop Andrew acquired at least fourteen other slaves, most or all of whom were inherited from her late husband Thomas Greenwood of Greene County, Georgia. Their names were "Nick, George, Tom, Orlando, Elleck, Edward, Addison, James, Jefferson, Peggy, Susan, Lillah and her two children Laura and Allen." Two other Greenwood slaves residing in the Andrew household during this period were named "Orange" and "Nancy."

In 1855, by marrying his third wife, Emily Sims Woolsey Heard Childers, in Dallas County, Alabama, Bishop Andrew acquired another "parcel" of slaves, numbering at least twelve. Among these were "Loy, Rose, Sal, Martin, Hasly, Nancy, Selvy, Eliza, Jim, William, Wilson, and Louise."

At least nine children were born to enslaved women who were the Bishop's property. These include the three children of Miss Kitty; three other slaves, five years old and under—postdating his 1844 marriage to his second wife, enumerated in the 1850 census; and three mulatto children, five years old and under—postdating his marriage to his third wife, enumerated in the 1860 census. There may, of course, have been other slaves who are not referenced in the documentary record.

In this chapter, I attempt to reconstruct the lives and legal trajectories of all these enslaved person, with the exception of Kitty and her children, whom we have already considered.

The John and Mary Andrew Slaves

At the outset, it is important to emphasize that James Osgood Andrew, his three wives, and other close kin had all grown up in contexts in which owning African American slaves appeared normal and desirable. The Bishop's grandfather, James Andrew; his paternal uncle, Benjamin Andrew; and his father, John Andrew, were all slaveowners.[1] Family oral history holds that the Bishop's grandfather and great-uncle were slaveholders in Dorchester in the Massachusetts Bay Colony before coming south to South Carolina and Georgia, where they continued to own slaves. Bishop Andrew's father, John Andrew, a farmer, Methodist minister, and schoolteacher, seems to have acquired and lost slaves throughout his life. The Bishop's biographer Rev. George G. Smith notes that after John Andrew returned home to Liberty County, Georgia, from military service in the Revolutionary War, "He found his slaves gone and his property much injured."[2] Some years later, John Andrew received at his wedding to his third wife, Mary Overton Cosby (the future mother of James Osgood), some slaves as dowry from his bride's parents. G. G. Smith writes that James Osgood's father-in-law, the father of Mary Cosby Andrew, "evidently gave his wife some negroes and though John Andrew on principle was opposed to slavery, he received them, and mentions with sorrow that he had to punish one by whipping. He thought, however, the demand of the church for emancipation or expulsion was unwise."[3]

Smith further notes that in 1794, when his son James Osgood Andrew was born, John Andrew was in reduced circumstances, but "evidently owned a home and a few slaves." An unsuccessful businessman, John Andrew seems to have lost nearly as many slaves as he acquired. Georgia Court records indicate that on several occasions his slaves were sold by the court in order to settle his debts. For example, in 1799 the Wilkes County, Georgia, Inferior Court issued a writ against John Andrew, on behalf of a Thomas Fontaine, allowing him to claim as a levy "the following negroes as property of said Andrew, viz.: Bob, Bess, July, Moses, Bob,

Joe & Davy." These seven slaves were advertised and sold at the Wilkes County courthouse for $725.[1] In 1812 the Elbert County, Georgia, sheriff seized the following slaves of John Andrew: "Maria, a woman named Tamer and her 5 children, Nelson, Milsy, Synthia, Jefferson & Louisa, a woman named Bess and her three children, Evelina, Sam, and Eady, a woman named Cloe and her 3 children, Milinda, Madison, and Billey and 3 other women named Silvia, Milly and Tenor." These eighteen slaves were sold to Thomas B. Scott of Putnam County, the highest bidder, for $3,792.

James Osgood Andrew must have grown up knowing these enslaved persons, as they moved in and out of his father's household. From an early age, he was clearly socialized into the dominant southern white sensibility that slaveowning was the preeminent sign of respectability and social prestige and that rights of ownership over enslaved people were to be assertively pursued and defended.

John Andrew died in March 1830; no probate records survive of his estate, so it is not certain that he willed slaves to his wife and children, although this seems likely. James Osgood Andrew's tax records through the 1820s as late as 1829 indicate no ownership of slaves. However, the 1830 census for Athens, Clarke County, Georgia, indicates that James O. Andrew owned two slaves: one male slave, between ten and twenty-four years old (born 1806–20), and one female slave, between thirty-six and fifty-five years old (born 1775–94).[5] Given that his father John Andrew had just died, it seems likely that James inherited these two slaves from him.

I have not been able to determine the identity or the fate of the female slave owned by James Andrew in the 1830 census. Ten years later, the 1840 census records only one female slave, aged between twenty-four and thirty-six (born 1804–16) in the John Andrew household; this woman presumably was Kitty, even though she was born around 1822. Of the older enslaved woman enumerated in 1830 as born between 1775 and 1794, there is no trace. Presumably, she died or was sold before 1840.

The male slave in the 1830 census was evidently "Jacob," whom James Osgood Andrew mentions in an 1853 *Southern Christian Advocate* series recounting his travels two decades earlier. Jacob, he reports, traveled with him to Florida on horseback for his health in the autumn of 1833. "In October, I left home, in company of Jacob, a little negro boy who lived with me, and whose health had been for some time poor. He was thought to be consumptive, and as I hoped that a horseback ride through that mild climate might be of service to his health, I purchased a horse, rigged him out and took him along with me."[6] The only other mention of Jacob is a passing reference in Rev. Smith's biography: "Jacob and herself [Kitty] were the only slaves Bishop Andrew ever really owned."[7]

It appears likely that Jacob died during or soon after this trip. The 1834, 1835, and 1836 tax digests for Clarke County indicate that Bishop Andrew owned no slaves in those years. So Jacob probably passed away between the fall of 1833 and the summer of 1834, when the tax rolls were recorded. The 1840 census for Bishop Andrew's household in Covington, Georgia, lists only one male slave, aged between ten and twenty-four (born 1816–30); this was probably Billy, discussed below, inherited earlier that year by the Bishop's first wife, Ann Amelia, from her mother, Catherine Stattler McFarlane.

The 1830 census in Clarke County also indicates that John Andrew's widow, Mary Andrew, owned two slaves, presumably inherited from her late husband John, who had passed away a few months earlier. In 1840 Mary Andrew was living next door to her son Bishop Andrew near Covington, the seat of Newton County, a few months before the Bishop moved a mile or so north to Oxford. At this point she owned nine slaves, seven more slaves than she had owned in 1830. Presumably, she had purchased these in the interim or they had come to her through probate judgments associated with her late husband's estate or through children born to her female slaves.

At least one of the slaves belonging to Mary Andrew came into Bishop Andrew's partial possession. In June 1843, three years before her death, Mary Andrew gave her slave "Ben" to her three sons, Hardy H. Andrew, James O. Andrew, and William Andrew, specifying that James and William should act as trustees.

In the 1850 census, William Andrew is listed as residing in James Andrew's household in Oxford. Hardy Andrew, who resided near his brothers in Oxford, died in May 1854. So Ben must have been in Bishop Andrew's possession for some of this time. At some point, the Bishop may have transferred Ben (who, the deed had specified, was partially for the use of Mary Andrew's grandchildren) to the household of his daughter Henrietta and her husband Thomas Meriwether at Mount Airy, about three miles from Oxford. In November 1864 Bishop Andrew's granddaughter Annie reports in a letter to Bishop Andrew that the slave Ben, "Mary Ann's child," escaped from the Meriwether household and joined the columns of General Sherman's troops as they marched through Georgia. Annie further reports that Ben did not want to flee, but that "Old Catherine," who seems to have been the eldest slave on the farm, "made him go."

The Bishop's mother Mary Andrew died in 1846, in Oxford, Georgia; no probate records of her estate have survived, so it is not clear how her slaves, apparently at least eight in number, were disposed of. It is possible that Bishop Andrew acquired one or more of them at some point and that others were distributed to Mary Andrew's other children and grandchildren.

Slavery and the McFarlane Family

In marrying his first wife, Ann Amelia McFarlane of Charleston, in May 1816 James Osgood Andrew became connected to another family long linked to slavery. Through the McFarlanes, at least two slaves, perhaps more, would in time come into Bishop Andrew's possession. As noted in Appendix 3, it is even possible that Miss Kitty herself came from the McFarlane family. We should thus explore the McFarlanes' involvement with the peculiar institution in some detail.

Ann Amelia's father, Rev. Alexander McFarlane (ca. 1773–1803), was an enigmatic figure. A Methodist minister, sea captain, and merchant, he appears to have been directly involved in the Atlantic slave trade. Originally from Manchester, England, McFarlane lived for a time in Nova Scotia before coming to Charleston, South Carolina. (Since many Tory sympathizers, black and white, as well as slaves had been relocated from Charleston to Nova Scotia at the end of the American war of independence, it is not all that surprising that McFarlane would have found his way from Nova Scotia to Charleston.) McFarlane served as a Methodist pastor in Charleston in the 1790s, responsible, it is said, for the "colored congregations," a responsibility in Charleston that his future son-in-law, James Osgood Andrew, would assume two decades later.

On at least two occasions, Rev. McFarlane was involved on behalf of Methodist organizations in helping enslaved women purchase their freedom. In May 1799 William Payne (his sometime business partner and creditor) sold a woman known as "Dolly Watters" to McFarlane, with the understanding that she would be able to obtain her freedom by repaying the Methodist Society the price of her purchase. Similarly, in June 1801 McFarlane purchased a woman known as "Fanny" from John McKee, and then arranged for her transfer to a black man named "Quamino" on behalf of an organization known as the "Black Methodist Society."[8]

References to slaves appear from time to time in the McFarlane family documents. A letter in March 1797 to Alexander McFarlane from his wife Catherine concludes with the postscript, "Dolly says I must remember her to her dear Master and her dear old Master." Since at the time Alexander was visiting his father James McFarlane in Manchester, England, it would appear that Dolly had initially been owned by James, and then passed on to his son, Alexander.[9]

In July 1801 Alexander McFarlane's business difficulties increased and he seemed eager to raise capital, quite possibly for an upcoming slave trading expedition. He sold two slaves, Dolly and Ben, to his mother-in-law, Eve Catherine McNeal. (This Dolly presumably was a different person than the "Dolly Watters" who was promised her freedom in 1799.)[10]

McFarlane was naturalized as an American citizen on February 8, 1798. He died on December 11, 1803, at age thirty, after a long tropical illness, in Rio Pongo, in Sierra Leone, West Africa. In *Family Album*, a genealogical book published in 1943, author Thomas McAlpin Stubbs (a descendant of the Mood family, collateral relatives of James Osgood Andrew's first wife, Ann Amelia McFarlane) is at pains to insist that Alexander McFarlane, as a devout Methodist, could not possibly have been involved in the slave trade while in Rio Pongo, at the time one of the most important embarkation points in the transatlantic slave trade.[11] The documentary record, however, indicates otherwise.

In 1801 disaster struck the firm McFarlane and Player, in which Alexander McFarlane was half owner. A fire swept through the company stores, destroying their valuable stock of sugar and other commodities. Around this time, the partners become embroiled in a set of complicated legal proceedings as numerous creditors sought to recover money that the firm owed to them. The ensuing bankruptcy case landed McFarlane and his partner, Joshua Player, in Federal District Court in 1802.

The year following the fire, the record indicates that Alexander McFarlane participated in a slave trade voyage. An extraordinary eyewitness account of the slave trade, written by him but probably published without his knowledge, appears in the *American Mercury*:

Rio Pongos, April 18, 1802
On Sunday last we were at Siera Leon, ready for sea, intending to proceed to Rio Pongos; a little before day light, Capt. Northrop,

the master of the vessel, awaked me with the information that they were firing ashore. As soon as the day dawned we discovered seven negroes swimming off to a sloop (who proved to be crew men, a set of industrious people, employed by the captains of ships to trade for them, from Siera Leon, to Cape Mount) lying about 100 yards from us. We thought it a false alarm, as with our glasses we could only perceive the settlers firing and no opponents. On our going ashore we saw a scene shocking indeed to humanity—22 miserable wretches cut and mangled in the most dreadful manner; several with their faces hewed to pieces, limbs cut and bodies lacerated cruelly.

After suffering them to lie 6 hours in the sun, they tied cords to their feet and dragged them to the sea side, where they had piled them upon the wharf, they offered them to us for half price. When we turned with horror for the scene, and went into the board; they threw them into the sea, as we got under way, the tide ebbing, had carried them along side, and all the sea-men on board saw the dismal spectacle—human beings floating about, a prey for sharks.

The account is prefaced by an editorial commentary:

We have often met with accounts of the cruel, and inhuman means made use of to get possession of the wretched Africans, and of the barbarity exercised towards them obtained—The flowing account which is given in a letter from a gentlemen in Barbados to his friend in this city, we think, for depravity and cruelty there has seldom been its equal. This letter after mentioning the arrival Barbados on the 21st ult. of the English brig *Byam*, with 200 slaves, says:

You can have no idea of the cruelty and barbarity made use of by the whites to get possession of these poor wretches; perhaps you may form some idea of it from inclosed letter, which the Capt. of the Byam gave me on his arrival. It seems that the infamous transaction mentioned in this letter, happened on a market day, when they were induced by the white inhabitants to bring their produce to market, and were then treated in the manner described.

Rio Pongo was at the time one of the most significant sites of slave trade activity. Although the author Alexander McFarlane does not directly acknowledge his own involvement in the slave trade, the letter's mention of a "Capt. Northrop" is telling. A William Northrop in fact captained the slave ship *The James*, which in 1802 sailed from Spanish Florida to Sierra Leone, returning with 117 slaves who were subsequently sold in the Americas. It should also be noted that the man to whom this letter was addressed, "Capt. Martin of the Byam," himself captained a slave ship. On this particular voyage, the *Byam* purchased 205 slaves in Rio Pongo, Sierra Leone, and sold the surviving 193 slaves at various ports in the Caribbean and British Guinea.[12]

In any event, an advertisement in the *Charleston Courier* in October 1806 leaves little doubt as to the involvement of MacFarlane's firm in the slave trade, emerging out of a later voyage:

BY WILLIAM PAYNE

On Thursday, the 16th instant, at twelve o'clock, north side of the Exchange, will be sold,

Eight New Mandingo Negroes, viz.

Four men, two Women, and two Boys, just arrived from Rio-Pongus, in the schooner Mary-Ann; being part of the Estate of M'Farlane and Player, bankrupts, and sold by order of the assignee. Conditions, cash.[13]

It would appear that McFarlane and Player had at least a 10 percent interest in the cargo of the *Mary-Ann*, which had begun its voyage with 103 slaves purchased in Rio Pongo, and which ended its voyage in Charleston with 90 slaves. Their share had evidently been assigned to William Payne, a prominent Charleston merchant who had been a major owner of an 1804 slave-trading voyage.[14]

By way of background it should be noted that the years 1804–7 saw the temporary resumption of the African slave trade into South Carolina. The period was marked in South Carolina by a bubble of excited speculation, as many prominent whites mortgaged their slaves to finance more slave purchases and slave-trading expeditions. It appears that Alexander McFarlane, hoping to recoup his business losses after the disastrous 1801 fire, was eager to be part of the renewed lucrative African slave trade back into Charleston and thus positioned himself in Rio Pongo, Sierra Leone, during 1803, just before the lifting of the embargo on slave transshipment. Since the voyage of the *Mary-Ann* began in spring 1804, after the embargo had been lifted, it seems likely that Alexander McFarlane, while in Rio Pongo before his death in December 1803, had set up an arrangement with the ship's owner and local slave brokers along the Pongo

River. I am unsure of the fate of the other eighty-two slaves who survived the voyage; they presumably were sold in Charleston or elsewhere in the low country.[15]

Captain MacFarlane's death in 1803 left his widow and children in severely reduced circumstances, but they do seem to have owned a few slaves during the period leading from the captain's death to Ann Amelia's marriage to James Osgood Andrew in 1818. Captain MacFarlane's widow, Catherine Stattler McFarlane, inherited from her husband the enslaved woman Maria, whom he had purchased in 1799. When she died in 1816, thirteen years after the death of her son-in-law, Eve Catherine McNeal willed the slave Dolly (the one she had purchased from Alexander) to her daughter Catherine Stattler McFarlane, Ann Amelia's mother.

By 1840, when Catherine Stattler McFarlane herself died, Ben had been manumitted and Dolly was long dead. The 1840 court inventory of Catherine Stattler MacFarlane's estate makes no mention of Dolly or Ben. It does list four slaves—Maria, Sarah, Lucy, and Billy. Maria is presumably the "Maria" whom Alexander McFarlane purchased in June 1799 from James Hartley, and whom Catherine Stattler then inherited from her husband when he died in 1803. Sarah, Lucy, and Billy are presumably the children of Maria.

In her 1840 will, Catherine Stattler McFarlane, Ann Amelia's mother, mandates the distribution of these four slaves:

> To Catherine Mood, my negro girl Maria. To my daughter, Anne A(melia) Andrew, my boy Billy. To Catherine Amelia Mood (grand-daughter) my little negro girl named Sarah. To James O Andrew, my girl Lucy in trust until Alexander M Wynn comes of age when said negro with her increase is to be delivered to said A. M. Wynn.[16]

Note how the structure of the divided enslaved family is partly reduplicated in the structure of the recipient family network. The eldest slave Maria went to the matriarch's eldest daughter and namesake, Catherine ("Kitty") McFarlane Mood. Catherine McFarlane Mood's daughter, Catherine Amelia Mood, in turn received Maria's evident daughter Sarah. Maria's other apparent daughter, Lucy, went to another grandchild of Catherine Stattler, Alexander McFarlane Wynn. Alexander Wynn was the son of Catherine Stattler McFarlane's daughter Elizabeth and Thomas L. Wynn. Elizabeth had died in 1827, three weeks after giving birth to Alexander. Named for his grandfather, Alexander McFarlane, the infant boy was baptized by Rev. James Osgood Andrew beside his mother's coffin in Charleston.[17] James Andrew would serve as guardian for Alexander McFarlane Wynn until at least 1848, when he turned twenty-one. Finally, Billy, the one male slave in the lot, went to Catherine Stattler MacFarlane's other surviving daughter, Ann Amelia McFarlane Andrew, the Bishop's first wife. (The transfers of the McFarlane slaves are summarized in Figure 8.1.)

As anthropologist Marcel Mauss long ago noted in his classic essay, *The Gift*, gifts partly embody the spirit or personhood of the donor, allowing him or her to exert influence or control over the recipients, even if the donor is not physically present and even if he or she is no longer alive. Such was the case with bequests of enslaved people. As with other instances we have examined—including the family of Esther, the slaves of Henry Harper, discussed in chapter 2—the enslaved family of Maria was mapped onto the white family of the dying matriarch. In a symbolic register, these gifts evidently provided Catherine with a sense of symbolic immortality across the generations of her posterity, helping to bind her white descendants to their venerated antecedents.

The Trajectories of the McFarlane Slaves

After Ann Amelia died in 1842, full legal title in Billy transferred to Bishop Andrew. Curiously, Bishop Andrew makes no mention of Lucy in his public defense offered to the northern bishop at the May 1844 New York Conference, although she was at the time residing in his household, laboring for him and acting under his full authority. Perhaps he felt that since he was only holding her as trust for his nephew, Alexander McFarlane Wynn, Lucy was not worthy of enumeration.

Lucy was presumably transferred to Alexander Wynn after he came of age around 1848. It is difficult to determine what then became of Lucy. During the late 1840s Alexander Wynn studied at Emory College, was ordained a Methodist minister, and married Maria Howard, daughter of the wealthy planter General Nicholas Howard (1787–1849) and Judith Campbell (1791–1843) of Columbus, Georgia. Wynn and his new bride, Maria, moved in 1849 to California on Methodist Church business. By 1850, according to the census, "Alex M. Winn" was living in Stockton, San Joaquin, California. A few months earlier, in late 1849 California had been admitted to the Union as a free state, so no slaves were enumerated in the 1850 federal census for California. This same census lists no women named Lucy living in Stockton. Perhaps the slave Lucy was left

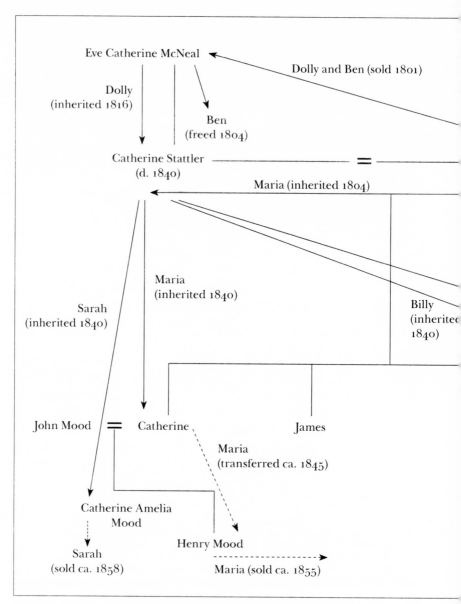

FIGURE 8.1. The McFarlane slaves (broken arrows are speculative)

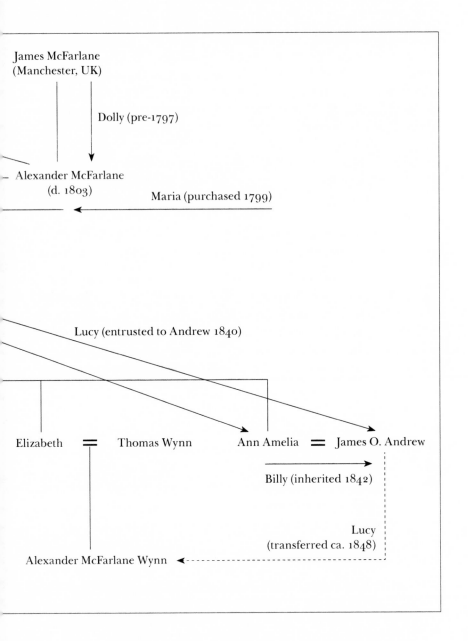

James McFarlane
(Manchester, UK)

Dolly (pre-1797)

Alexander McFarlane
(d. 1803)

Maria (purchased 1799)

Lucy (entrusted to Andrew 1840)

Elizabeth ═══ Thomas Wynn   Ann Amelia ═══ James O. Andrew

Billy (inherited 1842)

Lucy
(transferred ca. 1848)

Alexander McFarlane Wynn

with one of Maria Howard's siblings in central Georgia, or perhaps she was sold before the Wynns left for California. By 1856 Rev. Wynn was serving as a Methodist minister in Columbus, Georgia; in part due to poor health he was relocated in 1859 out to nearby Talbotton, in Talbot County, near his wife Maria's family. In the 1860 census, the Wynns are settled in Talbotton and appear not to own any slaves. In 1870 Rev. Alexander M. Wynn is residing in Columbus, Georgia, with two black domestic servants in household. It is possible that the Wynns' former slave Lucy is the "Lucy Brannon" born around 1805 listed in the 1870 census as a domestic worker, born in South Carolina, living in Oneal's precinct in Talbot County, but there is no positive evidence of this.

A little more information is available about Billy. The Bishop's great-nephew, Methodist cleric Rev. Francis Asbury Mood, recalls in his memoir,

> Amelia (the author's grandmother) married James O. Andrew afterward Bishop and prominent in the history of the Methodist Church in the United States as the occasion of the division of the church into Northern and Southern branches. One of the negroes who was involved in the conscience agonies of our northern brethren was a negro boy named Billy of whom he became the owner by the death of my Grandmother. We knew him as "Black Billy" to distinguish him from "Billy" my brother William. He was a fat greasy looking thick lipped good natured negro, the last creature in the world that in our boyish minds would have been the occasion of a trouble either in the church or out of it.[18]

Without specifically naming him, Bishop Andrew refers to Billy in his May 1844 public letter to the bishops of the New York General Conference, immediately after he explains the particulars of the Kitty case:

> About five years since, the mother of my former wife left to her daughter—not to me—a negro boy, and as my wife died without a will, more than two years since, by the laws of the State he becomes legally my property. In this case, as in the former [meaning Kitty], emancipation is impracticable in the State, but he shall be at liberty to leave the State whenever I shall be satisfied that he is prepared to provide for himself or I can have sufficient security that he will be protected and provided for in the place to which he may go.[19]

In a letter dated May 14, 1844, from the fateful New York Methodist Conference, Bishop Andrew writes to his daughter expressing concern for his

wife Ann Leonora and the slaves Billy and Orange: "I am very anxious
to hear how she is and how Orange and Billy have got."[20] Two days later,
the Bishop writes to his wife Ann Leonora,

> Robert mentioned to me that Billie and Orange were sick and I am
> anxious to hear how they are. I fear you have had a fatiguing time
> nursing them and I wish I were there to help you in your work.[21]

What became of Billy? The 1850 slave schedule in Oxford, Georgia, lists
seven black males born between 1822 and 1830 in the Andrew household, one of whom is likely to have been Billy. During 1855–56, following
his marriage to his third wife, Bishop Andrew moved with his remaining
slaves to Summerfield, Alabama, 250 miles west of Oxford. The 1860
slave schedule for Bishop Andrew's household in Summerfield, Alabama,
does not list any male slave over fifteen years old, that is to say, born
before 1845, whereas Billy must have been born by 1830 or earlier. Yet,
it is possible that the Bishop still owned him in 1860 and he was either
rented out or working on the Tranquilla plantation in Union when the
census was enumerated.

Quite possibly, Billy is the "William Neal" recorded in the 1870 Freedmen's Census residing near Summerfield in Union, Alabama, born 1826
in South Carolina. If so, he would have been about fourteen years old
when transferred into Bishop Andrew's household in Oxford in 1840 and
about twenty-nine when Bishop Andrew moved his slaves to Summerfield, Alabama, in 1855.[22] According to the 1870 census William Neal
was married to Harrit (Harriet?) and had a three-year-old son, Charles.[23]
In the early 1870s William Neal entered into a series of sharecropping
agreements with white landowners in Dallas County, including Edward
Ikelheimer and J. H. Burns.[24] In the 1880 census, a William Neal, evidently the same man, is listed as a widower, residing with his son Charles
in Morehouse Parish, Louisiana, where both are working as farm laborers. In the 1900 census, Charles Neal is married with three children,
the eldest named William, in Morehouse Parish, Louisiana. (Charles
Neal records in this census that his father was born in South Carolina.)
There is no sign of the elder William Neal, who presumably passed away
before 1900.[25]

After they were transferred to Bishop Andrew's household in 1840,
there is no evidence that Lucy and Billy were ever able to regain contact with their apparent sister Sarah or with Maria, who was probably
their mother; Sarah and Maria must have remained in Charleston, South

Carolina. As noted above, Maria had been inherited by Catherine "Kitty" McFarlane Mood, a sister of Bishop Andrew's wife Ann Amelia, and Sarah had been willed to Catherine McFarlane Mood's young daughter, Catherine Amelia Mood. The 1840 census in Charleston for the household of John Mood, the husband of Catherine McFarlane Mood and the father of Catherine Amelia Mood, lists only two slaves, who must have been Maria and Sarah—one female slave between thirty-six and fifty-five years old and one female slave under ten years old. One decade later, the 1850 slave schedule for the Mood household in Charleston lists a fifty-seven-year-old female black slave who is likely to have been Maria and an eighteen-year-old female slave, likely to be Sarah, Maria's apparent daughter.

It appears that Maria was then at some point passed on to Catherine and John Mood's eldest child, Rev. Henry McFarlane Mood, who seems to have sold her. In a letter dated September 1, 1857, Henry M. Mood explains that he no longer owns his previous "black family," that is to say, the slaves he had owned when stationed a few years earlier in Graniteville, South Carolina: "We have none of the black family we had when in Graniteville. Sallie married in Charleston and we sold her there. Mariah broke open my storehouse the present year, and stole our meat, beside other thefts, and we felt obligated to sell her."[26] Maria's apparent daughter Sarah, who had been willed to Henry Mood's sister, Catherine Amelia Mood, may also been sold out of the McFarlane-Mood family around the same time. An advertisement placed "in the late 1850s" in the *Charleston Courier* by William Ward Wilbur, the husband of Catherine Amelia Mood, states:

VALUABLE NEGROES

By Wilbur and Son

    This day, the 17th instant, we will positively sell at the Broker corner of State and Chalmers Street, at 11 o'clock to the highest bidder

    Tom, an accomplished and reliable house servant, as well as a good flower and vegetable gardener, and of unexceptional character.

    Sarah, about a 32 years old, a cook, washer and field hand.

Conditions cash. Purchaser to pay for papers.[27]

Legally, the property of Catherine Amelia Mood, including slaves specifically willed to her, would have been the legal property of her husband William W. Wilbur to dispose of as he wished, unless the original instrument specified that the husband was prohibited from doing so. No such prohibition was articulated in the 1840 will of Catherine Stattler McFarlane.

The saga of the McFarlane slaves illustrates with particular poignancy the dynamic we sketched out in chapter 2. Inheritance and dowry transfers, which were integral to the reproduction of white elite familial relations, often ruptured kinship bonds among enslaved persons of color. Through the posthumous gifts of her slaves, Catherine McFarlane sought to extend the bonds of lineage to her children and grandchildren. Yet the net result of these transfers, compounded by subsequent dowry transfers, was the fragmenting of at least one enslaved family. It would appear that Maria and her children, Billy, Sarah, and Lucy, were by the eve of the Civil War scattered across South Carolina, Georgia, and Alabama, and were probably never able to rediscover one another.

The Greenwood Slaves: Prior to 1844

The profound impact of inheritance and marriage transfers on enslaved families is even more powerfully illustrated through the aftermath of Bishop Andrew's second marriage, which led to his most legally intricate involvement with slave ownership. On January 14, 1844, James Osgood Andrew wed Ann Leonora Mounger Greenwood, the widow of the planter Thomas Greenwood of Greensboro, the county seat of Greene County, Georgia, about halfway between Oxford and Augusta. As I have suggested, it would be too simple to assert, as is often claimed, that Leonora Ann "owned" all the slaves that Bishop Andrew was accused of possessing. She rather had in her possession a set of slaves whose legal status was undergoing jural and practical negotiation during this entire period. This legal process generated a great deal of documentation, including court-ordered inventories of slaves, slave distribution lists, and accounts of income and expenses associated with slaves. From these documents it is possible to reconstruct significant aspects of the lives of the enslaved persons who were linked in one way or another to Ann Leonora Greenwood, her children, and Bishop Andrew during the years prior to emancipation. (The major transfers of these slaves are summarized in Figure 8.2.)

Ann Leonora Mounger's first husband, Thomas Greenwood, died at some point before September 1825. He had four children by a previous 1805 marriage to Nancy Mitchell, daughter of the slaveowner and Revolutionary War veteran Jacob Mitchell, an established Greene County

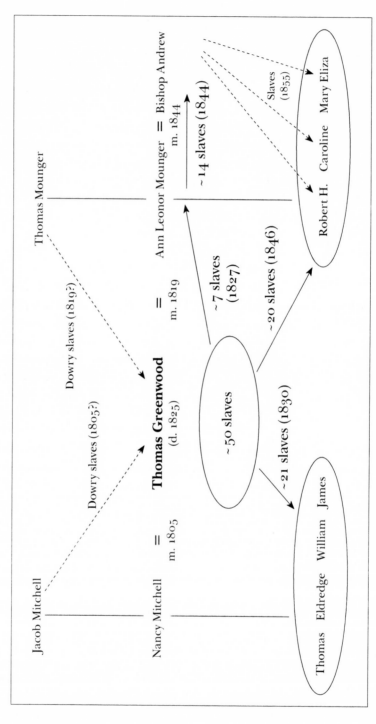

FIGURE 8.2. Slave transfers in the Greenwood estate, 1805–55 (broken arrows are speculative)

planter who also passed away in 1825. These children, as well as Ann Leonora's children, all had partial claim on the slaves in the Thomas Greenwood estate, some of whom had initially come from the Jacob Mitchell
estate.[28] Matters were complicated further by the fact that Ann Leonora
herself came from a slaveowning Georgia family and may have possessed
some slaves of her own given by or inherited from her father, Thomas
Mounger (who died in 1809), or from her mother, Lucy Grimes Mounger
(who died in 1840).

A few months after Thomas Greenwood's death, a December 1825 inventory of his estate lists the following forty-six slaves: the adult men Daniel, Isaac, Sam, Dick, Charles, George, Will, Henry, Solomon, Nicholas,
Harry, and Lace; the "boys" Little George, Nelson, Ben, Oswell, Jacob,
and Joe; and the women and young children (Luckey and three children, Rofe, Maria and child, Lizzy and child, Delsey and child, Bitsey [or
Betsy], Henney, Hariett, Little Harriet, Critty, Phiby, Alfa, Peggy and two
children, Ann, Elenor, Martha, Adrian and child, Phillis, and Reason).

For at least the next two decades the Thomas Greenwood estate was
overseen by two court-appointed administrators—Isaac Mitchell, brother
of Thomas Greenwood's first wife, Nancy Mitchell, and Ann Leonora's
sister's husband William Weaver. (The ordinary court had evidently
sought to balance the interests of the two wives' families by appointing a
mature man from each family.) In an initial division of the estate in 1827,
twenty of the slaves were reserved by the court for the orphaned children of Thomas Greenwood and his first wife, the late Nancy Mitchell
Greenwood, and twenty-one others reserved for the children of Thomas
Greenwood and his second wife, Ann Leonora Mounger Greenwood.
The Greene County ordinary court, in its distribution to Ann Leonora's
children, states,

> We set apart to Thomas, Robert, Caroline and Mary E. Greenwood,
> the following negroes by name and valued as follows, to wit:
>> Daniel $500
>> Harriet, 400
>> Solomon, 500
>> Maria and child Harid, 525
>> George, 475
>> Betsy and 3 children, 750
>> Little George, 500
>> Charles, 450

Jacob, 300
Philba, 150
Ben, 350
Lucky and 3 children, 800
Martha, 400.

These slaves were collectively valued at $6,300. In turn the court reserved slaves to the children of Thomas Greenwood's first wife Nancy Mitchell in these terms:

We set apart to Thomas Edwin, Eldridge L, William M, and James D Greenwood the following negroes:
Doch, 500
Henna and Mara, 500
Harriet and child James, 400
Will, 500
Nelson, 500
Diley and 3 children, 850
Nick, 500
Osborn, 400
Liza and 2 children, 650
James, 200
Rose, 275
Joe (?) 300
Critty, 275
Adriann, 400.

This second lot of slaves was valued at $6,250—roughly the same amount as the first lot. It is clear from subsequent documents in the loose probate records that these slaves were not immediately distributed to Thomas Greenwood's heirs, some of whom were still minors, but were supervised by the administrators; in many instances the slaves were rented out to local planters and the income generated was held in trust for the heirs.

In the same 1827 ruling, the Greene County court assigned to Ann L. Greenwood the following slaves from the estate:

Ann, a yellow girl, at $450
Peggy, Lander, and Alexander at $700.00
Harry, a man at $500.00
Elenor and child Dolphus at $150.00
Total: $1,800.00

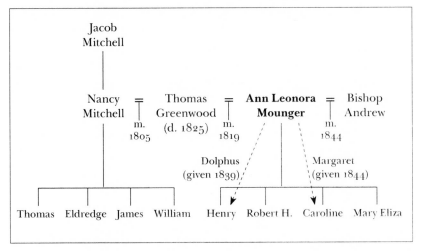

FIGURE 8.3. Additional slave transfers by Ann Leonora Mounger Greenwood

In a subsequent legal document Ann Leonora affirms that these seven slaves are her "proportionate part or share of the negroes of the estate of my deceased husband Thomas Greenwood." Yet, as late as 1830, while living in Greensboro Ann Leonora still had at least sixteen slaves in her household. Some of the remaining slaves in her household were evidently held on behalf of her children; according to one document she charged the Greenwood estate a boarding fee for maintaining her children's slaves. She transferred one of the slaves she had acquired in 1827, the twelve-year-old slave Dolphus or Adolphus ("the son of Eleanor") to her son Henry F. Greenwood in November 1838. Five years later, on March 23, 1843, apparently because he had recently come of age, she officially distributed to her son Henry Greenwood his share of the estate—the eight slaves, "Big George, Little George, Charles, Reason, Angeline, William, Isaac, and Phebe," as well as nine hundred dollars in cash. (Slave transfers by Ann Leonora are summarized in Figure 8.3.)

It would appear that some of the slaves in the Greenwood estate were sold off to meet various expenses. In December 1835 the Georgia State Senate passed "a bill to authorize Ann Leonora Greenwood, as Guardian of the minor children of Thomas Greenwood, late of Green county, deceased, to sell the negroes belonging to said minors."[29]

We do know that not all of the slaves in the estate survived to be sold or distributed to the white heirs. In 1840, four years prior to the 1844

Andrew-Greenwood marriage, the slave named Jacob, who had been valued at three hundred dollars in 1827, was rented out by the Greenwood estate administrators to a white man in Columbus, Georgia, about 150 miles from Greensboro; the estate paid for his hat, his shoes, shifting, and spool, and his travel expenses to Columbus.[30] However, Jacob's stay in Columbus was tragically short. In early 1841 the estate successfully sued to recover damages associated with Jacob's death while in Columbus. The estate also paid a sexton to bury him and a coroner to conduct an inquest into his death.

In spite of this loss, renting out slaves was profitable for the Greenwood heirs. For instance, an 1844 Greene County court document details the "Hire of Negroes belonging to Robert, Caroline and Eliza Greenwood for 1844." (Since Henry had received his share of the estate the previous year, he no longer shared into the profits generated by the commonly held slaves.) That year, the rent of at least fifteen slaves netted $525, which when divided into thirds paid out $175 to each white child.

The Greenwood Slaves: 1844–54

On January 13, 1844, the day before her marriage to Bishop Andrew, Ann Leonora Greenwood deeded to her daughter Caroline "Carrie" Greenwood "my slave girl Margaret." Knowing that any slaves in her possession were about to become the legal property of her new husband, Ann Leonora was clearly eager to secure her daughter's legal claim to Margaret. Soon afterward, Caroline moved with her mother to Oxford. She resided in the Bishop's household for two years before she married Dr. Henry King of Greensboro in 1846, in a ceremony performed by Bishop Andrew. For at least the year of 1845 slave Margaret probably resided in the Bishop's household in Oxford, unless Caroline rented her out back in Greene County.

Working through the complex legal records related to the Greenwood estate, it is difficult to sort out which of the slaves associated with the estate were held in Oxford and which were in various locations in Greene County or elsewhere in Georgia after Ann Leonora married Bishop Andrew in early 1844. Some were rented out, others were clearly in the Andrew household or on the Bishop's land holdings, and some seemed to have been moved from location to location.

One of the slaves in this mobile group was "Orange," who is described in one document in the following terms: "Orange not found on acct of

Health." Orange's health was clearly poor from 1839 onward, since the associated legal papers record multiple payments to a Dr. Foster Graves for "visits to Orange." Estate records from 1840–43 indicate Orange was too sick to bring in any income through rent.[31] We know that Orange was part of the Bishop Andrew household that year, since his illness was referred to in two of the Bishop's letters to his wife in May 1844, quoted above. Two years later, on June 2, 1846, Orange, valued at $525, was transferred out of the Bishop Andrew household to Ann Leonora's son Robert H. Greenwood, along with seven other slaves, Sarah Jane, Sarah Ann, Daniel, Betsey, Grandeson, Lucy, and Delia. Robert Greenwood presumably is the "Robert" referred to in Bishop Andrew's May 1844 letter about the two ill slaves, Billy and Orange. It would appear that Robert H. Greenwood, born around 1822, was living with his mother Ann Leonora and stepfather James Osgood Andrew in Oxford during this period, along with his newly acquired slaves. By 1860 Robert H. Greenwood was residing in the home of his brother-in-law Dr. Henry King and his sister Caroline in Greensboro; he then served in the Civil War as a private, first in Phillips Legion (Company A, the Greene Rifles) and then in Georgia's Forty-fourth Infantry (Company K, Greene Volunteers), primarily in Virginia. He spent much of 1862 and 1863 hospitalized with a gastrointestinal illness until returning to active duty, serving under General Robert E. Lee in the Army of Northern Virginia until the surrender at Appomattox Court House.[32] By 1870 he was working as a teacher back in northern Greene County in Militia District 140.

Our major source on the identity of the Greenwood slaves owned by Bishop Andrew is the legal deed drawn up between Bishop Andrew and his closest friend, Augustus Baldwin Longstreet, then president of Emory College. To review: Shortly before leaving for the New York Conference in April 1844, James Andrew legally transferred to President Longstreet—for the token price of ten dollars in total—ownership of fourteen enslaved persons: "Nick, George, Tom, Orlando, Elleck, Edward, Addison, James, Jefferson, Peggy, Susan, Lillah and her two children Laura and Allen." Andrew added to this a stipulation that "the said Augustus B. holds the said negroes to and for the joint use of myself and my wife Leonora during our natural lives, and upon the death of either, to the use of the Survivor." In other words, James and Ann Leonora Andrew retained full use of these fourteen slaves' labor, who continued to reside in their household. The deed seems to have been drawn up by Longstreet, at the time reputed to be "the cleverest lawyer in Georgia,"

as a legal device to shield Bishop Andrew from charges of slave ownership at the upcoming New York Methodist Conference. (The strategy, of
course, failed, and the Bishop's slaveownership quickly became a matter
of national controversy.)

It should be noted that in 1844, when he designed these deeds, Longstreet was scarcely a stranger to the Greenwood and Mounger families
and their slaves. The 1820 census indicates that when he was a judge
and planter in Greensboro, the seat of Greene County, Longstreet resided directly next door to Thomas Greenwood and his wife Ann Leonora, who were fellow Methodists and slaveowners. (In 1820 Longstreet
owned twenty-seven slaves in Greene County.) Since Longstreet resided in
Greensboro from 1817 to 1827, he presumably attended Thomas Greenwood's funeral in 1825. He probably also was personally familiar with
many of the slaves named in the April 1844 document. Longstreet had
long been close to Ann Leonora's natal family; his popular novel *Master
William Mitten: or, a Youth of Brilliant Talents, Ruined by Bad Luck* is largely
based on Ann Leonora's older brother J. H. T. Mounger and his unusual
dancing horse "Snap-Dragon," and features scenes in which slaves speak
about the horse in dialect.[33] As an attorney and superior court magistrate, he would have long been familiar with the Greenwood probate case,
which involved the distribution and supervision of over fifty slaves over
the course of several decades. Longstreet's wife, Frances Eliza Parke, was
from Greensboro and was a close confidante of Ann Leonora Greenwood
Andrew, whom she saw on a daily basis in Oxford after Ann Leonora's
marriage to Bishop Andrew in January 1844. Yet again, we are struck by
the intricate bonds among the many slaveholders and enslaved persons in
this complex antebellum legal and social drama, which stretched in time
across multiple generations and geographically across multiple counties
and states.

The 1850 slave schedule of the federal census in Oxford indicates that
Andrew had in his household twenty-four slaves, which presumably included the fourteen slaves named in the April 1844 deeds, less any who
had died in the interim, plus Kitty, Billy, and any children borne to the
enslaved women between 1844 and 1850. (Ownership of enslaved children was reckoned solely through the maternal line; the owner of an
enslaved woman was the owner of all the children she bore.) Six of the
slaves listed in 1850 were children under the age of seven; of these, as
we shall see, three were surely Kitty's children, so the remaining three

young slaves are likely to have been the offspring of the Greenwood enslaved adult women, Peggy, Susan, and Lillah.

Note that of the seven slaves transferred in the 1827 court order to
Ann Leonora, only three at most are mentioned in the 1844 Andrew-
Longstreet deed. One is Peggy. The other two might be her two sons,
who had been listed in 1827 as "Lander" and "Alexander." Lander might
be the same person as "Orlando" and Alexander might be "Elleck." (It is
perhaps significant that Bishop Andrew listed Orlando and Elleck next
to one another in the 1844 document.) Dolphus, as we have seen, was
given by Ann Leonora to her stepson Henry Greenwood in 1839. The remaining three slaves mentioned in 1827—Ann ("the yellow girl"), Harry,
and Elenor—may have died between 1827 and 1844 or may have been
given to one of Ann Leonora's children. The other eleven slaves mentioned in the 1844 deed may have been the offspring of Ann, Peggy, or
Eleanor. Alternately, they may have resulted from informal transfers of
slaves within the extended white Greenwood family.

The records indicate that even among the Greenwood slaves who were
securely owned by Bishop Andrew and Ann Leonora, not all were kept
within the Andrew household. On March 30, 1853, for instance, Bishop
Andrew hired out two of his slaves named in the 1844 deed, Alleck and
Allen (Lillah's son), for one hundred dollars to his brother Hardy Andrew.[34] Following Hardy's death that spring, the two slaves appear to
have continued to labor on his farm, since the Hardy Andrew estate paid
Bishop Andrew for their services for the entire year.

Three years into her marriage with Bishop Andrew, on August 5, 1847,
Ann Leonora Greenwood transferred to her daughter Mary Eliza Greenwood ten slaves, "Horace, Milledge, Martha, Harriet, her child named
Luisa, Elisha and her four children named Ellen, Edgar, Oscar and Melerian," along with $129.42 in cash as settlement, Mary Eliza affirms,
of "my claim arising from the Estate of my father Thomas Greenwood,
decd." Many of the adult slaves on this list were recorded in the December 1825 court inventory of the Greenwood estate, but none of them
were mentioned in the 1844 Longstreet-Andrew deed; they may have
been residing in Oxford, Georgia, prior to the 1847 transfer, or they may
have been rented out in Greene County as part of the trust arrangements
maintained for Thomas Greenwood's heirs. Mary Elizabeth Greenwood
would, significantly, spend the rest of her life residing in Oxford, where
she married Emory faculty member Luther M. Smith. After her death

in 1859, her property, including her slaves, all passed fully to Professor Smith. As we shall see, most of these enslaved persons resided in Oxford up until emancipation.

The "Greenwood Slaves": 1854–64

Ann Leonora Greenwood Andrew, the Bishop's second wife, died at her home in Oxford on June 10, 1854, after several years of being an invalid. It seems likely that the Greenwood enslaved families would have been highly apprehensive at this point, anticipating that they might be sold off or distributed in the settlement of the long-running Greenwood inheritance case.

Several sources insist that after the death of Ann Leonora Greenwood, Bishop Andrew did indeed divide up and distribute this human "property" to her children. An obituary of Bishop Andrew by Dr. Mitchell in the *Southern Christian Advocate* asserts,

> In the case of his second wife, who owned a large estate, and at her death, by will or otherwise, it all reverted to the Bishop during his lifetime, but rather than be involved with care and responsibility, he immediately turned it all over to her children, amounting to thousands of dollars.[35]

Similarly, the *History of Greene County* states, "Mrs. Andrew died in 1854 and the law reinvested the Bishop with his wife's property. The Bishop promptly gave the slaves to Mrs. Andrew's children."[36]

I can find no will or legal documents detailing such a division of enslaved persons, but surmise that it must have taken place. A comparison of the 1850 slave schedule in Oxford and the 1860 slave schedule in Summerfield suggests that hardly any of the adult Oxford slaves were transferred to Alabama, where the Bishop moved in 1855. Of the twenty-seven slaves listed by age and gender in the 1850 slave schedule, only six at most can be matched up with those recorded in the 1860 slave schedule. Two female slaves listed in 1850, born around 1817, could be the same women as the two female slaves listed in 1860 as born around 1815. An enslaved woman listed in 1850 as born around 1832 could be the same woman as one of the women listed in 1860 born around 1830. As we shall see, the three young slaves in 1850 who are almost certainly Kitty's three children also match up nicely with three young people in the 1860 census. But seven adult female slaves and twelve adult male slaves listed in the 1850 schedule are missing from the 1860 schedule.

Many of the Greenwood slaves appear to have been transferred back to Greene County, Georgia, after 1854, probably before Bishop Andrew moved to Alabama.[37] The 1860 census shows Ann Leonora Greenwood Andrew's daughter Caroline Greenwood as married and living with her husband, Henry H. King, in Greensboro, Georgia, the Greene County seat. Henry King at this point owned property worth fifteen thousand dollars, most of which presumably was in slaves. Also residing in this household was Caroline's brother, Robert Greenwood, who had received his share of the family slaves in 1846. Curiously, neither Henry King nor Robert Greenwood are listed as slaveowners in the 1860 slave schedule for Greene County. However, William W. D. Weaver, the maternal uncle of Caroline and Robert, who had long served as the administrator of the Thomas Greenwood estate, is listed in 1860 as holding seventy-eight slaves in Greene County. In 1842 he is listed in a court record as renting Betsy and her child from the Greenwood estate. It is possible that he was in 1860 still acting in a trustee capacity for his niece and nephew or renting their slaves. Alternately, Henry King, Caroline Greenwood King, and Robert Greenwood may have rented out their slaves to other planters in the county, as had been done with most of the Greenwood slaves from 1827 until 1844. Hence, the slaves would not have been recorded under the names of the Greenwood heirs in the census schedule, although they would have been their legal property. (The likely transfers of the Greenwood slaves after 1854 are depicted in Figure 8.4.)

The Greenwood Ex-Slaves as Freedpeople

Except when mother-child bonds are specified in the legal documents, determining the kinship links among the fifty or so enslaved persons that constituted the Thomas Greenwood estate is difficult. However, reconstructing aspects of their lives under slavery is possible, and in some instances we can trace them and their descendants into the postemancipation period. Although divided by the court distribution and by the complications of Ann Leonora's marriage to Bishop Andrew, a number of the enslaved people in the Thomas Greenwood estate appear to have retained bonds with one another and, in some cases, chosen to reside close to one another after freedom came.

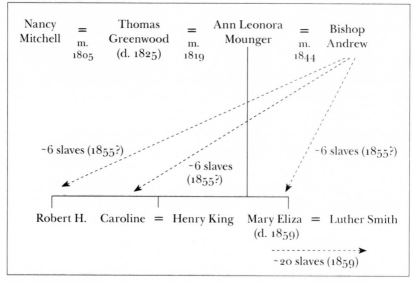

FIGURE 8.4. Likely slave transfers by Bishop Andrew after the death of Ann Leonora Mounger Greenwood (1854)

In Appendix 5, I review in detail the likely fates of the former Greenwood slaves following emancipation in late 1864. With one exception, their direct involvement with James Osgood Andrew began with his marriage to Ann Leonora Greenwood in January 1844 and came to an end soon after Ann Leonora's death in June 1854, as the Bishop distributed nearly all of them to her adult children, Robert H. Greenwood, Caroline Greenwood King, and Mary Elizabeth Greenwood Smith. The sixteen or so slaves distributed to Robert and Caroline were evidently taken back to Greene County, where most of them had resided prior to 1844. They appear to have been rented out to wealthy planters, returning to the cotton fields in the northern sections of the county. There they seem to have redeveloped close connections with kin and comrades from the wider circle of Greenwood/Mitchell slaves, from whom they had been separated during their decade-long sojourn in Oxford. In a number of cases, as detailed in Appendix 5.A, they appear to have developed or rekindled matrimonial alliances with other enslaved people in the Greenwood estate, whom they had probably known since childhood. After emancipation came in late 1864 the majority of these newly freed families were enmeshed in the increasingly brutal local system of sharecropping and agrarian convict labor in northern Greene County, termed by many "slavery by another name." Some, however, found their way to Atlanta and gradually made their way north in the Great Migration, taking their place in the emerging African American working and middle class in Chicago and other northern cities.

Yet, as chronicled in Appendix 5.B., life was rather different for the eight or so enslaved persons distributed to Mary Elizabeth Greenwood Smith. Falling under the legal control of her husband, Emory College professor Luther M. Smith, especially after Mary Elizabeth's death in 1859, they and their families remained in Oxford, Georgia. Without unduly romanticizing the challenges faced by freedpeople in postwar Oxford, it is clear that the town did afford a degree of economic, social, religious, and educational autonomy for persons of color after emancipation. The former Greenwood-Mitchell-Andrew slaves were within a few years able to disentangle themselves from sharecropping contracts and established themselves as independent farmers, owning land that they appear to have obtained as payment from Emory College for construction and service labor on campus. Their enduring relationships of patronage with powerful Emory white leaders brought in continuing income, mainly through service jobs for the men on campus and work as cooks and laundresses for the women in the town's off-campus student boardinghouses.

The Oxford African American community developed a vibrant base in Rust Chapel Methodist Church, which detached itself from the Methodist Episcopal Church, South, and allied itself with the northern Methodist Episcopal Church. The new church's attached school, replaced in time with a successful Rosenwald school, prepared many Oxford young people for study at Payne College in Augusta, or later, the noted Washington Street High School in Covington. Close relations of clientage with powerful Emory-related white families provided a degree of economic and social security, and protected, by and large, persons of color in Oxford from the immediate brunt of Klan-related violence and intimidation. Many of the Greenwood descendant families in Oxford were thus able in time to send their children and grandchildren to higher education at Clark, Spelman, and Morehouse in Atlanta, setting many on the road toward middle-class, professional careers.

As detailed in Appendix 5.D., the most puzzling anomaly is the enslaved family of Thomas and Henrietta Greenwood, who for some reason were not given to any of the white Greenwood heirs but were instead taken by Bishop Andrew to Summerfield in 1855, along with Billy and

Kitty's three children. After emancipation they were caught up in share-cropping arrangements and rural impoverishment. Their predicament was much closer to that of the thirteen or so enslaved people whom Bishop Andrew acquired in Summerfield through his third marriage in late 1854, to whose stories we now turn.

The Childers Slaves in Summerfield, Alabama: 1854–65

Bishop Andrew's third marriage, on November 24, 1854, to Emily Sims Woolsey Heard Childers (often called "Aunt Emma" in her family circle), brought him into legal possession of a cohort of slaves, most or all of whom had been inherited from her third husband, George Childers, who had resided with her in Summerfield, Alabama, before his death in 1853. She may also have inherited some slaves from her previous husbands, Franklin Heard and A. B. Woolsey. All these individuals, it should be noted, had been closely associated with one another years earlier in Augusta, Georgia, and had been friends with Bishop Andrew. Emily Sims Woolsey had been one of Bishop Andrew's congregants at St. John Methodist Church in Augusta in the early 1830s.

George Childers became a prominent planter north of Selma, Alabama; he also seems to have had extensive agricultural interests to the west of Selma, in the district known as Union. It was also in this area that his wealthy stepson, Emily Sims Woolsey's son Benjamin Woolsey, acquired and operated a plantation from the 1840s onward. The connections to Union were to prove important, as we shall see, for African Americans linked to Bishop Andrew's family.

In early 1853 George Childers died and left to his widow Emily the following thirteen slaves: "Levy, Rose, Sal, Martin, Hasly, Nancy, Selvy, Eliza, Jim, William, Wilson, Louise, and Nelson." Less than two years later, Emily married Bishop Andrew; these slaves, and any others she might have owned, would have at that point legally been transferred to him. Around the time of their marriage, Bishop Andrew also acquired the house that Emily had acquired after George Childers's death. This house still stands in Summerfield, a block off of the main road to Selma.

In the 1860 slave schedule, Bishop Andrew is listed as owning eleven slaves in Summerfield, residing in three slave houses. It may be impossible to know how these eleven persons were divided up among these houses, and if some of them considered themselves married to one another. The Andrew slaves would have constituted 1 percent of the total enslaved population in Summerfield in 1860, which amounted to about eleven hundred slaves owned by about forty-six white persons.

With the assistance of his new stepson Benjamin Woolsey, Bishop Andrew acquired a tract of land in Union, about eight miles west of Selma, that he named Tranquilla Plantation.[38] Bishop Andrew's slaves appeared to have labored on Tranquilla during part of the Civil War, in 1862 and 1863, perhaps longer.

When precisely were the enslaved people owned by Bishop Andrew freed? For those in Oxford or in Greene County, Georgia, freedom came in November 1864. We know that a number of slaves belonging to members of Andrew's extended family joined up with General Sherman's columns in their march through Georgia. Some returned; others never came back. In Summerfield and Union, Alabama, emancipation followed on the heels of General Wilson's raid through Dallas County in early April 1865. Many self-emancipated freedpeople from Dallas County joined the Union Army columns in its push toward Montgomery, Alabama, and Columbus, Georgia, some as enlisted soldiers and others as camp followers. As we saw in chapter 7, such was the case for at least one of Kitty's children, Alford Boyd, who attached himself to General Wilson's army as a cook.

The Andrew/Childers Freedpeople, Dallas County, Alabama: Post-1865

We know that for those who remained in rural Georgia and Alabama, freedom was a gradual and highly contested process; within the first year of legal freedom a number of freedpeople entered into sharecropping agreements with their former masters. Ku Klux Klan activity intensified over the course of the 1870s, even though federal troops were repeatedly dispatched to Summerfield to protect freedmen's families. The records of the Bureau for Freedmen, Refugees, and Abandoned Lands for Alabama provide testimony of the intensive challenges freedmen faced, subjected by continuous efforts by white landowners and political figures to marginalize and exploit them economically and socially.

Some former Andrew slaves remained in Summerfield and perhaps also in the adjacent precinct of Union, near the apparent area of Tranquilla Plantation. As noted above, the 1870 census lists a "Thomas Greedwood" (surely Thomas Greenwood) living next door to the Bishop in Summerfield; this was presumably the "Tom" mentioned in the 1844

Longstreet-Andrew deed. Two households away from Bishop Andrew resided a "Martin Andrews," born 1845, who is presumably the "Martin" named in George Childers's will, assigned to his widow Emily Sims Woolsey Childers. This household also contained a "James Sanders," who is perhaps the "James" named in that will. James Sanders was married to Emma, who is, as we have seen, almost certainly Miss Kitty's youngest child. "Rose" may be the Rose Causby, born 1845, married to an Armsted Causby in Summerfield. "Wilson" and "Nancy" may have become the married couple of Wilson Hunter, born 1826, and Nancy Hunter, born 1840, living in Union, Dallas County, with six children. Nelson may have been Nelson Briggs, born 1797 in Virginia, residing in Summerfield in 1870.[39]

Whatever his personal feelings about the more than forty people whom he possessed over the course of his life, their circumstances do not appear to have particularly preoccupied Bishop Andrew in the years after emancipation. His surviving correspondence from 1865 onward makes no mention of freedpeople. His 1871 will enumerates many whites to whom he is grateful, but no people of color are mentioned. The enslaved people with whom the Bishop's life had been for so long intertwined were now on their own, free to make their own way across the challenging terrain of the post–Civil War era.

The Bonds of Matrimony:
Slavery, Kinship, and Fields of Influence

Beyond the mass of historical detail, what have we learned from part 3's consideration of the enslaved persons owned, held, or controlled by James Osgood Andrew from his youth up until the end of the Civil War? First and foremost, this enterprise of historical social mapping helps us refine the model of slavery as a kinship system sketched out in chapter 2. The operations of enslavement in this extended social arena were substantially conditioned by the organization of kinship among the white actors, especially by the processes and bonds of marriage, which anthropologists term "affinal ties," as well as parent-child bonds, which anthropologists characterize as "filial ties." The varied trajectories of these enslaved people were largely conditioned, if not fully determined, by successive marriage alliances among the slaveholding class and by associated family bonds across the generations. Marriages within white slaveowning families not only helped reproduce white family members but also helped reproduce and extend intricate networks of white control over enslaved people. Embedded within webs of white affinity and filiation, the enslaved persons we have encountered thus embodied a complex set of histories and property claims that stretched back for many decades.

To illustrate this point, let us briefly review the multiple white matrimonial bonds that formed the background of this story and consider how these affinal links helped shape the overall architecture of enslavement within the overlapping social networks we have explored. To begin with, the very first enslaved people James Osgood Andrew encountered in his life were probably dowry gifts given by his maternal grandfather to his father (one of whom, G. G. Smith reports, John Andrew flogged). The slave named Jacob and the unidentified woman owned by Andrew in 1830 evidently came to him through his parents' marriage and his father's death—as did Ben, transferred to him and his brothers on behalf of his children, nieces, and nephews by his mother sixteen years after his father passed away. Billy and Lucy, in turn, came into his possession in 1840 as a result of his first marriage, as bequests from Ann Amelia's mother, Catherine McFarlane. Lucy herself was implicated in another white marriage, that between Ann Amelia's sister Elizabeth and Thomas Wynn, both deceased, the parents of the child, Alexander McFarlane Wynn, for whom Bishop Andrew held Lucy in trust. As we have seen, both Billy and Lucy traced their lineage back to slaves owned by Ann Amelia's parents and maternal grandmother. Catherine McFarlane's gifting of Billy, Lucy, Maria, and Sarah may be understood as an effort, conscious or unconscious, to bind together her extended family across four or more generations. This effort, as we have seen, led to the scattering of a once-united enslaved family across the Deep South.

The Bishop's second marriage brought him into an even more complicated kinship configuration of human bondage, which was also shaped by the contours of previous white marriages. The enslaved people under the supervision of his second wife, Ann Leonora Mounger Greenwood, were legally governed by bequests from her own parents, by her previous marriage to her late husband Thomas Greenwood, by Thomas Greenwood's earlier marriage to his first wife Nancy Mitchell, and by Thomas Greenwood's links to his father-in-law, Jacob Mitchell. These kinship histories conditioned the complex distribution of the slaves across three decades, from 1825 to 1855. Some Greenwood slaves were assigned to Nancy Mitchell's children, others to Ann Leonora Mounger Greenwood's children, and still others to Ann Leonora herself. This latter group was the primary cohort that came under Bishop Andrew's legal control, but he also exercised some sort of supervisory control over several slaves who had been assigned to Ann Leonora's children. These included Orange, who resided in his household, and Nancy, whom he rented from the Greenwood estate, paying rent that ultimately went to the Greenwood heirs, his new stepchildren. Bishop Andrew was highly mindful of the weight of these enduring matrimonial connections when he decided, soon after Ann Leonora's death in 1855, to distribute most of her slaves to her adult children.

Similarly, the next set of slaves the Bishop came into possession of were governed not simply by his marriage to his third wife Emily, but also by her prior matrimonial history. Most of the slaves Andrew owned in Summerfield had been willed to Emily by her third husband, B. M. Childers. Yet the practical management of these slaves' labor, at least during 1864 and early 1865, was ultimately governed by a legacy of Emily's first marriage, to Mr. Woolsey. Emily's son by that marriage, B. M. Woolsey, who was now Bishop Andrew's stepson, assumed supervisory responsibilities for the slaves working at Tranquilla Plantation during the final eighteen months or so before emancipation. Slavery in these instances really was a family business, and the life possibilities of enslaved families were intimately embedded within overlapping circles of white kinship loyalties.

At the same time, while white kinship relations established the framework within which antebellum kinship relations among enslaved African Americans developed, white-dominated structures of power did not entirely determine all features of kinship among those held in bondage. As we have seen, although they were divided and rented out by the court-appointed administrators, the over fifty enslaved persons within the Greenwood estate did manage to contract matrimonial alliances and to nurture kinship bonds with loved ones, even if these bonds were not protected by the force of law. The fact that several of the Greenwood slaves retained the surname "Mitchell," a name that must have predated the 1805 marriage of Thomas Greenwood to Nancy Mitchell, through six decades until emancipation gives us a hint of the strength of kinship consciousness among enslaved persons of color. In turn, during the post–Civil War period, the numerous Greenwood freedpeople in Oxford and Penfield were able to reconstitute family groups, as were the former Childers and Andrew freedpeople in Summerfield, Alabama. To be sure, the terms under which these families pursued social, emotional, and economic goals were not entirely those of their own choosing. In many instances, those who had been owned or controlled by Bishop Andrew and his in-laws were forced into relations of economic dependence upon their former white owners or renters, at times enforced through sharecropping contracts, black codes, and the threat of organized racial violence by the Klan. Yet many of these newly freed families were able to establish important zones of economic and social autonomy, through farming their own land and through churches, schools, and fraternal organizations. Some were able to move to Atlanta and join the Great Migration to the industrial North, even as they retained important links to rural kin.

This work of historical reconstruction thus causes us to revisit in significant ways the predominant white mythic, sentimental representations of James Osgood Andrew and his connections with slavery. With the exception of Kitty herself, since the 1840s the enslaved persons owned or held by James Osgood Andrew have been rendered invisible in mainstream discourse, either ignored entirely or figured as an anonymous mass, lumped together as "his second wife's slaves." (If Jacob and Billy are mentioned, they are invariably confused with one another.) As noted in part 1, this rhetorical strategy has reinforced the ideological reading that Bishop Andrew's slaveholding was an "accident" of history. According to the standard narrative, Bishop Andrew was trapped in an impossible position not of his own making through an honest matter of the heart, an act of marriage, for which he should be regarded as essentially blameless. By extension, the position of all southern slaveholders was rendered morally defensible, or at least sympathetic.

Yet dramas of chattel slavery such as this one are never fully reducible to a single narrative line or a singular perspective. The predicaments and trajectories of these many enslaved people were highly variegated, arrayed across a complex spectrum of relative privilege and subordination. To comprehend the gestalt of a slave-based society we need to take seriously the dynamic intertwining of kinship configurations among masters and slaves, all exercising elements of agency and strategy, admittedly operating from drastically divergent positions of power and authority. The actors in this history, in slavery and in freedom, operated under fields of influence anchored in the overall organization of a general slavery-oriented kinship system. Their descendants' life possibilities, in turn, were governed in part by this antebellum matrix of slave-oriented kinship and the webs of agrarian patron-client relations that endured in slavery's aftermath. Yet their families' trajectories were also shaped by a great range of other institutions and fields of influence, as more and more African Americans detached themselves from rural impoverishment and began to adopt working-class and middle-class orientations in urban areas.

The historical record thus tends to undercut or at least complicate an implicit theme running through the dominant "myth of Kitty." Conservative white retellings attempt, on the one hand, to present the circumstances of Bishop Andrew's slaveholding as extraordinary and, on the other hand, paradoxically imply that these atypical conditions are illustrative of the comparatively benign nature of slavery itself. Yet the historical trajectories of the multiple enslaved families controlled by Bishop Andrew during his life, while eminently worthy of our careful attention, are not in and of themselves atypical. They encompass a great range of familiar outcomes, from rural sharecropping to the great migration, from rural tenantry to higher education. Rather than illustrating the unique and poignant predicament of James Osgood Andrew, we may approach these lives as representative of the grand, multiple narratives of African American historical experience, forging new possibilities out of freedom's inspiring and elusive promise.

Chapter Nine

Saying Something Now

W HAT ARE THE social and ethical consequences of revisiting a powerful myth, such as the contested stories of Bishop Andrew and Miss Kitty? Are such efforts most likely to exacerbate old wounds, polarize communities, and deepen suspicions across lines of race and related distinctions? Or might there be ways, through alternate engagements with such deeply held narratives, to contribute to mutual understanding, bridge building, and social transformation? These questions are vital ones, as scholars and activists in diverse locations ponder how interventions in public history might best be framed and articulated. Are there ways for public scholars to pursue serious academic research while responsibly contributing to the building of what Martin Luther King Jr. long ago termed the "beloved community"? In short, how might a commitment to documenting the intersection of myth and history help redraw the contours of our body politic?

In retrospect, initial efforts to revisit the "myth of Kitty" had decidedly mixed results. Beginning in spring 2000 my Oxford College students and I worked closely with local African American church congregations to research the campus's early African American history, and to restore African American grave plots in the city cemetery. The work elicited a wide range of responses, ranging from exhilaration and joy to rage and condemnation. As we have seen, the story of Kitty became quickly entangled in a wider set of struggles, over the desegregation to the cemetery and the city police force, the distribution of political power in the city and the county, and continuing debates over race and social justice within the Methodist Church. In some instances, as white leaders in the community began to shift their position on the cemetery, they also began to discuss other possible readings of the Kitty story. One older white man, a great-grandson of one of the Emory College faculty's leading slaveowners, quietly acknowledged to me that he had long suspected that the full story of Kitty and James Andrew had not been properly aired. "Seems to me we might have another Sally Hemmings story right here in town," he said with a broad smile to a group of my students. "Can't hurt to talk some of this through." He chuckled, "We're all family after all, aren't we?"

Yet some white residents were infuriated that any questions were being raised about the standard narrative. When the class mounted an exhibition about Oxford's African American history in the college library, some white visitors took great exception to exhibition text that indicated that the precise relationship between Kitty and Bishop Andrew remained a matter of debate. Outraged letter writers to the college dean and the university president asserted that "all of this nonsense" was a libel against the Bishop and the Methodist Church, and suggested that the class was falling under "communist influence." At a public lecture I gave in the college chapel on the varying white and African American versions of the story, several prominent audience members stood up to denounce the "lies" being circulated about James Osgood Andrew and Emory's history. Such accounts, they claimed, were a "slur on southern heritage." When I tried to explain that I was simply trying to document the varying versions of the story, a well-known white attorney and political figure retorted, "You aren't documenting anything. You are just spreading scandal!" A few days later, a middle-aged white woman whom I had long regarded as a friend approached me at a public gathering and asked me angrily, "Why are you doing all these terrible things, stirring up so much trouble about Kitty and Bishop Andrew, and make a mess of things in the cemetery?" I was, she told me with tears in her eyes, breaking the heart of Martin Porter, who had devoted his life to preserving the city's proud heritage. "He is such a dear man, who loves this college and this town. You and your students have no right to be doing this!" The same week, an older white woman angrily remonstrated with J. P. Godfrey, who was leading the struggle on the city council to desegregate the cemetery and who had publicly spoken on alternate versions of the Kitty-Andrew story.

"What would you like me to do?" J.P. asked, taken aback.

"I just want you to go away," she responded, "Just go away!"

The week after my public lecture on Kitty, I received three puzzling business cards from an anonymous person or persons. One was placed on my office door, one under my car windshield wiper, and another on my library carrel. Each had a large drawing of a single eye on it, with the words, "The eye of Oxford is watching you." Several of my African

American friends recalled that the same iconography had characterized business cards reading "The Klan is Watching You," sent to persons who had angered the Klan the night before they or their houses were shot at. The source of the cards was never determined, but the incident certainly shook my students and me.

And yet, amid all the anger and recrimination, there were beautiful and moving moments during this period. I will never forget our first day of work in the African American section of the city cemetery, as we began to clear out the weeds and privet blocking access to many old gravesites.

Cemetery restoration work in rural Georgia has an uncertain edge to it. Many of us had helped the multiracial Moore's Ford Memorial Committee restore nearby cemeteries where the four victims of the 1946 lynching at Moore's Ford are buried. For five decades, local Klan members had routinely desecrated successive attempts to mark the graves of the four young African American victims, until a massive, televised multiracial effort finally restored all the cemeteries, and the headstone smashing stopped.

We were mindful of this recent history on the first day of the project, as Rob, a silent, burly ex-marine, a white man in his fifties who kept company only with his two large German shepherds, strode purposely toward the cemetery. J. P. Godfrey and I walked forward, a little nervously, to meet him, but Rob had no time for chitchat. Looking at the forty students working with limited efficiency on the privet and bramble, Rob declared, "Never did set right with me, the town treating this ground like that." He immediately got to work, teaching the young men in my class, to their unending delight, how to use chainsaws and how to bring down dead tree branches and haul them away in his pickup. Rob came to every work session over the subsequent year, up until the day he was diagnosed with a terminal illness. His final months were often agony, but he was no longer a loner; women in the Mount Zion and Rust Chapel congregations took turns bringing him covered dishes and sat on the porch with him chatting, their children and grandchildren dispatched to take his dogs for regular walks. His internment, at his request, in the African American cemetery was well attended by his African American neighbors. Cemeteries, as we have seen, do not simply serve to help us remember the dead; they also serve to produce kinship, to expand the bonds of family, and Rob, somewhere along the way, was adopted, without any fuss, into the beloved community.

I once asked Norah Simonson, an older African American woman, if she had ever harbored any resentment toward Rob, who hadn't ever marched during the movement, hadn't ever protested gerrymandering or the thousand indignities imposed on local African Americans every day, during the many years after he came back from Vietnam. She smiled at me, "He was a hard worker, and you know, sweat-producing labor is soul-cleansing labor. He's family now, that's all I can say." One day, gazing at Rob hacking away at a tree limb, his tanned torso perspiring in the sun, Deacon Henry had joked, "You sweating like an old field hand. Never thought I'd seen the day." In a rural southern context, "sweat-producing labor" by a white man, toiling on behalf of the very African Americans who worked the land as slaves and sharecroppers, is of course deeply resonant.

Recalling Rob, I find myself thinking of the question posed to anthropologist Judy Rosenthal by her Ewe informants in southern Togo: "Why should [you white Americans] not pay your debts to the slave spirits the way we Ewe do? You would be better off for it. Some of them died violently. Their spirits are powerful; they can help, heal, and protect you when you need them, if you honor them fully."[1] As he labored, did Rob come, in a sense, to be possessed by the dead men and women of the cemetery, by those who had worked the land on behalf of his own white ancestors?

Saying Something Now

In any event, the enduring legacies of slavery were on everyone's mind in early April 2000, when J. P. Godfrey, Rob, and many others attended a community meeting in the fellowship hall of Mount Zion, after my students and I came across, in the probate records at the county courthouse, receipts paid to slave-catchers. One script reads,

> Conyers, GA. October 2, 1864. Estate of Dr. Cody To John W. Allan For arresting four negroes viz. Rose and her 3 children and expenses connected with the same
> $500
> by cash $200
> Balance $300

Rose and her three children had escaped from the Cody plantation and run westward through artillery fire in a futile attempt to reach General

Sherman's Union lines. Since a number of Oxford's African American families, including J. P. Godfrey's, were known to be descended from slaves owned by Dr. Jeptha Cody, the document was of particular interest to us. Several students wanted to exhibit the document in the exhibit we were putting up in the campus library about the cemetery. Yet other students worried that this receipt, raw evidence of a woman risking the lives of her children in wartime, was too painful to show in public. What did community members think? After a long silence, Deacon Henry rose to speak:

> All my life, I've heard white folks saying slavery was just a regular social security system, looking after people cradle to grave, and I never said anything. This woman, Miss Rose, I don't know who her kin were, she could be lying right out there in the cemetery, all these years. But she said something. She said to her children we are going to be free even if we walk into the mouth of the cannon. Yea, even if we walk through the valley of the shadow of death. Nothing holding us back. She said something.

Alice Thompson of the church mother board nodded and said, "She saying something now."

Two weeks later, on the exhibition's opening night in the college library, there was singing and constant conversation, joking and laughing in front of all the family photos and elegant heirlooms local families had lent for the show. But when people got to the corner where the slave-catcher's receipt hung, conversation always stopped, as each person slowly deciphered the old script and pondered the caption. Miss Alice's husband, James, took off his trademark hat and stood still. Miss Alice squeezed my hand and said quietly, "She saying something now."

The Work of Documentation: By the Dead Possessed

What might this book's revisiting of a single mythic narrative, revolving around a single graveyard in the Georgia Piedmont, suggest about documentary projects more broadly? What precisely does it mean for the living to insist that through stones, scraps of paper, or preserved images, the dead are "saying something now"?

In a celebrated passage of *The Savage Mind*, Claude Lévi-Strauss ponders why in funeral games among the Fox Indians the team personifying the living conspires, by cheating, to ensure that they will ultimately lose to the team playing the spirits of the dead. Why should the living go out of their way to lose if life is assuredly better than death? For Lévi-Strauss, that is precisely the point: in order to reproduce the world of the living, it is necessary to produce the dead as truly dead, to be firm with them and not allow them to return fully to the world of life. And thus the living must convince the dead, by temporarily lending them their living bodies, that it is in fact desirable to be dead, to accept permanent residence on their side of the great divide. "By ruling that they should always win, the dead are given the illusion that it is they who are really alive, and that their opponents, having been 'killed' by them, are dead. Under the guise of playing with the dead, one plays them false and commits them." For there is a truth universally acknowledged in archaic societies, which "resolutely sid[e] with the living," and that truth is: "death is a hard thing; sorrow is especially hard."[2]

Part of the burden of sorrow is that in giving voice and substance to the dead, who have been robbed of human speech and corporeal presence, the living risk becoming instruments of the dead's will, subordinated by precisely those forces that the living seek, respectfully yet forcefully, to domesticate. Among the Ngoni people of rural eastern Zambia, with whom I lived for twenty-eight months in the late 1980s, the three nights of the funeral process are organized around stately dances and hauntingly beautiful songs, in which the mourners enact the sorrowful progress of the dead, and so gently ease the recently departed soul toward its resting place in the outer groves, far beyond the village of the living. Come the final morning, after the body has finally been interred, the entire community gathers back in the village center for the closing funeral oration; a respected senior man is aggressively challenged by a representative from the other half of the kingdom: how did our sister, how did our brother, who once was healthy, come to die in this place? The lengthy response must be declaimed sonorously, detailing the lineage of the deceased, the accomplishments and challenges of a life well lived, and most important, all known details of the final illness up to the very last breath drawn. Without such a forced elicitation of the details of the process of passing away, I was often told, the deceased would never remain in the grove but would continue to roam among the village.

The underlying principle, for the Fox Indians or for the Ngoni, is surprisingly comparable to our notion of "documentation," derived from the classical Latin term *documentum*, a lesson or example, from *docere*, to pull out, to bring to light, to make evident, to teach. (Only in medieval

Latin did *documentum* come to be applied to an *instrumentum*, a record in writing, as in a parish register or death certificate.) The loss of a human life from the visible world demands an accounting, a tangible act of revelation on behalf of the dead through a living voice and breathing body, in order, paradoxically, to help the dead become truly dead.

These *documenta*, these lessons to the living and to the dead, are necessarily multiple. Nearly always, after the official giving of evidence has in principle concluded the Ngoni funeral, at least one of the singers falls prey to the dead, beginning to shake, twitch, snort, and shout out with all the telltale signs of *vizimu* spirit possession. Even in the face of a masterful, authoritative documentary narrative, the dead are not easily consigned to their place and must be enabled to speak by and through living tongues.

Too often, I suggest, readings of "heteroglossia" inspired by the writings of Mikhail Bakhtin assume that the clamoring multiple voices at stake in modern or postmodern narratives are only those of the living. A useful corrective might be Roland Barthes's famous meditation on death and photography, *Camera Lucida*, a book structured around an elusive photographic image of his late mother, whom he simultaneously knows intimately and yet is entirely distanced from. In contemplating her image and other images of the dead, he is increasingly enmeshed in a central paradox of memorial undertakings, which seek to bring the invisible into the visible world; through the image, the dead come once again to live, yet in a manner that makes us all the more uncannily aware of their ultimate absence. In gazing upon the photograph of a condemned prisoner on the eve of his execution, Barthes ponders, "He is dead and he is going to die."[3]

Documentarians and ethnographers routinely traverse this paradoxical territory. We seek to give voice to the dead, rendering their former words and experiences in media that themselves hover between the tangible and intangible, alive and inanimate—shadows captured on film, temporary museum installations, printed words on the turned page. In so doing, we take on, at times, some of the enigmatic qualities of spirit mediums, of those possessed by our invisible antecedents. Our labors, whether formally framed as fiction or nonfiction, are not simply acts of homage to the departed, but ritual acts of propitiation directed toward them, by lending them our bodies and our voices.

As Lincoln's Gettysburg Address reminds us, the graveyard is, in many respects, the archetypal space of the *documentum*. Each grave is an externalized example or lesson in which the living make visible transformed aspects of their predecessors to be seen by their descendants; often, they do this in a manner that crosses, in both directions, the great divide between this world and the next. In classical antiquity, written phrases carved on stone tombs and mausoleums were understood not only as messages to posterity but as especially efficacious prayers to be transmitted to the other world through the benevolent agency of the recently departed; in the presence of the stones, in turn, oracles might divine the intentions of the departed, often in their imputed voices. In the Shakespearean speech that inspired Lincoln, Marc Anthony lends his voice to the fallen Caesar, by reading his "will" and letting him momentarily live again. In a similar fashion, as we have seen, Longfellow in meditating about the village churchyard in Cambridge takes on the voices of the "mute" slaveowner and the slaves buried at her head and feet, in order to pose difficult existential challenges to his living readers.

The dead continue to speak through the living in twentieth-century literary evocations of memorial space. Consider the poetic graveyard of Edgar Lee Masters's *Spoon River Anthology*, in which each page is an alternate headstone offering the words of those who lie buried in a small town's cemetery, "on the hill." Two-thirds of the way through the text we encounter Richard Bone, the stonemason who, when alive, chiseled the epitaphs of the town's dead. At the poem's end he acknowledges that even as he came to know his neighbors, warts and all, "I made myself party to the false chronicles / Of the stones / Even as the historian does who writes / Without knowing the truth / Or because he is influenced to hide it."[4]

At a manifest level, the mason discloses the fictions he has carved over the years, comparing himself to an ignorant or compromised scribe. In that sense, he seems entirely unlike the omniscient poet, who speaks so truthfully for the dead, in such exhaustive detail, throughout the anthology. Yet, in the poem's middle, Bone recounts his shift from ignorance to insight in these telling words: "later, as I lived among the people here, I knew how near to the life / Were the epitaphs that were ordered for them as they died."

The phrasing betrays a subtle aspect of the labor of inscription, a careful undertaking that hovers between the realms of life and death. In working so closely to create words for those who can no longer directly speak for themselves, even when he is, in a literal sense, inaccurate, Bone becomes "near to the life" of those who are now dead. Note the careful parallelism: "as I lived" is matched with "as they died"; "here" is echoed in the next line's rhymed "near." Like his name, cleaned like a buried corpse down to the "bone," his written words resemble those he has carved on the bonelike stones. He and his words have become one with those of the possessed poet, through whose reconstructed headstones the dead seem to live, if only for a little while.

Seven decades later, in another poetic reconstruction of our buried inner lives, another gravestone comes alive to wander, for a time, among the living. The pinkish headstone of Toni Morrison's Beloved, against which Sethe had to submit to the sexual predations of the stone carver, reemerges years later as Sethe's alternate self, inhabiting the mysterious visitor Beloved, who uncannily embodies the infant daughter killed at Sethe's hand back in slavery times. At the book's end, it falls to the older women of the free community, those who keep its stories and its secrets, to send Beloved back, for "this is not a story to pass on." The unquiet dead may temporarily take refuge in the body of the living, but subsequent narrative memory depends on the repression of this wellspring of pain. A wandering inscription, Beloved must ultimately be returned to her initial, lonely fixity on the silent headstone. And thus the living Sethe, at long last, is free herself to "be loved" and to become her "own best thing."[5]

The dead even hover around documentary texts that appear to be resolutely about the living. Consider, in *Let Us Now Praise Famous Men*, how James Agee describes a mirror on the bureau of the Gudger family house:

> The mirror is so far corrupted that it is rashed with gray, iridescent in parts, and in all its reflections a deeply sad thin zinc-to-platinum, giving to its framings an almost incalculably ancient, sweet, frail, and piteous beauty, such as may be seen in tintypes of family groups among studio furnishings or heard in nearly exhausted jazz records made by very young, insane, devout men who were to destroy themselves, in New Orleans, in the early nineteen twenties.[6]

The family members who gaze into the ancient mirror come to see themselves framed in sepia, passing through the looking glass to join those who are already dead. The noble poor of central Alabama, whose life is being praised so lavishly in such fine detail, become most beautiful when they are envisioned as virtually dead. In Agee's mirror the forgotten men of the nation's antipodes are recast as our common ancestors.

Along similar lines, the year before Agee and Evans traversed the middle South, Walter Benjamin reflected in "The Work of Art in the Age of Mechanical Reproduction":

> It is no accident that the portrait was the focal point of early photography. The cult of remembrance of loved ones, absent or dead, offers a last refuge for the cult value of the picture. For the last time the aura emanates from the early photographs of the fleeting expression of a human face. This is what constitutes their melancholy, incomparable beauty.[7]

Walker Evans, for his part, begins his parallel text of photographs that precedes Agee's *Let Us Now Praise Famous Men* with his famous melancholy images of hard-bitten faces, but he concludes the entire sequence with three striking images: a new gravesite, marked by a simple headstone; a plate resting on a mound of earth; and finally a gourd tree or "martin house," of the sort erected in central Alabama to attract the mosquito-eating little blue-black birds. In these treetop shelters martins come to rest, and then, like souls taking wing as the old song has it, some bright morning when this life is over, they'll fly away.

Agee, in turn, ends his written text with a passage from Ecclesiasticus 44:1–14, in the Old Testament's Apocrypha:

> Let us now praise famous men and our fathers that begat us.
> . . . There be of them, that have left a name behind them, that their praises might be reported.
> And some there are which have no memorial; who perished as though they had never been; and are become as though they had never been born; and their children after them.
> But these are merciful men, whose righteousness hath not been forgotten. . . .
> Their bodies are buried in peace; but their name liveth for evermore.

Here, then, is the genealogy of the craft of historical reconstruction and mythic revisiting. Agee and Evans's collaborative work, the model of all subsequent American documentary undertakings, is itself begat by a scriptural reference to the buried bodies of the dead, to our common ancestors who live on through the reported, documented praises of their living descendants.

Responsible documentary work demands that we strive to honor all the dead, in the diverse material forms through which the living seek to make them manifest. Between the covers of the book, in the bureau's aged mirror, in the tattered document hanging in the corner, in the melancholy faces of the photograph, or on the weathered faces of the headstone no less than on the ceremonial playing fields of the Fox funeral game, within Kitty's long-contested cottage, or on the mantelpiece of Sally's Angel Room, the dead are all, through us, "saying something now." In succumbing to their insistent demands, in letting them speak through our borrowed voices and crafted objects, we commit them, and ourselves, to the rejuvenated society of the living.

Family Plots

In this light, it is perhaps not surprising that in Oxford, Georgia, the most productive reimaginings of race and community, along with the richest retellings of Miss Kitty and Bishop Andrew, have centered on the city cemetery—where Oxford residents, white and black, have been interred since the 1830s. In the years that followed the formal desegregation of the cemetery in 2001–2, new members of the city government have been eager to better conditions throughout all precincts of the cemetery. The city administration decided to name the flower garden in the African American cemetery "Ellen's Garden," in honor of my wife Ellen Schattschneider, who had planted the flowers with her students. (Advocates judged that naming the garden for a white faculty member would emphasize the multiracial nature of this remembrance initiative and make full council support easier to obtain.) In 2008 a brick walking path and gazebo were installed near the oldest graves in this section, with a plaque bearing the inscription,

ELLEN'S GARDEN

In this historic cemetery are buried the many African American forefathers and foremothers who, in slavery and freedom, helped to build and developed the community of Oxford, Georgia, including Emory College. Among those at rest here were farmers, ministers, laborers and educators.

Community members and students from Emory University in the year 2002 planted this cedar tree and flower garden, which is named "Ellen's Garden" as an expression of thanks to Professor Ellen Schatt-

schneider who with her students and colleagues worked tirelessly to
pay respect and to beautify this historic site.

Mayor and City Council
City of Oxford, Georgia
2008

In the summer of 2008 the city leadership, along with prominent white
and African American citizens from Oxford and Covington, gathered for
a dedication ceremony in the African American section of the city cemetery. Those present spoke of their shared commitment to honoring all
at rest in the cemetery and to bringing to light the many diverse histories
of the city's families, black and white.

Afterward, we walked across to the Andrew family plot and looked at
the headstone of Miss Kitty. Forrest Sawyer, president of the new African
American Historical Association of Newton County, joked gently with a
white woman member of the city council, who had worked hard to fund
the gazebo and marker. "I used to think Miss Kitty was just the loneliest
woman in the world," Forrest said, "being all alone over here, with no
one even remembering her kinfolk. But now I think she's resting a little
better, resting a little better. Thank you, sister, thank you."

The following summer, while doing research in Georgia, I came across
Nathan Boyd's Freedman's Bank application, filed in Atlanta in 1871.
This quickly led to two further discoveries. First, that in 1875 Nathan
died in Atlanta and was buried in the colored paupers' section of Oak-
land Cemetery, the city's most prominent burial ground. Second, consulting the census records, I saw that in 1870 Alfred Boyd was residing in the small town of Keosauqua, Iowa, married to a woman named
Malvina. Ellen and I thus decided to drive to Keosauqua and see what
we might find. A chain of evidence, gathered in Keosauqua, other small
Iowa towns, and the Iowa State Archives led to my contacting Lynn
Walker Webster, a direct descendant of one of Malvina's brothers in Des
Moines. An avid genealogist, Ms. Webster had for many years tried to
find Alford and Malvina's descendants without success. We talked every
day as I labored in the Iowa States Archives and drove across the region to consult old probate records. When I finally discovered the name
of the church, Allen Chapel AME in Rockford, Illinois, with which Rev.
Boyd's descendants were likely to be associated, it turned out that she
had known the current pastor, Rev. Virgil Woods, since he was a child;
Ms. Webster contacted him, and we made the final connections. Two

weeks after arriving in Iowa, I found myself at the moment described in this book's prologue, on the front steps of the home of Lee Caldwell, Rev. Alfred Boyd's great-grandson.

Mr. Caldwell was fascinated by the story I had to tell. He explained that he knew very little of his great-grandfather's childhood, and nothing of his parentage. He had certainly heard nothing of Miss Kitty or Bishop Andrew. He recalled that his great-grandfather's name had actually been "Alford," although it had been listed as "Alfred" on official documents. He knew that he had been born in slavery and that he had served in some capacity in the Civil War. He also noted that his adult daughters Darcel and Cynthia, who lived near one another in a city on the East Coast, were the family historians. They had been very close to his mother, Bertha Caldwell, who had been raised by Alfred/Alford and his wife Malvina, and they had, he thought, recorded her stories of the family's history.

Three weeks later, Cynthia invited Ellen and me into her suburban home. We spent eight delightful hours with her and her sister Darcel around the dining table, going through old family photographs and records, gradually putting together pieces of the puzzle. They shared their father's infectious sense of humor and his love of a good story. The story they had heard, as noted in chapter 7, was that great-great-grandfather Alford Boyd had served as a cook attached to the Union Army, but had not formally enlisted when given the opportunity.

In the year and a half that we have known one another, Darcel and Cynthia have carefully familiarized themselves with the historical materials explored in this book. Although I still by force of habit speak of "Miss Kitty," the sisters now speak of their great-great-great-grandmother as "Catherine Boyd," since they consider "Kitty" a diminutive slave name. They reason that since Alford and Malvina named their first child "Catherine," which must have been in honor of Alford's mother, and since Nathan wrote his late wife's name as "Catherine" in the 1871 Freedman's Bank application, that is the name by which she should be known. Darcel and Cynthia are both determined that the memories of Nathan and Catherine Boyd be treated with respect and have carefully pondered the precise circumstances of their lives. The questions of whether Bishop Andrew was father to Kitty/Catherine, or if she was his concubine, have become deeply personal matters to them. DNA testing, they note, might cast light on the question of biogenetic relatedness but not on the social and psychological connections among the various parties.

As of this writing, the family is still puzzling over the related question of Alford's relationship with Bishop Andrew. One sister is inclined to think that he headed north with the Bishop's blessings; the other tends to the theory that Alford escaped and cut his ties with his former owner. They wonder if Andrew gave assistance to his black sons. Did he encourage Alford to follow in his footsteps as a minister of the gospel, in keeping with the Methodist discipline of his youth—albeit within a black-led denomination? Did the Bishop perhaps advise Russell Nathan on finding employment in the prominent Washington family of the Dahlgrens? Or did the young men forge these pathways entirely on their own?

As Emory University laid plans to host an international conference on slavery and universities in February 2011, Darcel and Cynthia began to discuss visiting Oxford and Atlanta. They hoped to see the graves of their great-great-great-grandparents Kitty and Nathan. They agreed to join in some sort of dialogue with the descendants of slaveowners and enslaved families. (One sister joked that she didn't know "which side of that table to sit on—masters or slaves—since we might be descended from both sides!")

The news of the sisters' possible journey to Oxford, perhaps more than anything else, brought together white and African American residents of Oxford. In May 2010 the historically white Allen Memorial Chapel of the United Methodist Church hosted a preliminary planning meeting for interested parties. Participants began to conceive of a kind of roundtable or talking circle in Old Church, on the final day of the conference, at which the descendants of enslaved families as well as the descendants of slaveowners would engage in dialogue about this difficult, shared history. All agreed that the day should culminate in placing flowers at Miss Kitty's gravesite and in the historically African American cemetery, near the plaque at Ellen's Garden.

At this meeting, a white woman who has long played a leading role in the restoration of Kitty's Cottage turned to J. P. Godfrey and said, "I realize we made serious mistakes with the cottage, not consulting people and making sure the whole history was represented. I am so very glad we are finally working together now." The memory of Miss Kitty, which had so long divided the city, finally, with the prospect of her descendants' return, promised a significant reconciliation—centered, appropriately, on a memorial space.

Grace United Methodist, a historically African American church with deep ties to families long ago enslaved by Emory's founders, then offered to host a worship service on the final day of the Slavery and University conference, honoring all the descendants of the enslaved, including Miss Kitty's family. Mike Watson, the resident bishop of the North Georgia Conference, a white man who also serves on the Emory Board of Trustees, agreed to preach at the service and participate in the day's other events, including the talking circle at Old Church in Oxford. Within the space where slave masters and the enslaved once worshipped together, and apart, the living would join in the collective labor of memorialization and honest, difficult dialogue.

All involved were especially fascinated with the story of Kitty's eldest son, Alford Boyd, who found his spiritual vocation within the larger Methodist fold inside the African Methodist Episcopal Church—the church in which his descendants still worship. Given that the AME Church split in the early nineteenth century from the Methodist Episcopal Church over questions of race and social equality, the "return" of his and Miss Kitty's descendants to Oxford's Old Church signaled, for some, the promise of a truly united Methodist compact, transcending two centuries of racial division. J. P. Godfrey remarked that it is to his mind providential that Miss Kitty's great-great-great-granddaughters were to be welcomed to Grace and Old Church by Rev. Sharma Lewis, the first African American woman district superintendent of the Atlanta-Decatur-Oxford district of the Methodist United Church. "To think," he told me quietly, "that I have lived to see this day."

Unravelings

Outside of Newton County itself, the anticipated return to Oxford by Miss Kitty's descendants inspired new mythic imaginations and new memorial undertakings. African American artist Lynn Marshall-Linnemeier first became fascinated with the story of Miss Kitty/Catherine Boyd when she participated several years ago in the Transforming Community Program's seminar at Emory. As the prospect of the trip by the great-great-great-granddaughters was discussed, Marshall-Linnemeier began to conceptualize a sculptural and multimedia installation in Miss Kitty's honor, titled *Unraveling Miss Catherine's Cloak*. The work, she explained, would evoke the Yoruba ritual costume known as the *Agan*, associated with Egungun ancestral masquerade performances. The piece, she initially thought, would incorporate elements of a nineteenth-century woman's dress. Scanned archival documents and old family photographs would be sewn into the structure along with heirloom lace pieces, stuffed feathered birds, and cowry shells. The names of all known enslaved persons owned by James Osgood Andrew would be sewn into panels around the cloak's outer boundaries. The artist wrote,

> Rendered in white, the assemblage includes a cloak, bodice, skirt and head covering. The head covering, reminiscent of the bridal veil, celebrates innocence and purity. Feather white doves (the kind used in wedding and Christmas decorations) mounted on branches and placed in birdcages complete the installation. The doves symbolize Catherine's (and the community's) existence of being free (at least in their own heads) and enslaved simultaneously.[8]

This work was conceived as part of Marshall-Linnemeier's multiyear initiative, *The Journey Projects*. The artist resides in communities for weeks or months, engaging in dialogues across lines of difference. The resulting artworks are donated to the community and become a focal point for continuing conversation and exploration.

During 2010 the Emory University President's Commission on Race and Ethnicity (PCORE) became increasingly interested in exploring the possibility of an official university apology for or acknowledgment of the institution's role in slavery and segregation. After a great deal of discussion and negotiation, the executive committee of the university's board of trustees unanimously issued the following statement of regret on January 13, 2011:

> Emory acknowledges its entwinement with the institution of slavery throughout the College's early history. Emory regrets both this undeniable wrong and the University's decades of delay in acknowledging slavery's harmful legacy. As Emory University looks forward, it seeks the wisdom always to discern what is right and the courage to abide by its mission of using knowledge to serve humanity.[9]

The public release of the statement made it easier, two weeks later, for Miss Kitty's descendants, Darcel and Cynthia Caldwell, to travel to Atlanta for the conference and the associated memorial events. They were at that point in mourning for their father, Lee Bradley Caldwell, who passed away in November 2010. (I had attended his funeral at Allen Chapel AME Church in Rockford, Illinois, the same church his great-grandfather Rev. Alford Boyd had pastored in the early twentieth century, and helped to eulogize him.) Darcel and Cynthia decided to honor their father's memory by attending the conference and visiting Oxford.

On their first day in the Atlanta area, in the company of J. P. Godfrey, Rev. Avis Williams, my wife Ellen, and me, the sisters paid an initial quiet visit to the Oxford cemetery, to pay their respects at Miss Kitty's grave. We then all went over to Bethlehem Baptist Church, the county's oldest African American house of worship, for a moving conversation with Pastor Hezekiah Benton, who had so long supported my research. Darcel, Cynthia, and Rev. Benton had a remarkable talk about the predicament of the many black fathers in this story, including Nathan Boyd, who had seen his children taken away from him in 1855; Alford Boyd, who had raised his granddaughter Bertha; and their late father Lee Caldwell.

The next afternoon, we all gathered in Oakland Cemetery in Atlanta to lay a wreath in honor of Miss Kitty's husband, Nathan Boyd, the sisters' great-great-great-grandfather. In the sleet and hail, Rev. Williams read from the book of Ecclesiastes, by coincidence choosing the same passage Darcel and Cynthia had read three months earlier at their father's funeral service in Rockford. In her spoken remarks, Cynthia noted that this moment was not only in memory of Nathan, but in remembrance of all the fathers of color, in slavery and freedom, who had seen their children taken from them, and who had continued to love and cherish their posterity across the divides of time and space.

We then drove over to Emory's main campus, where Darcel and Cynthia met the university's vice president and historian Gary Hauk, who officially welcomed them to the university inside the board of trustees' conference room and gave them golden pins commemorating Emory's 175th anniversary. We walked over to the university library, where university archivist Kate Donovan Jarvis had kindly laid out many of the key documents related to slavery at Emory, including the Graves grocery book showing the items Kitty had purchased on account in the 1840s. I found this moment enormously moving—to be present as Darcel and Cynthia consulted the manuscript records I had so long worked with and which had, at long last, in Darcel's words, helped to "close the circle." We then attended a formal dinner hosted by University President James Wagner, who graciously welcomed the sisters to Emory.

For the next two days the Caldwells attended the Slavery and University conference with Ellen and me, pondering the many haunting and poignant stories of enslaved persons owned and rented by colleges across the nation. On the conference's final afternoon, during my talk on the story of Miss Kitty, the sisters allowed me to recognize them in front of an audience of several hundred scholars, and they were acknowledged with thundering applause. At a reception that evening, they had a chance to meet the great African American historian Evelyn Brooks Higgenbotham, and there was animated discussion of the fact that their great-great-uncle, Russell Nathan Boyd, had been married by Evelyn's grandfather, Rev. Walter Henderson Brooks, at Washington, D.C.'s Nineteenth Street Baptist Church in 1883. Also present was Dr. Joseph Pierce Jr. and his wife Aaronetta, two noted African American patrons of the arts who reside in San Antonio, Texas. Dr. Pierce's great-grandfather, we all noted, had been the white Methodist bishop George Foster Pierce, third president of Emory College and avid defender of his friend Bishop James Osgood Andrew. The evening, we all agreed, was a most remarkable "family reunion."

The next day, Sunday, we gathered for a day of remembrance and reconciliation in Newton County. At a service of remembrance at Grace United Methodist, attended by Emory's officials, faculty, and conference attendees, I read aloud from the will of Henry Harper, detailing the family of Esther, sold apart in the 1840s. So many children lost, and yet, I noted, some had in turn been found, as the congregation recognized Darcel and Cynthia. Cynthia spoke beautifully to the congregation, thanking them for their kindness. "She was yours, before she was ours, and now she belongs to all of us." An eight-year-old member of the church youth wing presented the Caldwells with greeting cards prepared by children in the Sunday school, welcoming them home. Bishop Mike Watson, the resident bishop of the North Georgia Conference, preached a powerful sermon on reconciliation and the continuing struggle for liberation. The sisters were tearfully embraced by scores of congregants, many of whom had labored for weeks to prepare the *Unraveling Miss Kitty's Cloak* quilt with Lynn Marshall-Linnemeier.

After a lunch held at Oxford College by the dean in honor of the sisters, we gathered in Old Church, Oxford's neoclassical house of worship built in 1841. Lynn's artwork was hanging, rolled up, from the high rafters of the church, waiting to be "unraveled." After an invocation by Rev. Benton, the mayor of Oxford read aloud an official proclamation by the Oxford City Council, declaring February 6, "Descendants of Catherine (Kitty) and Nathan Boyd Day," and handed the framed document to the sisters. Cynthia and Darcel each then spoke to the assembled. They again expressed their gratitude to Emory officials who had so warmly welcomed them and to the Oxford and Covington residents who had cherished the memory of Catherine, "their ancestral mother," across the generations. The sisters had, they noted, come to think of themselves as belonging to a new set of families, to the extended Emory family as well as the Newton County family. Cynthia declared, "Yes, Kitty's children have come home."

Then, as she pointed to the Emory 175th anniversary pin that Emory vice president Gary Hauk had given her, Darcel addressed the crowd:

> As I stand here today, a descendant of Miss Kitty, our ancestral mother —she was the symbol, she was just the representative, of so many people who are not known, who have been lost. For the families who cannot trace their great-great-grandmothers and grandfathers, their aunts and uncles, this is for you. . . . This pin says, "Emory 175 years." This morning, I asked myself should I wear this or not, since this is Kitty's Day. But I said to myself, I'm going to wear it. Because I feel this is to represent Kitty, to represent *all* the people that worked to help build Emory University.

Her voice rising, she declared triumphantly, "This is *my* pin! This is *your* pin!" The assembly responded with tumultuous applause.

President Wagner then read the statement of regret by the board, and J. P. Godfrey delivered a community statement of response, thanking the board and urging them to establish a university scholarship for the descendants of the enslaved families involved in Emory's early history. White and African American community members joined in a talking circle, reflecting on the complex burdens of slavery and the enduring struggles for reconciliation. Lane Norton, one of Bishop Andrew's white collateral relatives, shared with us the story of a beloved talisman, a half dime dating from the mid-nineteenth century, passed down to her father from a woman who had been enslaved.

After the talking circle, we adjourned to the city cemetery. The burial ground was bathed in the golden light of a brilliantly clear winter late afternoon. Darcel and Cynthia placed the wreath, provided by the Oxford Historical Shrine Society, at Miss Kitty's graveside, and spoke to all those who were gathered. We all walked to the historically black burial ground for a final prayer in memory of the enslaved foremothers and forefathers of Oxford.

An interview with Darcel appeared in a local newspaper, in which she remarked,

I'm moved by the generosity and friendship of the people here. . . . My sister and I are just two examples of the descendants of people who don't know who their families are. With the focus and attention on this subject, I hope to serve as a steward for all the rest of the people who cannot experience this.[10]

Recalling that day, the Caldwell sisters and I agreed that its most poignant moment took place in Oxford, as Lynn's artwork was unraveled from the high ceiling of Old Church. Lynn, Darcel, and Cynthia gradually lowered the rolled work by guide ropes, revealing a thirty-foot-long, multicolored quilt that billowed out from the rafters down along the floor of the stage. As the work unraveled, fifteen students and community members slowly read aloud the names of the seventy enslaved residents of antebellum Oxford whose identities my students and I had unearthed a decade earlier. Lynn's artwork, we saw, had altered as she began to work with members of the Grace United Methodist congregation and other community members. Rather than a three-dimensional, freestanding sculpture in the cemetery, she came to think of it as a grand quilted design, evoking the names of all enslaved persons known to have resided in antebellum Georgia, as well as scanned photographs from Oxford and Covington family lines. Darcel and Cynthia had sent along the lovely photograph of Alford and his wife Malvina, which Lynn enlarged and printed out on cloth to become a center point of the expanding piece, surrounded by stuffed white cloth doves.

Other African American families explored in this book, including the Mitchell, Henderson, and Stone family lines, were also included in the work. One large panel incorporated an enlarged photograph of Professor Joseph Pierce Sr., the African American mathematician and president of Texas Southern University, who was the grandson of Bishop George Foster Pierce, who had spoken against Reconstruction and in defense of Bishop Andrew from this very pulpit. Professor Pierce's son and daughter-in-law proudly sat in the audience as the work was unveiled.

At the close of the talking circle, Rev. Avis Williams contemplated *Unraveling Miss Kitty Cloak*. She noted the aquamarine borders of the great quilt, which had just descended from the roof like a multicolored waterfall thundering forth. Avis quoted from the words of the memorial architect Julian Bonder, who had spoken the day before at the conference on the challenges of constructing a memorial to slavery and the slave trade. "In the end," Julian had reminded us, "the only witness remaining is the water." Here, noted Avis, we see the water as witness, sewn together with the love and labor of this community, bound together by shared sorrow and joyous hope for the future.

After the talking circle, members of the Emory and Newton County communities gathered with great animation to gaze upon Lynn's remarkable work, alternately laughing and crying with one another as they reached out to touch the fabric and its scores of images.

I find it deeply appropriate that this work is a collectively stitched quilt. Miss Kitty supported herself and her family as a seamstress. The common labor of contributing to this composite piece, in effect, stitched together many persons across time and space. The allusions to a wedding dress and bridal veil encourage viewers to ponder the mysteries of Kitty's marital status or statuses: was she in fact Nathan's bride, and if so, what kind of marriage was possible within slavery's coils? Was she "married" to Bishop Andrew, perhaps against her will? The conjugal symbolism also recalls the ritual aesthetics of Yoruba spiritual initiation; in these traditions, the novice is often dressed as the bride of the *orisha* or divinity, as she or he is gradually moved along the enigmatic thresholds of the visible and invisible worlds. The work of reclothing is, in this respect, akin to the work of spirit mediumship, often figured as a form of rebirth into the shadowlands between the living and the dead. Kitty, Nathan, James Osgood Andrew, and the other players of the drama are emphatically no longer alive, yet our persistent, attentive labor summons them up in new and enduring ways.

Although Lynn drew and painted a number of evocative images of Miss Kitty in the early stages of the project, she chose in the final work not to include a direct image of Catherine/Kitty. This, too, strikes me as how it should be. For so long, diverse parties have sought to impose a particular vision on Kitty, forcing her to conform to their fundamental assumptions and habits of judgment. An absent visage, only deftly hinted at, helps restore to Kitty a measure of mystery and autonomy, inviting our imaginations without providing easy answers. H. Y. McCord Sr., who more than anyone established the canonical modern white myth of Kitty, often remarked that he would have given anything to see Kitty's face. In contrast, in Marshall-Linnemeier's artistic vision, Kitty/Catherine's face rests just beyond the horizons of our sense perception; she is simultaneously rendered intimately present and beyond our easy comprehension.

Equally apt is the motif of unraveling, signaled in the project's title and in the manner in which the fabric descended from Old Church's high ceilings in the presence of her descendants and the whole community. The work of reconstructing Kitty's garment, a process dependent on the effort and imagination of so many different people, is necessarily incomplete and provisional. In striking contrast to McCord's stone tablet, which purported to tell the entire story in the most fixed and permanent of media, this cloak is in a continuous state of becoming and unbecoming. In Homer's *Odyssey*, Penelope each night confounds her suitors by unraveling the funeral shroud she claims to be weaving for the father of Odysseus. In this fabric sculpture Kitty herself holds at bay her insistent suitors, past and present, through a cyclical process of creative destruction that escapes completion and finitude.

In Marshall-Linnemeier's work, then, we glimpse the puzzling entangling of the mythic and historical, the imaginative and the material, in the paradoxical enterprise of documentation. Here are summoned up all the figures who have intersected in this epic drama over a century and a half. Some of these images are fantastical: the Mammy, the Loyal Slave, and the Tragic Mulatto. Here we also glimpse traces of Miss Kitty's unknown parents and her puzzling relationship with James Osgood Andrew and Ann Amelia McFarlane. In this composite bridal gown and funeral shroud we recall her matrimonial bond to Nathan, her early death in slavery, and Nathan's own poignant death as a freedman, deprived of his fortune and of knowledge of his children's fate. At the same time, through the icons of fertility in the piece, we are reminded of Catherine/Kitty's many descendants, whose lineage continues to this day. Here we also glimpse the many chroniclers of Kitty's story, among them James Osgood Andrew, Augustus Baldwin Longstreet, George Foster Pierce, George Gilman Smith, Warren Candler, and H. Y. McCord, in whose hands the story was used, in turn, to justify chattel slavery and postslavery apartheid. Through the hand-stitched work of present-day community members, we encounter the growing tangible commitment of white and African American neighbors to struggle, through the burdens of a difficult and enigmatic past, for a measure of justice and mutual understanding. Along the cloak's edges we catch sight of recuperated names, celebrating the lives of the nearly forgotten men and woman who, with Kitty and her children, were fellow slaves of Bishop Andrew. Catherine's capacious restored cloak shelters a multitude of voices and presences.

This then is the legacy of myth when it is revisited through art and documentation, in the fullest senses of these terms. When all voices had seemed silenced, when all stories had seemed completed, a new telling emerges to be articulated, even as it is unraveled. Through the shared work of imagination and social engagement, those who have for so long been lost are unexpectedly restored to us, in ways that we cannot quite grasp. A family that had once seemed lost is now found again. In continuous new configurations of the mythic imagination, the dead call upon us to speak for them and through them. When we least expect it, we discover a truth at once new and eternal: the dead, conjoined with the living, are saying something now.

Guide to Persons Mentioned in the Text

(Enslaved persons listed by first name, unless surname is known; freedpersons listed by family name.)

Addison. Slave acquired though the Bishop's January 1844 marriage to Ann Leonora Greenwood. From the Thomas Greenwood estate. Mentioned in the April 1844 Longstreet-Andrew deed.

Alexander. Slave. Presumably, a son of Peggy, mentioned in the 1827 transfer to Ann Leonora Greenwood. Perhaps the same person as "Elleck."

Allen. Slave. Son of Lillah and brother of Laura. Acquired though the Bishop's January 1844 marriage to Ann Leonora Greenwood. From the Thomas Greenwood estate. Mentioned in the April 1844 Longstreet-Andrew deed. Rented out by Bishop Andrew in 1853 to his brother Hardy. Possibly Allen Parham (b. ca. 1835) in the 1870 census for Penfield, Greene County, Georgia.

ANDREW, Ann Amelia McFarlane. First wife of James Osgood Andrew. Died April 24, 1842, in Oxford, nursed by Kitty.

ANDREW, Elizabeth Mason. Born 1817. Eldest daughter of James Osgood Andrew and Ann Amelia Andrew. Later Elizabeth Lovett, wife of Robert Watkins Lovett. Nursed Kitty on her deathbed. Died 1856.

ANDREW, James Osgood. Elected bishop, Methodist Episcopal Church, in 1832. From 1845, senior bishop of the Methodist Episcopal Church, South. Died 1871.

ANDREW, James, Jr. Son of James Osgood Andrew.

ANDREW, John (Rev.). Father of James Osgood Andrew. Died March 10, 1830.

ANDREW, Hardy H. Brother of James Osgood Andrew.

ANDREW, Henrietta. Daughter of James Osgood Andrew and Ann Amelia. First wife of Thomas Meriwether.

ANDREW, Mary Catherine. Born 1833. Daughter of James Osgood Andrew and Ann Amelia. Attended Wesleyan Female College in Macon in 1847. Died 1858.

ANDREW, Octavia ("Occie"). Born 1835. Married Rev. John Wesley Rush.

ANDREW, Sarah. Daughter of James Osgood Andrew and Ann Amelia. In 1840, married Lamar, John Oswald. In adulthood, she became a "feeble minded invalid," nursed by her mother.

ANDREW, Mary Cosby. Wife of John Andrew. Mother of James Osgood Andrew. Died in Newton County, Georgia.

ANDREW, William H. Brother of James Osgood Andrew.

ANDREWS, Martin. A former slave of James Osgood Andrew, residing two households from him in 1870 in Summerfield, Alabama. (See "Martin")

Ann. Slave of the Thomas Greenwood estate. "A yellow girl." Assigned in 1827 to Ann Leonora Greenwood.

Anthony. Slave of Rev. Stephen Shell. Brother of Nathan (Boyd).

BANKS, Malvina. Wife of Alfred Boyd. Married April 4, 1866, in Van Buren County, Iowa.

BEAL, Ann. Wealthy woman in Augusta, Richmond County, Ga. Died 1832. Widow of Archibald Beal (d. 1811). Possible source of Kitty.

Ben. A slave sold by Alex. McFarlane along with Dolly to his mother-in-law Eve Catherine McNeal in 1801/1802. Manumitted October 19, 1804.

Ben. Slave partially owned by James Osgood Andrew from 1843 onward, a gift of his mother Mary Andrew.

Billy. (Also known as "Black Billy.") Slave in 1840, willed by Catherine Stattler McFarlane to her daughter Ann Amelia Andrew. Inherited by James Osgood Andrew after Ann Amelia's death in 1842.

BOYD, Alfred, or Alford. Probably born June 1844 in Oxford, Georgia. Husband of Malvina Boyd, married 1866 in Van Buren County, Iowa. AME minister by 1885 in Iowa. Died 1926.

BOYD, Barbara. Daughter of Alfred and Malvina Boyd. Born 1871.

BOYD, Mary Catherine. Eldest child of Alford and Malvina Boyd. Born 1867. Married Louis Bradley, Rock Island, Illinois, 1888.

BOYD, Cordelia Syphax. Second wife of Russell Nathan Boyd. Mother of Edna Boyd. Died July 4, 1924.

BOYD, Edna. Born January 20, 1896, Washington, D.C. Daughter of Russell Nathan Boyd and Cordelia Syphax Boyd. Married Daniel Gary. School-teacher in the District of Columbia.

BOYD, George Russell. Son of Russell Nathan Boyd and Tulip (née Cook) Boyd. Born July 25, 1885. Died at age forty-five, December 29, 1937, in Washington, D.C.

BOYD, Malvina Banks. Born ca. 1840. Married Alford Boyd in April 1866, in Keosauqua, Iowa. Had at least one child during slavery. She and her siblings were slaves in Callaway County, Missouri; escaped and led by Union soldiers to Mexico, Missouri; taken then by Quakers to Keosauqua, Iowa. Died August 8, 1930.

BOYD, Maurice (or Morris). Born around 1875. Iowa. Son of Alford and Malvina Boyd. Died in Cook County, Illinois, April 9, 1924.

BOYD, Nathan. Husband of Kitty (Catherine). Father of Alfred (Alford), Russell Nathan, and Emma L. Born ca. 1809 in Newberry, South Carolina. Willed in 1822 to Stephen Shell. Died June 6, 1875. Buried Oakland Cemetery, Atlanta, Georgia.

BOYD, Nathan. Son of Alford and Malvina Boyd. Born around 1873 in Iowa.

BOYD, Russell Nathan. Kitty's second son. Born around 1846. Messenger and librarian at the U.S. Department of State. Died in Washington, D.C., in 1921.

BOYD, Samuel. Son of Alford and Malvina Boyd. Born 1868, Iowa.

BOYD, Shawter (or Shorter). Born around 1878, Mahaska County, Iowa. Son of Alford and Malvina Boyd.

BOYD, Tulip Victoria Cook. Daughter of George Cook and Marcelena Washington, of Washington, D.C. First wife of Russell Nathan Boyd, married 1883 in Washington, D.C. Died before 1895.

BROWN, William. Brother-in-law of Stephen Shell. Born 1786. Married Rev. Stephen Shell's daughter Susan Shell of Newberry District, South Carolina, in 1812. Inherited the slaves "John Wesley" and "Dick" (brother of Nathan Boyd) in 1822–24. Died 1856 in Newton County, Georgia.

CALHOUN, John. U.S. senator for South Carolina and secretary of state. Took great interest in the 1844 Methodist General Conference dispute. Mentor to Augustus Baldwin Longstreet.

CANDLER, Warren. Senior bishop, M.E. Church, South. President of Emory College and chancellor of Emory University. Champion of the story of Kitty and of James Osgood Andrew.

CAPERS, William (Rev.). Methodist minister. Delivered funeral sermon for Ann Amelia Andrew.

CARLTON, Wilbur Allen. Born 1890. Faculty member at Oxford College of Emory University. President of the Oxford Historical Cemetery Foundation. Author of *In Memory of Old Emory* (1962). Died 1971.

CHILDERS, Elizabeth. Died 1851. Wife of George Childers. He later married Emily Sims Woolsey.

CHILDERS, Emily Sims Woolsey. Wife of George Childers. She later became the third wife of James Osgood Andrew, marrying him on November 24, 1854. Died January 4, 1872, in Dallas County, Alabama.

CHILDERS, George. Married to Emily Sims Woolsey Heard, in Summerfield, Georgia. Died in 1853 in Dallas County, Alabama.

COOK, George (free man of color). Washington, D.C. Married to Marcelena Washington. Father of Tulip Victoria Boyd, first wife of Russell Nathan Boyd.

COOK, Tulip Victoria. First wife of Russell Nathan Boyd, married 1883. Daughter of George Cook and Marcelena Washington.

COSBY, Mary Overton. Mother of James Osgood Andrew. Born December 11, 1791. Married John Andrew, evidently his third wife. Died January 26, 1846, in Oxford, Georgia.

DAHLGREN, John (rear admiral, U.S. Navy). Russell Nathan Boyd employed as his house servant in 1869. Married Madeleine Vinton in 1865. Died July 12, 1870.

DAHLGREN, Madeleine Vinton. Wife of Admiral John Dahlgren. Daughter of Congressman Samuel Finley Vinton and Romaine Madeleine Bureau, and the widow of Daniel Convers Goddard, first assistant secretary of the newly created U.S. Department of the Interior.

Daniel. Slave in the Thomas Greenwood estate, distributed to Robert H.

Greenwood. Possibly Daniel English in 1870 in Greene County, Georgia, Militia District 140.

Delsie. Slave of Rev. Stephen Shell of Newberry, South Carolina. Sister of Nathan (Boyd).

Dolly. Slave of James McFarlane, and then of his son Alexander McFarlane from the 1790s onward. Sold by Alexander McFarlane to his mother-in-law, Eve Catherine McNeal, in 1801, and then bequeathed to Catherine McFarlane (Alexander's widow) in 1816.

Dolly (Waters). Slave. Sold in 1799 by William Payne to Alexander McFarlane, acting for the Methodist Society, "in expectation she will be freed as soon as she can pay the Society the money they advanced for her." Free by 1802.

Dolphus (Adolphus). Born ca. 1826. Slave in the Thomas Greenwood estate. Child of "Elenor." In 1827, assigned to Ann Leonora Greenwood; she later gave Dolphus to her son or stepson, Henry F. Greenwood, in 1838.

Edgar. Son of Elisha. Brother of Ellen, Oscar, and Melerian. Slave in Thomas Greenwood estate; transferred by his widow, Ann Leonora Greenwood, to her daughter Mary Elizabeth Greenwood in 1847. Later evidently acquired by Mary Elizabeth's husband, Luther Smith, in Oxford.

Edward. Slave of James Osgood Andrew. Earlier the property of Ann Leonora Greenwood.

Elleck. Slave of James Osgood Andrew. Earlier the property of Ann Leonora Greenwood.

Ellick. Slave of Professor George Lane. Died 1848.

Ellen. Daughter of Elisha. Sister of Edgar, Oscar, and Melerian. Slave of Thomas Greenwood; transferred by his widow, Ann Leonora Greenwood, to her daughter Mary Elizabeth Greenwood in 1847. Later evidently acquired by Mary Elizabeth's husband, Luther Smith, in Oxford.

Elisha. Mother of Ellen, Edgar, Oscar, and Melerian. Slave of Thomas Greenwood; transferred by his widow, Ann Leonora Greenwood, to her daughter Mary Elizabeth Greenwood in 1847. Later evidently acquired by Mary Elizabeth's husband, Luther Smith, in Oxford.

Eliza. Slave of George Childers, bequeathed in 1853 to his widow Emily Woolsey Heard Childers; after 1854, slave of James Osgood Andrew in Summerfield, Alabama.

Elenor. Mother of Dolphus (Adolphus). Slave of Thomas Greenwood, assigned to Ann Leonora Greenwood in 1827.

Emma L. Slave of James Osgood Andrew. Daughter of Nathan Boyd and Catherine ("Kitty") Boyd. Born ca. 1848 in Oxford, Georgia. Sister of Alfred/Alford and Russell Nathan Boyd. Slave in Summerfield, Alabama, ca. 1855–65. Evidently married to a James Sanders by 1870; by 1880 appeared to be widowed with four children in Union, Alabama; then married an Abe Neal. Evidently residing in Pine Bluff, Arkansas, as of 1920 with her son Will L. Long.

Fanny. Slave of Lovey Powers in Augusta, Georgia. In 1832 court inventory, valued at $350.

Fanny. Slave transferred to Alexander McFarlane in Charleston, South Carolina, evidently for the purpose of freeing her in 1801.

FISH, Hamilton. U.S. Secretary of State. Hired Russell Nathan Boyd as laborer in 1875.

Frances. Slave of Emily Tubman, who sold slave Frances and her daughter Mary in 1841 to Milton Brown of Houston County, Georgia, for eight hundred dollars, on condition Frances never come within seventy-five miles of Augusta or Tubman's plantation in Columbia County. Perhaps mistress of the late Richard Tubman.

GARY, Daniel M. Husband of Edna Syphax Boyd, the daughter of Russell Nathan and Cordelia Boyd. Married May 3, 1924. Died June 18, 1951.

GARY, Edna Syphax Boyd. Daughter of Russell Nathan Boyd and Cordelia Syphax Boyd. Married Daniel Gary on May 3, 1924. Died 1978.

George. Slave of James Osgood Andrew, acquired through his marriage to Ann Leonora Greenwood in 1844. Perhaps later George Daniel of Greene County.

George. Slave of Rev. Stephen Shell. Brother of Nathan (listed by Nathan in 1871 bank account application). Delivered to Stephen Shell the younger in 1823. Perhaps later George Ansley of Newton County.

GRAVES, Iverson Lea. Son of Solomon Graves. Born June 20, 1799. Early trustee of Emory College. Died October 22, 1864, at Mount Pleasant, his plantation in Newton County.

GRAVES, Nicholas. Freedman. Married Rena Thompson, daughter of Lander Thompson (evidently the Lander, son of Peggy, both conveyed to Ann Leonora Greenwood in 1827).

GREEDWOOD, Thomas [Probably "Thomas Greenwood"]. Freedman. Born around 1825. According to the 1870 census, living next to James Osgood Andrew in Summerfield, Alabama. Probably the slave "Tom" from the Thomas Greenwood estate, acquired by James Osgood Andrew in 1844 from his marriage to Ann Leonora Greenwood.

GREENWOOD, Ann Leonora. Daughter of Thomas Mounger and Lucy Grimes Mounger. Widow of Thomas Greenwood of Greene County, Georgia. Second wife of James Osgood Andrew (married in January 1844). Died June 10, 1854, in Oxford, Georgia.

GREENWOOD, Caroline ("Carrie"). Daughter of Ann Leonora and Thomas Greenwood. Resided in Oxford from 1844 onward. Later married Henry King of Greensboro, Greene County, Georgia.

GREENWOOD, Henry F. Son of Thomas Greenwood of Greene County, Georgia. Son or stepson of Ann Leonora Greenwood.

GREENWOOD, Mary Elizabeth ("Eliza"). Daughter of Ann Leonora and Thomas Greenwood. Resided in Oxford from 1844 onward. Later married

Professor Luther M. Smith in Oxford. From 1847, owned the Greenwood slaves Horace; Milledge; Martha; Harriet; Harriet's child named Luisa; Elisha and her four children named Ellen, Edgar, Oscar, and Melerian; as well as some of her mother's slaves after 1854. Died in Oxford October 31, 1859.

GREENWOOD, Nancy Mitchell. First wife of Thomas Greenwood (married 1805). Daughter of Isaac Mitchell. Mother of four children. Died prior to 1819.

GREENWOOD, Thomas Edwin. Planter and slaveowner in Greene County, Georgia. Husband of Ann Leonora Mounger Greenwood, who later married James Osgood Andrew. Died around 1825.

GRIMES, Lucy. Wife of Thomas Mounger. Mother of Ann Leonora Mounger, the second wife of James Osgood Andrew. Died March 1, 1840.

GRIMKE, Francis (Rev.) Pastor of Fifteenth Street Presbyterian Church in Washington, D.C., where Russell Nathan Boyd served as deacon.

GUINN, R. J. Major. Trustee of Salem Campground.

GWIN, William. Chief messenger, U.S. State Department. Russell Nathan Boyd, a laborer and messenger at the State Department, resided with him and his family during the 1880s in Washington, D.C.

Harriet. Slave of Rev. Stephen Shell. Sister of Nathan (Boyd).

Harriet. Slave of Thomas Greenwood, transferred to his daughter Mary Elizabeth Greenwood by her mother, Ann Leonora Greenwood Andrew, in 1847. Presumably acquired by Mary Eliza's husband, Luther M. Smith, in Oxford.

Harry. Slave of Thomas Greenwood, distributed to his widow Ann Leonora Greenwood in 1827. Evidently, then acquired by James Osgood Andrew upon his marriage to her in 1841.

Hasly. Slave of George Childers, bequeathed in 1853 to his widow Emily Woolsey Heard Childers; after 1854, slave of James Osgood Andrew in Summerfield, Alabama.

HAYGOOD, Atticus. President of Emory College (1879–84); ideological promoter of the "New South"; author of Our Brother in Black. Before the Civil War, supervised the black church in Oxford.

HEARD, Emily Sims Woolsey. Third wife of James Osgood Andrew, her fourth husband. (See Andrew, Emily Sims Woolsey Heard.)

HEARD, Franklin. Second husband of Emily Sims Woolsey Heard Childers Andrew, third wife of James Osgood Andrew.

Horace. Slave in the Thomas Greenwood estate. Distributed to his daughter Mary Elizabeth Greenwood in 1847 by her mother, Ann Leonora Greenwood. Presumably, later acquired by Mary Elizabeth's husband, Luther Smith, in Oxford.

Isaac. Slave of Rev. Stephen Shell. Brother of Nathan Boyd. Delivered (with his mother "Judi" or Judith) to Lemuon Shell in 1823, after the death of Rev. Shell.

Jacob. Slave of James Osgood Andrew, who took Jacob with him to Florida in the early 1830s. Perhaps inherited from John Andrew, James Osgood's father. Probably dead by 1840.

JARRELL, Charles Crawford (Rev.). Born 1874. Methodist minister and Emory faculty member. Oxford, Georgia, essayist in the *Wesleyan Christian Advocate*. Nephew of Methodist historian George G. Smith. Died 1961.

Jim. Slave of George Childers, bequeathed in 1853 to his widow, Emily Woolsey Heard Childers; after 1854, slave of James Osgood Andrew in Summerfield, Alabama. May be the "James Sanders" who marries Emma, the apparent daughter of Miss Kitty, residing two doors from Bishop Andrew in Summerfield in 1870.

James. Slave from the Thomas Greenwood estate, acquired by James Osgood Andrew through his marriage to Ann Leonora Greenwood in 1844. Later, James Mitchell (father of Tom Mitchell), freedman of Oxford, Georgia, and patriarch of the Mitchell-Wright clan of Oxford.

Jefferson. Slave from the Thomas Greenwood estate, acquired by James Osgood Andrew through his marriage to Ann Leonora Greenwood in 1844.

Joseph. Slave of Rev. Stephen Shell. Brother of Nathan Boyd.

Judith. Slave of Rev. Stephen Shell. Mother of Nathan Boyd. According to the 1824 return, "Judi and child Isaac" delivered to Lemuon Shell in 1823.

KING, Caroline Greenwood. Daughter of Ann Leonora Greenwood and Thomas Greenwood. Married in 1846 to Henry King of Greensboro, Greene County, Georgia. Died December 16, 1874.

KING, Henry. Husband of Caroline Greenwood. In 1846, married Caroline Greenwood, daughter of Ann Leonora Greenwood, in ceremony performed by J. O. Andrew.

Kitty. Catherine Boyd. Slave of James Osgood Andrew. Born around 1822. Acquired by Bishop Andrew after 1832 and before 1840. Mother of Alfred (Alford), Russell Nathan, and Emma L. Died April or May 1851 in Oxford, Georgia.

LAMAR, John O. Married Sarah Andrew, daughter of James Osgood Andrew and Ann Amelia McFarlane, in 1840.

LANE, George. Emory College professor, close friend of James Osgood Andrew. Witness with A. B. Longstreet to the Kitty interview of December 1841. Died 1848 in Oxford, Georgia.

Lander. Slave of Thomas Greenwood. Son of Peggy and brother of Alexander. In 1827 assigned to Ann Leonora Greenwood. Acquired by James Osgood Andrew, after his marriage to Ann Leonora in 1841. Evidently becomes Lander Thompson, carpenter, son of Peggy Thomas, and husband of Sarah J. Thompson.

Laura. Slave of James Osgood Andrew. Daughter of Lillah, sister of Allen. Acquired in January 1844 upon Bishop Andrew's marriage to Ann Leonora

Greenwood. Perhaps later Laura Digby, freedwoman residing in Oxford in 1870.

Lillah. Slave of James Osgood Andrew. Mother of Laura and Allen. Acquired in January 1844 upon Bishop Andrew's marriage to Ann Leonora Greenwood.

LONG, Will L. (Dr.). Son of Emma Sanders (Kitty's apparent daughter). African American dentist. Widower of Cora Long. Evidently, no children. Died July 3, 1952, in house fire, Pine Bluffs, Arkansas.

LONGSTREET, Augustus Baldwin (Rev.). Born September 22, 1790. Methodist clergyman, attorney, judge, newspaper publisher, fiction writer, pro-slavery and Confederate partisan. President of Emory College, University of South Carolina, University of Mississippi. Close friend and confidant of James Osgood Andrew. Died in 1870.

LONGSTREET, Hannah. Mother of A. B. Longstreet. Died February 12, 1833, in Augusta, Georgia.

LONGSTREET, James (General, CSA). Nephew of Augustus Baldwin Longstreet, who in 1832 gave him eight slaves.

Louise. Slave of George Childers, bequeathed in 1853 to his widow Emily Woolsey Heard Childers; after 1854, slave of James Osgood Andrew in Summerfield, Alabama.

LOVETT, Robert Watkins. Born 1818. Physician and Methodist minister. Son-in-law of James Osgood Andrew. Graduated Emory College in 1843, then married Elizabeth Mason Andrew, Bishop Andrew's daughter. Died 1912.

Loy. Slave of George Childers, bequeathed in 1853 to his widow Emily Woolsey Heard Childers; after 1854, slave of James Osgood Andrew in Summerfield, Alabama.

Lucy. Slave. In 1840, willed in trust by Mrs. Catherine Stattler McFarlane to her son-in-law James Osgood Andrew, until her grandson Alexander M. Wynn came of age.

Lucy. Slave of Lovey Powers. In 1832 court inventory, has three children—Lewis, Zelda, and Dennis—valued at eight hundred dollars.

Luisa. Slave of the Thomas Greenwood estate. Daughter of Harriet. Transferred in 1847 to Thomas Greenwood's daughter Mary Elizabeth Greenwood by her mother, Ann Leonora Greenwood.

Maria. Slave purchased by Alexander McFarlane in 1799, later willed by his widow Catherine McFarlane in 1840 to her daughter Catherine "Kitty" McFarlane Mood.

Margaret. Slave owned by Ann Leonora Greenwood, given to her daughter Caroline Greenwood in 1844, the day before Ann Leonora's wedding to James Osgood Andrew. Possibly becomes the freedwoman Margaret Armor of Greene County, Georgia.

Martha. Slave of the Thomas Greenwood estate. Transferred to his daughter Mary Elizabeth Greenwood by her mother, Ann Leonora Greenwood, in

1847. Presumably acquired by Mary Elizabeth's husband, Luther M. Smith. Might become the freedwoman Margaret Brown in Oxford, Georgia, born around 1820.

Martin. Born 1845. Slave of George Childers, bequeathed in 1853 to his widow Emily Woolsey Heard Childers; after 1854, slave of James Osgood Andrew in Summerfield, Alabama. Postemancipation became freedman Martin Andrews. Married to Mariah, living two households away from James Andrew in 1870, in Summerfield, Alabama.

Mary. Daughter of Frances, both slaves of Emily Tubman. In 1841 Emily Tubman sold slave Frances and her daughter Mary to Milton Brown of Houston County, Georgia, for eight hundred dollars, on condition Frances never come within seventy-five miles of Augusta or Tubman's plantation in Columbia County.

Mary. Slave of Rev. Stephen Shell. Sister of Nathan Boyd.

MASON, Thomas (Rev.). Married to Elizabeth McFarlane, sister of Ann Amelia McFarlane Andrew.

Matilda. Slave of Rev. Stephen Shell. Sister of Nathan Boyd. Delivered to George Shell, son of Rev. Stephen Shell, during 1823.

MCCALLISTER, Samuel Ward. Socialite and inventor of "The Four Hundred." In 1877, visited the U.S. Department of State with Rev. G. G. Smith and meets "Kitty's son," Russell Nathan Boyd.

MCCORD, H. Y., Sr. Born 1855. Businessman, Emory University trustee member. Active at Salem Campground. Champion of the Kitty story, moved Kitty's Cottage to Salem Campground and erected cenotaph to her memory in Oxford City Cemetery.

MCFARLANE, Alexander. Born 1773. Son of James McFarlane of Manchester and Birmingham, England. Father of Ann Amelia McFarlane, who married James Osgood Andrew. Businessman and Methodist minister, evidently involved in the Atlantic slave trade. Died in 1803 in Rio Pongo, Sierra Leone.

MITCHELL, Nancy. First wife of Thomas Greenwood. Married April 25, 1805. Mother of Thomas E., Eldredge L., William M., and James Greenwood. Died before 1819.

MCFARLANE, Ann Amelia. Born 1796 in Charleston, South Carolina. First wife of James Osgood Andrew. Died in 1842 in Oxford, Georgia.

MCFARLANE, Catherine "Kitty" (later Mood). Sister of Ann Amelia McFarlane. Daughter of Alexander McFarlane and Catherine Stattler.

MCFARLANE, Catherine Stattler. Widow of Alexander McFarlane. Charleston, South Carolina. Mother of Ann Amelia, the first wife of James Osgood Andrew, James McFarlane, and of Catherine "Kitty" Mood. Died April 1, 1840 in Oxford.

MCFARLANE, Elizabeth (later Mason). Sister of Ann Amelia McFarlane Andrew.

MCFARLANE, James S. Physician. Born ca. 1800 to Alexander McFarlane and

Catherine McFarlane in Charleston, South Carolina. Moved to New Orleans. Married Eliza Norman in 1820. Brother of Ann Amelia McFarlane; brother-in-law of James Osgood Andrew. Died in New Orleans September 9, 1862.

MCNEAL, William. Resided in Charleston, South Carolina. Third husband of Catherine Reader Stattler McNeal, the mother of Catherine Stattler, who married Alexander McFarlane.

MEANS, Alexander. Methodist clergyman, educator, scientist, and physician. President of Emory College. Born in Statesville, North Carolina, February 6, 1801. Close colleague of James Osgood Andrew at Emory College. Died in Oxford, Georgia, June 5, 1883.

Melerian. Child of Elisha. Slave of the Thomas Greenwood estate. Transferred in 1847 to Mary Elizabeth Greenwood by her mother, Ann Leonora Greenwood. Perhaps later acquired by Mary Elizabeth's husband, Luther Smith, in Oxford, Georgia.

MELTON, Wightman F. Born 1867. Six-term mayor of Oxford, Georgia. Taught at Emory 1908–34. Chair of English and Journalism, Emory University. Served as the *Atlanta Constitution*'s local correspondent for Emory University and published numerous articles in the paper. Died 1944.

MERIWETHER, Thomas. Husband of Henrietta Andrew, James Osgood Andrew's daughter.

MERIWETHER, Henrietta Andrew. Daughter of James Osgood Andrew, married to Thomas Meriwether. Died 1862; buried in Oxford cemetery.

Milledge. Slave of the Thomas Greenwood estate. Transferred in 1847 to Thomas Greenwood's daughter Mary Elizabeth Greenwood by her mother, Ann Leonora Greenwood.

MITCHELL, Jacob. Father of Nancy Mitchell, first wife of Thomas Greenwood. Grandfather of her four children, named in his will.

MITCHELL, James. Slave of Bishop Andrew. Probably the "Jim" in the 1844 Longstreet-Andrew deed. Father of Tom Mitchell, grandfather of "Billy" Mitchell.

MITCHELL, Katie. Purported African American informant of H. Y. McCord Sr. on location of Kitty's grave. No such person existed. Perhaps refers to Katie Gaither.

MITCHELL, Nancy. First wife of Thomas Greenwood (married 1805). Daughter of Jacob Mitchell. Died before 1819.

MITCHELL, Tom (Tommie). Slave of James Osgood Andrew, son of James Mitchell.

MOOD, Catherine "Kitty" McFarlane. Born Charleston, July 22, 1798; died there January 31, 1857.

MOOD, James Amos. Nephew of Ann Amelia Andrew. Resided in Charleston, South Carolina.

MOOD, John. Born 1792. Husband of Catherine McFarlane Mood, the sister of Ann Amelia McFarlane Andrew. Died 1864.

MOUNGER, Ann Leonora. Born 1801. Married Thomas Greenwood in 1805; married James Osgood Andrew in 1844. Daughter of Thomas Mounger and Lucy Grimes. Died 1854.

MOUNGER, Thomas. Father of Ann Leonora Mounger, second wife of James Osgood Andrew. Died 1809.

Nancy. Slave of George Childers, bequeathed in 1853 to his widow Emily Woolsey Heard Childers; after 1854, slave of James Osgood Andrew in Summerfield, Alabama.

Nathan (Boyd). Born ca. 1809. Slave of Rev. Stephen Shell, then slave of Stephen Shell the younger. Evidently married Catherine (Kitty) around 1843 in Oxford, Georgia. Father of Alfred (Alford), Russell Nathan, and Emma L. Died 1875.

Nelson. Inherited from George Childers by Emily Childers in 1854. Evidently acquired by James Osgood Andrew through the Bishop's 1854 marriage to Emily Sims Woolsey Childers in Summerfield, Alabama.

NEWTON, Louie. White Baptist writer in Georgia; wrote about Kitty's Cottage.

Nick. Slave of the Thomas Greenwood estate. Acquired by James Osgood Andrew at his marriage to Ann Leonora Greenwood in 1844.

Orange. Slave of the Thomas Greenwood estate. Resided in Bishop Andrew's household in Oxford in the 1840s, where he was often ill. Perhaps owned by Bishop Andrew or his stepson Robert Greenwood. Postemancipation evidently Orange/Warren Dennis of Greene County.

Orlando. Slave of the Thomas Greenwood estate. Acquired by James Osgood Andrew at his marriage to Ann Leonora Greenwood in 1844. May have been the "Lander" (son Peggy, brother of Alexander) transferred in 1827 to Ann Leonora Greenwood.

Oscar. Son of Elisha. Brother of Ellen, Edgar, and Melerian. Slave of the Thomas Greenwood estate. In 1847, transferred to Mary Elizabeth Greenwood by her mother, Ann Leonora Greenwood. Presumably acquired by Mary Elizabeth's husband, Luther Smith.

PARKE, Frances Eliza. Born in Greensboro, Greene County, Georgia. Married Augustus Baldwin Longstreet in 1817, who through this marriage acquired at least twenty slaves. Close friend of Ann Leonora Greenwood, Bishop Andrew's second wife.

PAYNE, William. Creditor of Alexander McFarlane in Charleston, South Carolina. In October 1806, auctioned "eight mandingos" in Charleston to settle the debts of the firm McFarlane and Player.

Peggy. Slave of the Thomas Greenwood Estate. Mother of Lander and Alexander. Acquired through the Bishop's January 1844 marriage to Ann Leonora Greenwood. Evidently, postemancipation is Peggy Thomas, mother of Lander Thompson, in Oxford, Georgia.

Peter. Slave of Rev. Stephen Shell. Brother of Nathan Boyd. Bequeathed to Rev. Shell's daughter Milly Yeargain.

PIERCE, George (Bishop, Methodist Episcopal Church, South). Longtime associate of James Osgood Andrew. Delivered James Osgood Andrew's memorial sermon in 1871.

PLAYER, Joshua. Business partner of Alexander McFarlane in Charleston, South Carolina.

POTTER, Rev. Colored Methodist minister. Died November 1851. Oldest extant headstone in the Oxford, Georgia, African American cemetery.

"POWER, Mrs." Identified as the original owner of Kitty, in G. G. Smith's account of Augustus Longstreet's record of the 1841 interview with Kitty. Her actual identity is unclear.

POWERS, Ann. Born ca. 1749, evidently in Augusta. Buried in April 1839 in City Cemetery, Augusta. Possibly the source of Kitty.

POWERS, Eliza Olivia. Daughter of Lovey Powers; married to Joshua B. Hartford.

POWERS, Lovey. Born ca. 1777. White woman, single mother in Augusta, Georgia. Owned several slaves. Possibly the source of Kitty. Died 1832.

READER, Phillip. Son of Eve Catherine (Reader Stattler) McNeal. Lived in Charleston, South Carolina. After 1816, shortly after his mother's death, his estate went to his sister Catherine McFarlane.

Richard. Slave of Rev. Stephen Shell. Father of Nathan (Boyd). Purchased by Stephen Shell from Hibbert(?) Tucker in Newberry, South Carolina, on August 23, 1803. Delivered to Deverick Yeargain, husband of Millie Yeargain, Rev. Shell's daughter.

Richard or "Dick." Slave of Rev. Stephen Shell. Brother of Nathan Boyd. Delivered to William Brown, husband of Susanna Shell Brown, in 1823; evidently taken to Covington, Georgia.

Rose. Slave. Escaped from the estate of the late Dr. Jeptha M. Cody, Newton County, Georgia. Mother of three children. Captured October 2, 1865.

Rose. Slave of George Childers, bequeathed in 1853 to his widow Emily Woolsey Heard Childers; after 1854, slave of James Osgood Andrew in Summerfield, Alabama.

RUSH, John Wesley (Rev.). In 1854, married Octavia Andrew, James Osgood Andrew's daughter.

Sal. Slave of George Childers, bequeathed in 1853 to his widow Emily Woolsey Heard Childers; after 1854, slave of James Osgood Andrew in Summerfield, Alabama.

Samuel (Buckner). Brother of Malvina Cook, wife of Alford Boyd; he and his siblings were slaves in Callaway County, Missouri; escaped and led by Union soldiers to Mexico, Missouri—taken then by Quakers to Keosauqua, Iowa.

SANDERS, Charles Haney (Rev.). Born 1798. One of the original founders and trustees of Emory College, and the first elected treasurer of the board of trustees. Stephen Shell served as coadministrator of his estate after Sanders's death in 1851.

SANDERS, Emma. Probably Kitty's daughter. In 1850 slave schedule, a two-year-old black girl listed (born 1848). 1870 census Summerfield. Married to James Sanders, residing two doors away from Bishop Andrew. Perhaps the same Emma Sanders residing with four children in the 1880 census in Union, Dallas County, Alabama (no husband). Perhaps the same Emma Sanders residing in 1920 in Pine Bluff, Arkansas, with a son, Dr. Will L. Long (dentist), and his wife Cora.

SANDERS, Jacob. Freedman. Born in the 1840s. Perhaps related to James and Emma Sanders. Married to Ann Sanders. In 1880 resided in Summerfield, Alabama. Their children, it is interesting to note, include an Emma (born 1870) and a Kittie (born 1873).

SANDERS, James. Freedman, married to Emma Sanders. 1870 census Summerfield, Alabama. Presumably the slave "Jim" bequeathed by George Childers to his widow, Emily Childers, and then owned by James Osgood Andrew when he was married to Emily Childers from late 1854 onward.

Sarah. Slave of Catherine Stattler McFarlane, willed by her in 1840 to her granddaughter Catherine Amelia Mood, the daughter of Catherine McFarlane Mood and John Mood. Perhaps sister of Billy and Lucy, and daughter of Maria.

Selvy. Slave of George Childers, bequeathed in 1853 to his widow Emily Woolsey Heard Childers; after 1854, slave of James Osgood Andrew in Summerfield, Alabama.

SHELL, Lemuon. Brother of Stephen Shell the younger and son of Rev. Stephen Shell. Grew up in Newberry, South Carolina. Relocated to Mississippi, major slaveowner.

SHELL, Stephen D. (Rev.). Methodist minister and slaveowner in Newberry, South Carolina. Father of Stephen Shell (the younger). Died December 11, 1822, aged sixty-eight. Bequeathed his slaves to his children.

SHELL, Stephen D. (the younger). Son of Rev. Stephen Shell. Born Newberry, South Carolina. Inherited slaves Nathan and his brother George. Moved to Newton County, Georgia, perhaps in early or mid-1830s. Clerk at the court. Died impoverished on January 27, 1885, at the home of his brother's children, in Houston, Mississippi.

SIMS, Emily Wingfield. Born in Washington, Wilkes County, Georgia, November 20, 1798. Daughter of John and Mildred Sims. Married January 26, 1820, to Abraham Minthorne Woolsey. Her fourth husband was James Osgood Andrew, married in 1854.

SMITH, George Gilman (Rev.). Biographer of James Osgood Andrew. Died 1913.

SMITH, Luther M. Married in 1849 to Mary Elizabeth Greenwood (daughter of Ann Leonora Greenwood and stepdaughter of Bishop Andrew). 1848 graduated Emory College. Emory faculty member. President of Emory College post–Civil War. In 1865 married Callie Anne Lane (1843–77), daughter of Professor George Lane of Oxford.

SOULE, Joshua. (Bishop, Methodist Episcopal Church, South). Close friend of James Osgood Andrew.

STANSELL, Joel (Rev.). Grandfather of Major Robert J. Guinn. Ordained by Bishop Andrew.

STATTLER, Catherine. Born August 28, 1777, in Charleston, South Carolina. Daughter of John Stattler and Eve Catherine Stattler. Married Alexander McFarlane; mother of Ann Amelia McFarlane, who married James Osgood Andrew. Died 1840.

STATTLER, Eve Catherine. Married John Stattler, mother of Catherine Stattler, mother of Ann Amelia McFarlane, who married James Osgood Andrew.

STATTLER, John. Married Eve Catherine. Maternal grandfather of Ann Amelia Stattler McFarlane, who married James Osgood Andrew.

Susan. Slave of the Thomas Greenwood estate. Acquired by James Osgood Andrew through his marriage to Ann Leonora Greenwood in January 1844. Postemancipation, probably Susan Daniel, freedwoman of Greene County, Georgia.

Sylvie. Slave of Rev. Stephen Shell. Sister of Nathan Boyd.

SYPHAX, Cordelia S. Second wife of Russell Nathan Boyd, married in 1895.

SYPHAX, Fred B. Born around 1882. The brother of Cordelia Syphax (Boyd), resided with her and her husband Russell Nathan Boyd in Washington, D.C.

Tom. Slave of the Thomas Greenwood estate. Acquired by Bishop Andrew through his 1844 marriage to Ann Leonora Greenwood. Presumably, postemancipation, is the freedman Thomas Greedwood/Greenwood of Summerfield, Alabama, later Thomas Andrew.

TUBMAN, Emily. Married to Richard Tubman, Columbia and Richmond County planter, businesswomen. Best known for arranging to transport her late husband's slaves to Liberia in spring 1837. Possible source of Miss Kitty.

TUBMAN, Richard. Born 1766, Maryland. Married to Emily Tubman. Died in 1836; his will attempted to manumit his slaves.

TURNER, Nathan. Coadministrator with Stephen Shell of the estate for Charles Haney Sanders from 1851 onward.

Wade. Slave of Rev. Stephen Shell. Brother of Nathan Boyd.

WASHINGTON, Marcelena. Free woman of color. Mother of Tulip Victoria Cook Boyd, first wife of Russell Nathan Boyd; married to George Cook.

WATKINS, Sadie. In 1908 married George Russell Boyd. Son of Russell Nathan Boyd, in Boston, Massachusetts. Died 1916.

WEAVER, William D. Brother-in-law of Ann Leonora Greenwood, who was James Osgood Andrew's second wife. Administrator of the estate of Thomas Greenwood.

WIGHTMAN, Rev. Methodist leader. Friend of James Osgood Andrew.

William. Slave of George Childers, bequeathed in 1853 to his widow Emily Woolsey Heard Childers; after 1854, slave of James Osgood Andrew in Summerfield, Alabama.

Wilson. Slave of George Childers, bequeathed in 1853 to his widow Emily Woolsey Heard Childers; after 1854, slave of James Osgood Andrew in Summerfield, Alabama.

WILSON, James H. (General, USA). Led Wilson's Raid, through Summerfield, to Selma, Alabama, to Macon, Georgia.

WOOLSEY, Abraham Minthorne. Son of Major Benjamin M. Woolsey. Born 1794. Married 1820, Emily Wingfield Sims. A prosperous merchant in Augusta, Georgia; moved to Mobile, Alabama, and died there in 1836.

WOOLSEY, Benjamin Minthorne. Born August 15, 1823. Second child for Abraham Minthorne Woolsey and Emily Wingfield Sims. Handled financial and farming affairs for his stepfather James Osgood Andrew.

WYNN, Alexander McFarlane. Born 1827. Son of Sarah Harriet McFarlane Wynn, the sister of Ann Amelia McFarlane. Baptized by Rev. James Osgood Andrew next to his mother's coffin. His guardian from 1846 was Bishop Andrew, who held the slave Lucy in trust for him. Educated Emory College. Died 1906.

WYNN, Sarah Harriet McFarlane. Fourth daughter of Alexander and Catherine McFarlane. Sister of Ann Amelia McFarlane, James Osgood Andrew's first wife. Mother of Alexander McFarlane Wynn; died giving birth to him February 7, 1827.

Zelda. Slave of Lovey Powers. Daughter of Lucy.

Timeline

1783. End of American Revolutionary War.

1791, December 11. Mary Overton Cosby marries John Andrew.

1792. South Carolina imposes embargo on slave imports; lasts through 1803.

1794, May 3. James Osgood Andrew born in Wilkes County, Georgia.

1796, June 28. Ann Amelia McFarlane (future wife of James Osgood Andrew) born in Charleston, South Carolina. Daughter of Alexander McFarlane and Catherine Stattler McFarlane.

1798, April 27. Stephen Shell born in Newberry, South Carolina.

1801. Georgia law enacted banning manumission of negro slaves.

1802, April 18. Alexander McFarlane writes eyewitness account of slave trade atrocities in Rio Pongo.

1803, August 23. Rev. Stephen Shell in Newberry, South Carolina, purchases slave Richard (father of the future Nathan Boyd) from Harbert Tucker.

1803, December 12. Death of Alexander McFarlane from tropical illness in Rio Pongo, Sierra Leone.

1804, January 1. Resumption of the South Carolina slave trade (through 1807).

1805, April 25. Thomas Greenwood marries his first wife Nancy Mitchell in Greene County, Georgia.

1806, October 16. Auction of eight mandingos in Charleston—assigned to William Payne, to settle the debts of McFarlane and Player.

1809. Approximate birth of Nathan Boyd, future husband of Kitty. Child of Richard and Judith, in the household of Rev. Stephen Shell in Newberry, South Carolina.

1812, December. James Osgood Andrew admitted on trial and sent as junior preacher to the Edisto District, South Carolina.

1816, May 1. James Osgood Andrew marries Miss Amelia McFarlane in Charleston, South Carolina.

1817. Augustus Baldwin Longstreet marries Frances Eliza Parke in Greensboro, Georgia; he thus acquires about thirty slaves, and moves to Greensboro to reside with his wife and parents.

1818, June 25. Emily Harvie Thomas, recently arrived in Augusta, Georgia, weds Richard Tubman.

1819, March 9. Thomas Greenwood marries his second wife Ann Leonora Mounger in Greene County, Georgia.

1820-22. James Osgood Andrew pastor at St. John Methodist Church in Augusta, Georgia.

1822. Probable year of Kitty's birth, evidently in Augusta, Georgia.

1822, December 11. Death of Rev. Stephen Shell (aged sixty-eight years) in Newberry District, South Carolina. He wills his son Stephen Shell the negro slave "Nathan" (the future Nathan Boyd).

1822–25. A. B. Longstreet serves as Superior Court judge, Ocmulgee Circuit, in Greensboro, Georgia.

1825. Death of Thomas Greenwood in Greene County, Georgia.

1827. Greene County court assigns slaves from the Thomas Greenwood estate to Ann Leonora Greenwood, her children, and the children of Thomas Greenwood's first wife Nancy Mitchell.

1830, March 10. Death of John Andrew, the father of James Osgood.

1830. Federal census in Athens, Georgia, indicates James O. Andrew owns two slaves and that his mother, Mary Andrew, owns two slaves.

1831–32. James Osgood Andrew again pastor at St. John Methodist Church in Augusta, Georgia, assisted by George Pierce.

1832, April 12. Death of Lovey Powers, age fifty-five, in Augusta, Georgia.

1832, May 22. James Osgood Andrew and John Emory elected Methodist Episcopal bishops in Philadelphia, Pennsylvania.

1833, July 1. Richard Tubman drafts will, specifying his desire to emancipate his slaves posthumously.

1836, July 10. Richard Tubman dies. His widow Emily begins the process of attempting to manumit his slaves.

1836 (fall). Georgia Legislature committee declines to endorse Emily Tubman's request to manumit her late husband's slaves. She begins correspondence with American Colonization Society and Maryland State Colonization Society on resettling the slaves in Liberia.

1836–37 (winter). James Osgood Andrew and his family move to Newton County, Georgia, from Augusta. Initially reside at the property Chestnut Grove near the Georgia Manual Labor School in Covington.

1837, March. Death of Hannah Fitz-Randolph Longstreet, mother of A. B. Longstreet.

1837, April. Around forty-two slaves from the Richard Tubman estate are transported by the Maryland State Colonization Society to "Maryland in Africa" in Liberia, where they found Mound Tubman.

1838, December. A. B. Longstreet admitted into Methodist ministry. Elected president of Emory College.

1839, April 3. Burial of Ann Powers, age ninety years, in Augusta City Cemetery.

1839. Emory College opens.

1840, February 10. A. B. Longstreet delivers inaugural address as president of Emory College in Oxford, Georgia.

1840, April 1. Mrs. Catherine Stattler McFarlane (mother of Ann Amelia McFarlane Andrew) dies at the home of her son-in-law James Osgood

Andrew in Oxford, Georgia. She wills Ann Amelia her slave "Billy" and her slave "Lucy" in trust to James Osgood Andrew in trust for her grandson Alexander McFarlane Wynn.

1840 (fall). Bishop Andrew's family relocates from Chestnut Grove to Oxford.

1840, December 5. James Osgood Andrew, on a western tour, writes to wife Amelia in Oxford about Kitty's coffee and the importance of her preserving her chasteness.

1841, December. Kitty, interviewed by A. B. Longstreet and George Lane, attests that she is unwilling to be sent to Liberia, and thus remains in slavery.

1842, April 24. Ann Amelia McFarlane Andrew (first wife of James Osgood Andrew) dies in Oxford, Georgia, at age forty-six. Kitty nurses her.

1843, June 23. Newton County. Mary Andrew, mother of James Osgood Andrew, gives her slave Ben to her sons Handy H. Andrew, James O. Andrew, and William Andrew (and daughters and grandchildren) with James and Williams as trustees.

1844, January 14. Bishop Andrew marries his second wife, Ann Leonora Greenwood of Greensboro in Greene County, Georgia. She brings at least fourteen slaves into the marriage.

1844, April 12. Longstreet "purchases" fourteen slaves from Bishop Andrew for ten dollars, but then names Andrew their trustee. Their names are "Nick, George, Tom, Orlando, Elleck, Edward, Addison, James, Jefferson, Peggy, Susan, Lillah and her two children Laura and Allen."

1844, May. The New York Methodist General Conference, at which delegates vote to request Bishop Andrew discontinue serving as bishop as long as he is a slaveowner. Southern delegates move to detach from the northern church.

1844, June. Evidently birth of Alfred Boyd (son of Kitty) in Oxford, Georgia.

1844, June 4. Secretary of State John C. Calhoun writes to Rev. Capers and asks him and A. B. Longstreet to stop off in Washington, D.C., to discuss the New York Conference and the case of Bishop Andrew.

1845. James Osgood Andrew becomes presiding bishop of the Methodist Episcopal Church, South, at the founding Conference held in Louisville, Kentucky.

1845. Augustus B. Longstreet publishes his theological defense of slavery, *Letters on the Epistle of Paul to Philemon, or the Connection of Apostolical Christianity with Slavery*, in Charleston, South Carolina.

1846, June 2. Robert Greenwood, son of Ann Leonora Greenwood, receives eight slaves as his share of the estate of his father Thomas Greenwood.

1846, August 25. Likely birth of Kitty's second son, Russell Nathan Boyd.

1847. George Pierce elected president of Emory, succeeding A. B. Longstreet, who becomes president of the University of Mississippi.

1847, August 5. Mary Elizabeth Greenwood, daughter of Ann Leonora Greenwood, receives ten slaves as her share of the estate of her father Thomas Greenwood.

1848, July 19. Emory College Board of Trustees deeds land for a "church for the col'd people" in Oxford.

1848–49. Birth of Emma L., daughter of Miss Kitty.

1849, January 13. Mary Elizabeth Greenwood (daughter of Ann Leonora Greenwood) marries Luther M. Smith. Married by Bishop Andrew.

1851, April. Death of Miss Kitty in Oxford, Georgia, after a long illness.

1851, May 30. *Southern Christian Advocate* publishes James Osgood Andrew's death notice of a mulatto girl, Kitty.

1853. George Childers of Dallas County, Alabama, dies and bequeaths to his wife Emily W. Childers twelve slaves.

1854. James Osgood Andrew publishes his *Miscellanies*, including the (reprinted) "Biographical Sketch of Mrs. Ann Amelia Andrew," in which Kitty's kissing the dying mistress is described.

1854, June 10. Death of second wife of James Osgood Andrew, Ann Leonora Greenwood, in Oxford, Georgia.

1854, November 24. In Dallas County, Alabama, Bishop Andrew marries his third wife, Emily Sims Woolsey Heard "Aunt Emma" Childers.

1855. James Osgood Andrew and his third wife travel to California on church business; this year he relocates his household from Oxford, Georgia, to Summerfield, Alabama.

1856, July 23. Death of Elizabeth Mason Andrew Lovett, daughter of James Andrew and his first wife Amelia, in Oxford, Georgia.

1859, October 31. Mary Eliza Greenwood Smith, wife of Luther M. Smith, Emory professor and Methodist minister, dies in Oxford, Georgia. Her slaves entirely pass to him.

1860, November. Election of Abraham Lincoln.

1861, January 11. Alabama votes to secede from the Union.

1861, April 12. Fort Sumter in Charleston Harbor fired upon, beginning the Civil War.

1862, January 23. James Osgood Andrew writes to his son-in-law Thomas Meriwether from his new plantation, Tranquilla, that he has turned planter.

1864, November. General Sherman's troops march through Newton County, Georgia, liberating slaves. Some join the Union columns.

1865, April 2. Skirmish at Summerfield, Alabama, between Confederate forces and General Wilson's Union troops. Union Army captures Selma, Alabama. Bishop Andrew during fighting hides at home of a friend.

1865, April 3. Col. John Noble leads his 3rd Iowa Cavalry from Selma through Summerfield, Alabama. Returns on April 6 to Selma.

1865, April 8. 137th United States Colored Infantry in Selma, organized by Major Martin R. Archer.

1865, May 25–26. Grand Review in Washington, D.C. Victorious Union armies parade. Many U.S. Colored Troops and African American camp followers present with Sherman's army on May 26.

1865, August 9. 3rd Iowa Cavalry mustered out in Atlanta and returns to Davenport, Iowa.

1865, August 20. *Keosauqua* (Iowa) *Republican* reports that the men of the 3rd Iowa Cavalry had returned home earlier in the week.

1866. James Osgood Andrew retires as bishop, Methodist Episcopal Church, South.

1866, April 4. Alfred Boyd marries Mrs. Melvina Banks in Van Buren County, Iowa.

1867. Mary Catherine Boyd born to Alfred and Malvina Boyd, in Van Buren County, Iowa.

1869. Washington, D.C., City Directory lists Russell Boyd as a servant (colored) living at 402 L Street North, the home of Rear Admiral John A. Dahlgren.

1870, July 9. Death of Augustus Baldwin Longstreet in Oxford, Mississippi.

1870, July 12. Death of Rear Admiral John A. Dahlgren at his home in Washington, D.C.

1871, February 22. Birth of Nathan Boyd, son of Alford and Malvina Boyd in Iowa.

1871, March 1. Death of Bishop James Osgood Andrew in Mobile, Mobile County, Alabama (in the Franklin Street Parsonage) at the home of his daughter Octavia and son-in-law Rev. J. W. Rush, after he had gone to New Orleans on church work.

1871, March 5 (Sunday). James Osgood Andrew buried at Oxford, Georgia.

1871, March 27. Russell N. Boyd opens a Freedman's Bank account in Washington, D.C.

1871, May 23. Nathan Boyd opens Freedman's Bank account in Atlanta, Georgia.

1874, June 28. All branches of the Freedman's Bank close their doors.

1875, June 6. Nathan Boyd buried in Atlanta cemetery. List of Colored Paupers, Oakland Cemetery.

1875, July 1. Russell N. Boyd hired as a laborer at the Department of State by Secretary of State Hamilton Fish.

1877. Rev. George Gilman Smith reports meeting, with Judge McCallister, "Kitty's son" at the U.S. Department of State in Washington, D.C.

1883. Rev. George Gilman Smith publishes *Life and Letters of James Osgood Andrew*, which contains an account of Kitty and of meeting Kitty's son in 1877 at the U.S. Department of State.

1883, October. Russell Nathan Boyd marries Tulip V. Cook, who will be the mother of his son George Russell Boyd. Marriage conducted at 19th Street Baptist Church by Rev. Walter Brooks.

1884. A. Boyd appointed as AME pastor to Newton and Marshalltown, Iowa (evidently his first appointment).

1885, July 25. Birth of George Russell Boyd, to Russell Nathan Boyd and Tulip (née Cook) Boyd in Washington, D.C.

1893, August 1. Russell Nathan Boyd appointed assistant messenger at State Department (salary: $720 per year).

1895. Russell Nathan Boyd marries his second wife, Cordelia Syphax. Marriage conducted by Rev. Francis Grimke at 15th Street Presbyterian.

1896, January 20. Birth of Edna Boyd to Russell Nathan Boyd and Cordelia Boyd.

1898. Warren Akin Candler elected bishop of the Methodist Episcopal Church, South.

1903, October. Russell Nathan Boyd travels to London, England, as part of the U.S. delegation demarcating the boundaries of Alaska at the 1903 London Tribunal.

1915. December 1. Russell Nathan Boyd appointed messenger at the State Department (salary: $840 per year).

1916. Death of Sadie W. (Watkins) Boyd, wife of George Russell Boyd, in Boston.

1921, February 1. Russell Nathan Boyd dies in Freedmen's Hospital, Washington, D.C.

1924, May 3. Edna S. Boyd marries Daniel M. Gary. Married by Rev. Francis Grimke.

1924, July 4. Death in automobile accident of Cordelia Syphax Boyd, in car with her daughter Edna S. Boyd Gary and new son-in-law Daniel Gary near Bryantown, Maryland.

1926, May 13. Death of Alfred Boyd, following an automobile accident.

1937, December 29. George Boyd, 45, dies, Freedman's Hospital, Washington, D.C.

1937–1938, winter. H. Y. McCord purchases the land of the former Bishop Andrew estate in Oxford, Georgia.

1938, December. Kitty's Cottage moved to Salem Campground on motor truck from Oxford to Salem Camp Ground.

1939, May 10. Methodist churches north and south reunited at a conference in Kansas City, Missouri.

1939, July. Kitty's Cottage Museum opens at Salem Campground.

1939. Installation of the Kitty tablet in Oxford City Cemetery by H. Y. McCord Sr.

1939, December 15. *Gone with the Wind* premiere at Loew's Theater, Atlanta. Three hundred thousand people line the streets.

1941. Death of Warren Akin Candler, followed by burial in Oxford Cemetery.

1951, June 18. Death of Daniel Gary, husband of Edna Boyd Gary.

1952, July 3. Dr. W. L. Long, retired dentist and son of Emma Sanders, dies in a fire in Pine Bluff, Arkansas.

1965, March 1. Oxford Historical Cemetery Committee takes responsibility for the historically white section of Oxford City Cemetery.

1966. November 5. Dedication and Act of Unveiling a Marker in Remembrance of Bishop James Osgood Andrew, Oxford, Georgia.

1966. Erection of the Oxford and Emory College State Historic Marker, by the Georgia State Historical Commission, including an entry on Kitty's Cottage.

1970, June 18. North Georgia Conference, United Methodist Church unanimously adopts resolution that Oxford should be designated a historic shrine of the Methodist Church. Resolution mentions Kitty's Cottage and her burial in Oxford.

1976. Publication of John Jakes's *The Furies* (book 4 of the American Bicentennial Series), which has a fictional journal sequence on Bishop Andrew and the 1844 Methodist Conference.

1978, July 20. Death of Edna Syphax Boyd Gary (Kitty's granddaughter) in Washington, D.C.

1992. Board at Salem Campground offers city of Oxford the possibility of taking back Kitty's Cottage.

1994. Kitty's Cottage transported back to Oxford, Georgia. Initially in Oxford cemetery, then placed to right of Old Church.

1995, January 30. Oxford Historical Shrine Society takes responsibility (by vote) to preserve Kitty's Cottage.

1999. Kitty's Cottage moved to the rear of the Old Church lot.

2000. Oxford Historical Cemetery Foundation arranges for the placement of a small stone marker to Kitty in the Andrew family plot, Oxford cemetery.

2007, "Juneteenth." June 19. Ancestral Walk to Kitty's Cottage; Renaming of Miss Kitty to a Ewe name by First Afrikan Presbyterian Church of Lithonia, Georgia.

2009, July–August. Mark Auslander contacts and meets Catherine "Kitty" Boyd's great-great-grandson and great-great-great-granddaughters.

2011, January. Emory Board of Trustees issues "regret" for the university's "entwinement with slavery."

2011, February 2–6. Darcel and Cynthia Caldwell, Miss Kitty's descendants, visit Atlanta, Georgia, to attend Emory University's conference on slavery and universities, and are "welcomed home" to Oxford and Covington.

Kitty's Possible Origins

A. Ann Powers (d. 1839)

A woman named Ann Powers was buried on April 3, 1839, in the Augusta City Cemetery. She died at age ninety and was, according to cemetery records, a lifetime resident of Augusta, Georgia. An Ann Powers is listed among the early members of St. John Methodist Church, so she would have been an early parishioner of Rev. Andrew. The 1830 census indicates that she owned three female slaves under ten years of age, and two female slaves between the ages of thirty-six and fifty-five. So she could have owned Kitty, who would have been about eight years old in 1830. Years earlier, her husband Nicholas Graham Powers had deeded her two slaves: Charity, a negro woman about nineteen years of age (born about 1798) and Charity's child Alfred, two years of age (born about 1815). The name Alfred might be significant, given that Kitty named her eldest son "Alfred." If Charity were in fact Kitty's mother, then Alfred would have been Kitty's brother, and she could have named her son for him.

By the time Ann Powers died in April 1839, Bishop Andrew had been gone from Augusta for at least three years. It would have been difficult to transfer Kitty to the Bishop at this point. It is conceivable, if unlikely, that Augustus Baldwin Longstreet, the Bishop's close friend, might have played a role in such a transfer. Longstreet, at that point a Methodist minister, remained in Augusta during 1839 and ministered to the ill and dying during the yellow fever epidemic that ravaged the city. In principle, the dying Ann Powers could have arranged for a transfer of Kitty to the Bishop through Rev. Longstreet, who was to move to Newton County in early 1840 and take up residence, as Emory College's new president, near his close friend Bishop Andrew.

However, Ann Powers left no will and there is no documentary evidence that she arranged for any of her slaves to be transferred out of her family. Like Lovey Powers she was clearly of modest means, and often had difficulties paying her debts and taxes. Some years earlier, her son Jeptha signed himself into an indentureship under harsh conditions with a local artisan. In 1812, the sheriff held a sale of her house and lot to satisfy her debts to two creditors. It is difficult to imagine that her heirs and creditors would have allowed any slave from her estate to be transferred to Bishop Andrew.

Why, then, in the 1841 document authored by Augustus Baldwin Longstreet, does he refer to Kitty's original mistress as a "Mrs. Power"? Given that Longstreet was Andrew's closest friend, it seems unlikely that he was misinformed. More likely, he was engaged in a degree of deception or misdirection to hide

Kitty's actual origins. As an attorney practicing in Augusta in the 1830s, who was frequently in the county courthouse, he presumably would have known of the deaths of the slaveholding Lovey Powers and Ann Powers (he probably knew Ann Powers, a Methodist, quite well) and might have judged theirs a plausible name to use. Perhaps Longstreet and Bishop Andrew were eager to screen the identity of Kitty's father, who may well have been a prominent white citizen in Augusta. (Recall, as noted in chapter 3, the possibility that the "December 1841" interview text was in fact composed by Longstreet in April 1844, specifically as "insurance" against attacks by northern delegates at the upcoming May 1844 New York General Conference.)

Let us thus turn to several alternate scenarios of Kitty's origins.

B. Ann Beal or Beall (d. 1832)

Ann Beall, an Augusta woman who died in 1832, the same year as Lovey Powers, fits many of the criteria articulated by Andrew and Longstreet. She was a wealthy widow and active member of St. John Methodist Church, James Andrew's congregation. She owned twelve slaves in 1830, including one female slave under ten (recall that Kitty would probably have been about eight in 1830). She made elaborate provisions for a number of her slaves in her will, using language rather similar to that which Bishop Andrew would later use. The will's fifth section, for example, provides,

> 5th I give and bequeath to my friend Milton Anthony my two negroes Salira and Nancy in [sincere?] trust and confidence that he will make them as free as the law will permit, and grant them his kind protection for that purpose.

In the sixth provision she sets aside,

> ten acres of land . . . whereon the negro houses are . . . [to] permit my old and faithful servants Dinah, Isaac and Sue to reside and support themselves thereon under the protection of Executors during the material lives of said servants and the survivor and them.

The ninth provision holds, "I give and bequeath my negro man Caesar and his blacksmith tools to James Coleman in trust and confidence that he will [provide?] Caesar during his life (or so long as Caesar shall be able to contribute) . . . with a blacksmith shop and allow him the use of the tools aforesaid and in further confidence that he will receive of . . . Caesar the sum of forty dollars per year and pay to the trustees of the Methodist Episcopal Church in the City of Augusta." The seventeenth provision provides, "17th I will that my boys Bob and John be sold by my Executors at private sale and that they be consulted in choosing their owners or at any rate it is my express desire that my executors take good care to sell them to purchasers that will treat them well."

No mention is made in the will or associated probate records of a slave girl named Kitty. However, this is one of the very few Augusta antebellum wills that uses the phrase "make them as free as the law will permit" in reference to her slaves, very close to the wording Andrew would later use in his 1851 obituary of Kitty, "and make her as free as the laws of Georgia would permit." It is possible that Kitty was one of Ann Beall's slaves, and that she made a private arrangement with Bishop Andrew to care for her. Still, without legal sanction to receive a slave it is unlikely the Bishop would have consented to do so. As with Lovey Powers, the time frame does not appear quite right, since Ann Beal died in 1832 and Bishop Andrew evidently did not acquire Kitty until after 1836.

C. James McFarlane (ca. 1800–1862)

It is conceivable that Longstreet and Andrew were both prevaricating and that Kitty was not in fact acquired in Augusta. Perhaps instead she came from Charleston, South Carolina, where James Andrew spent a good deal of time and which was the home of his first wife, Ann Amelia. In the 1900 census, Kitty's eldest son, Alfred Boyd, asserts that both his father and mother were born in South Carolina. He is certainly correct in the case of his father, since we know that Nathan Boyd was born in Newberry, South Carolina; perhaps he was correct in his mother's case as well.

Might Kitty have come out of Ann Amelia's family, the McFarlanes, from which the Andrews were to acquire in 1840 at least two slaves, Billy and Lucy? (Is it simply coincidence that the nickname of Ann Amelia Andrew's sister Catherine McFarlane Mood was "Kitty"?) Might the enslaved girl Kitty have been fathered by Ann Amelia's elder brother, the physician James McFarlane? In the early 1830s, Dr. McFarlane appears to have left Charleston for New Orleans. Might he at this point have wished to divest himself of a mixed-race daughter and arranged to place her with his sister and brother-in-law? In 1840 Dr. McFarlane appears to be living with a mulatta woman in New Orleans's First Ward. Might this woman have had some connection to the mulatto child Kitty? In any event, by 1850 Dr. McFarlane owned nine slaves and was well established in New Orleans political and social circles. Might Bishop Andrew and Augustus Longstreet have wished to defend his reputation by continuing to conceal the actual circumstances of Kitty's origin?

D. Hannah Longstreet (d. 1837) and
Augustus Baldwin Longstreet (1790–1870)

It is also possible that Augustus Baldwin Longstreet had an even more direct hand in the Kitty story. Perhaps he himself was Kitty's father and prevailed upon his close friend Bishop Andrew to take responsibility for Kitty in the mid-1830s. Once again, there is no direct evidence for this scenario, but several circumstances suggest it might be plausible.

Longstreet had grown up in Augusta, but in March 1817 he married Frances Eliza Parke, a wealthy young Methodist woman in Greensboro, Greene County, Georgia, about fifty miles west of Augusta. Through the marriage he acquired about thirty slaves and sizable land holdings. He moved from Augusta to Greensboro, residing with his wife and her parents. He farmed and served as a judge in the county for some years on the Ocmulgee circuit. During this period, he must have been very familiar with Ann Leonora Greenwood, the future second wife of Bishop Andrew, and the complex transactions regarding the slaves in her late husband's estate, discussed in chapter 9. While in Greensboro, he later recalled, Longstreet acquired a slave for each of his children, naming each slave for the white child he or she was to care for. In 1827 Longstreet was converted to Methodism by his wife's brother. The conversion was said to have been occasioned by his deep grief over the death of his eldest child, Alfred Elmsley (1820–24), who had died three years earlier.

Around this time, Longstreet returned to Augusta from Greensboro and concentrated on his law practice, acquiring an elegant estate known as Westover. He also published and edited a newspaper, the *States Rights Sentinel*, in which he printed his humorous stories, largely based on his experiences as a circuit-riding lawyer and magistrate in Middle Georgia. These sketches were published to great acclaim in 1835 in book form: *Georgia Scenes, Characters, Incidents, Etc. in the First Half Century of the Republic.*

Around 1832 Longstreet resolved to quit farming and to dispossess himself of most of his slaves. His motivations for this course of action are unclear. He implies in various writings that he had not been a successful farmer and that his slaves had been cheating him. In any event, over the next several years he did reduce the number of slaves he owned. In June 1832 he transferred to his nephew and ward James Longstreet (the future Confederate general), for the token sum of ten dollars, eight slaves: "carpenter Dennis, Guss for Augustus, Daniel and Zanya, Charity and her children, Joe and Ned and Little May daughter of Nelly." In May 1834, as noted above, he transferred five slaves to Richard Tubman, to settle a debt. These slaves were "Vicky 29–30, Alfred a boy 14, Stephen a man about 35, Matilda a girl about 18, and Violet about fifty." (Alfred, it should be noted, was almost certainly named for Longstreet's own first child, Alfred, who had died ten years earlier; both the white Alfred and the slave Alfred were born the same year, 1820, when Longstreet was still living in Greensboro.)

Longstreet wrote in a published letter that around 1834 he resolved to get rid of all his slaves, and sold forty to fifty slaves to a "'pious friend of my old boyhood."[1] I have found no record of such a transaction. In spite of his claims, he continued to own slaves for decades afterward. In 1840 he is listed in both the Augusta and Oxford censuses. In Augusta he owns no slaves. He is, however, the guardian of six free persons of color, including two free women of color, age ten to twenty-four years, and one free women of color, age twenty-four to thirty-five years. In the Oxford census he is listed as owning fifteen slaves and providing for one free male of color, between ten and twenty-four years old, and one free woman of color, under ten years old. By 1850 Longstreet was living in Oxford, Mississippi, where he owned ten slaves, as president of the University of Mississippi. In 1860 he was the president of the University of South Carolina and owned seven slaves.

Perhaps there really was a wealthy Methodist woman's death associated with the transfer of Kitty, and this woman was in fact A. B. Longstreet's mother, Hannah Fitz-Randolph Longstreet, who passed away in the spring of 1837. During the period that Augustus is said to have decided to divest himself of slaves, Hannah also relieved herself of several slaves. According to the 1830 census, she owned sixteen slaves, including two girls under the age of ten; she thus could have owned Kitty, who was about eight years old at the time. In February 1833 she gave to a trustee three slaves, "Maria and her two children, Joe and Ellen," on behalf of her married granddaughter Hannah M. Baird.

Hannah Longstreet died in early 1837, within the "window" of the time period in which Andrew acquired Kitty (between 1837 and 1840). Her will and estate inventory mention only one slave, Leah, assessed at $699. Leah appears to have been somewhat favored. Hannah's will specifies, "I desire that my negro woman Leah be sold to a Master or Mistress of her own choosing, provided one can be found who will give for her within twenty five per cent of what my executors may think her fair value." (In other words, Leah could be sold to an owner of her own choosing, provided the buyer paid at least seventy-five percent of Leah's assessed value.)

What happened to Hannah Longstreet's other twelve or so other slaves, whom she had owned in 1830 but were not listed in the 1837 inventory of her estate? Might one of these have been Kitty, illegitimately fathered by Augustus Longstreet around 1822, when he was still residing on his plantation in Greensboro? If this were the case, one could imagine the following scenario: Longstreet deposited Kitty as a young girl with his mother Hannah. When Hannah died in early 1837, he needed to secure a residence for Kitty. Perhaps Longstreet's wife, a pious Methodist, absolutely refused to have Kitty, whom she knew to be Longstreet's illegitimate daughter, live with them, and perhaps Longstreet could not bring himself to sell Kitty off. He thus prevailed upon his dear friend Bishop Andrew, then in the process of relocating to Newton County, to take Kitty with him and to claim he had inherited her from an unnamed woman in Augusta.

In any event, soon after Bishop Andrew's departure for Newton County around 1836, Longstreet was ordained as a Methodist minister. He was reportedly the only minister to stay behind in Augusta in 1839 during the terrible yellow fever epidemic, ministering to the sick and dying. This same year he was elected the second president of Emory College. In January 1840 he moved to Oxford, Georgia; he was to reside in the lot adjacent to Bishop Andrew and his slaves, including Kitty, for the coming decade. The next year, 1841, he conducted the famous interview with Kitty.[2]

An intriguing piece of circumstantial evidence suggests a possible Longstreet-Kitty connection. A bank application was submitted during the Reconstruction era by a free man of color named William Longstreet, who bears the same name as the father of Augustus Baldwin Longstreet. On February 20, 1871, this William Longstreet, born around 1841 in Augusta, Georgia, and working as a farmer and a cook, applied for a Freedman's Bank account in Louisiana. (He was then living at Franklin and Market streets in Shreveport, Louisiana.) He lists as his father "Dennis" and lists among his nine siblings "Nelly," "Matilda," and "Kitty." We know from Augustus Longstreet's 1832 deed to his nephew James that he owned a carpenter named Dennis and another slave named Nelly, the mother of "Little May." From Augustus Longstreet's 1834 transfer to Richard Tubman we know that another of his slaves was named Matilda, born around 1826. Presumably, then, this William Longstreet was a former slave of Augustus Baldwin Longstreet, as were his parents and siblings.[3] Might William Longstreet's sister Kitty have been "our" Kitty, who was born around 1822? If so, did she and William share a common mother, an enslaved woman, or a common father, Augustus Baldwin Longstreet himself?

If Longstreet really did have such an intimate connection with Kitty, then the 1841 interview between Longstreet, George Lane, and Kitty was an elaborately staged ruse to shield Longstreet from any public acknowledgment of his status as Kitty's father. Such a scheme might well have appealed to Longstreet, who seems to have found great humor in elaborate tricks and practical jokes. His proclivity for deception is suggested by a famous scheme of his, proposed to General Robert E. Lee, that he and several other whites infiltrate Union lines near Charleston, South Carolina, by imitating the voices of negro slaves, and then place dynamite aboard Union naval vessels to sink them. (Lee refused to authorize the mission, emphasizing Longstreet's value to the Confederacy and the great risk of his being captured.)

In any event, Longstreet certainly was among the South's most prolific and articulate advocates, just as he was Bishop Andrew's most intimate friend and vocal defender. He drafted the elaborate double deed in April 1841 to disguise legally the extent of James Andrew's slaveholding. He, more than anyone else, was responsible for Bishop Andrew's refusal to resign the episcopacy over the issue of slaveholding in 1844. He strenuously advocated for the southern church's schism from the Methodist Episcopal Church. Soon after the fateful New York Conference, he published an 1845 commentary on the scriptural foundations of slavery, *Letters on the Epistle of Paul to Philemon or the Connection of Apostolical Christianity with Slavery*. This was followed by his satirical *Letters from Georgia to Massachusetts* (1848), evidently published at his own expense. In this pamphlet he makes extensive reference to the injustices heaped upon Bishop Andrew and denounces the hypocrisy of northern abolitionists for not attending to the plight of exploited New England mill girls.[1] He was a passionate defender of "nullification" (the right of individual states to ignore or overturn federal legislation), a confidant and family friend of South Carolina senator John Calhoun, and a noted backer of secession on the eve of the Civil War.

However, we must acknowledge that no direct evidence exists of Longstreet being Kitty's father or having had anything to do with Kitty beyond the 1841 interview. He left Oxford in 1847, four years before Kitty's death, to assume the presidency of the Centenary Institute in Louisiana. He then served as president of the University of Mississippi in Oxford, Mississippi, and moved to South Carolina to preside over South Carolina College in 1857. While in South Carolina on the eve of the Civil War he was a prominent advocate of secession, resisting what he termed "abolition aggression." After shots were fired on Fort Sumter, Longstreet returned to Mississippi in 1861 to resume presidency of the University of Mississippi. In December 1862 federal troops reached Oxford, Mississippi, and, using Longstreet's papers as kindling, burned his house. Most of his papers thus no longer exist. Important evidence on the question of Kitty's origins may forever be beyond recovery.[5]

After his house was burned, Longstreet relocated to Oxford, Georgia, and then to Columbus, Georgia. After the war he returned to Oxford, Mississippi, where he resided with his granddaughter. He died July 9, 1870, in Oxford, Mississippi, nine months before the death of his close friend Bishop Andrew.

E. John Andrew (d. 1830) or James Osgood Andrew (1794–1871)

Alternately, perhaps Miss Kitty was Bishop Andrew's half-sister, fathered by John Andrew, the father of James Andrew. If so she might have been the female slave (between ten and twenty-four years old) listed in the 1830 census as owned by Mary Andrew, John Andrew's widow in Clarke County. Kitty's birth year is usually given as 1822, but perhaps she was a little older. Perhaps the older female slave (between thirty-six and fifty-five) owned by James Andrew that year was Kitty's mother. Under this scenario, Kitty would have resided for her childhood first with John and Mary Andrew and then with the widowed Mary Andrew, until she was transferred to James Andrew at some point in the 1830s. Unfortunately, since no will or estate records associated with John Andrew have survived, determining which slaves he owned at the time of his death is impossible.

It is also possible that James Osgood Andrew himself was Kitty's father. (He was, it should be noted, residing in Augusta, serving as the pastor of St. John Methodist Church in 1822, the year Kitty was evidently born in Augusta.) If he was the father, perhaps Kitty resided with James's mother Mary Andrew, until Mary moved to Newton County around 1837. At that point, James may have asserted he had acquired Kitty in Augusta through a bequest. Although this possibility strikes me as unlikely, I should note that at least one elderly African American woman in Oxford told me in 2001 that her late father had told her, when she was a child, he was sure Kitty was in fact the daughter of Bishop Andrew.

Kitty's Children

A. Emma (ca. 1848–ca. 1925), Daughter of Kitty

In the 1880 census eight other black families named Sanders are listed as residing in Union Beat. It seems a fair inference that Emma had moved to Union to be close to her late husband's relatives, who may have come off of the nearby Saunders plantation. In 1850 Ethelbert W. Saunders in Union had thirty-five slaves. The Saunders plantation, it is interesting to note, in 1850 was very close to the plantation of "G. E. R. Childers," on which thirty slaves were held. This appears to have been George Childers, the future husband of Emily Sims Woolsey, who would in time be the third wife of Bishop Andrew. The precise connections between these parties are hard to disentangle, but it seems clear that close relations existed among enslaved black families in Summerfield and Union, linked through the white Andrew, Childers, and Saunders families. By 1880 many African Americans in Union district seem to have been laboring as sharecroppers on land owned by Benjamin Woolsey and his fellow white planters.

Intriguingly, a black Sanders family that may be linked to "our" Emma is enumerated in the 1880 census residing in Summerfield. A married couple, Jacob and Ann Sanders (the latter listed as a mulatta) are living with a ten-year-old mulatta girl named Emma Sanders (born about 1870). This Emma is listed as the stepdaughter of Jacob; presumably she is the daughter of Ann Sanders through a previous marriage or liaison. Also in the family is a seven-year-old girl named "Kittie." The precise relationship between the couple Jacob and Ann Sanders and the couple James and Emma Sanders is unclear, but perhaps this girl Emma was named for "our" Emma, the daughter of Kitty/Catherine Boyd, and the girl Kittie was named in memory of Miss Kitty/Catherine Boyd herself.

The subsequent fate of Miss Kitty's daughter Emma Sanders/Emma Neil is unclear. There is no surviving 1890 federal census. The 1900 and 1910 censuses do not contain any strong matches for an Abe Neil, an Emma Sanders, or an Emma Neil. However, the 1920 census lists an Emma Sanders, an African American woman born in Georgia in 1846 residing in Pine Bluff, Jefferson County, Arkansas. She is residing in the home of her son, "Will L. Long," a dentist listed as born in Georgia around 1873. Will L. Long's obituary in 1952 lists him as seventy-three years old, which would put his birth around 1879, consistent with the birth year of approximately 1878 given for "William," Emma's young son in the 1880 census in Union, Dallas County, Alabama.[1] The fact that Emma's son has the last name of "Long" would suggest that his father was named "Long," although his mother Emma has retained her earlier last name.

Dr. Long's 1952 obituary in the state's leading African American newspaper, the *Arkansas State Press*, asserts that he came to Pine Bluff in 1915 from the small Jefferson County, Arkansas, town of Moscow, several miles southeast of Pine Bluff.[2] He worked in the dental office of the noted African American dentist Dr. W. J. Parker, who with his son had a practice on Main Street in Pine Bluff. Dr. Long then started his own practice in rural towns surrounding Pine Bluff. After several years of rural practice, he moved back to Pine Bluff, where he continued his practice until his eyesight became impaired.[3]

It appears Dr. Long married at least twice. In the 1920 Pine Bluff City Directory, Emma Sanders is listed as residing at 519 East Thirteenth Street, Pine Bluff, with Will L. Long, "physician," and his wife "Cora," which is consistent with the 1920 census listing of his wife as Cora. There is no listing in the city directory for Emma Sanders in 1922 or any other subsequent year, nor is she listed in the 1930 census, so she may have passed away between 1920 and 1922, or perhaps she resided with Dr. Long during his rural sojourns. Dr. Long's wife Cora must have died soon after the 1920 census, since on October 21, 1921, he married an Ellen Scott, age twenty-two; the couple is listed in the city directory in 1927, but by 1929 Dr. Long is listed as residing alone. Ellen must have died during the late 1920s, since in the 1930 census Dr. Long is listed as a widower.

After this, Dr. Long does not appear in the city directory until 1946, so perhaps he continued his practice in rural towns. From 1946 onward he resided on North Elm Street in Pine Bluff. He passed away in a house fire at age seventy-three, with his seventy-year-old nurse, Ms. Maggie Dean, on July 3, 1952, at his house at 412 North Elm in Pine Bluff. (A family of three people, evidently boarders, survived the fire.) His funeral arrangements were handled through the prominent African American–owned funeral home, P. K. Miller's, which buried him on July 5 in the private P. K. Miller memorial cemetery. The funeral home's records indicate that the funeral was paid for by Mr. R. McNew, a prominent local white real estate agent. According to probate records, the same white businessman provided surety for Dr. Long's estate as it was probated; another white man, K. N. Alexander, served as the estate's administrator. So it would appear that Dr. Long was friends with at least several prominent members of the white business community in town. He does not appear to have had children.

I am not sure if Dr. Long received formal dentistry education. He is not listed in the records for Meharry in Nashville, Tennessee, where most black dentists practicing in early-twentieth-century Arkansas were trained. He may have studied at Howard University in Washington, D.C.

As of this writing I have been unable to trace the fate of the three other children of Emma Sanders/Emma Neil: Mary, Mark, and Ina.[1] Nor have I been able to reconstruct any aspects of Emma's life from 1880 to 1920. If her son really was in rural Jefferson County it seems possible that she might have resided with him, in Moscow or elsewhere. The 1900 and 1910 censuses did not record many African American migrant farm laborers and other low-income persons, and Emma and Mark may have thus escaped documentation.

Following its occupation by Union Army forces in 1863, the city of Pine Bluff had been perceived as a safe haven for African Americans, boasting strong black educational facilities and prosperous black middle class. Pine Bluff was widely considered a relative mecca for African Americans, where many black professionals flourished in comparative security during the period between the end of Reconstruction and the Great Migration. The African American community built in 1909 a Masonic temple, then the tallest building in the city. Many African American doctors and dentists had their offices in this building, so it seems likely that Dr. Long had his office there as well, after his time practicing in the county's rural areas.

B. Russell Nathan Boyd (ca. 1846–1921)

I am not sure how Kitty's second son acquired the first name "Russell." Was the name bestowed on him at birth, or did he take it on at some point later in life? In his 1871 Freedman's Bank application in Atlanta, his father, Nathan Boyd, refers to his second son as "Nathan," that is to say, as his namesake. As we shall see, Russell Nathan Boyd's elder brother, Rev. Alford Boyd (ca. 1844–1926), would name his first son, born in Iowa in 1869, "Russell." Perhaps Alford was honoring his brother. Perhaps uncle and nephew were both named for another relative or for a person admired by the family. If the latter, then the original "Russell" could have been the first name or the family name of an admired person. It might be significant that a white family by the name of Russell was prominent in both Summerfield and Union, Alabama. The 1860 slave schedule in Summerfield lists a "D W Russell" owning one slave and a "Wm Russell" owning five slaves; the 1860 slave schedule for Union (near the location of Tranquilla Plantation, where the Boyd children resided in the early 1860s) lists a James C. Russell (born about 1805) owning twenty-seven slaves. Might one of these white men have been so admired that the second Boyd son (whom his father remembered only as "Nathan") took on the first name "Russell" in his honor? Might Alfred Boyd then have decided to honor this person by naming his first son Russell in 1869?

C. The Children of Russell Nathan Boyd: George and Edna

Russell's only son, George Russell Boyd, seems to have had a mildly troubled youth, perhaps due to his mother's death, his father's remarriage, and the appearance of a new baby in the household. In 1899, the following article, evidently drafted or dictated by Russell Nathan Boyd, appeared in the *Washington Post*:

ABSORBED IN STORIES OF THE WAR.

George R. Boyd, a negro boy, fourteen years old, who has lived with parents at 1842 K Street, northwest, is missing and his father believes he has gone to the Philippines. The father is an old and trusted employee at the Department of State. He has been employed in the library of the department for

years. He is in good circumstances and has given his son every advantage
of education, but the boy lately became absorbed in the story of the war in
the Philippines and his father believes he has run away with the intention
of getting to the far off islands in some way.[5]

Whatever the cause of the boy's disappearance, the sojourn cannot have lasted
all that long, since he was back home in time to be recorded in the 1900 census.

In spite of his father's hopes for his educational success, George Russell does
not appear to have attended college. He held a series of manual and service
jobs throughout the remainder of his life. In 1908 he was married to Sadie B.
Watkins, an African American woman from Warrington, North Carolina, by
a justice of the peace in Boston. The couple lived in Dorchester and Roxbury,
Massachusetts. George worked as a janitor and waiter, Sadie at home as a dress-
maker. George is mentioned once in a local newspaper in December 1915, for
having been arrested during a police raid of a card game.

Sadie died in Boston at some point in 1916. By September 1918, when he registered with the Selective Service near the end of the First World War, George was
once again living in Washington, D.C., residing in his parents' home, now employed as a Pullman porter. (On his Selective Service card, he lists his half-sister
Edna as his next of kin.) The District of Columbia City Directory indicates that
he may have been married a second time, to a woman known as Eula or Eura,
in the mid-1930s, but no official records of such a marriage are available. Eula
is not listed in the 1937 entry under his name, so perhaps she died or separated
from him. He does not appear ever to have had children. George Russell Boyd's
final job was working as a laborer in a public school. He passed away at age fifty-
one in December 1937 of pneumonia in Freedman's Hospital, where his father
had died sixteen years earlier. His death notice in the *Evening Star* reads:

BOYD, GEORGE RUSSELL. On Wednesday, December 27, 1937. GEORGE RUS-
SELL BOYD, devoted son of the late Russell N. and Tulip Cook Boyd, beloved
brother of Edna Boyd Gary. Funeral on Friday, December 31 from 1:00 p.m.
at the home of his sister, 208 S. St NW. Relatives and friends are invited. Arrangements by Thomas Frazier Co.

Note that the death notice placed by Edna makes no mention of George Russell's
wives, Sadie or Eula; perhaps she did not approve of them or did not consider his
marriages with them to be significant. Edna arranged to have her half-brother
buried in Columbia Harmony Cemetery in northeast Washington in the same
plot as their father and her mother. (I have not been able to determine where
Tulip Victoria Cook, George Russell's mother, was buried.)

The loss of her father in 1921 may have propelled Edna into a more devout
position. The Fifteenth Street Presbyterian Church register records that on December 29, 1921, about ten months after her father's death, Miss Edna S. Boyd
was "after due examination having been previously baptized received into full
membership of the church and confession of faith."

Unlike her half-brother George Russell, Edna pursued a professional career. Her mother Cordelia Syphax had worked as a schoolteacher in the District of Columbia's public school system since at least 1890, and Edna followed her example. She was trained as a kindergarten teacher, and had a long career teaching in the District's elementary schools. On May 3, 1924, she married Daniel McKinley Gary, originally from Mayersville, Mississippi. Sadly, joy over the wedding was short-lived; two months later, on the July 4 weekend, Daniel, Edna, and her mother Cordelia drove down to the Maryland shore for a holiday. Near Bryantown, Maryland, they encountered a slick patch of pavement, and their automobile spun out of control. The accident fractured Cordelia's skull, and she was pronounced dead at the scene. An inquest found that no one was at fault, but the blow to Edna must have been horrific.

In the wake of the tragedy, Edna's married life does not appear to have been easy. Her husband Daniel is recalled by collateral relations as "a charming hustler" and a "card shark," who never held a steady job. He is variously listed in the city directory, census, and draft registration records as a musician, real estate broker, salesman, pharmacist, and manager of vending machines at an amusement company. He worked up and down the East Coast, spending more and more time in Harlem in New York City, where he was for a time a bandleader.

Soon after their marriage, Edna and Daniel moved into a row house at 208 S Street NW near the intersection of Rhode Island and Florida, in the Shaw neighborhood, popular among middle-class African American families. The 1930 census records Daniel's brother Carlyle, a real estate clerk, as living with them there. Edna was to reside there the rest of her life.

In the years after World War II, Edna's husband Daniel Gary became involved in a tangled legal case involving a gambling ring. In April 1950 the *Washington Post* reported that he had been subpoenaed to testify in front of a grand jury in Washington, D.C., on suspicion of jury tampering. At the time he was living apart from Edna, in the Teresa Hotel in Harlem. He was indicted, but his trial was repeatedly delayed because of a "heart condition." He died in 1951. We can only assume that the entire experience of her husband's public prosecution was deeply humiliating and heartbreaking for Edna. Nonetheless, Edna arranged to have her husband buried in Lincoln Cemetery, in Suitland, Maryland, just outside of Washington. Here many of the leading figures of Washington's African American community, including members of the Grimke and Syphax families, were interred.

In 1960 Edna, along with thousands of other local black families, faced a challenge born of enduring structural racism in the city of Washington. Metropolitan authorities declared that Columbia Harmony Cemetery would be terminated and all remains moved to a suburban location in Landover, Maryland. The Columbia Harmony Mutual Aid Society, established by former slaves in the 1830s, had run into financial difficulties, and support from the city government was not forthcoming. Ultimately, about thirty-seven thousand human remains were relocated, but no markers or headstones were moved and some remains were never in fact moved. The area of the cemetery is now occupied by the Rhode Island Metro rail station. Low-income families unable to afford the relocation of grave makers were deprived of the possibility of visiting the final resting places of their loved ones.

Edna arranged to have her parents' remains moved from Columbia Harmony to the suburban Lincoln Memorial Park, interred within the family plot in which she had already interred her husband Daniel.[6] She did not, however, arrange to move the remains of her half-brother George Russell from the site the city had moved them to in Landover. Perhaps she felt that her obligations to him had been discharged.

Near the entrance of Lincoln Memorial Cemetery in Suitland, Maryland (founded 1927), stands a large headstone. One side is inscribed "Gary," with the names Daniel (June 18, 1951) and Edna (1896–1978) underneath. On the other face of the stone is inscribed, "Boyd," above the names "Cordelia S., July 4, 1924" and "Russell N., Feb. 1, 1921." Under their names is inscribed, "To live in the hearts you love is not to die."

After retiring in 1968 Edna continued to reside at 208 S Street. During a long struggle with breast cancer she was at one point operated upon by one of her cousins, a physician in the Syphax family at Howard University Hospital. She passed away on July 20, 1978, at the age of eighty-two; her funeral was held at her house. Her obituary notes that she was active in the Retired Teachers' Association and a longtime member of 15th Street Presbyterian Church. She was buried in Lincoln Memorial Cemetery, in the same plot as her parents and her late husband.

Many older members of the extended Syphax family warmly remember Edna, recalling her kindness and devotion to her many elementary school students across the decades. Since neither she nor her half-brother George Russell had children, the line of Russell Nathan Boyd ended with her.[7]

The Greenwood Slaves, Postemancipation

A. Greenwood Freedpeople in Greene County, Georgia

The slaves Daniel and Phillis in the Greenwood estate (neither of them owned by Bishop Andrew) were separated from one another by a series of decisions by the ordinary court. Initially, Phillis was assigned to William Greenwood, a son of Nancy Mitchell and Thomas Greenwood. Daniel was initially assigned to the minor children of Ann Leonora Mounger and Thomas Greenwood, and in 1846 was distributed to Robert H. Greenwood. However, after emancipation, Daniel and Phillis appear to have been reunited. The 1870 Freedmen's Census records that residing together in northern Greene County Militia District 140, in the Penfield area, are Daniel and Phillis English, each eighty years, born around 1790. (Phillis's birthplace is recorded as "Africa"; one wonders if she might have been imported into South Carolina during the 1804–7 bubble discussed in Chapter 8.) Daniel and Phillis were surrounded by several other African American families bearing the surname English, including one headed by a younger man named Daniel English, born around 1825, who may be their son. They resided a few doors away from the nine-year-old Adam Daniel Williams, the future maternal grandfather of Martin Luther King Jr., and his parents the Baptist preacher Willis Williams and Lucretia "Creecy" Daniel Williams.[1] Nearby, in the same militia district, Robert H. Greenwood, to whom the slave Daniel had been transferred in 1846, resided and worked as a teacher.

Similarly, the Greenwood slaves Isaac and Delia (who also were never owned by Bishop Andrew) were separated by the 1830 and 1846 court distributions. Isaac was assigned to James Greenwood, one of Nancy Mitchell Greenwood's children, while Delia was assigned to Robert H. Greenwood, one of Ann Leonora Mounger Greenwood's children. Yet in the 1870 and 1880 censuses in Green County's Militia District 149, Isaac and Delia Fambrough, each born around 1810, are recorded as husband and wife, living in a multigenerational household with their children and grandchildren. So it would appear that the extended families of Daniel and Phillis, and of Isaac and Delia, managed to cohere, against great challenges, through slavery into the Reconstruction era.

It also seems likely that the "boy" Nelson—who in 1827 had been assessed at five hundred dollars and reserved for the children of Nancy Mitchell Greenwood—and Margaret—who had been transferred in 1844 at age eleven to Caroline Greenwood—in time became a married couple. The 1870 census for Green County Militia District 143 records a Nelson Wright, working as miller, born about 1816, and a Margaret Wright, born about 1835, married and living with two children.

What about the fate of the Greenwood freedpeople whom Bishop Andrew had owned? Five years after emancipation, the 1870 Freedmen's Census records a number of other African American men and woman living in Penfield District in northern Greene County with the same first names as the Greenwood slaves enumerated in the 1844 Andrew-Longstreet deed or related documents. For instance, the "Harry" mentioned in the 1825 estate inventory and 1827 distribution to Ann Leonora Greenwood and the "Susan" mentioned in the 1844 Andrew-Longstreet transaction may be the same persons as the married couple Harry Daniel, born around 1797, and Susan Daniel, born 1810, living together in 1870 in the Penfield area, in Greene County's Militia District 141. Perhaps the twenty-year-old black woman "Florida Daniel," born 1850, listed three lines from them in the 1870 census, is their daughter. Also bearing the surname Daniel in 1870 is George Daniel, a blacksmith born around 1818, residing in the village of Penfield; he may well have been the "George" mentioned in the 1844 deed. By 1880 George's son John Daniel, also a blacksmith, was residing in Skull Shoals, in the northwest of Greene County, quite close to where the ancestors of Dr. Martin Luther King Jr.—the widowed Lucretia Williams and her son Adam Daniel Williams—were now living as well, probably employed at the large cotton mills there. (Speculatively, given that Lucretia Williams, the great-grandmother of Martin Luther King Jr., was born Lucretia Daniel, it is possible Harry Daniel and George Daniel bear some kinship relationship to her.)[2]

In turn, "Elleck," mentioned in the 1844 Longstreet-Andrew deed, may be the same person as Ellick Armor, born 1805, residing in Greene County's Militia District 162 in Penfield. Fifteen households away dwelled Alexander Armor, born around 1818, who may be "Alexander," the child of Peggy and brother of "Lander" mentioned in the 1827 document distributing slaves to the widowed Ann Leonora Greenwood.[3]

In turn, the "Edward" listed in the 1844 deed may have become by 1870 Edward Davison, born 1800, residing in northern Greene County's Militia District 141. "Allen," the son of Lillah and brother of Laura, might have become the railroad worker Allen Parham, born 1835 or 1838, living in Militia District 161. Also in District 161 was Orange Dennis, born around 1822, who may have been the perennially ill slave "Orange," mentioned in Bishop Andrew's letters and the Greenwood estate records. In turn, "Jefferson" may have become Jefferson Wood, born 1805, or Jefferson Jackson, born 1810.

It would thus appear that the majority of the Greenwood slaves survived their sojourn under Bishop Andrew and returned to the Penfield region of Greene County, where they had lived prior to 1844. During the middle decades of the nineteenth century, Penfield was the site of the Mercer Institute and Mercer Female Academy, forerunners of Mercer University, which moved to Macon, Georgia, in 1871. Cotton cultivation was the economic mainstay of Penfield during much of the nineteenth century, and it is likely that many of the Greenwood slaves were returned to the cotton fields after 1855 or so. Conditions were clearly difficult during the early post–Civil War period, even after the passage of the Reconstruction Acts in 1867. The records of the Freedman's Bureau, which had a field office in Greensboro, detail a range of violent atrocities against many new freedpeople, some of them perpetrated as early as 1868 by "parties calling themselves the Ku Klux."[4]

I am not sure of the source of most of the last names adopted by the Greenwood slaves postemancipation. Hardly any of them adopted the last name Greenwood or Andrew. In some instances, they may have adopted the surnames of the white planters to which they were rented out for extended periods; since immediately after the Civil War, some of them continued on the land of these white planters, they may have found it expedient to take on the white family surnames.

Some former Greenwood slaves retained the last name "Mitchell," which had been the maiden name of Thomas Greenwood's first wife, Nancy, whom he married in 1805. Nancy's children—Thomas E. Greenwood, Eldridge Greenwood, James Greenwood, and William M. Greenwood—are listed in court documents as heirs of their grandfather Jacob Mitchell of Greene County. In 1820 Jacob Mitchell owned twenty-one slaves, some of whom may have been bequeathed to his grandchildren; years earlier some Mitchell slaves may have been given as dowry gifts when Nancy married Thomas Greenwood. As we shall see below, the slave James, owned by Bishop Andrew and mentioned in the 1844 document, almost certainly became James Mitchell (b. 1820), who remained in Oxford after emancipation.[5] In turn, another slave of Bishop Andrew listed in the 1844 Andrew-Longstreet deed, "Addison," appears to have become Addison Mitchell (b. 1830), living in Penfield, Greene County, in 1870, married to a woman "Nancy," born around 1832. Suggestively, a Greenwood estate document indicates that for the year of 1845 the Greenwood estate rented out a slave woman named Nancy to "J. O. Andrew" for forty-five dollars. (The year before she was rented out to William Greenwood for fifty dollars.) It is thus possible that the connection between Addison and Nancy dates back to 1845, when they were both laboring in Bishop Andrew's household in Oxford, one of them legally owned by the Bishop, the other only rented by him.

B. Greenwood Freedpeople and the Great Migration

Many of the descendants of the Greenwood freedpeople lived on as farm laborers and sharecroppers in rural Greene County, at least as late as the 1930 census. Some, however, moved to urban areas and joined the Great Migration, driven out by rural impoverishment and racist violence and drawn by the North's vast demand for industrial and service labor. Such was the case, for example, for Bishop Andrew's former slave Addison Mitchell and his wife Nancy. By 1880 the couple had moved out of northern Greene County and was living in Fulton County in Atlanta with their children on "Grady's Row." By 1889 Addison appears to have died, since his wife Nancy is recorded in the Atlanta City Directory for that year as working as a laundress. In the mid-1880s their daughter Georgia Mitchell (born in freedom on May 1, 1865) married David Wynn, listed as a "battery man" and lineman with Western Union Telegraph in Atlanta. By 1900 Addison's widow Nancy was residing with Georgia, her husband David, and their children in Atlanta.

I do not know how this family coped with the tumultuous events taking place in Atlanta during the early twentieth century, including the horrific Atlanta race riot of 1906. By 1910 Georgia's brother John Mitchell (born in 1870) had relocated to Chicago, where he worked as a janitor on "the Flats." Within a few years, the now-widowed Georgia Wynn and her children followed him to Chicago. In 1918, when they registered for the draft, Georgia's sons George and David Wynn were listed as working, respectively, as a "trolley man" and "checker," for Swift & Company, the vast meatpacking corporation in Chicago's famous Union Stock Yards. By 1920 Georgia Wynn and her brother John Mitchell were residing in the same household in Chicago, Illinois, along with Georgia's children George Dewey Wynn, now a Pullman porter; Dave Dorias Wynn, a butcher; Raymond, a shipping clerk; Maud, a clerk with a "mail order house" (perhaps Sears and Roebuck); and Marie, a "stock girl." John Mitchell was by then employed as a waiter in a railroad sleeping car. By 1930 Raymond Wynn was working as a sleeping car porter. In 1944 Georgia died at age seventy-eight in the Cook County Hospital. When he passed away at age fifty-four in 1952, her son George was working as a porter in a Chicago tavern, living with his sister Golden Butler. Both Georgia and George were interred in Lincoln Cemetery, a prominent African American cemetery in the Blue Island area of Chicago's far South Side. The family had, in short, fully transitioned to Chicago's working class.

Similarly, the family of the freedman "Orange," whose health was so feeble in the 1840s, in time headed to Atlanta and then northward. By 1880 Orange Dennis in Greene County had changed his first name to "Warren," the same name as one of his sons, Warren Jr. By 1900 Warren Dennis Sr. was living with his wife, his son Will, and his daughter-in-law Hattie in Atlanta, working as a day laborer. (As early as 1890 Warren's wife Parthenia Dennis is listed in the Atlanta City Directory, working as a laundress.) Ten years later, Will and Hattie were living in the city of Hobson, Alabama, a community celebrated at the time as one of the very few black-governed municipalities in the nation. By 1920 Will and Hattie and their children were living in Chicago, Illinois, in Ward 31. Will worked as a boot black in a shoe shop, his son Leon as a chauffeur in an auto shop, his son Napoleon as a laborer in a foundry, and his son Laventer as a porter in a bakery.

C. Greenwood-Andrew Freedpeople in Oxford, Georgia, post-1864

Although most of the Greenwood slaves were evidently taken by Ann Leonora's children to the environs of Penfield, Greene County, Georgia, after Ann Leonora's death in 1854, several former slaves of Bishop Andrew who were part of the Greenwood cohort continued to live in Oxford after Andrew departed for Summerfield, Alabama, in 1855–56. African American oral history in the Oxford Mitchell-Wright family is quite clear that the family patriarch, "Uncle Tommie Mitchell," was a slave of Bishop Andrew in his youth.[6] He clearly is the fifteen-year-old "Tom Mitchell" (b. ca. 1855), son of James Mitchell (b. 1820) mentioned in the 1870 census for Oxford. Tom was ten years old at emancipation, and thus too young to have been listed in the 1844 slave deed between Bishop Andrew and President Longstreet. However, his father, James Mitchell, listed as a blacksmith in 1870, must have been the "James" listed in the 1844 deed.

It seems a fair inference that Addison Mitchell (b. ca. 1830) and James Mitchell (b. ca. 1820) were brothers to one another; each bore the surname "Mitchell," they are listed next to one another in the 1844 Longstreet-Andrew deed, and both men named their sons "John" and "James."

In Oxford, James Mitchell's son Tom Mitchell eventually married Mary Robinson, daughter of Cornelius and Ellen Robinson. As noted in chapter 2, Cornelius and Ellen were former slaves of Alexander Means, a faculty member at Emory College who served as the college's president. Their child, Robert "Bob" Mitchell, worked at Emory College in Oxford, and then worked at Emory University after its establishment in Atlanta until his death. As we have seen, his son, Henry "Billy" Mitchell (b. 1883), worked at Emory at Oxford as its legendary janitor and groundskeeper, honored in 1966 by a plaque on the Oxford College campus. Billy Mitchell's daughter, Sarah Francis Mitchell Wise, was a respected citizen of Oxford; she and her son Henry "Billy" Wise worked closely with my students and me during our research on Oxford history from 1999 to 2001.

There is an elliptical reference to another former slave of Bishop Andrew's living in Oxford. This appears in a published account of Andrew's 1871 funeral in Oxford, written by Rev. James Osgood Andrew Clark (1827–94), professor of Latin at Emory College. Rev. Clark gives an account of the eulogy by Rev. William Martin, of the South Carolina Conference, which emphasized the late bishop's great service to the "colored people." Clark adds,

> When the writer of this [that is, Clark himself] returned home, his old cook-woman, who was present at the funeral, and who had long known the bishop and was a member of his family, remarked, "how true was all that the South Carolina brother said about Bishop Andrew's labor among the colored people.[7]

The phrase "member of his family" surely means that the "old cook-woman" had been a slave of Bishop Andrew. Like so many of his white contemporaries when discussing persons of color, Rev. Clark does not give this woman's name. Who might she have been? She is likely to have been Mary Ann Mitchell (b. ca. 1816), who, according to the 1870 census, lived two doors away from Rev. Clark.[8] She was married to James Mitchell, former slave of Bishop Andrew, and may have belonged to the Bishop as well.

Recall that in the 1827 document transferring seven slaves to Ann Greenwood from her late husband's estate, three slaves, "Peggy, Lander, and Alexander," are listed in the same line and are collectively valued at seven hundred dollars. Given the conventions of the day it is likely that Peggy was the mother of the children Lander and Alexander. The 1870 Freedmen's Census for Oxford, Georgia, records a household headed by "Lander Thompson," employed as a carpenter, born around 1822. Living in his household is a Peggy Thomas, presumably his mother, born around 1802, also as well Lander's wife, Sarah Jane. Sarah Jane may well be the same "Sarah Jane" rented out by the estate in the 1840s and then assigned to Robert H. Greenwood in 1846. Also in the household are Lander and Sarah Jane's children, Charles, Gabriel, and Harriet. Presumably, Peggy Thomas, who would have been about twenty-five years old in 1827, is the same person as the slave "Peggy" listed in the 1827 document. Her son, Lander Thompson, is probably the young slave "Lander," who would have been five years old in 1827. (As suggested above, Lander may also be the "Orlando" listed in the January 1844 Andrew-Longstreet deed.) Peggy Thomas may have been related to Lewis Thomas and his descendants, one of the largest and oldest African American families in Oxford; according to family oral history, Lewis and his family had been owned by James R. Thomas, Emory College's president from 1855 to 1867, who owned eight slaves in 1860.[9]

In any event, by 1880 Lander and Sarah Jane Thompson and their two younger children, Gabriel and Harriet, were residing together in "Wyatt's" (463rd Militia) district, Newton County, near the present-day town of Porterdale. Their eldest daughter "Rena" is evidently the same person as Rena Graves, born around 1850, who married Nick Graves in Oxford around 1870. Nick Graves, one of the founding trustees of Rust Chapel Methodist Church, had been owned by Iverson Lea Graves, one of the first trustees of Emory College, who held about thirty-one slaves in Newton County in 1860. (Nick, born around 1848, was probably the twelve-year-old male in the 1860 slave schedule of the Iverson Graves plantation in Mount Pleasant.) Lander's mother Peggy is not listed in the 1880 census, so is likely to have passed away by then.

By 1900 Nick and Rena Graves had seven living children, including John Wesley Graves (1869–1929), who served as Emory University's chef after the Atlanta campus was established in 1917. John Wesley's son Artie Graves (ca. 1900–1997) is buried in the northwestern section of the Oxford City Cemetery, in the plot next to his mother Victoria Graves (1873–1970).

In addition, it is quite possible that "Laura," described in the 1844 Longstreet-Andrew transaction as the daughter of Leilah and brother of Allen, is the same person as Laura Digby, born 1840, who lived in Oxford after the Civil War. In 1870 Laura and her husband Elbert Digby resided directly next door to Nicholas and Rena Graves in Oxford. Laura's eldest son, Ishmael, born around the time of emancipation in 1865, appears to have been fathered by a different man, since in 1880 he is listed only as Elbert's "stepson." By 1880 the Digbys had moved to the nearby town of Sheffield in the adjacent county of Rockdale (formerly a part of Newton County). Laura must have died prior to 1887, when Elbert married a second wife.

Living a few households away from the Digbys and the Graveses in Oxford in 1870 was Martha Brown, married to a Phillip Brown. Martha Brown was born in North Carolina around 1820; it is possible that she was the "Martha" assessed at $350 in the 1825 inventory of the Greenwood estate and listed in the August 1847 transfer of ten slaves from Ann Leonora to her daughter Mary Eliza Greenwood. Similarly, Millidge Cook, born around 1830 and living in the household of Bishop Andrew's former slave James Mitchell, is likely to be the "Milledge" distributed in 1847 to Mary Eliza.

To summarize, at least a dozen former slaves of Bishop Andrew and his second wife Ann Leonora Greenwood came to reside in Oxford after emancipation, through two likely routes. Some were slaves belonging to the Thomas Greenwood estate transferred to Mary Eliza Greenwood in 1847; Bishop Andrew must have transferred others to Mary Eliza, after Ann Leonora's death in 1854. As noted above, in January 1849 Mary Eliza married Professor Luther M. Smith, then teaching at Emory College in Oxford. After Mary Eliza herself died in October 1859, her slaves (including the ten slaves transferred to her by her mother in August 1847) became the full legal property of her husband, Professor Luther Smith. In 1860, the year after his wife Mary Eliza's death, Professor Smith owned twenty-eight slaves. As slaves, they must have been kept in Oxford at Professor Smith's household or on his nearby plantation until freedom came to Newton County at the end of 1864. As it happens, after the death of his first wife Mary Eliza Greenwood in 1859, Professor Smith married Callie B. Lane, daughter of Professor George Lane, who had conducted the interview of Kitty in 1841 with Augustus B. Longstreet. The former Greenwood-Andrew slaves evidently were housed with Professor Lane's former slaves, whom Callie appears to have inherited.

The 1860 slave schedule for Luther Smith's holdings only lists the gender and age of slaves, but the listings are consistent with what we have inferred about Bishop Andrew's former slaves in Oxford. For instance, Martha Brown, born about 1820, may be the female slave listed as "forty years old." Lander Thompson, born around 1822, and James Mitchell, born around 1820, may be the two male slaves listed as "thirty-seven years old" in 1860. Millidge Cook, born around 1830, may be the thirty-one-year-old male slave. Rena (later Rena Graves), born around 1850, might be the nine-year-old female slave.

After emancipation, some of these freedpeople may have continued to work for Professor Smith, who became president of Emory College soon after the Civil War. Indeed, the 1870 census records that James, Nancy, and Tom Mitchell, along with Milledge Cook, resided in Oxford a few doors away from Professor Smith. We do know that Tom Mitchell worked for most of his life for Emory, and it is possible that this labor relationship was anchored in his family's long-term connection with Professor Smith and his late wife Mary Elizabeth Greenwood.

D. A Greenwood Slave in Summerfield, Alabama: Post-1855

Although several sources insist that Bishop Andrew divested himself of all Ann Leonora's slaves after her death, it would appear that the Bishop took at least one of the Greenwood male slaves to Summerfield, Alabama, in 1855. The 1870 census in Summerfield, the first census in which all persons of color were listed by name, records a black man living next door to Bishop Andrew named "Thomas Greedwood," married to a woman named Henrietta. He is listed as born around 1825 in Georgia; she was born around 1849 in Alabama. I surmise that he was in fact a "Thomas Greenwood," who had taken the name of his family's earlier owner, Thomas Greenwood of Greensboro, Greene County, Georgia. It is puzzling, to be sure, that no adult male slave appears in the 1860 slave schedule in Summerfield for the Andrew household, but perhaps this man was rented out or located elsewhere during the census taking. He may well be the "Tom" mentioned in the 1844 Longstreet-Andrew deed. If so, he would have been about nineteen years old at the time of Ann Leonora Greenwood's marriage to James Andrew and would have been born around the time the slaveowner Thomas Greenwood died.

Curiously, by the time of the 1880 census, Thomas and Henrietta had changed their last name from Greedwood/Greenwood to "Andrew," presumably in honor of Bishop Andrew, who had owned Tom from 1844 until emancipation. Tom Andrew is in this census listed as a blacksmith, born in Georgia. He and Henrietta had five children: Jessie, Annie, Janie, Joseph, and Winnie.[10]

Chapter 1. The Myth of Kitty

1. Martin Porter is a pseudonym.

2. Porter was referring to Bishop Warren Akin Candler, a senior bishop in the Methodist Episcopal Church, South and the first chancellor of Emory University, who strongly opposed the reunification of the northern and southern wings of the Methodist Church. I discuss Candler and his role in the revival of the Andrew-Kitty story in subsequent chapters.

3. Porter never knew of Bishop Andrew's obituary of Kitty, which specifies that she died in April 1851. I only came across the obituary after Porter's death, so to my regret I was never able to tell him about it. I reprint and offer an analysis of the obituary below in chapter 3.

4. Porter refers here to G. G. Smith's footnote in his 1882 biography about meeting a son of Kitty, employed as a messenger in the U.S. Department of State in Washington, D.C. I discuss the life of this man, who must have been Russell Nathan Boyd (ca. 1846–1921), in chap. 8. Porter's use of the term "boy" in referring to the messenger, who would have been over thirty at the time of his encounter with Smith, often rankled his African American listeners.

5. Margaret Watkins is a pseudonym.

6. Present-day Emory University consists of multiple campuses. The core university campus, founded in 1917, is in the Druid Hills neighborhood of Atlanta. Nearby are the Briarcliff and Clairmont campuses, devoted to research units and graduate student housing. Several hospital complexes in the Atlanta area also bear the Emory name and are affiliated with the university in one way or another. The original campus, about forty miles to the east of the Druid Hills site, in Oxford, has since the creation of Emory University in 1917 successively housed an "academy" and a two-year feeder college, now termed "Oxford College of Emory University."

7. Bourdieu, "Structures, Habitus, Practices," in *Logic of Practice*, 52–79.

8. Comaroff and Comaroff, *Of Revelation and Revolution*, vol. 1: *Christianity, Colonialism, and Consciousness in South Africa*; vol. 2: *Dialectics of Modernity on a South African Frontier.*

9. Comaroff and Comaroff, *Of Revelation and Revolution*, vol. 1: *Christianity, Colonialism, and Consciousness in South Africa*

10. Davis, *Methodist Unification*; Thomas, *Methodism's Racial Dilemma.*

11. Richey, *Methodist Conference in America*; Davis, *Methodist Unification*, 3.

12. Hatch and Wigger, *Methodism and the Shaping of American Culture.*

13. Davis, *Methodist Unification*, 3.

14. Goen. *Broken Churches, Broken Nation.*

15. On the varied Methodist responses to emancipation and reconstruction, see Hildebrand, *The Times Were Strange and Stirring*; Montgomery, *Under Their Own Vine and Fig Tree*; Walker, *Rock in a Weary Land*; Minnow, *Northern Methodism and Reconstruction*; Hagood, *Colored Man in the Methodist Episcopal Church*. On the role of white Protestants, especially Methodists, in creating a post–Civil War racial concept of white national citizenship, see Bennett, *Religion and the Rise of Jim Crow in New Orleans*.

16. Clarke, *Dwelling Place*. For a telling case of the ideological contortions required by a Christian slaveowner facing the rape of a young enslaved woman in his own household, see Clarke's discussion on 142ff.

17. On Brown University and the Atlantic slave trade, see the report of the Brown University *Steering Committee on Slavery and Justice* (2006). Recent work on slavery at William and Mary includes Brophy, "Considering William and Mary's History with Slavery"; Meyers, "First Look at the Worst"; Oast, "Forgotten Masters."

18. This argument is developed in Comaroff, "End of History." Also see Campbell, "Settling Accounts?"

19. Woolfork, *Embodying Slavery in American Culture*.

20. Personal communication with author.

21. Lévi-Strauss, *View from Afar*, 158.

22. Ellison, *Juneteenth*, 257. Hickman's meditation also appears in book 2 of Callahan and Bradley's edited compendium of Ellison's unfinished second novel, known alternatively as *Juneteenth* and *Three Days before the Shooting*... See Ralph Ellison, *Three Days Before the Shooting*..., ed. John F. Callahan and Adam Bradley (New York: Modern Library Edition, 2010), 307, 1066. The extended passage in which this phrase appears was first published by Ellison as "Night Talk," *Quarterly Review of Literature* 15 (1969): 317–29.

23. See Schneider, *American Kinship*. Schneider is, of course, aware that in practice sexual intercourse often takes place outside of marriage. For him, however, "culture" is limited to the ideal operations of a system, to the formal rules and patterns of values that constitute a shared system of symbols, in contrast to what actual people do at the level of social action. A "cultural account" of American kinship for Schneider thus is restricted to analyzing underlying patterns and categories of thought. As perplexing as this approach may seem, it can illuminate crises and contradictions in underlying cultural categories.

24. Lévi-Strauss, *Savage Mind*, 21.

Chapter 2. Distant Kin: Slavery and Cultural Intimacy in a Georgia Community

1. Lévi-Strauss, *Elementary Structures of Kinship*.

2. Davis, "Slavery, Manufacturing and Productivity in Newton County, 1821–1860," 178.

3. These insights are developed in Comaroff and Roberts, *Rules and Processes.*

4. In some instances in Newton County, mothers and children were separated much earlier. In her 1826 will, Sarah Fielders stipulated that if her slave Becca should "hereafter have another child, I do give and bequeath [it] unto my daughter, Mariah Montgomery, to be delivered to her as soon as the child can be weaned from its mother" (Davis, "Slavery, Manufacturing and Productivity in Newton County, 1821–1860," 178).

5. Ibid., 177.

6. Ibid.

7. Stone, Unpublished memoir.

8. In 2000, as my students and I collaborated with African American congregations in restoring the African American cemetery in Oxford, we uncovered the Louisa/Louisa Means headstone and confirmed the veracity of this story.

9. Coleman Brown was killed in the Civil War; the African American–owned Lackey Funeral Home now occupies the site of his house in Covington. Coleman Brown's parents were the owners of the slave Richard, brother of Nathan Boyd, Miss Kitty's husband.

10. For examples of the disruptive effects of white dowry transfers of slaves of enslaved families, see Clarke, *Dwelling Place: A Plantation Epic*, 70ff.

Chapter 3. "The Tenderest Solicitude for Her Welfare": Founding Texts of the Andrew-Kitty Narrative

1. "Important Movement of the Methodists," *Barre* (Massachusetts) *Gazette*, June 14, 1844, 2.

2. Ibid.

3. "Division of the Methodist Church," *Pittsfield Sun*, June 27, 1844, 3.

4. Ibid.

5. *Mississippi Free Trader and Natchez Gazette*, June 19, 1844, 1.

6. *Southern Christian Advocate*, May 30, 1851, 208. It should be noted that the microfilmed pages are out of sequence; page 208 is interposed in the early June 1851 pages, and is very poorly microfilmed. It is especially difficult to decipher much of the text in column 1.

7. Few subsequent commentators on Kitty and Andrew were familiar with the 1851 obituary.

8. The essay may have been published earlier in the *Southern Christian Advocate*.

9. Andrew, *Miscellanies*, 389.

10. Quoted in "Has the Southern Pulpit Failed?" 599.

11. Douglass, "Slavery in the Pulpit of the Evangelical Alliance," 413–14.

12. "The Negro," originally published in the *Free Church Portfolio*, republished in the *Barre* (Massachusetts) *Gazette*, September 9, 1859, 2.

13. *Atlanta Constitution*, May 10, 1870, 1.

14. *Georgia Weekly Telegraph*, March 7, 1871, 1.

15. *Daily Evening Bulletin*, March 22, 1871, 1.

16. Smithson, *In Memoriam, Rev. Bishop James Osgood Andrew*, 12.

17. 1871 Minutes of the Annual Conference, MEC South 1871. *Memoir of Bishop Andrew*, 643.

18. Redford, *Organization of the Methodist Church South*, 161.

19. George Gilman Smith Jr., Methodist clergyman, author, and historian, was born in Sheffield, Newton County, Georgia, December 24, 1836, and died May 7, 1913, in Macon, Georgia. He held a pastorate in Cedartown, Georgia, when the Civil War began; he joined Phillips' Legion in the Confederate Army as chaplain, was wounded during Antietam (1862), left the army, and returned to Georgia. He held many pastorates in Georgia, 1871–1881. He published his biography of Andrew while he was a Sunday school agent for the Methodist Episcopal Church, South.

20. James Andrew to Amelia Andrew, Vicksburg, Miss., December 3–5, 1840, in Smith, *Life and Letters*, 303.

21. Billy is the second slave referred to in Redford's discussion. As we shall see in chap. 8, he was inherited by Amelia Andrew, the Bishop's first wife, in 1840.

22. Smith's source for his assertion that Kitty only moved to the house on Andrew's property after her "marriage" appears to be a letter written by Andrew's son-in-law, Dr. Robert W. Lovett (n.d.; Robert Watkins Lovett papers, MARBL). The relevant passage is discussed in chap. 5.

23. Cobb, *Inquiry into the Law of Negro Slavery in the United States*, 297.

24. See, for example, the 1833 Virginia case of *Elders v. Elders' Executors*, in *Virginia Reports*, 930–34.

25. *Cleland v. Waters*, 19 Ga. 35, 43 (1855).

26. Longstreet, *Augustus Baldwin Longstreet's Georgia Scenes Completed*, 263.

27. Smith, *Life and Letters*, 313.

28. The figure of the benevolent Christian black mammy appears elsewhere in Smith's published work. See, for instance, his *Harry Thornton*, 79. In this work, published three years after the Andrew biography, the saved white hero is taken to church by his kind black nurse "Aunt Betsy," who plants seeds of his later redemption.

29. Smith, *Life and Letters*, 313.

30. Ibid., 314.

31. Ibid., 314n.

32. My working assumption is that Smith, as a conscientious Methodist historian, would not knowingly publish an outright falsehood, but that he would find it entirely appropriate to leave out awkward details and direct the reader's attention away from any hint of Andrew's possible impropriety.

33. In private correspondence, Andrew notes that he had toyed with entering openly into his own defense. In an unpublished letter, to a fellow southern minister, he writes, "Now then is one curious fact in connexion with my slavery relations and the Episcopate. The last eight years have been decidedly the most prosperous the church has ever know [*sic*] and yet during all that time I have

been a slave holder. . . . The blessing came from God who knew all about it. Now what's the inference from this? I have been strongly tempted to enter the lists and give a shot at some passing game—but think on the whole it may possibly be best for me not to take any prominent position in the battle" (James Osgood Andrew, Oxford, to Rev. William M. Wrightman, Charleston, S.C., July 6, 1844).

34. Dr J. B. M. Ferris, Nashville, Tenn., February 21, 1882; unpublished chap. 16 of Smith's *Life and Letters of James Osgood Andrew*, 1106, Papers of George Gilman Smith, MARBL.

35. "Bishop George F. Pierce," *Atlanta Constitution*, February 3, 1884, 1.

36. Blight, *Race and Reunion*.

37. Savage, *Standing Soldiers, Kneeling Slaves*.

Chapter 4. "As Free as I Am": Retelling the Narrative

1. Boas, Introduction, 18; quoted in Lévi-Strauss, *Savage Mind*, 21.

2. "Some Noted Leaders among Early Georgia Methodists," *Atlanta Constitution*, December 4, 1904, 1.

3. For a detailed discussion of the political and cultural context of the fiftieth anniversary, see Blight, *Race and Reunion*.

4. Wrightman Melton, "How Mulatto Slave Girl Kitty Who Refused Freedom Brought Division of the Methodist Church in 1844," *Atlanta Constitution*, May 21, 1916, E4.

5. Felton, *Country Life in Georgia in the Days of My Youth*, 78.

6. Wade, *Augustus Baldwin Longstreet*, 274–75.

7. Warren A. Candler, "Forgotten History," *Atlanta Journal*, August 18, 1935, 18. Candler wrote regular columns in the *Atlanta Journal* during this period.

8. Cited in Pierce, *Giant Against the Sky*, 161–62. I have been unable to determine the identities of the enslaved women Mary and "Nan." The 1850 slave schedule for Samuel C. Candler's household in Carroll County lists only one female slave born before his wedding date in 1833, a young woman age eighteen, born around 1832; in all likelihood she was Mary. Seven years before Warren Candler's birth, the 1860 slave schedule for Samuel Candler's household lists adult female slaves born in 1820, 1822, 1832, and 1841, again with no names given. In 1870, the year of the first Freedmen's Census, the only African American living in the Samuel Candler household is a young man. The only African American woman named "Nancy" or "Nan" in the 1870 census for Villa Rica is Nancy Embry, born around 1830, a domestic servant in the household of the white family of Willis Bagwell. There are no African Americans named "Mary" living in Villa Rica that year of sufficient age to have been given as a dowry gift in 1833.

9. Buck, *Blessed Town*, 49. First published in 1986 by Algonquin Books of Chapel Hill, the Oxford Historical Shrine Society republished the book soon after the organization had completed restoring Kitty's Cottage.

10. On the complex negotiations leading up to the final unification of the

Methodist Church, see Thomas, *Methodism's Racial Dilemma*, and Davis, *Methodist Unification*. At the "uniting conference" in Kansas City in 1939, the concerns of white southern segregationists were largely assuaged by the creation of an entity known as the "Central Jurisdiction," to which African American members of the church were relegated. In 1968 the Central Jurisdiction was abolished with the merger of the Methodist and Evangelical United Brethren churches into the United Methodist Church.

11. Letter from "Dolly" to Bishop Candler, December 7, 1935, Burge Family Papers. Dolly is perhaps Dorothy Gray Bolton, married to Louis Davout Bolton, who occupied the Burge plantation in the 1920s.

12. The McCord marker has subsequently been referred to by many as a "cenotaph," that is to say, a memorial to those whose remains are buried elsewhere. However, McCord clearly believed he was erecting a memorial directly above Kitty's remains. I thus refer to it as a "tablet."

13. Stubbs, *Family Album*, 33.

14. White, "Old Oxford," 8.

15. Carlton, "History of the Oxford Methodist Church," *Covington News*, May 2, 1952, 20. In 1962 Carlton published a nostalgic memoir of early-twentieth-century Emory College, "In Memory of Old Emory." He later served as the founding president of the all-white Oxford Historical Cemetery Foundation, an organization that his son-in-law now heads.

16. Charles Jarrell, "Oxford Echoes," *Wesleyan Christian Advocate*, April 22, 1954, 12.

17. Charles Jarrell, "Oxford Echoes," *Wesleyan Christian Advocate*, June 17, 1954, 3.

18. Charles Jarrell, "Oxford Echoes," *Wesleyan Christian Advocate*, September 12, 1957, 12.

19. "Salem Camp Meeting to Start Friday," *Covington News*, August 6, 1953, 10.

20. *Emory Alumnus*, October 1960, 5–10, 58–59.

21. In 2006 the song was publicly revived with an alteration to the lyrics. The controversial line, "In the heart of dear old Dixie," was changed to "In the heart of dear old Emory."

22. Rast, "Slave Girl Who Divided a Church," 2.

23. *Methodist Book of Discipline*, 14.

24. Jakes, *Furies*, 99–110.

25. Ibid., 101.

26. Aiken-Burnett, "Emory College," in *History of Newton County, Georgia*, 118–24.

27. Stephenson, "Oxford, Town," 411.

28. Waterson, "Civil War," 243.

29. Hauk, *Legacy of Heart and Mind*, 13.

30. Ibid.

31. "Enigma: Kitty's Cottage and the Methodist Civil War," *Emory Magazine*,

Spring 1997, http://www.emory.edu/EMORY_MAGAZINE/spring97/enigma
.html (accessed February 1, 2011).

32. Logue and Logue, *Touring the Backroads of North and South Georgia*, 145.

33. *Atlanta Journal-Constitution*. September 28, 1997, 3H.

34. Peter Scott, "Oxford Cottage Rich in History," *Atlanta Journal-Constitution*
(precise date unknown, ca. 1997), in Oxford Historical Shrine Society collection,
Library of Oxford College of Emory University, Special Collections.

Chapter 5. "The Other Side of Paradise": Mythos and Memory in the Cemetery

1. Adams, *Wounds of Returning*, 17.

2. Wheatley, *Poems on Various Subjects, Religious and Moral*, 15.

3. Bishop Emory's last will and testament includes this passage: "To the colored servants now in my possession, for terms of years, viz. Alexander, Maria,
William, Mary and Nathan, I will their freedom, the males on the twenty fifth
day of December next after attaining the age of twenty-one, and the females on
the same day of December after attaining the age of eighteen years, respectively,
provided they take with them any child or children which either of them may
have, which I will to be free at the same time." Last Will and Testament of John
Emory, witnessed June 22, 1834, testated January 2, 1836, Baltimore County
Registry of Wills: 436–37. Maryland State Archives.

4. On the consequences of this clear-cutting, see Auslander, "Going by the
Trees."

5. See *http://www.buckinghamhemmings.com* (accessed July 18, 2010).

6. Jacobs, *Incidents in the Life of a Slave Girl*, in chap. 28, "Aunt Nancy," 186–87.

7. It would appear that Longfellow exaggerated the actual story for dramatic
effect. The only person of color buried in the white Vassal crypt appears to have
been Darby Vassal, who was born a slave in the Vassal household and died in
1861, nearly eight decades after emancipation in Massachusetts. Sixty years after
becoming free, he specifically obtained permission to be buried in the family
crypt of the white Vassal family in Christ Church. In April 1843 Miss Catherine
Graves Russell presented Darby Vassal with a paper that specified, "I have promised Darby Vassal that he and his family shall be placed in my grandfather's tomb
under the church in Cambridge, built by Henry Vassal, and owned by me, his
granddaughter" (William Cooper Nell, *Selected Writings, 1832–1874*, ed. Dorothy Porter Wesley and Constance Porter Uzelac [Baltimore: Black Classic Press,
2002], 619). Longfellow knew Darby Vassal well and would presumably have
been familiar with his plans to be buried in the white family crypt.

8. As we have seen, Porter was unfamiliar with Bishop Andrew's 1851 obituary
of Kitty, which would have given him the precise month and year of her death.

9. Durkheim and Mauss, *Primitive Classification*.

Chapter 6. "The Most Interesting Building in Georgia": The Strange Career of Kitty's Cottage

1. This chapter's subtitle alludes to C. Vann Woodward's classic study, *The Strange Career of Jim Crow*. As it happens, following the termination of his position at Georgia Tech in 1933, Woodward resided in Oxford, Georgia, where his father was dean of Emory's Junior College. It seems likely that during this time Woodward would have visited Kitty's Cottage and encountered white retellings of the Kitty-Andrew narrative.

2. From the unpublished chap. 16 of G. G. Smith's *Life and Letters of James Osgood Andrew*, 1082–83, MARBL, Emory University.

3. J. Marvin Rast, *Oxford Epitaph: A Chapter in History*, Addendum, sent to Special Collections by Rast on October 1, 1989, MARBL, Emory University.

4 Warren A. Candler, "Forgotten History," unpublished, undated manuscript, Warren A. Candler papers, MARBL, Emory University.

5. "Dolly" was probably Dorothy Gray Bolton, married to Louis Davout Bolton, who evidently occupied Burge Plantation in the 1920s. "Dr. Haynes" was presumably the Methodist minister, educator, and Emory alumnus Charles Myers Haynes (College 1921; Candler School of Theology 1924).

6. "Kitty's Cottage—A Shrine of Southern Methodism: Historic Cottage Now Permanently Located on Salem Camp Ground," *Atlanta Constitution*, June 4, 1939, 18.

7. For anthropological accounts of Salem Campground, see Kennedy, *Kinship and Pilgrimage*; Shore, "Spiritual Work, Memory Work."

8. Mary Louise Fleming, "Bishop Andrew and Kitty," unpublished manuscript (ca. 1985), in Papers of the Oxford Historical Shrine Society records, Special Collections, Oxford College of Emory University Library.

9. *Covington News*, July 31, 1986, 3A.

10. McElya, *Clinging to Mammy*; see also Wallace-Sanders, *Mammy*.

11. Patton et al., "Moonlight and Magnolias in Southern Education," 153.

12. Mitchell, *Gone with the Wind*, 16.

13. Mayor Ramsey recalls that he felt that the return to Oxford of President Haygood's desk, which had been stored in the cottage, was of greater historical importance than Kitty's Cottage (personal communication with author).

14. Minutes, Oxford Historical Shrine Society, January 30, 1995 (Oxford College of Emory University, Special Collections).

15. Jane Grillo, "Kitty's Cottage Is Center of This Weekend Tour of Homes," *Multi County Star*, December 5, 1995, 3.

16. Lisa Frederick. "Historic Kitty's Cottage Finds Its Way Back to Oxford: Slave Cabin Put on Tour of Homes," *Atlanta Journal-Constitution*, Rockdale Extra. November 20, 1995, JR3.

Chapter 7. Enigmas of Kinship: Miss Kitty and Her Family

1. Smith, *Life and Letters*, 312.

2. The letter discusses the question of whether Andrew should enter into his own defense: "Now there is one curious fact in connexion [*sic*] with my slavery relations and the Episcopate. The last eight years have been decidedly the most prosperous the church has ever known and yet during all that time I have been a slave holder. . . . The blessing came from God who knew all about it. Now what's the inference from this? I have been strongly tempted to enter the lists and give a shot at some passing game—but think on the whole it may possibly be best for me not to take any prominent position in the battle" (James Osgood Andrew, Oxford, to Rev. William M. Wightman, Charleston, South Carolina, July 6, 1844).

3. Stubbs. *Family Album*, 26.

4. *Ancestoring*, I.47. Augusta Genealogical Society. (This information is transcribed from records of John Marshall, sexton, who died January 22, 1833, after having served in that office since September 1, 1817.)

5. Richmond County, *Georgia Ordinary Court Estate Records 1789–1839*; Will Book A, 356. I have not been able to identify Lovey Powers's mother or to determine when she died.

6. Ibid., 125.

7. I do not know if there is anything to be made of the fact that Lovey Powers's granddaughter was named Emma, the same name that Kitty would give to her own daughter, born around 1848. Miss Emma Hartford, the granddaughter of Lovey Powers, died in 1839, along with her stepfather, Joseph Collins, in the yellow fever epidemic that swept through Augusta that year. If Kitty really did grow up in the Powers household, she would have known the white girl Emma well and perhaps would have been inclined to name her own daughter in her memory.

8. *Augusta Chronicle*, January 9, 1836, 2.

9. Ibid. Bridewell was New York City's principal prison and poorhouse.

10. Jonathan Ernst, "Freeing the Soul," *Augusta Chronicle*, September 9, 2001, http://chronicle.augusta.com/stories/2001/09/09/met_318236.shtml (accessed February 1, 2011).

11. Wiencek, *Imperfect God*.

12. Emily and Richard Tubman papers, Duke University Special Collections.

13. In Appendix 3, I review in detail several other possible scenarios for Kitty's origins.

14. Smith, *Life and Letters*, 300.

15. Ibid., 303.

16. Stubbs, *Family Album*, 32.

17. Harbert Tucker came from Virginia, where he served as a soldier in the Revolutionary War. He then relocated to Pendleton, South Carolina, where in 1790 he owned four slaves; perhaps Nathan's father Richard was one of these four. Tucker presumably acquired Richard in Virginia or South Carolina.

18. There is some evidence that Nathan's mother Judith was ultimately trans-

ferred to Permelia "Milly" Yeargain, Rev. Shell's daughter, and her husband Deveraux Yeargain, who owned Judith's husband Richard as well as Peter, the son of Richard and Judith. The Yeargains resided in Greenville, South Carolina. Deveraux Yeargain's will in 1849 makes mention of an elderly negro slave "Jude," bequeathed to his wife Permelia; Permelia is given fifty dollars to look after this old negro woman. It is possible that this woman was Nathan's mother, Judith. "Jude" is the only slave mentioned in the will by name.

19. William Brown, born 1786, married Rev. Stephen Shell's daughter Susan Shell of Newberry District, South Carolina, in 1812 and died 1856 in Newton County. One of their children was Coleman Brown, who married Fannie Reynolds, October 11, 1855, and who was killed in the Civil War in September 1862 (*History of Newton County*, 590). As noted in chap. 2, Coleman Brown received in 1862 as a gift from his father-in-law Judge Reynolds, the enslaved woman Mildred Robinson and her child, whom Judge Reynolds had purchased from Professor Alexander Means of Emory College.

20. *The Enterprise* (Covington, Ga.), February 6, 1885, 3.

21. The letter is copied out in the unpublished chap. 16 of Smith's *Life and Letters*, 1082–83.

22. Several black fraternal organizations in the 1870s and 1880s in South Carolina, Pennsylvania, and Washington, D.C., used titles such as the "Grand and Accepted Order of the Brothers and Sisters of Love and Charity." It is not clear if as early as 1871 these various groups were formally affiliated with one another. Nathan Boyd's organization was probably primarily a burial insurance society. Theda Skocpol and other scholars have argued that these early African American fraternal organizations were key forerunners of the NAACP and other civil rights organizations. See Skocpol, *What a Mighty Power We Can Be*.

23. Proceedings of [City] Council, Petitions: "Bill of Nathan Boyd, for care of a pauper, five dollars. Alderman Sparks moves to pay the bill. Adopted," *Atlanta Daily Herald*, October 25, 1873, 8.

24. Colored Paupers list. Oakland Cemetery archives, Atlanta, Georgia.

25. After the Civil War, many freedpeople placed notices seeking word of lost family members in African American newspapers. I have not found any such notices placed by Nathan or his children.

26. In 2008 I was allowed to consult the Summerfield Methodist Church record book, in private family possession. The African American members of the church were listed on the final pages. Sadly, the post-1855 pages, which might have listed Kitty's children, had been cut or razored out.

27. Smith, *Life and Letters*, 474.

28. Ibid.

29. No "James Sanders" is listed in the Registry of Voters for Dallas County in 1867; however, an African American man named James Sanders registered to vote in adjacent Perry County on June 18, 1867, in Precinct 1, Election District 20 (Alabama Department of Archives and History, Alabama 1867 Voter Registration Records Database).

30. Fleming, *Civil War and Reconstruction in Alabama*, 722. See also DeBow's Review, 1868.

31. Fleming, *Civil War and Reconstruction in Alabama*, 694.

32. P. M. Munro, "Sketch of Old Centenary Institute at Summerfield," parts 1, 2, and 3, *Selma Times Journal*, March–May 1934; see also Sledge, "Summerfield, Alabama."

33. Minutes of the Board of Trustees, Centenary Institute, Summerfield, Alabama (Special Collections, Alabama Department of Archives and History).

34. *Commercial Gazette*, n.d., Madeleine Vinton Dahlgren papers, Georgetown University Library Special Collections.

35. Dahlgren, *Washington Winter*, 35.

36. Ibid., 39.

37. Ibid., 244.

38. Madeleine Vinton Dahlgren papers, Georgetown University Library Special Collections, folder 2. The woman evidently was Eliza Harper, listed in the 1880 census as the only servant residing in the Dahlgren household in Washington; she was born in Maryland around 1856. Presumably, Madeleine brought Eliza to town from the Boonesville, Maryland, area where Madeleine's summer home was located.

39. In principle, Congress voted compensation for account holders. However, few depositors received compensation.

40. Hamilton Fish diary, Manuscript Division, Library of Congress.

41. Smith, *Life and Letters*, 314n.

42. *People's Advocate* (Washington, D.C.), October 13, 1883, 2.

43. *Afro-American Ledger* (Baltimore), November 20, 1901, 1.

44. Kate Tillman, Diary, George Washington University Special Collections.

45. Francis Grimke papers, Moreland-Spingarn Archives, Howard University.

46. *Washington Post*, April 5, 1902, 2.

47. *Washington Post*, October 6, 1906, 10.

48. I do not know if Alford served as a private cook to a Union officer or if he worked directly for the company's mess sergeant. The regimental records of the Third Iowa in the National Archives contain no mention of Alford Boyd or any other black personnel.

49. Iowa State Archives, manuscript collections.

50. On African American religious history in Iowa, see Hawthorne, "The Church."

51. It is perhaps only a coincidence that one of Bishop Andrew's daughters was named Mary Catherine Andrew (1833–57). Alford would have known her as a boy in Oxford.

52. *Cedar Rapids Evening Gazette*, May 24, 1902, 3.

53. *Cedar Rapids Daily Republican*, February 28, 1902, 3.

54. *Sioux County Herald*, September 26, 1906, 2.

Chapter 8. "Out of the Shadows": The Andrew Family Slaves

1. G. G. Smith incorrectly identifies Benjamin as the grandfather of James Osgood Andrew.

2. Smith, *Life and Letters*, 17.

3. Smith, "JNO. Andrews' Journal," *Wesleyan Christian Advocate*, January 2, 1908, 20–22. The term "expulsion" here refers to the early Methodist position that slaveholders should be expelled from the church.

4. Wilkes County Deed Books. Volume RR, 1798–1805.

5. The 1830 and 1840 federal censuses only list age ranges for enumerated free persons and slaves. The 1850 and 1860 slave schedules list actual ages for free persons and slaves.

6. James Osgood Andrew, "Reminiscences of an Itinerant," *Southern Christian Advocate*, 1852–53. African American readers of this passage are skeptical of the Bishop's phrasing. "Are you really saying that he just took this Jacob on a trip for his health?" asked Margaret Watkins rhetorically. "He just wanted a slave to look after him!"

7. Smith, *Life and Letters*, 321. As we have seen, numerous writers confuse Jacob with Billy, the slave whom Bishop Andrew acquired through his first wife, Ann Amelia, who in turn had inherited him from her mother, Catherine McFarlane, in 1840.

8. I know of no other reference from this period to a "Black Methodist Society," which might be a precursor to an AME congregation in Charleston. Quamino is an Akan name (from the region that was then the Gold Coast, now Southern Ghana) derived from one of the days of the market week. It is possible that Quamino was Fanny's husband. Free men of color in early nineteenth-century Charleston at times arranged to purchase their wives. See Kennedy, *Braided Relations, Entwined Lives*. This John McKee seems to be related to John K. McKee, the owner (and possible father) of Robert Smalls of Charleston. During the Civil War, Smalls was the first African American captain of a U.S. naval vessel and after the war served as a five-term U.S. congressman.

9. I am not sure if these McFarlanes were related to the prominent merchant Alexander McFarlane (d. 1755), based in Kingston, Jamaica, who purchased "121 slaves on two occasions in 1747" (Burnard and Morgan. "Dynamics of the Slave Market and Slave Purchasing Patterns in Jamaica," 214). This Alexander McFarlane bequeathed his astronomical instruments to his alma mater, the University of Glasgow, which erected the McFarlane Observatory to house them.

10. Eve Catherine McNeil manumitted Ben on October 19, 1804. After he was manumitted, she is listed as his guardian for some years.

11. Stubbs. *Family Album*.

12. By July 28, 1802, we know that Alexander McFarlane was back in Charleston, since on that day he legally attested that Dolly had repaid the Methodist Society and thus purchased her freedom. In September 1802 McFarlane was

involved in a carriage accident on Queen Street in Charleston, and was subsequently fined in a jury trial in February 1803. Given that he was ill in Rio Pongo, Sierra Leone, for eighty-three days before dying, he must have left Charleston for his final slave trading voyage before September 1803.

13. *City Gazette*, published as "City Gazette And Daily Advertiser," October 9, 1806. A similarly worded advertisement appeared the day before in the *Charleston Times*, October 8, 1806, 3.

14. McMillin, *Final Victims*, CD-ROM insert. It is perhaps relevant that on October 7, three days after the *Mary-Ann* docked in Charleston, the firm of Veree and Blair sold "29 African slaves" in Charleston. George Verree was one of the assignees to McFarlane and Player; perhaps, like William Payne, he was recovering his debts to the firm through this sale.

15. In *Final Victims*, McMillin notes that starting in fall 1806, a glut of African slaves appeared in the Charleston market, and that slave traders therefore sought to keep some of newly imported slaves off of the market, waiting for the cessation of the transatlantic trade in January 1808 to bring about a corresponding rise in prices. It is thus possible that not all of the *Mary-Ann*'s cargo was sold in October 1806.

16. The only child of Catherine Stattler McFarlane not to receive one of her slaves was her son, James McFarlane. By this time, James McFarlane was well established as a physician in New Orleans, and his mother may not have felt he was as needful of a bequest as her daughters and grandchildren. In any event, the will divides the proceeds of Catherine Stattler MacFarlane's house on Hassell Street in Charleston among all her children, including James (Will of Catherine Stattler McFarlane. Will Book I, p. 65, Charleston County Records [recorded March 27, 1840, in Newton County Will Book]).

17. Stubbs. *Family Album.*

18. Mood, *Autobiography of Francis Asbury Mood*, 4.

19. Smith. *Life and Letters*, 344.

20. Ibid., 355.

21. A footnote by Smith identifies Billy and Orange as "colored servants" (ibid., 356).

22. It may simply be a coincidence that in 1880 Emma Sanders married an Abe Neal in Union, Dallas County, Alabama. I do not know if Abe Neal and William Neal were related.

23. An African American named "William Neal" registered to vote on August 9, 1867, in Selma's Election District 13 (Alabama Department of Archives and History, Alabama 1867 Voter Registration Records Database).

24. Dallas County, Alabama, Deed Records, 1871 and 1873.

25. The 1930 census records that William Neal (the apparent grandson of Billy) is employed as a laborer in a paper mill and still residing in Morehouse Parish, Louisiana, with a wife, a son, and three nieces.

26. Stubbs, *Family Album*, 61–62.

27. Reprinted in ibid., 128–29n43.

28. When Jacob Mitchell died in 1825, he left some of his estate to the four sons of his late daughter Nancy, who had died prior to 1819: Thomas E. Greenwood, Eldredge L. Greenwood, William M. Greenwood, and James D. Greenwood. He bequeathed some slaves to his living children and to his granddaughters, but did not leave any slaves to his grandsons.

29. *Georgia House Journal for 1835*, 320.

30. This Jacob is not to be confused with Bishop Andrew's slave of the same name, who appears to have died in the early 1830s.

31. Robert Greenwood papers; Ordinary Court records, Greene County, Georgia. Georgia State Archives.

32. Records of the Georgia Forty-fourth Regiment, George State Archives. Robert Greenwood does not appear in the records of Greene County Confederate veterans authorized for a pension, so it seems likely he died before such pensions were authorized in the 1890s.

33. Letter, William H. M. Weaver to Mrs. E. F. Cauthen, April 5, 1934 (copy in Greene County Public Library, Greensboro, Georgia).

34. The one hundred dollars rent due was paid to Bishop Andrew by the Bishop's son-in-law, Thomas Meriwether, who acted as administrator for the Hardy Andrew estate (Hardy Andrew file, loose probate records, Newton County, Georgia).

35. Smith, *Life and Letters*, unpublished chapter, 1079, in MARBL, Emory University.

36. Williams, *History of Greene County, Georgia*, 123.

37. It is possible that Bishop Andrew sold some of the Greenwood slaves after his second wife's death and transferred the cash realized to the Greenwood white children. There are, however, no deed records extant detailing any such sales or transfers.

38. As far as I can tell, Andrew's plantation had no relationship to an earlier plantation called Tranquilla, owned by a George Walker, who died in the 1850s, located in the southeastern section of Dallas County.

39. Two African American men named "Nelson" are recorded in the 1867 voter registration rolls for Selma, a Nelson Briggs and a Nelson Jones, both in Precinct 13. No Nelson Jones is listed in Summerfield in the 1870 census.

Chapter 9. Saying Something Now

1. Rosenthal, *Possession, Ecstasy and Law in Ewe Voodoo*, 153.

2. Lévi-Strauss, *Savage Mind*, 31.

3. Barthes, *Camera Lucida*, 95.

4. Masters, *Spoon River Anthology*, 146.

5. Morrison, *Beloved*, 322.

6. Agee and Evans, *Let Us Now Praise Famous Men*, 141.

7. Benjamin, "Work of Art in the Age of Mechanical Reproduction," 226.

8. Lynn Marshall-Linnemeier, artist's statement, January 2011 (unpublished, shared with author).

9. "Emory's 'Regret' for Slavery Ties," *Inside Higher Ed.*, January 15, 2011, http://www.insidehighered.com/news/2011/01/25/emory_expresses_regret_for_its_ties_to_slavery (accessed February 11, 2011).

10. Sebastian Wee, "Kitty Boyd Descendents Get Respect," *Covington News*, February 9, 2011, http://www.covnews.com/section/15/article/17403/ (accessed February 11, 2011).

Appendix 3. Kitty's Possible Origins

1. Fitzgerald, *Judge Longstreet*, 45.

2. It may be entirely coincidental, but as we shall see below, Kitty was to name her first child, born around 1844, "Alfred." Might this have been in memory of the slave boy Alfred, sold by Longstreet to Richard Tubman in 1834? Was the enslaved Alfred, named for Longstreet's son Alfred, perhaps Kitty's own brother?

3. This freedman William Longstreet evidently died at some point between 1871 and 1880. His wife (apparently his widow) Elouise is listed in the 1880 census living with her married daughter, her son-in-law, and their children in Shreveport, Louisiana.

4. Longstreet, *Voice from the South.*

5. A modest collection of Longstreet's letters and manuscripts, primarily related to his time as president of South Carolina College, is preserved at the South Caroliniana Library, University of South Carolina in Columbia, South Carolina. A few papers are also at MARBL at Emory University.

Appendix 4. Kitty's Children

1. It is puzzling that in the 1920 census Will L. Long is listed as born in "Georgia," but this may be a simple mistake of the enumerator. In the 1930 census, oddly enough, Will L. Long is listed as born in Michigan.

2. It may not be directly significant, but Moscow, Arkansas, was the site of a Union-Confederate skirmish on April 13, 1864, in which the Eighty-third United States Colored Infantry (Second Colored Kansas Infantry) regiment distinguished itself in combat. (See Crawford, *Kansas in the Sixties*, 113.)

3. *Arkansas State Press*, July 11, 1952, 1.

4. In the 1900 census, a Mark Sanders, age thirty, is listed as living in Bells Precinct, Dallas County, Alabama, working as a farm laborer and residing as a boarder. He had been married for three years, but had no children; his wife's residence is not clear. An African American man named "Mark Sanders" does appear in the Selma City Directory as a laborer and paperhanger for 1913 and 1924; he appears to be the same Mark Sanders who is enumerated in the 1920

census in Selma, as born in 1897; and the same Mark Sanders, born around 1896 who on April 10, 1919, married a Hattie Lou Taylor in Selma. Although this man is too young to be the son of Emma Sanders listed in the 1880 census, born around 1875, the two Mark Sanderses may be related. (It is perhaps only a coincidence, but the elder Mark Sanders seems to have married in 1897, the same year that the younger Mark Sanders was born.)

5. *Washington Post*, September 6, 1899, 2.

6. Lincoln Cemetery records indicate that Russell and Cordelia's remains were reinterred on top of one another, in a single grave lot (D-69-9).

7. Having attended elementary school in the Washington, D.C., public school system from 1966 onward, and having lived in the District until 1979, it occurs to me that in principle I could have met Ms. Edna Boyd Gary. I am sorry not to have done so.

Appendix 5. The Greenwood Slaves, Postemancipation

1. After the death of Willis Williams in 1874, his widow Lucretia moved to Skull Shoals, Greene County, with her son, Adam Daniel, and Adam's twin sister Eve, where they worked as laborers. Adam in time studied at Morehouse College and became the Reverend A. D. Williams, serving from 1896 to 1902 as pastor of Bethlehem Baptist Church in Covington, the oldest African American church in Newton County, and as the second pastor at Ebenezer Baptist Church in Atlanta. His daughter Alberta Christine in 1926 married Rev. Martin Luther "Daddy" King Sr.; they were the parents of Martin Luther King Jr.

2. Daniel remains a common African American family name in Greene County to this day.

3. In 1870 these freedpeople resided near the wealthy white planter James N. Armor, who in 1860 owned sixty-nine slaves. He may have acquired some of them after 1855.

4. On the Klan terror campaign in Greene County, see Bryant, *How Curious a Land*, 130.

5. In some cases, descendent families were divided between agrarian and urban work; in 1930, for example, the son of Allen Parham, Alfred Parham (b. ca. 1865), was still working the land in Union Point, Greene County, Georgia, while Alfred's son, Frank Parham (b. ca. 1899), was apparently employed as a waiter in Evanston, Illinois.

6. *History of Newton County, Georgia*, 823.

7. Quoted in Smith, *Life and Letters*, 560.

8. It is possible that Mary Ann Mitchell was the same person as the slave "Mary Ann," the mother of "Ben," who joined General Sherman's Union Army column in November 1864, as reported by Bishop Andrew's granddaughter Annie.

9. Speculatively, perhaps Peggy married an enslaved man from the household of President James R. Thomas and thus acquired the last name Thomas. In 1860, as it happens, Emory College President Thomas resided next door to Professor

Luther M. Smith, Peggy's evident owner after 1855, so Peggy must have known the Thomas slaves well.

10. In the 1900 census, this same household was headed by a widowed Henrietta, whose last name was then Harris. Since her household included a seven-year-old boy named Nathan, whose father was born in Georgia, it seems likely that Thomas survived until at least 1893. Perhaps Henrietta remarried and took the name Harris after Thomas's death. (However, according to the Dallas County Colored Marriage records, no man named Harris married a woman Henrietta between 1880 and 1900.) Alternatively, perhaps Thomas and Henrietta together changed their family name a third time before his death.

Unpublished Manuscript and Archival Collections

Manuscript, Archives, and Rare Book Library MARBL, *Emory University*
James Osgood Andrew papers
Branham family papers
Burge family papers
Warren Akin Candler papers
Candler family papers
Graves family papers
Atticus G. Haygood family papers
Iverson family papers
Charles Crawford Jarrell papers
Augustus Baldwin Longstreet papers
Robert Watkins Lovett papers
Alexander Means papers
William M'Kendree papers
Orr family papers
Park family papers
George Foster Pierce papers
George Gilman Smith papers
Joshua Soule papers

Other Archival Sources
Hardy Andrew file, loose probate records, Newton County, Georgia
John Dahlgren papers, Manuscript Division, Library of Congress
Madeleine Dahlgren papers, Special Collections, Georgetown University
    Library
Hamilton Fish papers, Manuscript Division, Library of Congress
Georgia House Journals, Georgia State Archives
Greene County, Georgia. Ordinary Court Records, Georgia State Archives
Robert Greenwood papers. Georgia State Archives
Francis Grimke papers, Moreland-Spingarn archives, Howard University
Methodist Episcopal Church, South, Annual Minutes, 1871
Riggs Bank records, George Washington University Special Collections
Kate Tillman papers, George Washington University Special Collections
Emily and Richard Tubman papers, Duke University Special Collections
Alabama Department of Archives and History
Arkansas History Commission and State Archives

Georgia State Archives
Iowa State Archives
Maryland State Archives
Oakland Cemetery Archives, Atlanta
Oxford Historical Shrine Society records (housed in Special Collections, Oxford College of Emory University Library)
Richmond County, Georgia, Ordinary Court Estate Records, 1789–1839
South Carolina Department of Archives and History
South Carolina Historical Society
Stone, G. W. W., Jr. Unpublished memoir. Special Collections, Library of Oxford College of Emory University (Gift of Virgil and Louise Eady)
Weaver, William H. M., letter to Mrs. E. F. Cauthen, April 5, 1934 (copy in Greene County Public Library, Greensboro, Georgia)
Wilkes County, Georgia, Deed Books, 1789–1805

Newspapers and Periodicals
Afro-American Ledger (Baltimore)
Ancestoring (Augusta [GA] Genealogical Society)
Arkansas State Press
Atlanta Constitution
Atlanta Daily Herald
Atlanta Journal
Atlanta Journal-Constitution
Augusta Chronicle
Barre (Massachusetts) *Gazette*
Bulletin of Emory University
Cedar Rapids Daily Republican
Cedar Rapids Evening Gazette
Charleston Courier
Charleston Times
Christian Recorder
City Gazette (Iowa City, Iowa)
Columbus (Georgia) *Enquirer*
Commercial Gazette (Boston)
Covington News
Daily Evening Bulletin (San Francisco)
Emory Alumnus
Georgia Weekly Telegraph
Inside Higher Ed
Mississippi Free Trader and Natchez Gazette
Multi County Star (Covington, Georgia)
People's Advocate (Washington, D.C.)
Pittsfield (Massachusetts) *Sun*

Selma Times Journal
Sioux City Herald
South Carolina Methodist Advocate
Southern Christian Advocate
Washington Post
Wesleyan Christian Advocate

Books, Chapters, and Journal Articles

Adams, Jessica. *Wounds of Returning: Race, Memory and Property on the Post-slavery Plantation*. Chapel Hill: University of North Carolina Press, 2007.

Agee, James, and Walker Evans. *Now Let Us Praise Famous Men: Three Tenant Farmers*. Boston: First Mariner Books, 2001.

Aiken-Burnett, Hanna. "Emory College." In *History of Newton County, Georgia*, 118–24.

Andrew, James Osgood, *Miscellanies: Comprising Letters, Essays, and Addresses*. Louisville, Ky.: Morton and Griswold, 1854.

Auslander, Mark. "Going by the Trees: Death and Regeneration in Georgia's Haunted Landscapes." In "Ancient Mysteries, Modern Secrets" (Electronic Antiquity), May 2009, http://scholar.lib.vt.edu/ejournals/ElAnt/v12n1/auslander.pdf (accessed February 1, 2011).

Barthes, Roland. *Camera Lucida: Reflections on Photography*. New York: Farrar, Straus and Giroux, New York.

Benjamin, Walter. "The Work of Art in the Age of Mechanical Reproduction." In *Illuminations*, edited by Hannah Arendt, 217–51. New York: Schocken Books, 1969.

Bennett, James. *Religion and the Rise of Jim Crow in New Orleans*. Princeton, N.J.: Princeton University Press, 2005.

Blight, David. *Race and Reunion: The Civil War in American Memory*. Cambridge, Mass.: Belknap Press of Harvard University Press, 2001.

Boas, Franz. Introduction to James Teit, *Traditions of the Thompson River Indians of British Columbia*. Memoirs of the American Folklore Society 6. Boston: Houghton Mifflin and Company, 1898.

Book of Discipline of the United Methodist Church. Nashville: Abingdon Press, 2008.

Bourdieu, Pierre. *The Logic of Practice*. Stanford, Calif.: Stanford University Press, 1990.

Brophy, Alfred L. "Considering William and Mary's History with Slavery: The Case of President Thomas Roderick Dew." *William & Mary Bill of Rights Journal* 16, no. 2 (2008): 1091–139.

Brown University. Report of the Steering Committee on Slavery and Justice, 2006, http://brown.edu/Research/Slavery_Justice/report/ (accessed January 1, 2011).

Bryant, Jonathan M. *How Curious a Land: Conflict and Change in Greene County, Georgia, 1850–1885.* Chapel Hill: University of North Carolina Press, 1998.

Buck, Polly Stone. *The Blessed Town: Oxford, Georgia at the Turn of the Century.* 1986; repr. Oxford, Ga.: Oxford Historical Shrine Society, 2001.

Burnard, Trevor, and Kenneth Morgan. "The Dynamics of the Slave Market and Slave Purchasing Patterns in Jamaica, 1655–1788." *William and Mary Quarterly* (3rd Series) 58, no. 1 (January 2001): 205–28.

Butler, Octavia. *Kindred.* Garden City, N.Y.: Beacon Press, 1979.

Campbell, James T. "Settling Accounts? An Americanist Perspective on Historical Reconciliation." *American Historical Review* 114, no. 4 (October 2009): 963–77.

Carlton, W. A. "History of the Oxford Methodist Church." *Covington News*, May 2, 1952.

Clarke, Erskine. *Dwelling Place: A Plantation Epic.* New Haven, Conn.: Yale University Press, 2005.

Cobb, Thomas R. R. *An Inquiry into the Law of Negro Slavery in the United States.* Philadelphia: T. & J. W. Johnson and Company, 1858.

Comaroff, Jean. "The End of History, Again: Pursuing the Past in the Postcolony." In *Postcolonial Studies and Beyond*, edited by S. Kaul et al., 125–44. Durham, N.C.: Duke University Press, 2005.

Comaroff, John L., and Jean Comaroff. *Of Revelation and Revolution.* Vol. 1, *Christianity, Colonialism, and Consciousness in South Africa.* Chicago: University of Chicago Press, 1991.

——. *Of Revelation and Revolution.* Vol. 2, *The Dialectics of Modernity on a South African Frontier.* Chicago: University of Chicago Press, 1997.

Comaroff, John L., and Simon Roberts. *Rules and Processes: The Cultural Logic of Dispute in an African Context.* Chicago: University of Chicago Press, 1981.

Crawford, Samuel Johnson. *Kansas in the Sixties.* Chicago: A. C. McLurg and Company, 1911.

Dahlgren, Madeleine. *A Washington Winter.* Boston: James R. Osgood and Company, 1883.

Davis, Morris L. *The Methodist Unification: Christianity and the Politics of Race in the Jim Crow Era.* New York: New York University Press, 2008.

Davis, Theodore. "Slavery, Manufacturing and Productivity in Newton County, 1821–1860." In *History of Newton County*, 172–79.

Douglass, Frederick. "Slavery in the Pulpit of the Evangelical Alliance: An Address Delivered in London, England, on September 14, 1846." *London Inquirer*, September 19, 1846, and *London Patriot*, September 17, 1846. In *The Frederick Douglass Papers: Series One—Speeches, Debates, and Interviews*, vol. 1, edited by John Blassingame et al., 407–16. New Haven, Conn.: Yale University Press, 1979.

Durkheim, Emile, and Marcel Mauss. *Primitive Classification.* 1903; repr. Chicago: University of Chicago Press, 1963.

Ellison, Ralph, *Juneteenth*. Edited by John F. Callahan. New York: Random House, 1999.

Felton, Rebecca Lattimer. *Country Life in Georgia in the Days of My Youth*. Atlanta: Index Printing Company, 1919.

Fitzgerald, O. P. *Judge Longstreet: A Life Sketch*. Printed for the author, 1891.

Fleming, Walter Lynwood. *Civil War and Reconstruction in Alabama*. New York: Columbia University Press/Macmillan, 1905.

Goen, C. C. *Broken Churches, Broken Nation: Denominational Schisms and the Coming of the American Civil War*. Macon, Ga.: Mercer University Press, 1985.

Hatch, Nathan O., and John H. Wigger, eds. *Methodism and the Shaping of American Culture*. Nashville: Kingswood Books, 2001.

Hauk, Gary. *A Legacy of Heart and Mind: Emory since 1836*. Atlanta: Emory University, 2000.

Hawthorne, Frances E. "The Church." In *Outside In: African American History in Iowa, 1838–2000*, edited by Bill Silag, 386–401. Des Moines: State Historical Society of Iowa, 2001.

Haygood, Atticus. *The Colored Man in the Methodist Episcopal Church*. 1890; repr. Westport, Conn.: Negro Universities Press, 1970.

——. "Has the Southern Pulpit Failed?" *North American Review* 130. New York: Appleton and Company, 1880.

Hildebrand, Reginald F. *The Times Were Strange and Stirring: Methodist Preachers and the Crisis of Emancipation*. London and Durham, N.C.: Duke University Press, 1995.

History of Greene County, Georgia, 1786–1886. Edited by Carolyn White Williams; data by Thaddeus Brockett Rice. 1961; repr. Spartanburg, S.C.: Reprint Company, 1979.

History of Newton County, Georgia. Compiled and published by the Newton County Historical Committee, 1988.

Jacobs, Harriet. *Incidents in the Life of a Slave Girl: Written by Herself*. Edited with an introduction by Jennifer Fleischner. Boston: Bedford/St. Martins, 2010.

Jakes, John. *The Furies*. Garden City, N.Y.: Nelson Doubleday, 1976.

Kennedy, Cynthia M. *Braided Relations, Entwined Lives: The Women of Charleston's Urban Slave Society*. Bloomington: Indiana University Press, 2005.

Kennedy, Gwen Neville. *Kinship and Pilgrimage Rituals of Reunion in American Protestant Culture*. Oxford: Oxford University Press, 2005.

Lévi-Strauss, Claude. *The Elementary Structures of Kinship*. Boston: Beacon Press, 1969.

——. *The Savage Mind*. Trans. George Weidenfeld and Nicholson Ltd. Chicago: University of Chicago Press, 1966.

——. *The View from Afar*. Chicago: University of Chicago Press, 1985.

Longstreet, Augustus Baldwin. *Augustus Baldwin Longstreet's Georgia Scenes Completed: A Scholarly Text*. Edited by David Rachels. Athens: University of Georgia Press, 1998.

———. *A Voice from the South: Comprising Letters from Georgia to Massachusetts and to the Southern States with an Appendix*. Baltimore: Western Continent Press, 1847.

Logue, Victoria, and Frank Logue. *Touring the Backroads of North and South Georgia*. Winston-Salem, N.C.: John F. Blair, 1997.

Masters, Edgar Lee. *Spoon River Anthology*. New York: MacMillan, 1915.

McElya, Micki. *Clinging to Mammy: The Faithful Slave in Twentieth-Century America*. Cambridge, Mass.: Harvard University Press, 2007.

McMillin, James A., *The Final Victims: Foreign Slave Trade to North America, 1783–1810*. Columbia: University of South Carolina Press, 2004.

Meyers, Terry L. "A First Look at the Worst: Slavery and Race Relations at the College of William and Mary." *William and Mary Bill of Rights Journal* 16, no. 4 (April 2008): 1141–68.

Minnow, Ralph E. *Northern Methodism and Reconstruction*. East Lansing: Michigan State University Press, 1956.

Mitchell, Margaret *Gone with the Wind*. New York: Macmillan, 1936.

Montgomery, William E. *Under Their Own Vine and Fig Tree: The African American Church in the South, 1865–1900*. Baton Rouge: Louisiana State University Press, 1993.

Mood, Francis. *Autobiography of Francis Asbury Mood*. (typescript) South Carolina Historical Society archives.

Morrison, Toni. *Beloved*. 1987; New York: Vintage International, 2004.

Oast, Jennifer. "Forgotten Masters: Institutional Slavery in Virginia, 1680–1860." Unpublished PhD diss., College of William and Mary, 2009.

Patton, June, et al. "Moonlight and Magnolias in Southern Education: The Black Mammy Memorial Institute." *Journal of Negro History* 65, no. 2 (Spring 19980): 149–55.

Pierce, Alfred M. *Giant against the Sky: The Life of Bishop Warren Akin Candler*. New York and Nashville: Abingdon-Cokesbury Press, 1948.

Rast, J. Marvin. "The Slave Girl Who Divided a Church." *South Carolina Methodist Advocate*, April 1968.

Redford, A. H. *Organization of the Methodist Church South*. Published by the Methodist Episcopal Church, South. Nashville, 1871.

Richey, Russell. *The Methodist Conference in America: A History*. Nashville: Kingswood Books, 1996.

Rosenthal, Judy. *Possession, Ecstasy, and Law in Ewe Voodoo*. Charlottesville: University Press of Virginia, 1998.

Savage, Kirk. *Standing Soldiers, Kneeling Slaves: Race, War, and Monument in Nineteenth-Century America*. Princeton, N.J.: Princeton University Press, 1999.

Schneider, David. *American Kinship: A Cultural Account*. 2nd ed. Chicago: University of Chicago Press, 1980.

Shore, Bradd. "Spiritual Work, Memory Work: Revival and Recollection at Salem Camp Meeting." *Ethos* 36, no. 1 (2008): 98–119.

Silag, Bill, ed. *Outside In: African American History in Iowa, 1838–2000.* Des Moines: State Historical Society of Iowa, 2001.

Skocpol, Theda, et al. *What a Mighty Power We Can Be: African American Fraternal Groups and the Struggle for Racial Equality.* Princeton, N.J.: Princeton University Press, 2006.

Sledge, John Sturdivant. "Summerfield, Alabama: Historic Preservation in a Rural Context." MA thesis, Middle Tennessee State University, 1982.

Smith, George Gilman. *Harry Thornton, Story of a Georgia Boy: A Brand Plucked from the Burning.* Nashville: Southern Methodist Publishing House, 1886.

——. *The Life and Letters of James Osgood Andrew.* Nashville: Southern Methodist Publishing House, 1883.

Smithson, W. T. *In Memoriam, Rev. Bishop James Osgood Andrew. Together with Original Essays and Poems.* Compiled and published by Wm. T. Smithson, 1871.

Stephenson, Margaret B. "Oxford, Town." In *History of Newton County, Georgia,* 409–16.

Stubbs, Thomas McAlpin. *Family Album: An Account of the Moods of Charleston, South Carolina, and Connected Families.* Atlanta: Curtis Printing Company, 1943.

Thomas, James S. *Methodism's Racial Dilemma: The Story of the Central Jurisdiction.* Nashville: Abingdon Press, 1982.

Virginia Reports: Jefferson–33 Grattan, 1730–1880. Annotated by Thomas Johnson Michie. Charlottesville: Michie Company, Law Publishers, 1903.

Wade, John Donald. *Augustus Baldwin Longstreet: A Study of the Development of Culture in the South.* New York: Macmillan Company, 1924.

Walker, Clarence E. *Rock in a Weary Land: The African Methodist Episcopal Church during the Civil War and Reconstruction.* Baton Rouge: Louisiana State University Press, 1982.

Wallace-Sanders, Kimberly. *Mammy: A Century of Race, Gender, and Southern Memory.* Ann Arbor: University of Michigan Press, 2008.

Waterson, James. "The Civil War." In *History of Newton County, Georgia,* 242–61.

Wheatley, Phillis. *Poems on Various Subjects, Religious and Moral.* London. N.p., 1773.

White, Goodrich C. "Old Oxford." *Bulletin of Emory University* 34, no. 4 (February 15, 1948): 8.

Wiencek, Henry. *An Imperfect God: George Washington, His Slaves, and the Creation of America.* New York: Farrar, Straus and Giroux, 2004.

Woodward, C. Vann. *The Strange Career of Jim Crow.* New York: Oxford University Press, 1955.

Woolfork, Lisa. *Embodying Slavery in American Culture.* Champaign: University of Illinois Press, 2009.

CPSIA information can be obtained
at www.ICGtesting.com
Printed in the USA
LVOW11s0637290318

571589LV00001B/156/P